D1047063

The Rose Man *of* Sing Sing

The Rose Man of Sing Sing

A True Tale of Life, Murder, and Redemption in the Age of Yellow Journalism

James McGrath Morris

Fordham University Press

New York   2003

Communications and Media Studies, no. 8
ISSN 1522-385X

Library of Congress
Cataloging-in-Publication Data
Morris, James McGrath.
    The Rose Man of Sing Sing : a true tale of life,
    murder, and redemption in the age of yellow
    journalism / James McGrath Morris.
        p.   cm.—(Communications and media
    studies)
    Includes bibliographical references and index.
    ISBN 0-8232-2267-5 (hardcover : alk. paper)
    1. Chapin, Charles E., 1858–1930.
    2. Journalists—United States—Biography.
    3. Prisoners—United States—Biography.
    I. Title.   II. Series.
    PN4874.C45M67   2003
    070.92–dc21   2003006842

Printed in the United States of America
07 06 05 04   5 4 3
First Edition

Parts of chapter 19 of the present work appeared in
a similar version in James McGrath Morris, *Jailhouse
Journalism: The Fourth Estate Behind Bars.* Jefferson,
N.C.: McFarland & Co., 1998.

THIS ONE IS FOR YOU, PATTY.

"There is a concatenation of all events in the best of possible worlds; for, in short, had you not been kicked out of a fine castle for the love of Miss Cunegund; had you not been put into the Inquisition; had you not traveled over America on foot; had you not run the Baron through the body; and had you not lost all your sheep, which you brought from the good country of El Dorado, you would not have been here to eat preserved citrons and pistachio nuts."

"Excellently observed," answered Candide; "but let us cultivate our garden."

—Voltaire, *Candide*

CONTENTS

Preface

Charles Chapin's life story is so extraordinary that it could have been a novel. In fact, a best-selling author wrote one while Chapin was still alive. The present book, however, is based on years of research that began in the 1980s and took me to libraries in small towns of Kansas and upstate New York, to manuscript collections in Washington, Chicago, St. Louis, Albany, and New York, and to Sing Sing itself. As with any biography, I have sifted through a mountain of evidence in preparing a literary portrait. However, I have purposely chosen not to clog the text with discursive remarks on my methods or sources. All of that is reserved for the extensive notes.

This book could never have been written had writer Basil King and publisher George Putnam not talked Chapin into writing his memoirs while confined at Sing Sing. The memoirs, along with his two volumes of published letters, provided both an outline to Chapin's life story and a running commentary. But having been trained as a skeptical journalist and historian, I have accepted none of Chapin's versions of events without considerable research.

Chapin turns out to be quite truthful. To make that determination, I looked first to see if anyone contested Chapin's account. The book was published while many of his contemporaries were still alive. It was widely reviewed, but no one made any claim that any part of it was inaccurate. Further, when other witnesses to the events portrayed in the book read it, they did not dispute Chapin's account.

Second, all of Chapin's accounts were subjected to a battery of tests. For example, he mentioned having attended a show in a Washington theater, and then seen another show in Baltimore. The shows did play in those theaters at that time, something he could not have researched from his prison cell. In another place, Chapin recounted spending time in the Union League Club in New York as the guest of a member. The person was indeed a member at that time and had reason to be in New York, making it doubtful that Chapin could have made up the story. These are only small examples of the kind of fact checking that was used to test Chapin's memory.

Throughout the book, I also corrected Chapin's faulty memory with actual records and have indicated such in the notes. Where it is clear that he has purposely changed his recollection, perhaps to inflate his role in a particular episode, I have also indicated it. In many cases, however, it was mostly a matter of errors common to anyone writing a memoir fifty years later without the use of notes, diaries, or other records. One of his frequent mistakes, for example, involved time. He recalled being in Washington for a year; it was six months. Oddly, he thought he worked for the *Chicago Tribune* for four years; it was seven. In all cases, the dates I use have been corroborated by other sources.

I also depended on other records to fill in some enormous gaps. Chapin is extraordinarily vague about his childhood and his family. For example, he never says anything about the fact that his father deserted the family. My luck was the discovery of a large cache of affidavits in his father's pension file in the National Archives.

My only regret is how little I could learn about Nellie Chapin. I was never able to uncover any family records or photographs. All I could ascertain is that she died with no living relatives. From what little I did learn, she seemed to be quite a remarkable woman who would have gladly endured poverty with Chapin if only he had asked. The tragedy is that he never asked.

Chapin gained enormous credit and fame for his *Evening World*. But even with his ego, he knew that the paper was only as good as his reporters. So it is with this book. I have benefited greatly from the assistance of a large crew of people who have helped bring forth the Chapin story. I will endeavor to thank each in turn.

The Ragdale Foundation gave me quiet time at its wonderful writers' colony to piece together a critical part of this book and work on its overall architecture. Thanks are also owed to Jerry Ellis and Dave Garrow for their quiet assistance in procuring me this moment.

Laura Belt, my agent, never lost faith in this unusual biography. Patricia O'Toole gave me sage counseling and support at every turn. Adam Kernan-Schloss helped make sure I crossed my *t*s and dotted my *i*s by patiently reading chapter after chapter. Dean Sagar traveled with me to the wilds of upstate New York and saved me from one embarrassing error, which I don't intend to reveal now. James Percoco shared many of the book's turns and twists during our weekly caffeine-laced editorial meetings. Melissa Lipman kindly searched through reels of microfilm. Michael Olmert provided me with advice on acting and Shakespeare that gave me useful insights into Chapin's verbal viper-like sting. Edwin N. Carter, a clinical psychologist in private practice in Northern Virginia, put Chapin on "the couch." Glenn Florkow, of the Winnetka Police Department, who is researching an unsolved murder that Chapin wrote about, shared his expertise. Karen Kamuda, editor of the Titanic Historical Society magazine, *The Titanic Commutator*, published a version of chapter 14. Dave Smith, my school's principal, and my students were immensely patient with me and supportive of this project.

Special thanks are owed to Lynn Sniderman, Associate Librarian and Archivist at the Federal Reserve Bank in Cleveland. She was instrumental in helping me uncover critical elements in the heretofore-untold story of Chapin's prison paramours. Without her help and advice, the tale of Constance Nelson and Viola Cooper would have been incomplete.

David Siegenthaler with the Elgin Area Historical Society in Elgin, Illinois, enthusiastically dug up some remarkable information that often represented the missing piece in my own research. Wendy Schnur, reference manager at the G.W. Blunt Library of the Mystic Seaport Museum, provided both background and specific information about Chapin's days as a yachtsman. Carol Reif, at the Deadwood Public Library in Deadwood, South Dakota, laboriously photocopied articles relating to Charles's and Nellie's acting days there. Jim Sherer of the Kansas Heritage Center of

Dodge City helped find items related to Chapin's early use of a gun. Shirley Hagan, of the Brookfield Public Library in Brookfield, Missouri, located the Chapins' marriage certificate. Dina Young, at the Missouri Historical Society, helped me complete the fascinating tale of Hurd and Chapin in their pursuit of the *Titanic* story and to ferret out critical information about St. Louis in the 1890s. Travis Westly, in the newspaper room of the Library of Congress, helped me dig up items I would have overlooked had it not been for his skills. Paul Stavis, an attorney in Albany, tried to persuade the state to open up Chapin's clemency files. Our request, seventy-two years after his death, was turned down.

A number of authors were also kind with their time in answering my questions: Ralph Blumenthal, author of *Stork Club: America's Most Famous Nightspot and the Lost World of Café Society*; Denis Brian, author of *Pulitzer: A Life*; C. Joseph Campbell, author of *Yellow Journalism: Puncturing the Myths, Defining the Legacies*; Armond Fields, author of *Eddie Foy*; Brooke Kroeger, author of *Nellie Bly*; Paul Heyer, author of *Titanic Legacy: Disaster as Media Event and Myth*; Anita Lawson, author of *Irvin S. Cobb*; Leslie J. Reagan, author of *When Abortion was a Crime: Women, Medicine, and Law in the United States, 1867–1973*; Donald A. Ritchie, author of *Press Gallery: Congress and the Washington Correspondents*; Carlos A. Schwantes, author of *Coxey's Army: An American Odyssey*; Louis B. Schlesinger, editor of *Explorations in Criminal Psychopathology*; and Kenneth Silverman, author of *Houdini!!!*

Others who have helped me one way or another as I tracked down the odd fact or tidbit include, in alphabetical order: David Alvord, Oneida City Library, Oneida, N.Y.; David G. Badertscher, principal law librarian, Supreme Court, First Judicial District, New York, N.Y.; C. Michael Bright, U.S. Government Printing Office, Office of Congressional and Public Affairs, Washington, D.C.; Ellie Carson, Winnetka Historical Society, Winnetka, Ill.; Ruth C. Crocker, Department of History, Auburn University; Scott Cross, Oshkosh Public Museum, Oshkosh, Wis.; Kenneth Cobb, director, Municipal Archives, New York, N.Y.; Jackie Couture, archives, Eastern Kentucky University, Richmond, Ky.; Scott Cross, archivist at the Oshkosh Public Museum, Oshkosh, Wis.; Deanne Driscoll, for assistance with

Chapin's family tree; Elizabeth Ellis, Museum of the City of New York, New York, N.Y.; James W. Ely Jr., Department of History, Vanderbilt University, Nashville, Tenn.; William Estrada, Glenwood Cemetery, Washington, D.C.; James D. Folts, head, Reference Services, New York State Archives, Albany, N.Y.; Nancy and Marv Greenburg, Chicago, Ill.; Rosemary Hanes, Moving Image Section, Library of Congress, Washington, D.C.; David Hardin, attorney, Chatham, N.J., for help with the intricacies of estate law and terms such as *per stirpes*; Michael Horvat, American Private Press Association, Stayton, Ore.; Lena Goon, White Museum of Canadian Rockies, Banff, B.C.; Judy Grossnickle of Granger, Ind., who heard about my research and unsolicited sent me a copy of what may have been Chapin's last interview with the press; Kathy Killoran, Lloyd Sealy Library, John Jay College of Criminal Justice, New York, N.Y.; Mary King, librarian, Madison County Historical Society, Oneida, N.Y.; Jennifer B. Lee, Rare Book and Manuscript Library, Columbia University, New York, N.Y.; Larry Lorenz, Department of Communications, Loyola University, New Orleans, La.; Jerry Maizell, secretary, International Press Club of Chicago, Chicago, Ill.; John S. McCormick, Salt Lake Community College, Salt Lake City, Utah; Pat Montgomery, Utah State Library, Salt Lake City, Utah; Sharon Morris, reference librarian at the Kingston Library, Kingston, N.Y.; Nora S. Murphy of the Archdiocese Schools of New York, N.Y.; Sharon Neely, reference librarian at the Springfield-Greene County Library, Springfield, Mo.; Jeanne K. Reid, Warner Library, Tarrytown, N.Y.; Sister Marguerita Smith, archivist of the Archdiocese of New York, New York, N.Y.; Linda Rice, Condé Nast Publications, New York, N.Y.; John Stinson, Manuscript and Archive Division, New York Public Library, New York, N.Y.; Ginalie Swain, editor, *Iowa Heritage Illustrated*, Ames, Iowa; Chris Taylor, Atchison Historical Society, Atchison, Kan.; Mary Ann Thompson, Hays Public Library, Hays, Kan.; Ellen Trice, American Rose Society, Shreveport, La.; Lt. Ray Wilk, Sing Sing Correctional Facility, Ossining, N.Y.

Additionally, thanks are owed to librarians at the manuscript, newspaper, microfilm, and main reading rooms of the Library of Congress, Washington, D.C.; New York Public Library, New York, N.Y.; Columbia University, New York, N.Y.; New-York

Historical Society, New York, N.Y.; City Museum of New York, New York, N.Y.; and Utah State Historical Society. Anonymous librarians also unknowingly assisted at public libraries in Deadwood, Mont., Atchison, Hayes, Junction City, and Russell, Kan., Lake Forest, Ill., Springfield, Mo., Oneida, N.Y., and Arlington and Fairfax, Va., and at the libraries of American University, Washington, D.C., George Mason University, Fairfax, Va., Virginia Commonwealth University, Richmond, Va., and Virginia Tech, Blacksburg, Va., as well as librarians at the Oral History Research Office of Columbia University, and at the News Research Department of the *St. Louis Post-Dispatch.*

At Fordham University Press, this book found a very supportive home. Felicity Edge, the managing editor, and Lisa Weidman, the copy editor, strengthened the manuscript while preserving the narrative style I prefer. Thanks are also owed to the Imaging Zone, Springfield, Va., for its work on the illustrations.

Christopher and Elissa Morris, my brother and sister-in-law, lodged me on my research trips to New York. Helen Scorsese, my sister, gave me precious encouragement. Dave and Marge McGrath, my in-laws, gave me a Colorado refuge the equal of any writer's colony. My children were immensely supportive, and all have learned more than they care to know about Chapin. My son Benjamin was my "Watson" on trips across Kansas in search of clues about Chapin's days as an actor. My daughter Stephanie completed some last-minute research for me. My son Alexander always wished me good luck when I descended each night to my study in the cellar. Last, my wife Patty has always been an inspiration to me. I think I finally have a book worthy enough to dedicate to her.

The Gardens

On Tuesday, October 28, 1924, while eating breakfast in his Park Avenue apartment, writer Irvin S. Cobb discovered an annoyance that accompanied fame. There in the *New York Times,* for all to see, was the amount he had paid the federal government for its relatively new income tax. At least Cobb could take some comfort in the fact that he was not the only one whose tax payment had become public. In fact, for the past three days newspapers had entertained their readers by listing the tax payments made by the nation's best-known citizens. That he was among those the *New York Times* selected to publish probably confirmed his own sense of his literary importance.

The blame for this fiduciary unmasking of the rich and famous fell to a poorly written section of a new federal tax law passed by Congress in June. Befuddled tax officials interpreted the passage to mean they had to disclose the payment portion of an individual's tax return to any inquiring reporter or citizen. Thus, for a brief moment before Treasury Department officials regained their wits and resealed the records, the veil of tax secrecy was lifted. Wall Street financiers buzzed with the revelations. A garment industry businessman discovered his partner had lied about the poverty of their shared enterprise and was actually flush with cash. Even romantic matters were not immune from the disclosures. Along with the reporters who flocked to the tax offices in the New York Customs House, a number of women came seeking to compute the true income of their fiancés and husbands. "I am finally going to find out how much my husband makes," said an excited woman while another woman calculated how much alimony she should seek in her divorce.[1]

Although it paled in comparison to John D. Rockefeller Jr.'s incredible $7,435,189.41 payment—the only one above $1 million—Cobb's $5,762.20 payment listed in the *New York Times* gave authenticity to the rumor that he was the best-paid writer of the 1920s. It was, for instance, twenty-five times the amount paid by his neighbor, writer Fannie Hurst, described by critics as a female O. Henry. Money making aside, Cobb was certainly one of the United States' best-read writers. In 1923, ten of New York's leading editors, critics, and writers supping in an elegant restaurant erupted into an argument as to who were the best living U.S. writers. It was decided that each would mark his first and second choice in various genres on an anonymous slip of paper. "The outcome of the ballot," reported the magazine *Current Opinion*, "was such as to give Irvin S. Cobb a kind of primacy in contemporary letters." He appeared on eight of the ten lists.[2]

Cobb's fame was so extensive that he had even licensed his name to a line of cigars with his likeness on the box. The rendering was highly flattering. In life, Cobb's looks were a favorite of caricaturists. He was a huge man whose drooping cheeks, large jowls, and protruding eyes gave him an undeniable toadlike appearance. Over time, Cobb, a perpetual showman, came to regard his apparent homeliness as an asset. While covering World War I, he was the most easily recognized correspondent and was continuously mobbed by U.S. troops everywhere he traveled. As a result, he did nothing to diminish his distinctiveness; quite the opposite. He favored knickers, boots, and long jackets with numerous buttons worn closed, accentuating his barrel-like physique. In his hand, if not between his teeth, he always held a smoking cigar.

Famous and recognized whenever in public, Cobb could hardly blame the newspaper reporters for having a field day with his income-tax records. Before the money, the Park Avenue apartment, the country house, and the Algonquin lunches, Cobb would have been the first to write up such a story for his city editor when he—in his own words—"sweated between the decks" of a Park Row "slave ship"; he would have had no choice in the matter. Before he won his manumission from the tyrants who ruled the newsrooms in the heyday of yellow journalism, Cobb had toiled for Charles Chapin, the most accomplished, notorious, and feared city editor of them all. "Chapin," recalled Alexander Woolcott, a fellow Park Row escapee and one of New York's leading drama critics of the 1920s, "was the acrid martinet who used to issue falsetto and sadistic orders from a swivel chair at the *Evening World* in that now haze-hung era when Irvin Cobb was the best rewrite man on Park Row and I was a Christian slave in the galleys of the *New York Times*."[3]

For two decades, until his abrupt and dramatic departure from the scene in 1918, Chapin had set the pace for the city's vibrant evening press as city editor of Joseph Pulitzer's *Evening World*. Beginning in the morning and sometimes stretching late into the night, the buildings on Park Row shook as massive presses rolled out hundreds of thousands of copies of evening editions. On any street corner, New Yorkers heading home could buy one of a dozen papers filled with news as fresh as the ink, for as little as a penny, hawked by the young peddlers known as newsies. When the events warranted it, such as during the Harry Thaw trial or the sinking of the *Titanic*, evening papers would publish hourly editions that were consumed immediately by a news-hungry public. More than 2,600 newspapers battled daily for the hearts and minds of the nation's readers. This was the golden age of the newspaper. They were indispensable reading and definers of reality. As never before, the features of city life were mirrored in a daily pageantry of print.[4]

In the guerrilla warfare of yellow journalism, any editor who valued his job got a copy of the *Evening World* within minutes of its publication. He could order a rewrite of an *Evening World* exclusive for his paper, then sit at his desk and await the descent of the publisher from upstairs while constructing an explanation as to why only Chapin's paper had the story, "Tiny Tot With Penny Clutched in Chubby Hand Dies Under Tram Before Mother's Eyes." Editors were saved from being fired only because all publishers knew that Chapin was unbeatable. A kind of journalistic equivalent to the Civil War's renowned Bedford Forrest, Chapin knew where hell was going to break out and got there before it broke. The only strategy to beating Chapin would be to hire him, and Pulitzer continually feared that his nemesis William Randolph Hearst, whose checkbook seemed bottomless, would do just that.[5]

Chapin's professional life spanned the birth and adolescence of the modern mass media. In the 1880s, Chapin's sensational crime reporting in the legendary world of Chicago journalism made him one of the best known apostles of what was then known as "new journalism." In the 1890s, he arrived in New York just when the revolution Pulitzer had sparked was transforming Park Row into the epicenter of American journalism. And, as the city editor of Pulitzer's *Evening World* for two decades, Chapin became the model for all city editors, real and fictional. "Chapin walked alone, a tremendously competent, sometimes an almost inspired tyrant," said Cobb. "His idol, and the only one he worshiped, except his own conceitful image, was the inky-nosed, nine-eyed, clay-footed god called News." His faith afforded little comfort to others who did not share in his creed. Chapin was said to have fired 108 men during his tenure. Even Pulitzer's son was a victim. The fact that the father, who kept watch over his dominion with spies in the newsroom, remained mute when the ax fell on his son only served to elevate Chapin's fearful reputation. The smallest infraction could send one packing—and create another barroom tale. Among those told regarding Chapin's relish for giving a man the boot was one about a reporter who claimed his lateness was caused by having scalded his foot in the bathtub. When Chapin fired him several days later, he was said to have exclaimed, "I would have fired you earlier but I wanted to see how long you could keep on faking that limp." Tales of this sort were so frequently told that one witty repartee about Chapin was included in *Bartlett's Familiar Quotations*.[6]

"In him was combined something of Caligula, something of Don Juan, a touch of the Barnum, a dash of Narcissus, a spicing of Machiavelli," said Cobb. Chapin's harsh management style was, however, not entirely unique. Stanley Walker, city editor of the *Herald Tribune* and one of the few tenderhearted editors of that era, described the prototypical city editor as a brutal curmudgeon who would make one's blood run cold. "He invents strange devices for the torture of reporters, this mythical agate-eyed Torquemada with the paste-pots and scissors. Even his laugh, usually directed at something sacred, is part sneer. His terrible curses cause flowers to wither, as grass died under the hoof beats of the horse of Attila the Hun. A chilly, monstrous figure, sleepless, nerveless, and facing with ribald mockery the certain hell which awaits him."[7]

Chapin's talents, however, were legendary. "Quite possibly, viewed as a machine, he was the ablest city editor who ever lived," concluded Walker. His reputation was such that any man who developed similar traits or methods was said to be marked with the "Chapin stigmata." Journalists put up with Chapin's despotism because he was one of the most innovative and daring editors in New York. For a reporter, the journey to the *Evening World* always began with a letter from Chapin, delivered by personal courier, containing the request that the reporter "drop in some day and talk things over." Chapin drew together the city's best legmen, reporters, and writers with the promise of journalistic glory and sufficient money that they would abandon the comfort of their posts with rival newspapers, such as those owned by Hearst, to risk life under him. He pioneered the beat system that later became ubiquitous, and he lavishly spent Pulitzer's money to create a pool of writers who would translate the coarse facts streaming in by telephone into hard, crisp, jump-off-the-page prose that sold papers. "Such a rewrite battery as probably never has been assembled before, never has been since, and never will be again," said Donald H. Clarke, a reporter who left Harvard for Park Row in 1907.[8]

Now in late October 1924, events converged to resurrect memories in Cobb of those bygone days. The previous week, while in Montréal after a fishing trip on Lac La Peche, Cobb had lifted the receiver of his hotel telephone to hear the familiar, but distant voice of Ray Long, the editor of *Cosmopolitan*, calling from New York. Long and Cobb had been friends since working as low-paid reporters for rival Midwestern newspapers twenty-five years earlier, when they only dreamed of making it big in New York. Now as editor of one of the nation's most widely circulated general-interest magazines, Long had a budget lavish enough to afford Cobb, and he rewarded his friend with choice assignments.[9]

"You worked under Charley Chapin," Long said. "I heard you say once that he was one of the most vivid, outstanding personalities you ever encountered. I think there is a story in the entombing, the total eclipse behind prison walls of such a man."[10]

Indeed, the public memory of Chapin had faded in the six years since he had been sent to Sing Sing prison for murdering his wife of thirty-eight years with a pistol while she slumbered peacefully in her bed. The crime was zealously reported in all New York newspapers, whose editors relished the revenge of putting into headlines a crime committed by one who had been the ultimate composer of crime-filled front pages.

By 1924, however, Chapin, once the previously most-talked-about figure on Park Row, was rarely mentioned, even among the company of writers that Cobb kept. The old Chapin tales that used to earn the raconteur a drink were almost never told in bars where the ink-stained wretches of New York congregated. "The physical image of him as I last had seen him, humped over his desk in the Pulitzer Building on Park Row, was growing fainter in my mind," said Cobb. Coincidentally, just days before Long's call, Cobb had spotted an item in the *New York Times* that had also prompted him to think of his old boss. A dispatch from Ossining, New York, said that the state had published a report on what seemed to be an incongruity in conditions at the notorious Sing Sing prison. They credited, by name, the inmate who had brought about the change. It was Chapin.

> He has adorned the gruesome place with flowers, trees and shrubs, and the yard which five years ago was desolate and littered with stones and rubbish is now a thing of beauty. The rose garden is an inspiration to dark and troubled souls.[11]

From Montréal, Cobb sent word to his secretary to go to Sing Sing and make arrangements for a visit. He was not sure what reception awaited his request. A few years earlier, Chapin had refused a visit from Cobb. This time he accepted. Perhaps, Chapin wrote to a friend after the secretary departed, the visit will be "a chance for Cobb to get even for the hard knocks he had when I was his boss."[12]

Although it was an overcast day, by the time Cobb set out in the late morning of October 28, 1924, it was already ten degrees above average, certainly pleasant enough to spend the day outside. Most who made the trip to the New York State Penitentiary at Ossining took the train from Grand Central Station a few blocks south of Cobb's apartment. For a destination as grim as it was, the trip was breathtakingly beautiful. The prison was built on the banks of the Hudson River thirty-four miles north of New York City, giving rise to the expression "being sent up the river." The train tracks follow the contours of the river for miles, offering the passenger on the left side of the compartment an unfettered view of the Hudson, a river that inspired artists and gave rise to a school of painters whose best-known works hung in New York's great Metropolitan Museum nine blocks from Cobb's apartment.[13]

Whether one took the short walk or a cab ride from the Ossining station, approaching Sing Sing was like coming to a medieval fortification. Erected in the 1820s with stone quarried on the spot, Sing Sing was America's best-known and most-feared prison. Its massive stone walls, round stone towers, and heavy doors made its line of business clear to all comers. New York's most notorious criminals were, if lucky, confined here for life or else executed on Thursdays. Only in the prior decade had the prison begun to shed the last of its nineteenth-century practices under the rule of a new warden, Lewis Lawes. Rising from the ranks of prison guards, Lawes had been appointed by Governor Al Smith four years earlier during a wave of reform that saw many modernizations in prison life. Lawes, who dressed for the role of the enlightened reformer in tailored New York suits, enjoyed immensely showing off his fiefdom. He was publicity savvy. He knew the city's literati—even had hopes of joining its set someday—and never missed a chance to increase his visibility and promote his reforms. Cobb's visit could be a boon. It also pleased Lawes that Cobb was coming to do a story about Chapin. Of all his prisoners, Chapin was one of his favorites. The two had been immediately attracted to each other when they met in 1919, and an unusual friendship had evolved. In fact, over time, Lawes had given Chapin virtual free run of the prison. On many an afternoon, the inmate could be found reading magazines in a wicker rocker on the warden's porch overlooking the river, with the warden's daughter playing at his feet.

After exchanging pleasantries with Cobb, Lawes escorted the writer down into the prison yard, where they found Chapin. "Dear Chief," said the corpulent Cobb, who immediately took his old boss in his arms. Even though Chapin had gained thirty pounds and his five-foot-eight frame now held nearly 160 pounds, he was momentarily eclipsed by Cobb's embrace. When they separated, Cobb examined his former slave master, whom he had not seen since a few days before that baleful day in September 1918. He seemed unchanged, thought Cobb. "Only he was white now when he used to be gray, with the same quick, decisive movements, the same bony, projecting chin upheld at a combative angle, the same flashes of stern and mordant humor, the same trick of chewing on a pipe stem or cigar butt, the same imperious gestures, the same air of being a creature unbendable and uncrushable." But further consideration of Chapin would have to wait because what stretched out in front of Cobb were Chapin's gardens, a certain conversation stopper.[14]

Only a few years before, the yard—nearly as long and wide as two football fields joined end to end—had consisted of hard pack, covering decades of strewn construction debris and refuse. Only tiny patches of struggling grass and even tinier flower beds previously broke the monotony of the gray soil surrounded on all sides by gray stone edifices. Cobb knew this landscape well because he had used the setting for one of his short stories, written eight years earlier. Now what lay before him stunned Cobb. "There were spaces of lawns, soft and luxuriant, with flagged walks brocading them likes strips of gray lace laid down on green velvet," he wrote. Along the walks stood soft, puffy arborvitae trees and masses of neatly trimmed ornamental shrubs. Green vines, like veins, wove their way up the walls of heavy stone, quarried by the hands of those the state had confined here for more than a century. And everywhere Cobb looked were flowers, familiar and unfamiliar, some in full bloom and others done for the year. The array of plant life was such that the mind's eye and nose could imagine the summertime burst of color and perfume that had preceded his visit.[15]

Cobb and Chapin made their way down one of the flagstone paths. To their right, lining the bed along the six-story-tall old cellblock, was a herbaceous border 469 feet long, with more than

1,000 iris plants, 150 peonies, hundreds of other perennials, and 6,000 bulbs waiting for spring. The long narrow bed, however, served only as a complement to the massive rectangular garden running the length of the yard's center. At its midpoint was a fountain rising from a ten-foot-wide pool, upon the surface of which floated white and yellow water lilies. Leading to it were paths, lined with large, blue hydrangeas and benches for the inmates. And there, set in beds framed by narrow strips of lawn, were the rose bushes. They were so many as to defy counting. Chapin said they numbered about 2,000, and almost 3,000 if one counted the new arrivals in the greenhouses.

The rose gardens were, wrote Cobb, "of such size and richness and all so well tended, all so carefully laid out as involuntarily to make you think it properly should be the possession of a millionaire fancier." Chapin's handicraft had not stopped with the main yard. "Not an odd-shaped scrap of earth, nor a tucked-in corner behind a building or within a recess in the walls but was brilliant with flowers and grass. The eye strayed downward from wattled windows and guarded watchtowers to rest on zinnias and cannas and asters and all manner of autumnal blooms. It was like bridging two separate worlds of misery and despair, the other a world of sweetness and gentleness and hope and high intent."

From the center, Cobb and Chapin turned and proceeded down a secondary yard. It was the only open space in the prison without a wall on every side. It gave out onto the Hudson below and was planted in solid colorful blocks. At the end of this boulevard, Cobb and Chapin turned left again and came to the most macabre building of the compound, a low-lying brick structure that contained the electric chair. Chapin's touch was visible even here. "I saw how the approach to the new death house had been planted, so that the last outdoor thing a condemned man sees as he is marched into the barred corridor from which he does not issue again ever, is the loveliness of green grass and fair flowers," wrote Cobb. Next they toured a former garbage depot, now the site of Sing Sing's prized tulip beds. In May and June, after the jonquils and hyacinths that hedged the beds quit blooming, thousands of tulips would rise in a sea of color. (The sight had become so noted that even white-gloved ladies from Westchester garden clubs braved entering this den of criminals to gaze upon it.) They traveled through three greenhouses opposite the entrance to the death house, only yards from the lapping water of the river. They were built twenty years before, when prison officials had made an attempt to have the inmates raise vegetables, and had fallen into disrepair before Chapin restored them. In winter, flowers from the greenhouse would be brought daily to the prison chapel and hospital.

Returning to the center of the prison yard, Cobb made his last stop in a fourth greenhouse abutting the old death house, in which several cells had been converted into living quarters for Chapin. Prior to its new life, the glassed-in space had been the prison's morgue. Here, after an electrocution, the corpse was brought to be examined by state medical officials before being surrendered to the family. After lawmakers heard of two cases in which men had been accidentally electrocuted and later revived by physicians, they passed a law requiring that the brain of execution victims be opened and examined. "On the slab where a hundred autopsies had been performed," wrote Cobb, "potted flowers stood very thick, and in the sink where anatomists washed their tools when the job was done, sheaves of cut flowers were lying in cool clear running water." The fragrance of the potting soil and moist plant life and the sounds of the canaries chirping in gilded cages eliminated all trace of the building's past. Here Cobb turned to Chapin.

"Boss," he said, "in the old days down on the *Evening World,* I never would have dreamed that a time would come when you would be an expert florist."

"Nor I," Chapin replied.

"You ought to see him now," said Warden Lawes, who had rejoined the party. "He's up every morning at five o'clock and out here among these flowers and I guess he'd stay out here with 'em all night if he could. And he's got a whole library of books on flowers and knows 'em all by heart."

The immensity of the work was easily apparent. In all, if one counted the bulbs, seedlings, and plants under various stages of propagation in the greenhouses, there were as many as 50,000 plants that needed tending.

"I used to have a harder job than getting up at five o'clock," said Chapin. "I used to have to get Cobb up out of bed and down to the office by nine o'clock every morning."

They all chuckled. Then Chapin turned and tended an exotic shrub, pressing the mulch down around its roots.

"Well, it takes a lot of personal attention to make flowers yield their best," he admitted. "Watering, for example. One plant wants a lot of water; another would be drowned if you gave it half as much."

As they walked back toward the entrance to the yard, completing their inspection tour, Chapin continued to fill in Cobb on his new life. "Mostly we talked about his flowers, or rather he did, larding his speech with technical terms and Latin names," wrote Cobb. "Nothing was said by either of us about repentance or atonement or regeneration or recapturing a man's self respect. Nothing much was said about the past. Nor about the future." But as Cobb contemplated, there wasn't much future to talk about in the case of a sixty-five-year-old man who was serving no less than twenty years, with little prospect for parole or pardon. "He didn't invite sympathy and I didn't bestow it," said Cobb.

"Have you got someone broken in to carry on this work after you go?" asked Cobb.

"I've got nine more years to stay here, so why hurry about getting another fellow to carry on," replied Chapin. Cobb simply smiled and looked wise. The next day, back in his New York apartment, Cobb wrote in the piece he prepared for *Cosmopolitan* that he thought Chapin would die in prison.[16]

As Cobb departed, George McManus, another colleague of Chapin's newspaper past, arrived for a visit. The day had turned into a virtual alumni reunion. McManus had worked on the *World* with Chapin a dozen years earlier. He had renounced the drudgery of Park Row when he created "Bringing Up Father," an immensely popular comic strip starring the unflappable Maggie and her up-to-no-good husband Jiggs, whom she often chased after with a rolling pin. The strip had been nationally syndicated and recently had been turned into a Broadway play called "Father" in which McManus sometimes played the lead character. McManus had decided to visit Chapin after attending the funeral of a mutual friend. The two reminisced for a while.

Finally done with his visitors, Chapin returned to his office for the first time since the morning. There was probably no inmate anywhere in the United States, or the world for that matter, who had an office like Chapin's. With three windows overlooking the Hudson, his carpeted, draped, and book-lined hideaway was more luxurious than any workplace he had had on the outside. There he found nine letters waiting. A prodigious correspondent, Chapin received and sent in one day the amount of mail that many inmates could hope to see in a month. After examining the envelopes, Chapin set them all aside except for one from the Federal Reserve Bank of Cleveland. The return address alone was enough to set his old heart racing. As he already knew, it contained another installment of his newest prison-romance-by-mail begun eight months earlier with Constance R. Nelson, a young editorial worker at the bank. He feverishly read all four closely written pages of the latest in an almost daily stream of saccharine letters. The mailbags between Ossining and Cleveland ferried the duo's fantasies of how they would devote their remaining years to each other when the governor issued their hoped-for pardon.

After eating supper, prepared for him by Larry, his private inmate-cook, and closing the greenhouses for the night, Chapin sat in his office as darkness and quiet fell over the prison. The other inmates were confined to their tiny, damp cells, but not Chapin. He was free to roam the dark prison all night if he wanted to. The stack of letters still lay unopened on his desk. Instead of tending to them, he reread Nelson's. "The other eight are from very dear friends," Chapin pecked out on his Underwood typewriter later that night, "but only the one letter ever makes my heart beat faster, makes me glad to be alive, glad I've got someone who cares."[17]

He went to bed in his cell in the old death house. In the morning, he would turn sixty-six. Though he enjoyed unheard-of privileges for a prisoner, he was continually reminded of his descent from the life he had so relished. Gone were the cars, the horses, the yacht, and the luxury hotels. Gone were sounds of the clattering typewriters and jingling phones, leading to the roar of the presses as they churned out the evening edition. Gone, most of all, was his power. His only remaining dominion was his rose garden. "Roses respond to me when all else fails," Chapin had written earlier that year to Nelson. "Park Row would never recognize me. I don't even know myself, and to think I have so changed in so short a time."

"Do you think," he asked, "do you think that growing flowers did it?"[18]

Youth

Charles E. Chapin was born on October 29, 1858, in Oneida, a dozen miles from the geographical center of New York state. He was the second member of the second generation of his family to be born in Madison County, situated in the western end of the Leatherstocking region, so named because of the leather leggings worn by frontiersmen and made famous by James Fenimore Cooper's fictitious Natty Bumppo. Oneida was then a growing, prosperous community, one of many in a string of towns that had come to life across the top of the Empire State since the 363-mile Erie Canal was opened in 1825, connecting the Hudson River with the Great Lakes. Only four feet deep and dug almost entirely by hand, the canal was nonetheless a technological marvel. It cut travel time in half to what was then the West, slashed shipping costs, triggered the first westward movements of white settlers, and transformed New York City into the busiest port of the nation.[1]

Chapin's grandfather Samuel Chapin witnessed and benefited from the economic boom. A descendant of Massachusetts Puritan Deacon Samuel Chapin, Samuel came to Madison County in 1813 when his parents Rufus, a cabinetmaker and carpenter, and Polly joined the westward movement. Only a few years before their arrival, Madison County had been part of an untouched wilderness occupied by Oneida Indians, one of the six nations of Iroquois. New York's state legislature began purchasing tracts of land from the Oneida in 1795 and encouraged white settlers to move in. By 1840, most of the Oneida had left New York for Wisconsin. Later in life, Samuel would recount the frontier-like conditions under which they lived during those early years, cooking on a great log fire and wearing clothing made from his mother's own carding, spinning, and weaving. Charles Chapin's grandmother, Fannie, also came to Madison County as a small child soon after her birth in Hartford, Connecticut. Her parents, Elisha and Prudence Sage, paused their westward-bound ox train in the summer of 1816 at the onset of labor pains. Before the wagon had come to a stop in the center of Scanandoah, a small Indian village, Fannie's brother Russell Sage had completed his entry into the world. Two years later, the Sages and their seven children made their stay in Madison County permanent with the purchase of a foreclosed farm.[2]

Fannie and Samuel were married in 1830. Within a year, they had their first child, a boy they named Samuel. Charles Chapin's father was the second born, arriving June 22, 1832. They named him Earl. By the end, the union of Samuel and Fannie produced nine boys and three girls. To support his growing family, Samuel pursued a skilled trade as a mechanic in a carriage shop, and then repairing watches and clocks. Soon he opened a jewelry business in Vernon, in adjacent Oneida County. There he was fortunate to become acquainted with Sands Higinbotham, who was buying up land in Madison County in a speculative venture. In 1834, Higinbotham moved onto his land, deeded a right of way to New York Central Railway, and persuaded the railroad to include his newly constructed Oneida Depot as a stop on its new line. On July 4, 1839, a long train rumbled into town, passing by a forest of cut stumps, piles of brush, and stacks of logs stripped of bark. When the train departed with its load of excited excursionists, one local historian noted that a few members of the Oneida Nation had been among those witnessing the spectacle. "Fancy could read sadness in their faces at this last inroad of a scarcely understood civilization upon the domain of their ancestors and their own homes," she wrote. "If, with the transient and soon gratified feeling of curiosity, they were, in the main, mourners upon the scene, it need be no marvel."[3]

Higinbotham's gamble paid off. One no longer had to be situated on the banks of the canal to reap its economic benefits.

Within a few years, Higinbotham induced a number of merchants to open stores in his growing village. Among them was Samuel Chapin, who moved his jewelry store, now called S. Chapin & Sons, from Vernon to Oneida. By the 1850s, it was a prosperous family enterprise. Samuel's eldest two boys worked as jewelers, and two others toiled as clerks. But to call S. Chapin & Sons a jewelry store is not quite accurate, though the family always referred to their trade as that of jewelers. In addition to watches, clocks, jewelry, silverware, and plated ware, a customer could also find pianos, melodeoans (a kind of accordion), and other musical instruments for sale or rent, perfumes, school books, stationery, and "a host of Yankee Notions" in the three-story brick building Samuel built on Main Street. As the town's first jeweler and premiere purveyor of finery, Samuel was well known. To be a Chapin was a mark of some distinction in Oneida. The eldest son, Samuel Jr., followed in his father's footsteps and made tending the family business his life's work. Earl was also trained as a jeweler by his father, but, as with many second born, he did not seem eager to remain under his dad's shadow, or his elder brother's, for that matter. Unlike Samuel, who remained in the house with his father, Earl moved out. In fact, Earl would become the only one of Samuel's offspring to eventually move away from Oneida.[4]

Earl's separation from the family began in March 1854 when, at age twenty-two, he boarded a train in Oneida and headed for Erie, Pennsylvania, 270 miles west. The object of his journey was to complete his romantic pursuit of Cecelia Ann Yale. Earl had known Cecelia for several years. She had been born in Homer, in neighboring Cortland County, on October 20, 1837, and had lived in Oneida between 1846 and 1854 when her family had moved to Erie. The two were married in a simple ceremony, presided over by a Methodist pastor, in her father's new home in Erie on March 27, 1854. Following the wedding, the couple moved to Perry, in western New York. They remained there only six months before coming back to Oneida, where Earl went back to work in his father's store. In 1857, Earl and Cecelia had their first child, whom they named Fannie in honor of Earl's mother.[5]

In the summer of 1858, Cecelia was expecting her second child. The summer had been a fine one in Madison County as evidenced by the abundance of prize-winning fruits and flowers at the just-concluded Lenox township and Madison County fairs. But stormy weather of an entirely different sort loomed that fall as the birth of their child approached. In Illinois, Abraham Lincoln had issued his famous warning that "a house divided against itself cannot stand." Closer to home, William H. Seward, then one of the nation's most prominent Republican leaders, repeated this dire forecast in a speech in nearby Rochester, New York. "It is an irrepressible conflict between opposing and enduring forces," Seward said, "and it means that the United States must and will, sooner or later, become either entirely a slaveholding nation, or entirely a free-labor nation." Three days later, on Friday, October 29, 1858, Cecelia gave birth to Charles, whom they named after Earl's brother who had died in infancy.[6]

Before Charles turned three, the irrepressible conflict erupted. A patriotic fever consumed the North, especially in counties such as Madison, which Lincoln had won in 1860. "A whirlwind of patriotism," is how Ralph Waldo Emerson described it. At night, torches lit up cities and towns as massive recruiting rallies were held. "The whole population, men, women, and children seemed to be in the streets with Union favors and flags," wrote a Harvard professor. A Philadelphian described his city as being in "a wild state of excitement." Oneida was no exception to the war fever. On April 23, 1861, a meeting was called for Deveraux Hall in the center of Oneida. All of the town's leading families attended, the Oneida Saxe Horn Band played national airs, and patriotic speeches were made, followed by resolutions of support for the war. The pro-war sentiment in town was such that the one citizen who publicly admitted that he was of a different mind was "induced to mount a dry good box while Gen. John M. Messinger administered the oath of allegiance," recorded one local historian. "It is unnecessary to say that this summary proceeding had the desired effect," he added.[7]

Earl Chapin and another townsman urged those at the meeting to join the volunteers for the cause. But he himself did not sign up for the company, which went off to the war with a Syracuse regiment. His reasons are not known. However, the Chapins's house burned to the ground that year, and he may have felt he had to stay. Eventually Earl did join. On January 12, 1864, he

signed up for a three-year tour with Company B of New York's
157th Regiment. The regiment, formed in 1862, was a battered
company by the time Earl became a member. It had fought at
Chancellorsville and Gettysburg, as well as six other substantial
battles. Now, as the war's tide had turned, what fighting was left
would seem like small skirmishes in comparison. The regiment
was stationed in South Carolina and Florida. In the North, it was
rumored that new volunteers would not be welcomed into the
thinned ranks of these war-weary soldiers. But it turned out to be
quite the contrary. Members of the 157th welcomed the new recruits, including Earl, with open arms and helped them pitch
their tents and learn to brew coffee on the improvised sheet-iron
stoves with fruit cans for a stovepipe.[8]

Earl reached the 157th on May 8, 1864, in Fernandina, Florida,
after nearly four months in various training barracks. At first he
was put in charge of ordnance, then was reassigned to work as a
clerk in the headquarters at Hilton Head, South Carolina. He
didn't miss any action, as his regiment saw none, aside from a
small skirmish in Florida, between July and the end of the year.
In October, while at Hilton Head, Chapin sought and received a
furlough to go home for thirty days because he faced foreclosure
on his property. Upon his return to Hilton Head, he continued
to work as a clerk until February. Then he took the unusual step
of obtaining a transfer to the 103rd U.S. Colored Infantry being
organized in Hilton Head to serve garrison and guard duty in Savannah. The Union began permitting the formation of these regiments of black soldiers in 1863, but they were almost universally
commanded by whites. In addition to a promotion to Second
Lieutenant, Earl may have seen some potential for further ad-
vancement in a post many other whites spurned. But by July, after
never having seen action and having been home at least once, if
not twice, Earl's Civil War service was over. He resigned "for personal reasons" and was discharged on July 28, 1865.[9]

After several years back home, Earl decided the family should
leave Oneida. The family now comprised two more boys, Freder-
ick and Frank, in addition to Charles, and two girls, Marion and
Fannie. In 1869, they boarded a westbound train and resettled in
Junction City, Kansas, near Fort Riley and where a number of
Civil War veterans had moved. "It was the end of the railroad,"

said John Frederick Glick, a German Civil War veteran who rode
the train as far as it would take him. Named for the intersection
of the Republican and Smoky Hill rivers, Junction City was one
of many Kansas towns that grew exponentially after the Civil
War, fueled by a steady flow of immigrants who were lured by
cheap land in the West, encouraged by the completion of the
transcontinental railroad in 1869, and fleeing uneasy economic
conditions in the East. In the decade before the Chapins arrived,
Junction City's population had quintupled to 5,526. Earl bought a
small plot of land and went into business selling watches and jewelry. Charles entered school, the only one of the Chapin children
to do so; his older sister and younger siblings remained at home.
But Junction City did not produce the riches for which Earl had
hoped, and the family soon picked up stakes.[10]

In the fall of 1872, the Chapins moved north to Atchison, Kansas. Although Junction City certainly had been a growing, prosperous community, Atchison looked like El Dorado. Situated on
rolling hills along the western side of a bend in the Missouri
River, the city was like a funnel through which virtually all westbound rail traffic poured. Selling supplies to this river of humanity
would be said to produce more millionaires per capita than any
other spot in the United States. On Monday, November 11th,
Earl made his stab at tapping into the potentially easy cash by
opening a jewelry shop in Atchison. "Mr. Chapin is a practical
watchmaker and desired to say that his work is warranted to give
satisfaction in all cases," read the advertisement he placed in the
Atchison *Daily Champion*.[11]

Charles was now fourteen, an age by which most boys of that
time were at work, but he held no aspirations to follow in his
father's trade. "The one idea that was firmly fixed in my mind was
that I wanted to be independent," he said. "I realized I must no
longer be a burden to my father, who had as much as he could do
to provide for my sisters and younger brothers. Most of all I
wanted to earn the means with which to acquire an education."
His only schooling thus far had been that of the one-room
schoolhouse in Junction City. His father's continued inability to
support the family made further schooling unlikely. "I reasoned
out of my small boy brain that if ever I was to amount to anything
I must work out my salvation in my own way, without help or

hindrance. Others had done it and come out on top and so must I. So I cut away and boldly set out to conquer the world."[12]

In the winter of 1873, Charles spotted a sign in the window of the *Daily Champion* that a boy was sought to deliver papers. The *Daily Champion* was one of the most prosperous and influential newspapers in Kansas at the time. It occupied a three-story brick building at the center of Commercial Street, an impressive ten-block gathering of stores, businesses, and professional offices. Colonel John A. Martin, the publisher, was also the town's postmaster, and the post office occupied the ground floor. Chapin walked up the flight of stairs to the paper's office on the second floor and applied for a delivery job at the counter. He was sent back to the circulation manager, who took one look at him and declared he wouldn't do. He needed strong boys, he said, with enough strength to carry heavy bundles of newspapers several miles each morning and deliver them to subscribers before breakfast. "I was a little chap, even for my age," admitted Chapin, "but had grit and persuaded the man to give me a trial." He succeeded, and soon Chapin was rising long before dawn every day, except Monday when the paper did not publish, to make it to the pressroom by 3:30 to gather the papers as fast as they came off the press, fold them, and head off into the dark of Atchison on a five-mile route with several hundred papers strapped to his shoulder. "Many of the streets on my route were so steep one took almost as many steps upward as forward and in the winter months I would often flounder through snow that was waist deep."[13]

For his efforts, Chapin earned four dollars a week, a decent sum for a boy, but not one matching his ambition. So he looked for ways to increase it. One morning, returning from completing his route, the operator of one of the town's two telegraph offices asked Chapin if he would deliver a telegram from President Ulysses S. Grant addressed to lawyer John James Ingalls, who had just been elected by the state legislature to the United States Senate. Ingalls, a graduate of Williams College, was an unusually literate politician. Between his several short-lived political posts and failed election bids, he had served as an editor of the *Champion* and helped found the *Kansas Magazine*. He told a biographer that he made it a daily habit to spend an hour with a Webster's dictionary, often committing to memory the Pope and Johnson couplets that were used to illustrate the meaning of a particular entry. The Ingalls house stood on a bluff overlooking the Missouri River, about a dozen blocks south of the business district. A ram- bling affair with a two-story wing, it was surrounded by a large yard almost one-half of a city block, giving a sense of seclusion from the growing city below. Although the Ingalls were not rich, Ingalls's law practice had made the family very comfortable.[14]

The Ingalls's maid answered the door and told Chapin the Senator was asleep. He insisted nonetheless that he be shown to the bedroom. Chapin knocked at the bedroom door, with no success. The door was ajar, and Chapin could see Ingalls in his bed, the blankets pulled over his head. He boldly pushed open the door. "Wake up, Senator," Chapin said. "I have an important telegraph message for you from President Grant." Ingalls rose, read the telegram, and began to laugh. "How did you know that it is important?" he asked.

"Any message from President Grant to a United States Senator must be important," replied Chapin.

Ingalls patted Chapin's head, reached for his trousers, and pulled from his pocket a silver dollar, which he proffered to Chapin.

"Nothing to collect on the message," said Chapin.

"The dollar is yours for being my little alarm clock and waking me up," explained Ingalls, who pulled the bellcord and, when the maid returned, ordered breakfast for two. Over breakfast, Ingalls peppered Chapin with questions about himself and his ambitions. In return for his answers, Ingalls told stories of famous statesmen who had begun life at the bottom like Chapin was doing and had made their way to the top. He loaned Chapin two books from his library and sent him on his way. Upon returning to the telegraph office with the receipt for the delivered message, the operator offered Chapin a permanent post to replace the messenger who had failed to show. Delivering telegrams would take place after his newspaper route and would pay $13 a month, plus "perquisites" of a quarter for all telegrams delivered more than a mile from the office.[15]

Chapin now earned more than $30 a month. For his father, on the other hand, Atchison was not an equal economic success. Competing with the town's two established jewelers was apparently tougher than he had presumed. By May 1873, the family was moving to Hamburg, Iowa. This time, however, they left without Charles, though he was only fourteen years old. Leaving Atchison would have meant giving up his two jobs and his ambitions. It may have been too much to ask. Nearly fifty years later when Chapin wrote his memoirs, he began them with a remembrance of Atchison because it was here, he said, that he "began life . . . the real living of the everyday world—as a newspaper man." But without his parents, he had to fend entirely for himself. This he accomplished by first getting permission from the pressroom foreman to sleep on a stack of paper, and by working out a plan with a restaurant on Commercial Street to act as cashier during the busy lunchtime in return for meals. "There are tender memories of my nest a-top the reserve supply of print paper, covered only with my quilt of many colors and fantastic designs," recalled Chapin years later. "It was there I learned the lesson of self-education; a lesson that was worth while."[16]

Unschooled as he was, Chapin nonetheless loved to read. He had continued to borrow books from Ingalls's library until the senator headed to Washington for the opening of Congress. At the newspaper, Chapin befriended a kindly editor who encouraged Chapin's reading. He selected books for the young boy and helped him divine the meaning of the more complicated ones. After a while, he lent Chapin a copy of the key to his bookcase, in return for keeping it orderly. Chapin was voracious. He read the essays of Emerson and Carlyle, the fiction of Balzac, Dickens, Dumas, Hugo, the philosophy of Aristotle, Epictetus, Montaigne, and Johnson, ancient and modern histories, the Bible—he loved its language—and Voltaire and Darwin, both of whom mystified Chapin, except for the former's *Candide*, which remained a favorite for life.[17]

Although Chapin's drive was remarkable, his pursuit of self-improvement was not. Many, if not most, in the newspaper world to which Chapin aspired had never attended college. There was, however, a strong belief among them in self-education. It was, after all, one from their ranks, Mark Twain, who is said to have quipped that he never let his schooling get in the way of his education. Thus, the path to success among newspapermen was constant study, especially of newspapers, which in and of themselves offered a virtual curriculum feeding the era's fashion of self-improvement.[18]

Chapin ran across a weekly paper published for boys and girls. It had a section devoted to instruction in shorthand by one of New York City's best stenographers. Chapin subscribed and soon purchased a set of advertised textbooks. He quickly mastered the art, practicing at night at public lectures and meetings. Chapin also learned Morse code at his telegraph job. His new skill saved the paper one night when the regular telegraph operator was drunk and fell to the floor while the evening's batch of telegraphic news was coming down the wire. "I let him lie there in a drunken stupor while I took every word of the report without once breaking in on the wire to ask that a sentence be repeated," said Chapin.[19]

At the paper, Chapin learned everything he could about its operation, from setting type to the feeding and operation of the press itself. He earned no pay for his effort, but did it because he had come to love newspapers and everything about them. "I had no boy friends and made no attempt to cultivate them," he said. "My associates were men, chiefly men from whom I could learn something useful and there wasn't a man in the entire organization of the newspaper office who didn't cheerfully explain to me anything I asked of him."[20]

One night while idling away time in the telegraph office, Chapin composed a short item, which he called "An Autobiography of a Hotel Office Chair." He left it on the desk and went across the street for his nightly dinner at the restaurant. When he returned, the sketch was gone. The evening press reports had begun to arrive, so he couldn't ask the telegraph operator if he had seen it. Maybe, Chapin thought, he threw it out. The next morning, Chapin found a note from the *Champion's* editor with two silver dollars attached. The note and money were thanks for an "exceedingly well-written little sketch." Better than the money or the thanks, Chapin found his little piece on the editorial page, double leaded to make it stand out. "Within an hour I read it not less than a dozen times," said Chapin. "Never were telegraph messages delivered with greater celerity than I delivered them that day. I felt as if I had wings." In coming days, the item was republished in Chicago and St. Louis. Chapin took now to studying the big-city papers and practicing rewriting the stories he read. Whenever he could, he would talk to the editor about his new ambition. Soon the editor said he would have a job within a year as a reporter. "I was elated over the promise and during the ensuing months I studied harder than ever." His exaltation, however, was burst by illness. "Whether it was because I worked too much and slept too little, or because I was sleeping in the foul atmosphere of a basement pressroom, I was stricken with a fever and when next I was able to sit up I was a miserable little skeleton of skin and bones."[21]

"All ambition was gone," he said. "Even that bright and happy dream of a newspaper career vanished with the delirium I suffered. There was but one thing in all the world I wanted. I wanted to see my mother. And home to her I went, as fast as a train could take me." By this time, his family had left Hamburg, Iowa, and had resettled in Freeport, a fifty-year-old Illinois city founded by German settlers along the Pecatonica River. Its only claim to fame was that it had been the site of the second Lincoln–Douglas debate.[22]

Chapin's illness was serious, the first of many bouts with ill health that would plague him during his life. As he recovered at home, he rediscovered a painting of a young girl that had previously hung in the living room and had entranced him. "I would sit in silent admiration of that lovely face, and smile back to the eyes that seemed to be smiling at me," he said. It now hung in his sister Marion's room. Once when she was not there, Chapin went into her room, removed the painting, and hung it above his bed where he convalesced. At dinner that night, Marion asked him, "Did you take mother's picture from my room?"

"Mother's picture?" said the surprised Chapin. "And then for the first time I was told that the portrait was painted by my father the year before they were married."[23]

That fall, Chapin had recovered sufficiently to take a train to Chicago in hopes of finding work as a reporter. "Not one of the editors appeared eager to grab me," he said. "The only one who listened to me seriously was the venerable Wilbur F. Storey, one of the greatest editors of his day." Storey owned and managed the *Chicago Times*, the best known of the city's papers. Notorious for its hell-raising style, the paper had been padlocked closed for

three days during the Civil War because of its anti-Federal sentiments, a distinction that its editor valued like a war medal.
"When I entered Mr. Storey's sanctum," recalled Chapin, "he was
tilted back in a big swivel chair, his long legs stretched across the
top of his desk." The editor listened carefully as the young boy
told him of his newspaper work in Atchison and of his ambition
to become a reporter. Storey even consented to read Chapin's one
clipping. In the end, the kindly publisher told Chapin that at sixteen he was still too young to be a reporter in Chicago. "Go back
to your home town or some other small city and get a few years
of practical training and when you have done this come to me
again," Storey said as he put his arm around Chapin and walked
him to the elevator. Discouraged, Chapin returned to Freeport
and called on his hometown papers. Even his offer to work for
free left them disinterested. One editor suggested he become an
apprentice at $5 a week. "I knew what that meant; I had seen what
was expected of apprentices," said Chapin. It was no more than
building fires to warm rooms for the editors, fetching coal, and
cleaning the presses. "Me, who had seen the product of his imagi-
native brain reprinted in two of the greatest newspapers in the
country, become a smutty face printer's 'devil?' Not much! I
wanted to set the world aflame by writing thrilling accounts of big
news happenings."[24]

The press wouldn't hire him, but Chapin's luck was such that
an opportunity arose for him to become a press lord, granted on
a small scale. In the winter of 1874, Chapin discovered the sheriff
was selling the remains of an insurance company that had gone
belly up. Among the effects were a printing press and a set of
type. "I happened along, chirped a low bid and down came the
auctioneer's hammer," said Chapin. "It was mine." Chapin
bought more than a press that day. He joined a nationwide do-
it-yourself printing craze that had captured the imagination of
just about every teenage boy in the nation, including the President's son. A decade earlier, a Boston druggist had discovered
that the miniature press he had created to print labels for his
medicine bottles was a hit with young boys. Soon, manufacturers
of all sorts of small, or "novelty" presses, as they were called,
found that in satisfying the needs of teenagers, they could expand
their sales beyond the limited tradesman market. An 1874 catalog

from W. A. Kelsey, one of the first manufacturers to see this new market, urged boys not to "rest until you own a printing Press, and see for yourselves the fun there is in it. Our word for it, you will never want for amusement or pocket money after you get a Press." Chapin's press would be the envy of any of these teenage would-be printers. It took nearly all of Chapin's savings to pay for it and a dray to get it home. His mother gave him two rooms on an upper floor to set up his printing business. "I remember making myself unpopular with the rest of the family by scrubbing inky type in the bathtub," said Chapin. "I worked most of that night putting my print shop in shape and the next day I printed business cards and circulars, announcing that I was prepared to do all kinds of commercial printing at prices much lower than any competitor."[25]

"Charlie Chapin Book & Job Printer," read his notices. "We are determined to do good printing, and are positive our prices will compare favorbly [sic] with any amateur printer in the world." He got orders from merchants and friends and was soon working day and night to keep up. "To gratify my ambition to write," said Chapin, "I began publishing a monthly magazine for boys and girls which I called *Our Compliments*." Just as in purchasing a press Chapin had joined a national craze, his launch of a publication was part of a related movement. The profusion of presses spawned an amateur journalism on a massive scale. In the 1870s, there were almost 1,000 amateur newspapers from Maine to California publishing fiction, essays, jokes, poetry, puzzles, and editorials, often copied from each other. *Our Compliments* was just one more.[26]

Soon Chapin's four-page sheet grew to eight pages. "Just think!" touted an advertisement, "*Our Compliments* is a neat 8 page monthly devoted exclusively to the boys and girls of America." As its main offering, the paper featured a serial about romance and life in the theater by a writer for whom Chapin predicted "a brilliant future." If readers, however, did not suspect the truth about Edwin S. Stone, "author of *Darkness before Dawn* and *Joe and Allie*," they certainly must have been suspicious when they read the work of "Tellie Graph" in subsequent issues. The paper was completely the product of Chapin's mind and hands. "I wrote nearly every line it in, set all the type and did the presswork." In the summer of 1875, Chapin took on a partner, Stanton S. Mills, of Rock Island, Illinois, and together the two redesigned the paper, enlarging its size and layout. Mills, who had four years of printing experience, took over manufacturing the paper, and Chapin continued as editor.[27]

One of the pleasures of amateur journalism was the social intercourse it offered to adolescents in an era when travel and communication were limited. By exchanging publications, the young printers made new friends from all parts of the country. In the East, an Amateur Press Association was being formed, and there was talk of participating in the great Centennial exhibit planned for Philadelphia. Chapin got the idea to create a western association of amateur editors. He appointed himself secretary of such an organization and issued a call for a meeting in Dubuque, Iowa, on November 25, 1875, "Every amateur editor, publisher, author, printer, puzzler and engraver are cordially invited to attend," he wrote in *Our Compliments*. The meeting took place, and the *Amateur Aspirant*, published by Chapin's friend Alexander Dingwall (who later became a well-known theater manager on Broadway), was designated the new organization's official organ. The idea, however, did not stick, and the organization never held a second meeting. Chapin, meanwhile, abandoned amateur journalism as, once again, the family decamped. In 1876, his father found work as a watchmaker at the Elgin National Watch Company in Elgin, Illinois. The plant was running twelve-hour shifts to keep up with demand after lowering the price for its pocket watch from $67.50 to $39.75. Chapin sold his presses and would, in following his family to Elgin, trade in the written for the spoken arts.[28]

Traveling Thespian

Years later, Chapin would call it "a false step," but in the spring of 1877 he became an actor. Rodney Guptill, an Elgin friend, invited Chapin to join an amateur dramatic club he was organizing. "I protested that I knew nothing about acting, that in all my life the only plays I had witnessed were *Uncle Tom's Cabin* and *The Gipsy Queen.*" Nonetheless, Chapin was soon talked into accompanying Guptill into Chicago to see renowned actor Lawrence Barrett who was touring in *Richelieu,* a popular play of murder and unwanted advances in the court of Louis XVI by Edward Bulwer-Lytton. Few actors were held in higher esteem at that time than Barrett, and Richelieu was his most widely admired role. Otis Skinner, who was a supporting actor in Barrett's cast, recalled "there was a tempestuous, torrential character to his acting in many of his parts that swept his audience into enthusiasm."[1]

"We went and I fell," said Chapin. Upon their return, Chapin agreed to perform in *Ten Nights in a Bar Room,* a classic melodrama loved by the temperance movement. "I was to be Willie, who gets killed by a gambler," said Chapin. Louis H. Yarwood, Elgin's librarian, who was also an actor and painter, directed the production, which was put on as a charity benefit in the DuBois Opera House on the third floor of the Grove Avenue building. "There was a storm of applause when the gambler killed me," said Chapin. "I suspect that it was because I was such a bad actor, but I was flatteringly mentioned in the newspapers and some of my friends said I ought to go on the stage." Impetuously, Guptill and

Chapin did just that. Another production was planned for June 13, 1877, to follow the success of their first. This time, two professional actors, James and Louie Lord, who ran a traveling theater company based in Chicago, were engaged to put on *Lemons*, a British comedy. The Lords played the two leading characters, but Chapin was given the role of Tom Brinkerhoff, and his name appeared fourth on the playbill. The glamour accompanying the Lords proved to be irresistible for Chapin and Guptill. Like boys running off to join a circus, they enlisted with the Lords on their next tour.[2]

In the second half of the nineteenth century, Americans were in love with theater, and the theater with them. "The theater is now extremely popular, perhaps even more popular than in any part of Europe," wrote Englishman James Bryce, who made three long trips through the United States at that time. In any decent-sized city, one could see classic drama or the newest theater offering for as little as a quarter. All the great English and European actors crossed the ocean for a dose of adulation and hard cash. It wasn't long before theater mania reached into the countryside. After the Civil War, railroads had begun to move scores of settlers and goods across the country. Dozens of enterprising theater troupes, like the one belonging to James and Louie Lord, saw opportunity in the new manner of travel and followed the rail lines into the West. They discovered that such tours could produce considerably more revenue than staying put, even in a metropolitan area. The successful companies, most commonly a husband and wife team, usually comprised a single star performer and a small group of principal players. James, who had considerable theater experience, managed the Lord troupe. Louie was the star of the company, having made a bit of a success of herself on Broadway in the early 1870s. A beautiful woman with magnificent blond hair that, when let down, reached below her waist and a melodious voice, Louie entranced critics and audiences alike, and, in this case, a young Chapin. "Louie painted an alluring picture of the life of a traveling thespian," Chapin recalled, "so we signed contracts for a tour of forty weeks and were enrolled as professional 'barnstormers.'"[3]

The tour began in September. Chapin was lucky. A decline of stock companies and radical changes in acting methods had left many beginners begging for jobs in the 1870s. Although Chapin was fortunate to land the job, he was also talented, despite his protestations to the contrary. He was a remarkably quick study of text, a skill honed from his consummate reading, and he had an intensity of character that was well suited for the stage. Each traveling company had a list of "lines," such as *juvenile, heavy man, walking gentleman,* or *old man* that would permit a troupe to stage the widest variety of plays. The leading roles were reserved for the actor–manager and his wife. Chapin was selected for leading juvenile.[4]

The Lords were among the first, and by many accounts the best, of the theatrical troupes on the road. But it was pioneering work in harsh conditions. Train travel was arduous and often supplemented by rough rides on stages with actors perched on trunks and scenery. Hotels were rudimentary, and the eight male actors frequently shared four beds in a room so small one had to stand on the bed in order to change clothes. "In those days few of the Western towns boasted of a theater," said Chapin, "so we carried our own scenery and gave many of our performances in courthouses, public schools, and vacant stores, borrowing lumber as we went along to build a raised platform on which we presented our plays." The work was unending. The actors unloaded the materials at each stop, built the stage, hung the scenery, strung planks across cracker boxes and nail kegs for seats, and served as ushers until a few minutes before the performance. A woman who saw the company perform while Chapin was on tour recalled, "their opera house was a court room—bare dirty walls—their scenery crude and their stage a low platform curtained off with cheap curtains strung on a wire."[5]

From Iowa to Colorado, from Montana to Texas, the Lords plied their trade. Audiences in small towns, large towns, and mining camps eagerly lined up to see performances. The troupe never gave a play twice in the same town. In one ten-day run in Topeka, Kansas, they performed a different play each night. As a result, Chapin spent all his hours learning a vast repertoire. The memorization alone was hard work, not to mention that Chapin still had a lot to learn about acting itself, as the *Hayes Sentinel* noted. "Chapin has fine histrionic powers," said its reviewer during his first tour, "but there is a trifle too much of the studied amateur in

his motions and his base voice occasionally drops into a weari-
some monotone." But over the course of several months, he be-
came schooled in such Shakespeare plays as *Othello* and *Richard III* and contemporary favorites such as *Damon and Pythias* (loved
by members of the Order of Knights of Pythias, whose lodges
could be found at most of their stops), *East Lynne*, *Rip Van Win-
kle*, *Hidden Hand*, and *Uncle Tom's Cabin*. The demand for this
last play was insatiable. At the time, there were more than fifty
"Tom Shows" on the road in the United States. By the end of the
barnstorming era, there was hardly a place in the nation that was
not visited by one or more Tom Shows; that is, except for the
deep South. Chapin himself was regularly called on to perform
the role of Uncle Tom and, when others were sick, washed his
blackened face between acts so as to play some of the white characters as well. There was no play that the troupe was too modest
to attempt, but quality theater was not always within their reach.
When there were not enough actors for the parts, some played
two or three roles. Chapin recalled seeing "armies of Richard and
Richmond assault each other in terrific combat when both armies
numbered seven men and a girl, the latter dressed in armor and
wearing a bushy beard."[6]

States, cities, and towns clicked by as the railroad-bound
troupe made its migration, and in time Chapin found himself
back in Junction City, Kansas, playing in its Centennial Hall to
large and enthusiastic audiences. The city took pride in its thespian son, and, on a return visit, the *Junction City Union* urged
readers to come out and see this "former Junction City lad. . . .
He lived here several years and is well and favorably known to
most of our people. Under the tutelage of J. A. Lord he is rapidly
developing into an accomplished actor, and this place will soon
be proud to boast that he was one of its citizens."[7]

Other Kansas towns rolled by, but none was as exciting as
Dodge City, the rowdy, emblematic western town of cowboys,
gamblers, prostitutes, buffalo hunters, and lawmen such as Bat
Masterson and Wyatt Earp. Dodge City was "the wickedest spot
outside of Hell," said Chapin. The Lords made two stops in
Dodge. The first was in January. The second came at the end of
their season in May 1878. The company was booked to play its
usual fare of romantic dramas such as *The Lady of the Lyons* or

31

*Traveling
Thespian*

Ruys Blas in the courthouse. On May 31, 1878, the Lords put on their last performance of the season and returned to Chicago. Chapin and Guptill, along with several other actors from the company, chose to remain in Dodge City for the summer and work in the new Theater Comique—known to cowboys as *com-ee-cue.* Also performing there that summer was a rival company whose leading stars were Eddie Foy and Jim Thompson. Foy, who later became a famous actor and progenitor of an acting family, was a handsome man who apparently garnered considerable attention from Dodge women. Trouble brewed when one Dodge actress fell within his sights. Lilly Conley, who had the elegant stage name of Simone de Montreau, was the object of Chapin's attentions, too, that summer. He felt threatened by Foy's appearance in Dodge. "He somehow got the impression," said Foy, "that I was making eyes at a girl with whom he was infatuated." In a town where stray bullets were as common as prairie dogs in the plains, Chapin took the Dodge City solution and grabbed a gun. One night, while Foy was resting in the one-room shack he was given for quarters, Chapin stood outside and shot twice through the window. "Fortunately," said Foy, "he was no Hickok in marksmanship, and he missed me, though not far." The authorities, however, didn't press charges, contending that Chapin was so unfamiliar with guns that he couldn't have done any harm.[8]

At the end of the summer, Chapin decided to sign up with the Lords for another season. This time, however, it was a problem-plagued tour. In October two members of the troupe bolted to form their own company, taking with them the Lords's advance man. But if it was hard for an established company to make a financial success of it, the renegades proved they could do no better on their own. Within a month, their company collapsed in Salina under a mound of unpaid bills, and the advance agent was back at work for the Lords.

In December, Louie became ill and couldn't perform, so the group holed up in Wamego, Kansas, while she recovered. The new year brought more misfortune. On Sunday, January 5, 1879, they arrived in Hays, Kansas, for a week's worth of performances in the Ellis County Courthouse. That night, Chapin and the others retired to their beds in the Gibson House, a two-story hotel that had been moved to Hays from Rome, a town a mile west that was depopulated by cholera. The servant girls who staffed the hotel went to bed in the second story of the adjoining building. One of the women left a lighted candle on top of a wash stand. "Not in a candle-stick, understand, but on the paper-covered boards," reported the *Hayes Sentinel*. When the candle melted, the stand and the bedding caught on fire. A passerby spotted the fire, the women were dragged to safety, and the hotel was evacuated. By the time it was brought under control, the servants' quarters and the Gibson House were in ruins. Only quick work saved the rest of Main Street. Chapin lost most of his wardrobe, valued at $70, in the conflagration. On Thursday night, the Lords put on a benefit performance of *East Lynne* to mitigate his loss. In the midst all this real-life drama, the *Sentinel* noted a change in Chapin the actor. "Chas. Chapin has greatly improved since the *Sentinel* greatly criticized him so severely last February and gives promise of something still better."[9]

In the spring, after stops in Wellington, Winfield, and Wichita, the Lords decided to go into western Kansas to look for a ranch with an eye to retirement. Chapin returned to Chicago where he took on the lead role in a romantic drama of his own making. While sitting in the parlor of a hotel, Chapin hailed a bellboy and asked him to bring his card to a woman. The bellboy gave the card to another by mistake. The recipient was a diminutive, fragile, and unassuming schoolteacher named Nellie Beebe. "There were mutual explanations and she smilingly withdrew," said Chapin. A week later, the two met again, this time in line to buy tickets to the theater. "There was a smile of recognition when she saw that I was the one to whose card she had responded," said Chapin.[10]

Weeks passed, and Chapin traveled to Iowa to join the Charles Thornton Combination, another theatrical company, checking into a hotel late at night. "When I went down to a late breakfast there was but one person in the room," he said. "It was the same lady. Fate!" Beebe signaled to Chapin to take a seat at her table. He discovered she had signed with the same company. The two tarried over their meal. Chapin learned that Beebe had given up teaching elocution and, on the advice of friends, was going to try acting. But, she confessed, she wasn't sure she was going to like it, and already there were aspects of stage life that worried her. By breakfast's end, Chapin was beguiled by this "young woman of unusual refinement and intelligence and personally very attractive." That night he carried her bags to the theater and back to the hotel after the performance.[11]

As the troupe made its way across the Midwest, Chapin was increasingly drawn to Beebe. "She was the sweetest, truest, the most lovable woman," said Chapin, "full of fun and the joy of living; bright, witty, and entertaining." By fall, Chapin had moved from carrying her bags to persuading Beebe to marry him. They planned to have the ceremony as soon as the season was over, but Chapin soon altered the arrangements after his twenty-first birthday on October 29, 1879. The following Tuesday morning, while the Thornton Combination was in Brookfield, Missouri, Beebe didn't descend for breakfast. Upon calling on her, Chapin found she had been ill most of the night. He obtained some medicine and counseled her to rest in her room. Later that day, Chapin was playing pool with his theater company's manager when, what he described as "a strange impulse" came over him. He placed the pool cue back on the rack, leaving balls on the table yet to be sunk.

"What's up?" asked the manager.

"I'm going to be married," replied Chapin.[12]

Dragging the manager with him, he left the billiard room. They headed to the home of J. P. Finley, an Episcopal minister. It was then four o'clock, and Chapin announced he wanted to be married at five. He then left the group and returned to the hotel where he persuaded Beebe to get some fresh air. "I walked her to the rectory and coaxed her to go in with me," he said. "Even then she didn't suspect, but when she was in the house and found our manager and his wife there in their Sunday clothes and the clergyman in official robe, she saw the trap I had sprung, but she played her part of the game and came out with a marriage certificate tightly clung in her hand." The only blemish on the matrimonial stroll was that Beebe had worn a black dress. "Black is an evil omen for a bride," she said to Chapin on the way back to the hotel, where the gang enjoyed a wedding supper with the first champagne Chapin ever tasted.[13]

Nellie and Charles spent most of 1880 back in Chicago and in Elgin with his mother, who was in sore need of company. On

May 5, 1880, Earl Chapin had left their home to seek work in Springfield, Illinois. Work in the local watch factory had dropped off, and Earl told his family he expected to find better wages at a similar factory in Springfield, 200 miles south. "He bade all of us good byes, kissed Ma and each of his children, and assured us just as soon as he could get settled, he would send his first wages home to bring us all to him," said Fannie, Charles's older sister. In the decade since they set off from Oneida, success had continued to elude Earl. The move to Springfield was yet one more effort to find his El Dorado. Time passed, however, and no one heard from him. Days turned to weeks, and weeks to months. Both Cecelia and Fannie wrote, but they received no reply nor did their letters come back undelivered, even though they had been sure to include their return address. Fannie persisted and, finally, sometime later, she met a person who told her that Earl was in Springfield but working for a jeweler, not at the watch factory. "I wrote asking if Earl Chapin was in his employ, and he replied that he was and was well." Apparently she never told Cecelia, perhaps in an effort to protect her mother from a truth she felt would hurt her. Equally unknown to Cecelia was what prompted his abandonment of her and the children. Neither she nor the children had a clue. "We had no reason whatsoever to ever suspect that he was going away with a view of deserting his family," recalled Fannie. "We had lived together with at least a reasonable degree of happiness," said Cecelia. "We had no trouble or difference whatever which would cause him to leave or remain away from home."[14]

But remain away is exactly what Earl did. In Springfield, the forty-eight-year-old father of five met and apparently fell for a young woman the age of his own daughter. The circumstance of his meeting eighteen-year-old Mary McCoy is not known, but she may have worked in the hotel where he lived. Nonetheless, from all accounts, they took up life as a couple, and a few years later they moved from Illinois to Springfield, Missouri, where in December 1884, Mary bore Earl a son whom they named Edward Gwynne Chapin.[15]

In the fall of 1880, the Lords decided to mount another season. Charles, along with Nellie, rejoined the group and passed the winter as newlyweds on tour. Nellie used her stage name Nellie

Thorne while Charles continued to use his real name. In November, the troupe arrived in Deadwood, in the Black Hills of South Dakota. Although it was certainly no cultural Mecca, Deadwood was overrun with cash-carrying miners ravenous for any kind of entertainment and willing to pay for it. The discovery of gold in 1875 abrogated the treaty that had previously reserved the isolated plateau in the southwestern corner of the Dakotas for the Sioux. In the spring of 1876, thousands of miners poured into Deadwood Gulch—so named because of the large number of decaying trees—and within a dozen months, transformed the wilderness as they had done in California and Colorado. The development was chaotic. A thousand houses sprouted before roads could be organized. The first path into the valley was so steep that freight companies locked the wheels of their wagons with chains, secured ropes around trees, and skidded their heavy loads down the incline. In 1877, a Nebraska reporter described what he found, "A year ago there was on the site of this town an impenetrable jungle; now it is the center of life and civilization—of a kind." Within a couple more years, Deadwood had become the "metropolis" of the barren Black Hills with more than 6,000 inhabitants. The boom underway was evident in the statistics for the stage lines that serviced Deadwood. In 1878, the stages transported 15,000 passengers, along with 500 pounds of mail a day, to and from Deadwood. Following right behind the miners were salon keeps and dance-hall operators who transformed Deadwood into a boisterous and lusty locale. Its rough-hewn streets, on which walked such legendary figures as Wild Bill Hickok and Calamity Jane, were soon dotted with saloons, burlesque houses, and opium dens. At night a din of boisterous voices, loosened by alcohol, intermingled with hurdy-gurdy music, rose from the valley into the surrounding hills. Not far behind the mavens of entertainment were theater impresarios. Within four years, more than 200 plays were performed. Some soon took to calling Deadwood the "Broadway of the West."[16]

Among the impresarios was Johnny Rogers, whose ambitious plans would bring the Lords to town. In the summer of 1880, Rogers had talked John A. Nye, a local entrepreneur, into constructing a 500-person theater on Main Street that, unlike any other in Deadwood at the time, would be built so as to keep the audience warm in the winter. Rogers's idea was to bring a more elevated form of theater to Deadwood than variety shows. The local paper was full of encouragement. It urged citizens who wanted "healthy, moral and legitimate amusement" to buy tickets. For the grand opening, he engaged the Lords for eight weeks. It was an arduous journey by train and stagecoach to get to Deadwood, but they came. On Monday morning, November 15, 1880, the troupe arrived on the Pierre coach. The next day's *Black Hills Daily Times* announced their arrival, calling them "a company of first-class artists from the east."[17]

"Amongst them is Miss Louie Lord, a lady who has a national reputation as a first class artist in every respect. Miss Nellie Thorne comes with the best recommendations as an excellent juvenile lady. . . . Mr. Fargo plays the old men and Mr. Chapin the juveniles. . . . Get your seats early, or you will have an opportunity of standing—and don't you forget it."[18]

On November 17, 1880, the Lords opened their season before a large audience with Henry J. Byron's comedy *Our Boys*. Three days later, as was the style, the Lord Company was already performing another play. This time they selected *Miss Multon*, also known as the *New East Lynne*, which was, oddly, a French version of what was then the nation's favorite play. It is the story of a young, beautiful, refined woman who leaves her husband and child for a dashing lover. Abandoned by her lover, she bears his illegitimate child and then returns home, disguised, and gains employment as a governess in her old household, now inhabited by a new wife.[19]

The performance was an enormous success. Louie Lord's performance could not have been excelled even by the well-known Clara Morris, who had made the role famous on the American stage, said the *Black Hills Daily Times*. "Everyone received their share of plaudits," continued the paper. "Miss Nellie Thorne particularly won the hearts of the audience by her naïve, childlike manner in the part of Janet. . . . Mr. Chapin was certainly properly cast in the character of Mons. Belin; his make up was perfect, and his clear enunciation admirably qualified him for this part."[20]

Among those in the audience that Saturday night were Seth Bullock, Deadwood's first sheriff and later friend to Theodore Roosevelt, whom he had met sharing coffee and beans on the tailgate of a chuck wagon, and Calamity Jane. Dressed in a corduroy suit, sombrero, and green kid gloves, the notorious grande dame of the West made her presence known wherever she went. That night was no exception, according to Chapin. "She and her escort clapped their hands in noisy appreciation until Lady Isabel eloped with Sir Francis and 'Calamity' showed her disapproval of the erring wife's conduct by marching down to the footlights and squirting a stream of tobacco juice over the front of Lady Isabel's pink satin evening gown." James Lord almost caused a fight in rushing to defend his wife's honor or, maybe, costume. "Trouble was avoided by the lady desperado tossing a handful of gold coin over the footlights to pay for the gown she had so ruthlessly desecrated." said Chapin. "Throughout the remainder of the performance she chewed up cud in courteous silence."[21]

Aside from this memorable night, the season continued much as it had when the Lords were on the road. Lots of hard work and continuous rehearsals filled the Chapins's days. By December, the troupe had performed *My Turn Next*, also known as *The Female Blue-Beard*, *Tim Conn,* also known as *Fortune's Toy*, *Our Gal*, *Guy Mannering*, also known as *The Gypsy's Prophecy*, and *Frou Frou*. It became too much for the frail Nellie. She became ill and was confined to her hotel room. She recovered, and the Lords's stay in Deadwood concluded with a performance of *A Celebrated Case* on December 24.[22]

As the season neared its end and the Lords packed up, Chapin accepted an offer from Rogers to stay. In February, Rogers left for Chicago to secure new talent. Weeks passed without any word from him. March turned to April, and at last news arrived in the form of a letter addressed to Rogers's wife. According to the letter, Rogers had reached Pierre, where he had become snowbound. Impatient for the eastern train tracks to be reopened, he had decided to take a skiff down the Missouri to Sioux City and then catch a train to Chicago from there. The river was ice filled, and the boat never made it.[23]

"When the news of the drowning came," said Chapin, "I sat up all night with a hysterical widow and in the morning awoke to a realization of my own predicament, for I was a long way from home, with no opportunity to obtain theatrical employment and but a few dollars in my pocket." The mayor offered to take up a collection to help Chapin get back to Chicago. Instead, Chapin went to the paper and got a job setting type. "I didn't have to earn my bread by setting type more than a couple of weeks, for the editor was summoned East by a death in his family, and the publisher asked me to fill the chair until the editor returned." Chapin held the job for six months, and he and Nellie continued to occasionally act. In July, for instance, they both had roles in a benefit at Nye's Opera House, where they had first played with the Lords, and Chapin had a role in another benefit performance.[24]

On July 28, Charles put Nellie on the stagecoach for Chicago. Describing her as "a sprightly and reliable actress and estimable lady," the *Black Hills Daily Times* said Nellie "has been in poor health for some time, and a journey to the states may lead to her recovery." Two weeks later, Charles followed. Just as reaching Deadwood had been hard, leaving nine months later was also a challenge. It took him two days of riding on the top of a stagecoach to reach a railroad station. But with him was a telegram he had received offering him the job as leading man with a company preparing to tour the west with a woman star. "Why a manager should send to the far-away Black Hills for an actor, had me puzzled until I found my old friend Rodney [Guptill] was in the company and knew that it was through him that I had been called."[25]

With Nellie in tow, Charles took off on his last theatrical adventure. Unfortunately, within a short time, the company went under, and the Chapins found themselves a long way from home and broke. With no hope of receiving the back pay owed, Charles and Nellie caught a train back to Chicago on credit proffered by the railroad company. But its generosity only extended so far. Upon arriving, Charles had to borrow money to pay for the tickets before the railroad would release their trunks.[26]

At Last, a Reporter!

Back in Chicago, penniless, his three-year acting career seemingly at an end, Chapin had to find work, fast. "I decided not to go near the theatrical agencies, for I had grown to detest the nomadic life of a barnstormer and was determined to turn my attention to something that gave greater promise for a future." He installed Nellie at a hotel and went out to call on the city's leading editors and publishers. This time, unlike seven years earlier in 1874 when he had made a similar set of rounds, he had better luck. The newspapers were at the beginning of a hiring binge that would last almost a decade. By nightfall, when he returned to his hotel, Charles was able to tell Nellie he had secured a position on the *Chicago Tribune.* His salary was the smallest of anyone on the staff, his assignments the least desirable. But he didn't care. "It was the life I had longed for from boyhood," he said.[1]

Of all the cities and all the times in which he could have started a career as a newspaperman, Chapin was fortunate in selecting Chicago. Outside of New York City, only Chicago approached the excitement, power, and prestige of Park Row. "For some reason difficult to fathom the most romantic and talkative reporters in America either work in Chicago or once worked there," recalled Stanley Walker of the *New York Herald.* Part of the reason for its aura was a notorious competitive spirit among the reporters. "A Chicago reporter," said the *Chicago Tribune*'s William Salisbury, "doesn't take an interest in a story unless he has to fight for it, or secure it by robbery, burglary, or any other means this side of murder." A hungry, ambitious reporter could go far in Chicago, and the city had no lack of tales to share.[2]

A brawling and exciting place, Chicago was like a magnet. Its burgeoning industries attracted thousands of rural Midwesterners looking for work. Its cosmopolitan atmosphere, tinged with a frontier-like brashness unlike the calcified society of New York, drew a large coterie of artists, writers, reformers, socialists, and anarchists; the mix would later create a social fire to match the incendiary one of 1871. More than 150 people a day moved into Chicago in the 1880s, doubling the city's size in a decade. By the time federal Census takers returned in 1890, Chicago's population topped one million, making it second in size only to New York City. Plans were underway for the construction of the city's first skyscraper, with a remarkable steel load-bearing frame known as the "Chicago Skeleton." There was construction everywhere one looked. And, outside the city, some of the nation's first commuter suburbs were rising along the rail lines that radiated from the city. It was an intoxicating atmosphere to anyone young and ambitious. "Chicago seemed so aspiring at this time," wrote Theodore Dreiser, who also came to the city in the 1880s looking for work as a newspaperman. "Its bad was so deliciously bad—its good so very good—keen and succulent, reckless, inconsequential, pretentious, hopeful, eager, new."[3]

Like those businesses that had risen from the ashes of the great fire of 1871, the surviving Chicago newspapers were more prosperous than ever. The *Tribune* had lost everything in the blaze except for a vault, a linen coat, and a box of matches. But a decade later, it was the leader among five English-language dailies (and countless foreign-language papers) that competed arduously for the city's attention. Although it did not always win its circulation wars with the others, the *Tribune* was uncontestedly *the* paper. "The *Tribune* is to Chicago what the *Times* is to London," said the *Journalist*, the trade publication of newspaperdom in the 1880s. "It is as old as the city. Its history is the history of Chicago. . . . Its reward is a supremacy which nobody questions, and which very few begrudge."[4]

The vigorous health of the press was not, of course, unique to Chicago. All across the country a mass media was emerging from the staggering changes resulting from the industrial revolution and the rise of the cities. Increased education generated readers, and gaslight, followed by electric light, increased the opportunity for reading. Greater wealth gave people leisure. Urbanization on an unprecedented scale created natural markets for purveyors of news, and city life, in turn, was a rich source of material about which to write. New methods of moving words—written by wire, verbal by telephone, and physical by train—revolutionized both the transmission of news and its dissemination. It was the beginning of the golden age of the newspaper, and Chicago was certainly a place to be. "At that time," recalled Dreiser, "although I did not know it, Chicago was in the heyday of its newspaper prestige."[5]

Anxiously, Chapin approached the apex of this heady world. The *Tribune* was situated in a five-story building made of Lake Superior red sandstone on the southeast corner of Dearborn Avenue and Madison Street. The paper had erected the building as if to thumb its nose to the fire that razed its previous incarnation. "I was frightened," recalled Chapin. "All the men on the staff were older and more experienced than I and I had misgivings that I'd ever be able to compete with them." At the start, he took his orders from Fred Hall, the city editor. Hall was the first city editor Chapin worked under, and he made an indelible impression on the young reporter. For the rest of his life, whenever Chapin considered how a city editor should act, he would think of Hall. A former secretary to Edwin Stanton, Lincoln's secretary of war, Hall had been with the *Tribune* since the end of the Civil War. He was easily the most recognizable member of the paper's staff. Bearded, blue-eyed, and spectacled, he was never without a yellowed, aging straw hat. His only item of clothing seemed to be a cardigan jacket so frayed that his shirt sleeves showed through at the elbows. From early morning to late evening, he could be found at his desk under a cloud of smoke, billowing from an ever-smoldering corn cob pipe. "A demon for hard work and a slave to his profession, he was intolerant toward shirkers," said Chapin. "Some called him a 'slave driver,' but he never asked one of his men to work nearly so hard as he did himself."[6]

Hall's other trait was an encyclopedic mind. There was nothing he did not seem to know. He was said to be an authority on Chinese metaphysics, to have read the twelfth-century poet Saadi in

the original Persian, and that he knew everything about theater—
something that Chapin could certainly appreciate—even though
he never seemed to attend any performances. More impressive to
Chapin was that Hall retained every tidbit of information about
anyone who was anyone in Chicago. "And he knew their secrets,
who and when they married, and how they got their money," said
Chapin. "He knew the city better than all the police force and the
letter carriers combined. He knew just how long it would ordi-
narily take a reporter to get to any part of it, cover a story and get
back to the office." A reporter who wished to remain on the staff
of the *Tribune* did not fail this man. There was a constant tension
in the newsroom generated by the expectations of the man in the
straw hat. Chapin was eager to please Hall. "At first I was given
only the smaller assignments to cover," said Chapin, "but no matter how unimportant the city editor considered them, they were
always important to me and I seldom failed to make the most of
my opportunities."[7]

Not long after joining the staff, Chapin's diligence paid off. A
tip was telephoned to the *Tribune* that there was some sort of
trouble brewing at a big steel corporation in the southern suburbs.
Hall sent Chapin to investigate. "He evidently didn't think much
of the tip," said Chapin, "for several of his star reporters were sitting idle in the office at the time." Braving foul weather, Chapin
reached the plant. He found the sheriff had closed the firm down,
hundreds of men were out of work, and the president had fled to
Europe. He returned to his desk and set to work writing up the
story. As a greenhorn, it had never crossed his mind to tip off
Hall to the significance of the story. "That was an astonished city
editor when he lifted a bunch of copy from my desk and read
what I had written about the collapse of the steel corporation."[8]

The life of the reporter thrilled Chapin. "I became so fasci-
nated with reporting that I regretted having wasted so much time
as a barnstorming player." A reporter had a front-row seat on all
that was exciting in Chicago. One night early in his career with
the *Tribune*, for instance, Chapin was ordered off to Hyde Park,
a lakefront community on the southeast side of the city, to report
on a vessel in distress. It was midnight by the time he reached the
edge of the lake. In the dark he could not make out the foundering ship itself, but he could detect lights offshore that came from

oil-soaked bedding set on fire by the crew as a signal. After Chapin persuaded men he found along the shoreline to build a bonfire to let the sailors know help was on the way, he went to telephone a rescue station. At dawn, the rescuers arrived with a boat on a wagon. Chapin joined them as they clambered through the waves and reached the imperiled crew. Life on stage seemed dull in comparison to the theater of the real world.[9]

On Wednesday, February 13, 1884, Chapin arrived at work in the late morning, at a time when most Chicagoans had already put in a half day's work. It was not unusual for a reporter to drift into the *Tribune* offices about lunchtime since publishing a morning newspaper often required the news staff to work into the night. But Chapin's chosen arrival time on this particular day turned out to be fortuitous. Just as he entered the building, a telephone call came in from the wife of *Tribune* editorialist Henry Demarest Lloyd. The couple lived in the small, well-to-do village of Winnetka, about seventeen miles north of the city, and that morning two of its most prominent citizens had been discovered hideously murdered. Hall told Chapin to get the story. He raced back out of the building and down the few blocks to the Van Buren Street station and caught the first afternoon train. Also on board were members of the county coroner and physician offices. As they rode northward, the only particulars known to them was that the victims were James L. Willson, an elderly, wealthy resident of Winnetka and President of the Village Board, and his invalid wife Clarissa.[10]

For the past four months, an equally mysterious murder in Lincoln, Illinois, had enthralled readers of the *Morning News*, the *Tribune*'s rival paper. The *Morning News* had taken a new tack in reporting crime news. Instead of being content to cover the activities of the police, *Morning News* reporters had been commanded by Melville E. Stone, the paper's publisher, to investigate and solve the murder. This new "detective journalism" sold papers and didn't go unnoticed by other members of Chicago's fourth estate. As Chapin rode the train toward Winnetka, the *Morning News* coverage—or one might say, investigation—of the Lincoln murder was still on the front page. Like many of his colleagues, Chapin was drawn to these new developments in journalism. But the closest he had come so far to detective journalism was to read it, especially in the pages of his rival paper. Thus far, Chapin's stories had been mostly the routine stuff of a city newspaper. Beat reporters in Chicago had developed a lingo of their own to describe news stories. Respectable scoops were called "pippins," and really big ones were called "bell-ringers." Chapin knew the Winnetka murders could be a bell-ringer.[11]

At last, the party alighted at Winnetka's train station. It was a chilly day, and a light snowfall dusted the ground as the group walked to the Willsons's home. The house was thought to be one of the nicest in the village. A two-story mansard building, it stood alone on the block, mostly concealed from view by great elm trees. Coming on foot from the station, the group arrived first at the back door, where they discovered a crowd of excited villagers. A police officer, along with some civic-minded citizens, had kept everyone at bay.

Chapin was permitted to accompany the investigators into the house, as was common in that era before modern forensics dictated that a crime scene be protected. The murderer had left his mark throughout the house. Furniture was overturned, papers were strewn all over, and blood was smeared on the wallpaper. Slowly and carefully, with Chapin tagging along, the group made its way from room to room. As they conducted their inspection, Chapin took careful note of what he saw and even did a little investigating of his own. In the living room, for example, he and the coroner studied a pair of vest buttons with broken threads still attached. Chapin found a third button and turned it over to the coroner. They concluded that the buttons did not belong to the murdered victim.[12]

As Chapin left the house to compose for his readers the horrors he had seen, a small army of reporters and investigators, including representatives of the famed Pinkerton Detective Agency, arrived. This murder could be a big break for Chapin if he did not bungle it. It involved prominent people, it was a mystery, and it was gruesome. In Chicago at the time, politics and crime were still the dominant paths to success for a reporter and the latter topic the surer one. The pursuit of the "objective" style of reporting was still years away, and a murder story afforded a creative reporter tremendous liberties. That night, Chapin filed his story. It was a startling account, more graphic, more complete, and more clever than anything his competition had. Hall was apparently pleased. The next morning, Valentine's Day, he gave Chapin's piece front-page treatment under the headline "Winnetka's Horror." Calling it a "double murder of the most revolting character," Chapin reconstructed for his readers both the discovery of the crime and its subsequent investigation. It was an effective technique because the horrors of the crime, which made for compelling reading, were not exhausted in the first paragraphs, but were promised to readers who followed the story to its conclusion.[13]

A young schoolteacher named Emma Dwyer had come to the Willson house in the morning, explained Chapin. She kept Mrs. Willson, 83, company on Wednesdays when Mr. Willson, 72, tended to business in Chicago. She found the kitchen door locked and, worried that the couple might be sick, clambered in through an open window. "Passing through the dining-room into the sitting-room she saw by the dim light struggling through the blinds Mr. Willson's body huddled in a heap behind the stove," wrote Chapin. Thinking Willson had fainted or otherwise collapsed, Dwyer rushed out through the kitchen to get Mrs. Murphy, the neighbor. Murphy, in turn, ran into the house and stumbled over Willson's body. "On raising the window-blind, the horrified woman saw that Mr. Willson was lying in a pool of blood, dead." Her screams brought others into the house. "The sight in the sitting-room was a ghastly one, but when the men proceeded upstairs it was one of the most horrible the human mind can realize," wrote Chapin. "Mrs. Willson lay half-naked on her bed, her head pounded into a mass of flesh, and broken bones, and gore, the pillow literally soaked with blood, the bedclothes covered with blood, and three walls of the room bespattered with showers of flying gore."[14]

With his readers hooked—that is, those who could stomach it—Chapin the writer turned into Chapin the investigator. First, he provided a complete description of the Willson abode. Two floor plans were even published with his article to mark where the bodies had been found. Second, he reconstructed the crime scene as he and the investigators had found it. He spared no details, even though later in life he confessed it was "the most gruesome sight I ever beheld."[15]

In the living room, Chapin wrote, they found "the bruised and perforated body of old Mr. Willson." Their investigation led them to conclude that Willson had been shot twice and then kicked to death by his assailant. "After he had fallen to the ground the murderer had jumped on him to stifle his dying cries," concluded Chapin. Willson's pockets had been rifled, and his gold watch ripped from its chain. Next, they traveled upstairs to what Chapin called "the second chamber of horrors," where they found Clarissa's corpse. "On the south wall, about four feet from where the old lady's body lay on the bed, were several spurts and splashes of blood," wrote Chapin, "and the opposite wall, about six feet from the body, was thickly spackled also, these two walls and the west wall, against which the head of the bed rested, being bespattered with showers of blood as though it were thrown on them from the end of a broom." Clarissa had been beaten first with a set of fire tongs, and then, when the handle fell off the tongs, the murderer completed the deed with a sword that had once belonged to her son, who had perished with yellow fever during the Civil War. "The victim's head was a pounded mass, swollen and covered with gore, leaving no feature recognizable," wrote Chapin.

Chapin added a coda to his gory portrayal of the scene. On a high shelf in the closet near the corpse they uncovered a small iron box. "It was found to contain an old rubber ball, a box of worn and variously assorted marbles, and a broken leather strap," said Chapin—all relics of the young dead son whose sword, cherished as a memento by his grieving parents, had now been used to kill his mother.

With his first installment, Chapin won the right to pursue the story, and in coming days he spared no opportunity to stir his readers. "The revolting tragedy enacted at Winnetka Tuesday night has thrilled the inhabitants of that usually peaceful suburb with an intense degree of excitement which only the capture and punishment of the guilty can subdue," reported Chapin the next day. Two days later, his rhetoric was even more inflammatory. It is the duty of the living, he wrote, to seek justice in this case. "The spirits of the dead have flown to the immortal realm of the great unknown, and their foul and inhuman murder has yet to be avenged. The blood-stained monster who crushed out their breath of life is free, with nothing to prevent him from committing another heinous crime."[16]

Detectives of all sorts joined in the pursuit of the guilty. "Stimulated by the promise of reward, every detective agency in the city has placed men at work on the crime, and an unusual number of amateurs have joined the search," reported Chapin, who clearly fell among the ranks of the latter as he tried to gather his own evidence. Suspicion began to focus on Neal McKeague, a Canadian and the town's butcher. The Pinkertons and Chapin descended upon the hapless man when he returned from a trip to Chicago. "He appeared to have perfect control and to answer without show of irritation any questions that were asked of him," said Chapin. But, he added, "I couldn't help thinking that McKeague knew more about the tragedy than he professed."[17]

McKeague had been the last to see James Willson alive when he had come to McKeague's store four blocks from his house to make a purchase the evening of the murder—a purchase, said McKeague, of meat to serve to a guest that night. "The fact that he was in debt to the murdered man and that no evidence of it has been discovered among the papers found in the house has attracted considerable attention, and the more so because there is no one to substantiate his story regarding the mysterious visitor," Chapin told his readers the day following the burial of the Willsons.[18]

On February 22, nine days after the murder, McKeague was arrested. "McKaigue [whose name Chapin took a while to spell correctly] is the young butcher whose name has figured so conspicuously in the newspaper reports of the murder, and on whom suspicion was centered from the first," Chapin excitedly reported. Only an hour before the police came to McKeague, Chapin had secured an interview with him and found him confident of his innocence. Now in custody, McKeague, Chapin, and the detectives all set off together for Chicago. The following day, McKeague was indicted for the murder of James but not Clarissa Willson. There still was no evidence linking McKeague to the latter's murder. Chapin rushed to the Cook County jail and found McKeague pacing in the corridor. "While walking about he was very nervous, his face was flushed, and his deep-sunken eyes wore an expression of anxiety. His strides were heavy and fast," observed Chapin.

"Have you any statement to make?" asked Chapin.

"No, sir; and you can go to hell," replied McKeague, who then muttered something Chapin couldn't hear and disappeared among the crowd of prisoners.[19]

Next morning, a Sunday, Chapin had better luck. He asked a deputy if he could be admitted to see McKeague. "Certainly," he replied, "but your errand will be a fruitless one, as you will only run the gauntlet of a shower of profanity." McKeague, he continued, had turned down at least a dozen reporters seeking interviews. To Chapin's surprise, McKeague greeted him cordially and extended his hand through the bars. "I have had quite an exciting experience since we rode down from Winnetka together, and, as you can see, it has resulted in my being locked up here," McKeague said. In a lengthy interview, McKeague continued his claim of innocence. "Do I look like a murderer?" he said. "You have seen and talked with me nearly every day since the murder was committed, and I don't believe you have ever seen anything unusual about my manner."

The two went over, point by point, the accumulated evidence, from the blood-stained clothing in his trunk to his odd behavior on the day the murder was discovered. In each case, McKeague had an explanation or a denial. When he concluded his interview, McKeague told Chapin he was welcome to come back anytime. "The *Tribune* has treated me fairly and has not tried to damage me by printing what was not true," he said. In the following days, while McKeague was in custody, Chapin continued his detective work. Some of it underscored the weakness of the case. "A *Tribune* reporter in searching for evidence at Winnetka yesterday," said Chapin of himself, "obtained information from three different persons which can explain the blood-stains found on McKeague's clothing."[20]

Any semblance of fairness that McKeague may have felt he received from the *Tribune* must have been shattered when he read the headline "Thou Art the Man!" The subhead proclaimed that "It is Declared that a Stronger Case of Circumstantial Evidence Was Never Known." But Chapin's copy betrayed an uneasiness with the state's case against McKeague. In fact, Chapin went so far as to offer the prosecution advice. "It is possible that the detectives have overlooked one very important point which might have assisted in establishing the innocence or guilt of the accused," he wrote. James Willson was severely kicked after being shot. "Blood must have spurted out of the bullet holes in Mr. Willson's breast and left an indelible stain on the murderer's shoes," he concluded. Find the shoes, and you have your man.[21]

Meanwhile, Chapin began reporting on new and intriguing developments about the case that would have no bearing on McKeague's innocence or guilt, but would certainly make for interesting copy. Many women seemed to be drawn to the young butcher. Chapin first noticed this phenomenon while McKeague was confined to jail. "Many women are among the curious who visit the place ostensibly to look at the inside of the building, but they are disappointed if they have to go away without seeing McKeague," he wrote. Sporting a thin, reddish mustache, McKeague was certainly an attractive, broad-shouldered man, possessing, in Chapin's words "shallow blue eyes of bead-like brilliancy [and] curly light-brown hair parted near the middle." But his looks alone couldn't account for this interest among females. He was certainly not the first attractive man to enter a Chicago court.[22]

Pretrial publicity caused the court to take almost a week to seat a panel of jurors from among the hundreds summoned. As the days passed, Chapin took careful note of the gentler sex's interest. On the first day of the trial, in May, Chapin identified by name the three single women who accompanied McKeague's family into the courtroom. Later, he reported how their ranks were swollen by a dozen more young women. There wasn't, it might be noted, much else to report during the opening days of the trial. But once the trial got underway, it wasn't long before it became the city's leading theatrical entertainment, and the *Tribune* allocated as much as half a page a day for Chapin's copy. The facts to be presented in court were already well known, the Pinkertons not having uncovered any new evidence, but Chapin found as much to report in observing the proceedings as in covering the substance of the trial. Nothing escaped his attention, including the new spring hats in the growing crowd of women. "Quite naturally they were large, and broad, and ornamented with bushy plumage, which made them at once the envy and the aggravation of all who had to take the back seats." The trial soon threatened "to become fashionable," he wrote. The only damper was the large contingent of elderly who now came, many viewing the proceedings with the aid of opera glasses or Brazilian pebbles. The aged and infirm seem to regard it as their cause, said Chapin. "Attendance seems a holy duty with them, for they come under many difficulties bent upon the trusty cane or hobbling upon crutches." If he failed to find what he needed in the audience, the parade of witnesses offered Chapin a means to sustain his readers' interest. For example, on the eighth day, an attractive and "buxom" woman who had been on a sleigh ride with McKeague was called to the stand. Her appearance generated considerable excitement. "She wore a jaunty purple jacket and a wide hat which served to subdue her rather strong but plump features," wrote Chapin. "There was a beseeching look in her large and liquid brown eyes and a well-rounded figure and a slight suggestion of double chin causes many to declare that she was as pretty as a picture."[23]

As the trial progressed, the audience grew in size. On some days, the bailiffs had to struggle to keep those standing from getting too close to the jury, who had been sequestered for the duration. Again, many were women. "They are a curious lot—not in looks, but in manners, jumping up to look at McKeague's trunk and clothing when they were offered in evidence, and straining their eyes in attempts to catch a glimpse of the celebrated buttons." Even if the case didn't attract a crowd, Chapin's account would certainly have generated one.[24]

For several more days, experts pontificated on the forensic evidence, and both sides called an endless parade of witnesses. The tide, however, seemed to be turning in the defendant's favor. Even Chapin, who thought McKeague guilty, was forced to remark that the defense's case "is certainly a strong one and well presented." The ranks of the women continued to grow. On the day McKeague himself took the stand, all the seats reserved for women were filled. "All the extra chairs possible were placed within the bar, but fully fifty women stood up all day," said Chapin.[25]

On May 24, all the evidence had been presented, and the court readied for the final arguments. Three days later, the case was turned over to the jury. On the first ballot, the jurors voted eight to four for acquittal. As the evening wore on, each vote brought them closer to a verdict. Finally, at one in the morning, the last juror folded, and the twelve were permitted to retire to their beds in the Revere House. The courthouse was packed in the morning as the jury was brought in. Chapin counted 600, nearly half of them women. The judge admonished the audience to remain quiet. But when the jury read its verdict—acquittal—the room broke out in applause. "It was noticeable that the women did most of the hand-clapping," reported Chapin.

McKeague caught up with the jurors as they donned their hats and coats to head home after nearly three weeks away from their families.

"Hereafter," said one of the jurors to McKeague, "you must be a good boy."

"Yes, indeed, I will as I have always been," replied the acquitted man.

"No, not at one time," said the juror. "However, we would rather you would give us a porterhouse-steak with a pin in it than all this taffy."

"You shall have it," said McKeague, now laughing loudly. "Yes, a porterhouse-steak without any pin in it."

Before he left, Chapin caught up for a word with McKeague himself. He found him in the bailiff's room, smoking a cigar in the company of the women who had testified on his behalf and surrounded by as many as nineteen other women. "Many of the females cried from joy," wrote Chapin.

"How do you feel?" he asked McKeague.

"Very happy."

"You expected to be acquitted?"

"I always thought that it could come out I was innocent. I knew it wouldn't be any different all along."[26]

Prosecutors decided not to pursue the second murder charge against McKeague, and he returned to his home country, Canada. Despite his discontent with the verdict and frustration that his first experience with detective journalism resulted in an acquittal, Chapin gained his first lengthy appearance in the *Tribune*. In all, he had written the equivalent of more than twenty full pages of the paper, most of which had been widely read as the city became captivated by the trial. It had been *his* story, and with it Chapin became an established part of the *Tribune* staff.

Chapin's work also caught the attention of Joseph Medill. As publisher of the *Chicago Tribune*, Medill was among the best-known figures in the city, this still being the era in which newspaper publishers were considerable public figures. Medill was the James Gordon Bennett of the Midwest. Like Bennett and his *New York Herald*, Medill treated his *Tribune* as his personal fiefdom, where he was known simply as "chief." He used it to promote the Republican party, to defend big business, and to assail almost every humanitarian or reform idea on the horizon. In 1884, the year of the Willson murder trial, for instance, he would recommend in an editorial that the problem of tramps in the city be solved by putting arsenic in the food distributed to them.[27]

"It was my good fortune to attract the attention of the good editor," recalled Chapin. Medill, who took an active role in the management of reporters, began to select Chapin for assignments in which he had a personal interest. "He had a way of bestowing praise that stirred in the recipient an ambition to do even better," said Chapin, "but he could be snappish and make one feel cheap if an article did not come up to his expectation." Once Chapin was so hurt by Medill's remarks, he went back to his desk and composed a letter of resignation. The next day Medill sent for Chapin. In his office, Medill recounted a mistake he had made early in his career. "I laughed so heartily," said Chapin, "that I forgot my injured dignity, for what he told me made him a bigger boob than I had been."[28]

The warm relationship between Medill and Chapin probably contributed to Chapin's willingness to enlist in the publisher's vendetta against labor when violence erupted at Haymarket Square. On May 1, 1886, nearly 300,000 workers in the United States, 40,000 in Chicago alone, participated in demonstrations calling for an eight-hour workday. Four days later, activists in Chicago held a rally on Haymarket Square to protest police brutality. As the gathering was ending, the police entered the square to disperse the crowd. Suddenly a bomb was thrown over the heads of protesters and into the lines of police officers, where it exploded in a deafening roar. The policemen drew their guns and fired an almost ceaseless stream of bullets into the crowd. When it was over, seven policemen had been fatally wounded, sixty injured, and an unknown number of protesters killed or injured. Most of the carnage, including among the police, resulted not from the bomb, but from the volley of police bullets.[29]

The night's events triggered America's first red scare. A hysteria focusing on the radical "menace" swept the nation, fueled in great part by a compliant press. Nowhere was the panic worse than in Chicago. The *Tribune* devoted its entire front page to the story, combining the dispatches of many reporters into one long tale of horror. Chapin, who reached the square after the carnage, was among those who got caught up in the press frenzy. When the city pursued eight anarchists, Chapin joined the chase. For example, on the night of May 6, he was among the first reporters with the police when August Spies, editor of the pro-labor newspaper *Arbeiter-Zeitung*, and Michael Schwab, a staff writer for the same publication, were arrested. The prisoners were kept out of contact with anyone on the outside, including their attorneys. "No one," explained the *Tribune*, "who was not thoroughly in sympathy with the police were permitted to see them."[30]

Chapin and Hugh Hume from the *Inter-Ocean* newspaper were among those passing that litmus test and were granted permission to approach the cells—known as sweat boxes for the lack of ventilation—of the arrested men around midnight on Wednesday night. Samuel Fielden, who had been one of the speakers in the square two nights before, was in an adjacent cell nursing a wound in his leg when Chapin and Hume arrived. He arose, rubbed his bloodshot eyes, and walked over to the bars. "His swarthy features, well covered with a thick growth of black hair and beard are repulsive, and his low brow and catlike eyes do not improve his appearance," Chapin told his readers. Fielden gave them an account of his life, from his childhood in England to his conversion to socialism after immigrating to the United States. "I have assisted in building up Socialistic Organizations in Chicago, and I am proud that we are now 3,500 strong in membership, not including several thousands of known sympathizers," he told Chapin and Hume. He offered no clue as to who had thrown the bomb.[31]

August Spies, who was in the adjacent cell, also claimed he had nothing to do with the bomb. As editor of the radical *Arbeiter-*

Zeitung, Spies had spoken at the rally, but told Chapin that his speech was the most temperate he had ever delivered. He believed the throwing of the bomb was an impulsive act, not prearranged. "Regarding the quantities of explosive found in his office he says that he was ignorant of their presence there," wrote Chapin. "He thinks they were probably placed there by the police in order to make a case against them. He had two cartridges in his desk, which he kept to show reporters, but they were perfectly harmless."

Chapin was, however, unconvinced by their claims of innocence. His article's lead made his view clear. "The Nihilistic agitators, Spies, Fielden, and their fellow-conspirators, remained in the cells below the detectives' quarters last night." Chapin was certainly one of Medill's boys.[32]

Marine Reporter

5

On a bright warm July morning in 1887, Chapin was making the rounds of the docks as the *Tribune*'s new marine reporter. The post was a potentially good beat in a port city like Chicago. Maritime news was considered important, and the stories that one could pick up on the beat, from wrecks to famous passengers, were often widely read. There also was a considerable sense of fraternity among the reporters from the different papers, much like that which existed among police reporters. Although they competed vigorously, they also found time to put aside their rivalries and socialize together frequently. Chapin thought his new post a sufficient elevation in status to change his listing in the city directory from "reporter" to "marine reporter." After five years of hard work, Chapin had made a comfortable place for himself at the *Tribune*. In fact, domestic life, too, had become remarkably stable for the Chapins. For the first time since their marriage, they had not moved in two years, choosing to stay put in a boarding house on Sedgwick Street in North Chicago.[1]

That morning, as on every day but Sunday, the docks were busy. Chicago had one of the nation's largest ports; some 2,000 schooners moved everything from apples to lumber, and grain to coal, back and forth across the Great Lakes. On most days, a tugboat would not have a moment's rest. While stopping on board the docked tugboat owned by Captain Dunham, Chapin said he overheard talk about the mysterious movements of a schooner. It seemed that on Saturday, the schooner *Blake* had taken a load of

wheat bound for a Canadian port on Lake Ontario. But instead
of heading out while the breeze was good, the *Blake* had been
towed to the North Pier, where the tug was dismissed and the
schooner was made fast for the evening. Shortly before eleven
o'clock, the captain of the *Blake* rushed ashore and excitedly entered the dockyard's office. He wanted a tug.[2]

"Which line do you use?" asked the man on duty.

"Any line," said the captain, "any that could come as soon as
possible."

The tug *Flossie Thielkie* responded to the call, and a few minutes later the *Blake* was towed out into the dark lake.[3]

Chapin concluded that under cover of darkness, the *Blake* had
taken on a cargo more sought-after than wheat. Earlier that evening, William McGarigle, a former county hospital warden, had
escaped from jail where he was awaiting sentencing on a corruption conviction. A foolish keeper had taken him to his house for
his weekly bath. While the sheriff chatted with McGarigle's wife
in the living room, McGarigle slipped out the bathroom window
to freedom. Chapin knew McGarigle, and he understood why
many might have joined in making the escape possible. Chapin
had first met him when he was a police reporter and McGarigle
was chief of police. When he became the warden of the hospital,
the two dined together frequently. "At all times genial and jolly,
liberal to a degree bordering on prodigality, he was just the sort
of man to attract others, and consequently his friends were legion," said Chapin.[4]

Unfortunately for Chapin, he wasn't the only one who had
picked up on McGarigle's trail and the schooner's odd nighttime
maneuvers. The escapee's physician, Dr. St. John, was questioned
the next day by a grand jury. Dr. St. John was part owner of the
Blake, and the state's attorney grilled him for two hours. When
he emerged, the *Tribune* said he "looked as though he had been
through the machinery of a steam laundry." Although Dr. St.
John had not confessed to helping McGarigle gain passage on the
schooner, the authorities were convinced that McGarigle was on
board the *Blake*, sailing toward Canada.[5]

By Thursday, sheriff deputies were heading by train up the
eastern side of Lake Michigan to the narrow Straits of Mackinaw,
three hundred miles north of Chicago, through which all vessels

must pass to reach Canada. "I figured that I could take a night train," said Chapin, "follow the sheriff's men to the straits, get there ahead of the schooner and be in time to report the capture of the fleeing boodler." Chapin wasn't, however, the only one with that thought in mind. Also on board the night train was Melville Stone, owner of the rival Chicago *Morning News*, along with his city editor. Three years earlier when covering the Winnetka murders, Chapin had hoped to emulate Stone's pioneering detective journalism. Now they were competing. Chapin became even more nervous when the sleeping car porter told him that Stone had wired ahead to reserve the fastest tug. "How could I expect to compete with such extravagant enterprise, when I had come away with not much more than railroad fare?"[6]

Friday morning, Stone, his editor, and Chapin arrived in St. Ignace, Michigan, at the edge of the straits. Unbeknownst to Chapin, a freelance reporter had already been out in the straits the day before in the tug *Pendell* with the Chicago deputies, and there had been no sighting of the *Blake* yet. Unconvinced that the *Blake* could have traveled 300 miles in such a short time, Stone took up the chase and hired the *Pendell* at $162 for the day and headed out into the straits with the detectives on board. Chapin had other ideas. Instead of rushing out onto the water, he began asking around. An old dock worker told Chapin that the *Blake* was well into Lake Huron by now. Chapin reported his findings in the next day's edition of his paper: "A *Tribune* reporter, sent out from Chicago to search for the escaped boodler, arrived in Mackinaw City early this morning and found the little burg laughing heartily at the stupidity of the Chicago detectives who have been lying in the straits all week waiting to nab McGarigle." Apparently, the *Blake* had slid undetected through the sheriff's dragnet Thursday morning on a brisk northwest breeze, while the men were dozing to make up for lost sleep during their three-day watch.[7]

The dock worker, who also claimed to monitor passing ships for underwriters, told Chapin he might still have a chance of catching McGarigle if he took a train to Port Huron and boarded the *Blake* as she was towed through the St. Clair River to Lake Erie. Chapin ran back to the train station and jumped on the southbound train just as it pulled out. "As I sank into a seat, gasping for breath and trembling from exertion, I began to speculate on the wisdom of what I was doing," said Chapin. "If the garrulous vessel reporter had misinformed me about McGarigle having safely run the gauntlet I would be ruined, for Stone and his city editor would have the story of his capture and no amount of explanation would ever satisfy my editor that I wasn't a fool."[8]

Chapin arrived in Port Huron at 10:00 P.M. and located a hotel room. After supper, he went to the docks and negotiated, on credit, the use of a fast tug, the *Orient*, from Captain Jimmy Lyons. If Chapin's information from the Mackinaw dockworker was correct, Lyons figured the *Blake* would be in sight in the morning. Chapin telegraphed a short dispatch to the *Tribune*, promising his readers he would soon catch up with the *Blake*. By return wire, the managing editor Robert W. Patterson replied:

STONE WIRES THE DAILY NEWS THAT MCGARIGLE HASN'T PASSED THROUGH THE STRAITS AND IS NOT EXPECTED UNTIL TONIGHT. YOU ARE ON THE WRONG TRACK AND WE ARE BEATEN. COME HOME.

Ignoring Patterson's orders, Chapin boarded Lyons's tug shortly after midnight, and they set off into Lake Huron. All day Saturday, Chapin and Lyons searched the lower end of the lake in his tug. They stopped every vessel for a distance of fifty miles. But it was to no avail. No one reported having seen the *Blake*. Maybe Patterson was right. Back in Chicago, the newspapers were in a complete state of confusion as to what was happening on the waters. Both the *Morning News* and the *Tribune* began publishing any dispatch that came in, even if it contradicted the one in the column above. Chapin's paper, however, now seemed more willing to bank on his being right. "The *Tribune* can depend on the report that the *Blake* passed down Thursday at 11 A.M.," read the front page.[9]

At midnight, Chapin's gamble finally paid off. The captain of the *Roanoke*, a propeller boat, said he had passed the *Blake* earlier in the day. Chapin and Lyons retired to Port Huron for a few hours rest, and at 4:00 A.M. on Sunday, the *Orient* steamed north again. "The weather had moderated some, but the wind was still blowing with sufficient violence to cause a tremendous sea," wrote

Chapin. "Great waves rolled over this little craft at every plunge, but she shook them off and raced through the white caps with a speed of nearly ten miles an hour." As the sun rose over the churning waters, Chapin and Lyons spotted smoke on the horizon. A full hour later they came upon four schooners under tow. The fourth ship was the *Blake*![10]

The rough sea would not permit the *Orient* to get close enough for Chapin to board, so they stood off and watched the parade of boats. Then without warning, the *Marsh*, which was third in the line of ships, dropped the tow line. At first, Chapin thought this was the moment when the *Blake* would break for the Canadian shore. Oddly, however, the Captain of the *Blake* requested a tow from the *Orient*. "This looked suspicious," said Chapin. He told Lyons to steam toward the *Marsh*. As Chapin made this request, the *Marsh* lowered a yawl off its stern. A crew member, accompanied by a tall man in an overcoat, dropped into the small boat. Bedlam reigned. Lyons ordered up a full head of steam from his engineer. The Captain of the *Blake* let loose a torrent of curses aimed at the pursuing boat carrying Chapin, and the crews on the other ships began to yell, cheering on the escapee. "The tug gave a leap that almost stood her on end, then the race began," said Chapin. The lone crew member on the yawl began madly scuttling, pushing the small craft toward shore as fast as he could while McGarigle lay in the bottom of the boat not daring to move. The *Orient* bore down on them. The gap between the two narrowed to less than a hundred feet, but suddenly Lyons turned the wheel and steered the tug back out into the open waters. It had become too shallow for the deep draft of a tug. "The shouts of laughter that rang from the decks of the schooners floated across the water, and the crews yelled in derision at the men aboard the tug, whom they had mistaken for officers," said Chapin.

With McGarigle safely on Canadian soil, Chapin ordered his tug alongside the *Marsh*. The waters were calmer, and the *Marsh* was not moving, so Chapin boarded easily. Captain Johnny Freer, whom Chapin knew from his beat, greeted him warmly, now realizing he had been mistaken in assuming the *Orient* carried police officers. Over steaming coffee, Freer told a tale that would further embarrass the already foolish-looking officers who were still waiting for McGarigle back in the Mackinaw straits. Several days earlier, Freer said, the detectives had boarded the *Marsh* while it traversed the straits. Freer, who was sympathetic to McGarigle's plight, invited the men below for a drink of "cherry bunce," a popular Canadian brandy. While they were drinking, Freer returned topside and spotted the *Blake* coming through the straits under a full head of sail. He then went back below and uncorked some more bottles. "The detectives relished the stuff and they had a rollicking, jolly time of it," Freer told Chapin. "When they came on deck I don't believe any one of them could have told a fishing smack from a steamboat. But by this time the *Blake* was out of sight."

Later that day, Freer overtook the *Blake* and warned her of the search now underway. The weather was rough, and at one point the two ships collided. During the brief instant they were together, McGarigle jumped from the *Blake* to the *Marsh*. "I recognized him as McGarigle and, with tears streaming down his face, he begged me to put him ashore. I told him I would and did," said Freer unapologetically. Chapin next interviewed Captain Irwin of the *Blake*. From him, Chapin garnered all the remaining details of the late-night transfer from the North Pier. One more interview was needed to complete his coup. Chapin summoned back the *Orient* and asked Lyons to drop him off at Point Edward, about half a mile below where McGarigle landed. As he walked along the shore, Chapin found the overcoat that McGarigle had worn discarded on a dock. At the station, Chapin discovered there would be no trains until after midnight, and that another man, who matched McGarigle's description, had asked the same question earlier. "Here all traces ended," said Chapin, "and although a careful search was made of both Sarnia and Point Edward he could not be found." Chapin asked that he be called by telephone if McGarigle surfaced from hiding, and he returned, exhausted from lack of sleep, to Port Huron.

At eight o'clock that night, a call came. McGarigle had been seen buying a hat. Chapin jumped into a rowboat and crossed the fast-moving river, reaching the town in about an hour. But McGarigle had again disappeared. Chapin spent another hour checking all the hotels and, at last, found his man in Jack Boyle's livery stable. Chapin walked up to McGarigle and extended his hand.

"It was warmly shaken and the big boodler linked arms with the reporter and together they walked up the street," Chapin wrote.

McGarigle looked haggard and worn down. "In walking he totters," said Chapin, "and several times he clutched the reporter's arm for support." Chapin took him to the Western Hotel, got him a room, and requested an interview. "I am worn out with worry and excitement and it would be simply torture for me to comply to the extent you desire," replied McGarigle. Instead, he promised to give Chapin a lengthy exclusive interview in the morning that would prove his innocence. Chapin persisted, however, in getting some answers to his questions. No, said McGarigle, Sheriff Matson was not in on the escape. Yes, the escape occurred as you have reported it. No, I have no money. If I had stayed in jail, I would have died from typhoid; my life depended on escaping.

As Chapin left McGarigle and returned to Port Huron, he knew there was not another member of the press within a hundred miles. The scoop was his. That night he filed his triumphant tale. In Chicago, Patterson stationed guards around the pressroom to prevent any leaks to rival newspapers. On Monday, his story consumed half of the front page. "This morning a *Tribune* reporter stood on the deck of the tug *Orient* and waved his hat at McGarigle as the escaped boodler planted his feet on British soil," read Chapin's lead. "McGarigle did not return the salute. He was in a hurry, and, although he has been dreadfully seasick, he ran away as fast as his long legs could carry him. He is now safe in Canada, and the detectives, deputy sheriffs, and newspapermen who are still waiting in the straits for the *Blake* to pass through might as well quit and go home." Not content with just one dig at the mistakes made by the detectives, Chapin described finding McGarigle's coat. "The reporter picked it up and will present it to Sheriff Matson as a souvenir of the most memorable event in his life." Chapin's remarkable story not only put all the pieces of McGarigle's escape together, but also reminded readers that the events confirmed Chapin's original hunch that the boodler had left Chicago on the *Blake*.[11]

Stone was beaten, and beaten badly. Years later, writing his memoirs, he still seethed at having lost the chase for the escapee and still clung to the idea he might have intercepted the *Blake* had it not been for Chapin. "My movements were betrayed by a rival newspaper, and McGarigle escaped," said Stone in 1920. "The story of this betrayal is told, in his interesting autobiography recently issued, by the offending reporter, Charley Chapin, who is serving out his sentence in Sing Sing prison for wife murder. If I could have caught him at the time, I should have been tempted to kill him, and might myself be the 'lifer' today."[12]

Chapin remained in Port Huron for several more days, but McGarigle stood him up for that promised interview. Canadian authorities refused a request for extradition on the grounds they did not recognize conspiracy convictions. At last, Chapin made his triumphant return to Chicago. Patterson summoned him to his office. There he presented him with a raise, two weeks vacation, and a cash bonus.

"I want to thank you for disobeying my orders," said Patterson.

"Would you mind telling me what you would have done if, after I disobeyed your orders, Stone had got McGarigle in the straits?" replied Chapin. The only answer that came was a laugh. The McGarigle scoop made Chapin one of the city's premier marine reporters. Three months later, his new status led to a tip that gave him another lake-related scoop.[13]

On Monday, October 31, 1887, the city's myopic focus on the upcoming execution of the convicted Haymarket anarchists was shifting to a developing story of disaster on Lake Michigan. The *Vernon*, one of the most noted "passenger propellers," as the new engine-powered crafts were called, was reported lost in an early winter storm that had swept across the lake over the weekend. Between thirty and fifty passengers were on board. The exact number was hard to determine because the only known passenger list had been on the ship. Among marine reporters, the *Vernon* was a well-known ship. She had been built to move fish to market and passengers to port rapidly. Alfred Booth commissioned the boat, and it had been completed August 16, 1886. Chapin, as a marine reporter, had witnessed the launching. It was an impressive new ship, and 5,000 people turned out to watch it slip into the water. The 177-foot craft had two boilers that turned a 565-horsepower engine capable of propelling the *Vernon* at fifteen knots. Reflecting the profitability of the Booth Fish Company, no expense had been spared in fitting the craft. Brass hardware was used everywhere, and the eighteen staterooms for passengers were luxurious. Once in the water, however, she became unstable when fully loaded because of a calculation flaw in her design. To overcome the press and maritime skepticism of her seaworthiness, Booth took 150 people for a cruise on August 28. On September 1, she was licensed for service.[14]

In October 1887, the *Vernon* was returning to Chicago after a journey to Cheboygan. As she made her way out into Lake Michigan Friday night, a gale developed. As it grew in intensity, the wind shifted to the north, a feared direction among sailors because it exposes a larger expanse of water to the winds, creating huge waves. On Saturday, while the high winds continued unabated, vessels ran across wreckage, drifting cargo, and even a survivor, but the pilots feared foundering in the rough waters if they stopped. In the afternoon, a boat picked up part of a pilot house. Attached to it was a carved sign with the name "Vernon."[15]

By Monday, the wreck of the *Vernon* was front-page news in all the Chicago papers. It was presumed that no one had survived, including the man who had been spotted on the roof of a cabin. But Tuesday, Charles Elphicke, a vessel owner, sent word to Chapin to come to his office in the Board of Trade. Elphicke was eager to show Chapin a telegram he had received from Captain Comstock of the *S. B. Pomeroy*, one of his schooners that had just anchored off Green Bay. During the night, it had come across a life raft bearing a survivor and a dead body. Elphicke gave Chapin a letter of introduction to the captain and agreed to tell no one else. Chapin rushed to grab a train to Green Bay.[16]

At 5:30 the next morning, Chapin arrived in Green Bay. The *S. B. Pomeroy* was anchored about two miles offshore. Chapin immediately rousted the crew of a tug, which he chartered to take him out to the schooner. On board the *S. B. Pomeroy*, Chapin found the survivor, Axel Stone, a watchman from the *Vernon*, still asleep. No matter, Chapin had him wakened, too. Twenty-eight years old, with a muscular body, Stone was still in considerable pain from his ordeal. "His legs are swelled to three times their ordinary size, and are discolored to the hips, while his hands are as big as boxing gloves," said Chapin. But his mind was clear and, over breakfast, he told his tale.[17]

Stone said there had been twenty-five passengers on board, and an immense amount of cargo. "Both holds were chock full, and between decks there was not space enough to stow a box of matches," said Stone. "I have sailed on vessels nearly all of my life and have made voyages to all parts of the world, but I never have seen a vessel so shamefully overloaded." With her passengers and cargo, the *Vernon* left Good Harbor, its last port of call before traversing the lake, on Friday night. Stone had the first watch that night. The wind began to pick up around nine or ten o'clock, and the waves soon began to build. "I have been out in storms that were a good deal worse, but I never was on a boat that acted as badly as she did," he said. Water began to run down into the engine room through hatches left open to accommodate the surplus of cargo. Stone urged the Captain to jettison some of the cargo, but he brusquely refused. At 1:00 A.M., Stone was relieved. Exhausted and scared, he turned in and fell fast asleep. Two hours later, he was thrown from his bunk onto the floor. Water poured in from the door and nearly filled his room. He grabbed his clothes, donned a life preserver, crawled through his window, and fell into the lake. "I am a good swimmer, but I was not six feet away from the steamer when she went down. Lots of people must have gone down with her, because I could hear them screaming above the racket made by the storm," Stone told Chapin, who was quickly scribbling notes.

In the turmoil, Stone still managed to spot a life raft about a quarter of a mile away. It took him a half-hour to reach it. On board were six members of the crew, wet and frozen, most with little clothing. They told Stone that the rising water in the engine room had finally extinguished the fires, leaving the boat powerless. As soon as it entered a deep trough between waves, it rolled over. All they had managed to do before the *Vernon* went under was to free the raft they were now in. Stone donned the clothing he had brought with him and began rowing. The rowing and his clothes, though wet, kept Stone warm, but the cold took a toll on the others. Within a day, only Stone was still alive. Bill, a fireman, had been the last to die. During the next days, Stone warmed himself as much as he could in the sun during the day, at one point drying his tobacco and having a long smoke on his pipe. Regularly he saw other ships, but none came to his rescue. In one case, he was sure the crew of a schooner saw him, but they continued on their way. Finally, after nearly forty-eight hours in the raft, Stone told Chapin he had felt the end was near. "I had lost my pipe, and Bill was dead, and I didn't have any company. Bill died in the middle of the raft and his clothes froze to it so he couldn't wash off. I was glad when darkness came so his eyes couldn't stare at me so. I put my head on his chest and fastened my arms tightly around him so I couldn't be washed off by the sea and fell asleep."

Later in the night Stone woke. A bright moon lit the lake, and he saw the *S. B. Pomeroy* nearby. His arms were now too stiff to wave a shirt, so he sat and shouted as loud as he could. The boat passed by, and once again he thought all was lost. Chapin learned from the captain what happened next. On board, the second mate thought he heard a faint shout and told the captain. Coming up on deck, Comstock spotted the raft in the "wake of the moon." He ordered that the yawl be lowered, and they rowed in the direction of the raft. A cloud darkened the water, and for a half-hour they pulled about aimlessly while Comstock continued to call out into the darkness. Finally, they struck the raft. Comstock jumped on board and lifted Stone into the yawl. As he did, he stumbled over something big and bulky. "Oh, that's Bill," Stone horsely whispered. "He's dead; don't mind him." Comstock went back on the raft, he freed the corpse from the raft's icy grip, and they rowed back to the *S. B. Pomeroy.*

After taking down Stone's story and conferring with Comstock, who corroborated the account with the bits and pieces the survivor had told him since his rescue, Chapin and Comstock went up to the deck. There the captain directed him to a heap of canvas. Chapin described what he found. "The reporter lifted one end of the sail and gazed upon the blackened face of Bill, the last of the six men who died on the raft with Stone. It was a horrible sight, and the covering was quickly replaced."

His notebook full, Chapin now had sole possession of one of the most dramatic lake survival stories in years. He decided to return to Chicago not just with the story, but with the survivor himself. "Stone being wholly without friends or money, and in such a low condition physically, the reporter offered to take him to Chicago at the expense of the *Tribune* and have him placed in a hospital there," Chapin explained to his readers. However, the coroner of Green Bay, "an officious little chap, accompanied by two policemen," had other ideas. He demanded custody of Stone and refused to give permission for him to leave until he testified before a jury holding an inquest on the dead body found on the raft. Chapin saw his story slipping from his grasp. The train for Chicago would leave at 1:25 that afternoon. He was "fearful that we would miss the train and fearing more that Axel would be compelled to tell his story for local newspaper men to telegraph to Chicago." Thinking on his feet, Chapin sent ashore and secured permission to talk to the coroner's jury. "I addressed the jury as eloquently as I could, describing the physical suffering of the unfortunate sailor." Stone, he said, needed immediate medical treatment if his life was to be saved. The jury was apparently swayed and agreed to Chapin's alternative plan. They would accompany him back to the *S. B. Pomeroy* and interview Stone during the ride to shore. By the time the journey was complete, the jury not only heard Stone's testimony, but also, at Chapin's urging, examined a defective life preserver found on the raft. Bill's death was ruled to be caused by exposure, freeing Stone to journey to Chicago.[18]

At the shore, a carriage and a physician were waiting for Stone and Chapin. "At the depot an enormous crowd had gathered to see the survivor, and for a time it looked as though both the reporter and the survivor would be sacrificed to the insatiate curiosity of the citizens of Green Bay," said Chapin. But Chapin managed to get Stone into a corner, where, by placing himself in front, he was able to ward off the crowd until the station manager came and escorted them to his office. "The doors were at once locked, the curtains pulled down, and he was given a chance to rest secure from the prying intrusions of the gaping, staring mob." But scarcely before the group got comfortable, the station manager answered a knock at the door.

"We are United States officers," said one of two men standing in the entrance.

"It makes no difference, gentlemen, there is no room for you in here," replied the manager.

"We must come in. We are United States officials, and we want to talk to this man," the man said, pointing at Stone and trying to force his way in.

"You can't talk to him," exclaimed Chapin, who joined the

manager in pushing the two intruders, who later were exposed as curiosity-bitten customs agents, out the door.

At 1:40 when the train pulled in, a police officer was on hand to clear a path through the crowd. On the train, passengers crowded the pair until Chapin secured seats in the parlor car, "the passengers in that being better bred and more courteous." At 9:30, the train reached Chicago. Getting off the train proved no easier then getting on. "Stone had hardly alighted from the train before he was beset by a horde of reporters, who offered him various amounts of money if he would come to the offices of their respective papers and tell his story." Chapin and Stone managed to reach a waiting carriage that whisked them to the *Tribune*. Getting in his digs at the competition, Chapin wrote that they were "followed by reporters in cabs, who chased after the carriage in hopes of getting for nothing an interview that the *Tribune* had obtained by superior enterprise."

The front page of the next morning's *Tribune* belonged to Chapin. Stone recovered after a few days in the hospital. By Sunday, advertisements appearing in the *Tribune* announced that Stone would be a featured attraction at Kohl & Middleton's South Side Museum. "Found floating with a corpse. Saved from a watery grave 'neath the Waves. Sailor Axel Stone, the only survivor of the Lost Steamer *Vernon*!" He soon earned enough money to return to his native Sweden. Chapin's story had turned Stone into a media celebrity.

Death Watch

Even if Chicagoans had wanted to put the events of May 1886 to rest, the *Tribune* certainly would not, at least not until its version of justice was meted out. Since the morning following the explosion at Haymarket Square, the *Tribune* had clamored for the arrest of the accused anarchists; once they were captured, the paper campaigned for their death. As execution day neared, Chapin was assigned to cover the hanging. "It was a nerve-straining task," said Chapin, "for I had known all of them for years and had frequently reported their meetings, long before anyone suspected they were anything more than harmless cranks." On Wednesday, November 9, 1887, he took his place among the reporters at the Cook County jail, a low brick building attached to the back of the county's ornate court house. The fourth estate was there in full force. Not only had Chicago's newspapers sent their best reporters, but also milling around were dozens of correspondents from faraway city papers, including the New York *Evening World,* launched by Joseph Pulitzer less than a month before to keep up with Randolph Hearst's entry into the wildly competitive Park Row. The reporters all knew the executions they would witness Friday would make the front page of their newspaper and other newspapers around the globe. The planned executions had become a rallying point for industrial workers the world over. Justice, in this case, was a two-sided coin. For business interests, the executions would preserve the rule of law. For workers, the executions would preserve the rule of capital. The fury around the hangings made it the most anticipated story of the year. But before the day arrived, one of the imprisoned anarchists detonated another front-page story.[1]

Louis Lingg was among the seven condemned to die by hanging on Friday and being kept in adjacent cells at the bottom of a four-tiered cellblock. In front of the cells were a caged visitor's room, which was filled during the day, and a smaller caged room where a guard kept a death watch. The evening Chapin joined the watch was uneventful and quiet. About the only thing he noticed was that the prisoners all smoked incessantly and that one of them in particular, Lingg, seemed unfazed by his approaching death. He ate a hearty meal of sirloin steak and two plates of chicken salad brought from Martell's restaurant. Lingg had remained the most defiant of the group throughout the trial and imprisonment. A twenty-one-year-old carpenter from Germany, he had told the judge at his sentencing that his death would not end the bomb throwing. "When you shall have hanged us, then—mark my words—they will do the bomb throwing! In this hope I say to you: I despise you. I despise your order, your laws, your force-propped authority. Hang me for it!" Only the week before, Lingg mailed the governor a letter refusing any kind of pardon that might be offered, demanding instead that he either be given his unconditional liberty or put to death.[2]

The waiter who brought his meal to the jail asked Lingg what he should bring for breakfast.

"Nothing," he replied.

"What? Don't you want anything?" said the waiter in surprise.

"No; yes, bring me some milk toast."[3]

But before the milk toast arrived the next morning, Lingg made a final defiant act. At 8:55 A.M., a detonation reverberated throughout the jail. It "snapped the terrible tension on the nerves of officials," wrote Chapin on the front page of the next day's *Tribune*, "and for a second all hearts stood still. Deputy O'Neill, who was in front of Lingg's cell, saw a puff of blue smoke roll from it and his call of 'It's Lingg' broke the silence and the men in the office rushed into the cage." As usual, Chapin's technique was a theatrical retelling of the events rather than a straightforward report on its conclusion. The reader would not learn of Lingg's fate until deep into the story.

After the explosion, the jailer and his clerk raced from their office. "As fast as keys could be procured and turned in the locks they made their way through the two doors into the cell of the arch-Anarchist," wrote Chapin, who was among the first reporters to reach the cell. They found Lingg lying on his bunk, his head hanging over the edge, bleeding profusely. The bedding, walls, and floor of the cell were spattered with blood, flesh, teeth, and bits of bone. It was immediately surmised that Lingg had inserted an explosive cap, normally used to detonate a larger explosive, in his mouth and set it off. No one knew where it could have come from. They carried Lingg from his cell to a table in a large bathroom across the corridor. Most of his jaw had been torn away by the explosion. Chapin's account did not make for pleasant breakfast reading. "The lips were almost wholly blown away. In place of the mouth there was a horrid, ragged aperture that extended nearly to the angles of the jaw. A trace of the form of the chin could still be seen, some of the upper lip with the mustache remained, while the nose was sunken and flabby and the eyes closed."[4]

Lingg's head was propped up with two or three pillows, and the assistant county physician tried to clean his wounds. Chapin used the doctor's examination as a pretext to continue his portrait of gore. "It was found that the upper jaw bone, including the teeth and the base of the nose, were completely torn, shattered and forced sidewise and downwards and the teeth gone; that the tongue had been horribly cut and mangled and all its attachments severed, necessitating the fastening of a cord to it to prevent its doubling back and closing the windpipe. A large hole, perhaps three-fourths of an inch in diameter, in the face near the left base of the nose was doubtless where the metallic cap came through." After being administered aid and hypodermic shots of brandy, water, and warm salt water, it was thought Lingg might live. He could not talk, so he resorted several times to writing messages on a reporter's pad. But by one o'clock, said Chapin, "it became evident that he could last but a few hours."

"Lingg died hard," Chapin wrote. "His athletic frame, splendid constitution, and superabundant vitality survived for more than six hours the injuries that would have killed a weaker man in a third of the time." In fact, the sheriff announced Lingg's death before it had actually occurred. A few Chicago reporters—out-of-town newspapermen were kept from the jail—deputies, and jail officials crowded into the bathroom to witness Lingg's last moments. Chapin described the martyr-like treatment of the dead man: "Just as the life was dying out of him a deputy took a pair of scissors and clipped off locks of Lingg's curly auburn hair and handed them about for souvenirs," wrote Chapin. "Bailiffs six hours before picked up bits of the dead-man's jawbone and teeth, which were scattered about his cell by the explosion. These were carefully put by for relics."

Chapin filed his lengthy account with his editor. When he was done, he rejoined the death watch. That evening, only four of the seven—August Spies, Albert Parsons, George Engel, and Adolph Fischer—still faced the gallows the next day. While Chapin had been working on his story, Governor Richard J. Oglesby had commuted the sentences of two of the remaining prisoners. Though the condemned finally fell asleep, Chapin and many of his colleagues didn't.

Sunrise illuminated a city in a virtual state of siege. Three hundred policemen armed with shotguns, rifles, and pistols surrounded the courthouse and jail. No traffic could come within a block of the jail. The courthouse rooftop and jail windows were manned with rifle-bearing officers. If this protection were insufficient, several regiments of militia were camped close to city hall, ready to spring into action with Gatling guns and cannons. Factories were locked shut for the day. Newspapers—especially those that had called for the death of the anarchists—banks, and other institutions of capitalism were under the watch of hired guards. A sense of apprehension descended over the city.

By 8:00 A.M., the condemned were awakened. They spent the early part of the morning writing letters, composing final statements, and eating their last meals. At 10:00 A.M., Chapin, other reporters, officials, and the jury gathered in the jail office and the courtyard. At 10:30 A.M., the large door leading into the jail itself was opened, and the crowd was escorted into the north corridor, where the gallows stood a full two-stories tall. The reporters took their seats at an assigned table, immediately behind the front benches reserved for the jury and doctors. All sat and waited. "The corridor was but dimly lighted by one of the barred windows high up on one side, and three or four dull incandescent lights on the walls served only to accentuate the gloom," wrote Chapin. More time passed. Someone lit a cigar, but the sheriff told him to extinguish it. It approached 11:45 A.M. "This long wait was excessively trying. To most of those present it was worse than the execution itself. Some of the newspapermen—especially those from other cities—affected a levity that was somewhat unbecoming, but that was possibly assumed to conceal a deeper feeling. For their own credit one hopes so. But the great majority of those present sat in solemn silence."⁵

Suddenly the bailiff appeared. He raised his hand and exclaimed in a low and excited voice, "Gentlemen of the jury uncover your heads." As one, they all removed their hats. Then muffled steps were heard. "They came nearer and each man's heart beat faster," said another reporter who witnessed the scene. Each condemned man was clad in white shrouds from his neck to his heels. Spies was the first, and he took his place in front of his assigned noose. The other three soon followed. A deputy caught the noose, placed it over Spies's head, and tightened it around his neck, leaving the knot lying under his left ear. He repeated this process with each man. Then white hoods were placed over each man's head. "For a moment or two the men stood like ghosts," wrote Chapin. "Suddenly from beneath the cap of Spies came the words in a thick voice: 'Our silence will be more powerful than the voices they are going to strangle today!'" The others each spoke. "Long live anarchy," said Engel. "This is the happiest moment of my life," added Fischer. "Then came the sound of Parsons' voice, distinct enough, but not so loud. 'Shall I be allowed to speak,' he said. 'O, men of America,' then, suddenly changing his inflection: 'Let me speak Sheriff Matson.' There was a moment's pause—only a moment's—and he began again: 'Shall the voice of the people be heard!' but as the sound of the last word left his lips it was lost in the loud 'bang' of the descending trap and the four men shot downward together."⁶

The bodies each reacted to their end differently. Parsons was still, while Spies writhed as his shoulders twisted, his chest heaved, and his legs drew up and down. Doctors stood by the men and reported the dying men's pulses to the crowd. Chapin took down a minute-by-minute account:

First minute—Spies, 119; Parsons, 62; Fischer, 62; Engel, 60.

Second minute—Spies, 104; Fischer, 98; Engel, 96; Parsons, 100 . . .

Seven and one-half minutes after the drop— Fischer, 22; no pulse perceptible in the others.

"As the white forms hung in the startling relief against the dark background of wall beneath the scaffold the sight was more ghastly than at any previous stage of the grim proceedings," wrote Chapin. The bodies began to twist in the air, and the doctors cut them from the ropes as the sunlight streamed in through the grated window above. "The spectators of the hanging, many of whom had been visibly affected by the scene, remained seated even after life had been declared extinct in each dangling figure. The only sound that could be heard for a few minutes was the distant rumble of wagons on the streets." The sheriff announced that it was time to clear the hall. "Then the men who had seen the Anarchists hanged filed slowly away, each turning as he reached the exit to look back down the long corridor at the four still, white figures appearing at that distance to be hanging against the wall."

Chapin was feeling so nauseous and faint he could hardly make it to the street. He followed his colleagues to a nearby saloon. He began drinking brandy, and that was the last thing he remembered. "In all the years since I have never been able to recall what happened to me afterward, not even leaving the saloon." He recollected only waking in his bed at home the next morning. The sun was up. It was six o'clock. "Then came the humiliating remorse of a drunkard." Chapin had prided himself on his dependability. But now he had failed, and he imagined the scene in the office when his editor must have pieced together a story because Chapin had failed to return that night. "I felt he could never forgive me and I buried my face in the pillow and cried." Later, he dressed and snuck out of his house to the street where he bought a complete set of the morning papers from a paperboy. He began with the *Tribune*.[7]

"August Spies, Albert H. Parsons, George Engel, and Adolph Fischer were hanged on the gallows in Cook County Jail yesterday," read the lead. "They met their death bravely and fearlessly; they were defiant to the end; as Infidels and Anarchists they lived, and as Infidels and Anarchists they died." Unquestionably, vintage Chapin. "As I read the story I grew more and more puzzled," said Chapin. "The introduction was precisely as I had planned to write it and the story described everything as my eyes had seen what had taken place. There were sentences that were undeniably mine."[8]

He hurried back to his boarding house and encountered a maid. He asked her what time he had come in the night before.

"Why, shortly after 10:00 P.M.," she replied. "You looked pale and tired," she said.

"I searched her face in an effort to discover whether she suspected that I was intoxicated, but her eyes beamed nothing but sympathy."

Following some breakfast, Chapin got up his courage to go to the office. In the elevator, he encountered Patterson, the managing editor. "You wrote a fine story of the execution," he said, putting his arm around Chapin, who mumbled his thanks, still too bewildered to know what to say. He tentatively entered the city room and nervously extended a cheery "good morning" to Hall. The city editor also praised his work and said he had been particularly pleased that it had been turned in before nine. One last stop remained for Chapin. He entered the proofreaders' room and picked up a sheaf of copy written in his hand. "There was no indication of trembling fingers, nor were there scratched-out words to betray unsteadiness of mind," he said. "I had never written more perfect copy." Fortified by seeing his copy, he slowly unraveled the events of the day before by speaking with his colleagues. It turned out he had left the bar after only one drink and had returned to the *Tribune*. There he had locked himself in a room and had written steadily for eight hours. Instead of alcohol numbing his mind, the work and events had. "An expert psychologist might explain it differently," he said. "I can't."[9]

As 1887 came to a close, Chapin's status as one of Chicago's best reporters was unquestioned. In that year alone, in addition to his stellar coverage of the executions, he had chased McGarigle into Canada and single-handedly beat everyone on the sinking of the *Vernon*, one of the worst maritime disasters in Lake Michigan history. Crime and maritime disasters were his trade, the front page his domain. Death of all sorts was one of the main ingredients of successful newspapers in their furious competition for readers. Murder or sensational stories of death, whether by accident, mob, or by hanging, made a reporter's reputation. Chapin, who had been an early disciple of this new creed, was now becoming one of its better-known apostles. Though the use of bylines was years away, everyone in the Chicago press recognized Chapin's work, especially the *Tribune*'s rivals. "I now began to get nothing but big stories to cover," said Chapin. "Frequently I was permitted to select my own assignments and often to create them."[10]

Chapin's success as a reporter brought him other dividends. He was now among the highest-paid *Tribune* reporters. As a result, he and Nellie moved from the boarding house on Sedgwick Street to better quarters on Pullman Avenue, and he was, at last, able to occasionally supply Nellie with the life's pleasures she coveted, such as jewelry, something which Chapin knew a great deal about as the son and grandson of a jeweler. He also came into proximity, in the course of his journalistic pursuits, with wealthy financiers such as Columbus R. Cummings, Calvin S. Brice, and General Samuel H. Thomas who put together railroad syndicates. Over time, Chapin became close to one source, a financier named William B. Howard. He evidently liked Chapin because he took him on a two-week, expenses-paid trip to New York, ostensibly to write about the construction of a new portion of the Croton aqueduct, for which his firm Brown, Howard & Co. held a seven-million dollar contract. They stayed in the Union League Club at 39th Street and Fifth Avenue. A four-story, brick, gabled affair, the club was the preserve of a thousand of New York's wealthiest citizens. "I frequently lunched there with his financial associates," recalled Chapin. "It was my introduction to the life of a millionaire. The taste for luxury I acquired in those two weeks I never got over." At one of these lunches, General Thomas told Chapin he had once been a reporter himself. Chapin immediately asked for the secret to his ascent to wealth. "Better stick to reporting," he warned. "You're a lot happier now than I am."[11]

Christmas of 1887 seemed especially promising, not just for the Chapins, but for most in Chicago. For the first time, Christmas trees could be found in many homes, thanks to a pair of entrepreneurs. At the Clark Street bridge, Herman and August Schueneman had tied up their fishing schooner loaded with young spruce trees cut from a Michigan forest, beginning the city's tradition of buying a tree from the "Christmas Ship." City residents joined in the popular custom of decorating a Christmas tree. The new rage, in particular, was to "frost" a tree by sprinkling water on it and dredging it in flour. If one had money, small electric lights wrapped in red, white, and blue crepe paper would make one's tree the talk of the neighborhood. But it was not solely the trees that caused Chicagoans to approach the holiday that year with considerable cheer. Since March, the economy had been improving steadily after a long slump, though some citizens worried about how the new federal regulation of railroads would affect their city, a crossroads of the nation's rail lines.[12]

John J. Glessner, an executive with the International Harvester Company, celebrated his prosperity with the delivery on December 23 of a Steinway piano in a case designed and hand-made by furniture-maker Francis Bacon at an incredible cost of $1,500. On the West Side of Chicago, William A. Macaulley also was savoring the better economic times in his home at 2 Arthington Street on Christmas Eve. The day before, his bosses had raised his salary from $110 to $125 a month, and had awarded him additional vacation days. His interest in a cigar factory was bringing in an additional $140 a month. But Macaulley's holiday reverie, if he was having one, was interrupted around 2:00 P.M. when the doorbell rang.

Ida Macaulley, a small, bespectacled woman, answered the door. There she found Chapin, asking to see her husband.

"What is your business with him?" she asked.

"It is of a personal character, and should be stated to him in private," replied Chapin.

"You must tell me before you can see him."

"I am a newspaper man and want to ask him some questions concerning the present whereabouts of his sister-in-law, Mrs. Mackin."

"I thought so," said Ida. "Come in."[13]

Chapin's journey to the Macaulleys's was prompted by a tip he had picked up during lunch. John Prindiville, a Chicago magistrate, told Chapin he had just issued warrants for the arrest of a man and a woman on charges of infidelity. This was no ordinary case, confided Prindiville. It began on a rainy night in October when the young woman, named Mollie Mackin, had disappeared in the company of her child, leaving behind only a short, baffling note for her doting husband. Since then, Harry Mackin had searched nonstop for his wife, breaking off only occasionally to go to the house of his sister Ida Macaulley for comfort. During the visits, he kept his sister and her husband up-to-date on his efforts. William Macaulley listened sympathetically and urged him to hire a detective agency.[14]

Despite his best efforts over the succeeding month and a half, Harry still had no idea where his wife was. Just a few days before, Harry had met William hurrying along in the street carrying a few bottles of wine, which he said he was bringing home. The following night, Harry called on his sister and asked if she had liked the wine her husband had brought home.

"Why," Ida replied, "he didn't bring me any."

Suspicion overcame him. The many business trips that William took came to mind, and the fires of his hunch were further stoked by the remembrance that his wife had spent considerable time in the Macaulleys's house tending his ill sister two years earlier. Harry immediately took to shadowing William. Within a day, he followed him to an apartment building, where he entered a flat recently rented to the "Williamses." Standing outside in the dark, Mackin spied through the frost-covered window of the second-story apartment the figure of his wife embracing a man.

On a subsequent night, as soon as William was with Mollie, Harry told Ida of her husband's infidelity. The next morning, the two went to Magistrate Prindiville and obtained the warrants for their respective spouses' arrests. They agreed Harry would remain with his wife and Ida with her husband until the officers came. Prindiville urged Chapin to come to court that afternoon to see the fireworks. Obviously, he didn't know Chapin very well. He was not the sort to wait for a story to come to him. Instead, Chapin learned from the city directory that William worked for Bartholomae & Roesing, a considerably large brewery on the West Side. "There I went in hopes of obtaining the story before he was locked up," said Chapin. Unfortunately, Macaulley had already begun his vacation and was not to be found. But the office consented to provide Chapin with his home address.[15]

Now inside the house, Chapin was ushered into the parlor. As he entered, a handsome young man with coal-black hair and a mustache stepped in from an adjoining room. "This is Mr. Macaulley," said Ida, suddenly leaning against the door and steadying herself with her hands as if she were going to fall. As Chapin passed by, he felt her hot breath touch his cheek. "Her bosom was violently heaving from suppressed emotion and her eyes flashed fiercely."[16]

Chapin told William he wanted to talk in private. William looked mystified, but led Chapin into the small room from which he had emerged. The room was small, and they stood near the window not more than a foot apart.

"What is it?" asked William.

"I want to ask you some questions about Mrs. Mackin," said Chapin.

William staggered. His face turned scarlet, and he looked away. "What about Mrs. Mack—"

"He never finished the sentence," wrote Chapin. "Almost like a phantom the fragile form of his wife appeared in the open doorway. She was white as a sheet. Her right arm was uplifted and in her hand she clutched a revolver." Macaulley was standing with his back to the door and could not see her. Before Chapin could warn him, she pointed the revolver at the back of his head and pulled the trigger.[17]

A muffled discharge, a puff of smoke, and Macaulley fell into Chapin's arms. "With the fierceness of an enraged tigress she sprang forward and again leveled the revolver, as if to fire a second shot." Chapin dropped Macaulley and seized Ida's wrists and removed the gun from her grasp.

"Let me kill him, let me kill the fiend," she shrieked.

Chapin pushed her out of the room and turned to William, who lay motionless on the floor. He attempted to lift him, but his weight was too much. He tried to talk with him, but heard only a gurgling groan. Chapin rose and crossed the parlor where Ida was pulling on her hair and shrieking. Another woman, who had been upstairs tending the children, burst in. "What happened?" she asked.

"I have killed Will, and I am glad of it," replied Ida.

Chapin rushed into the street, and at the third home he tried he was able to telephone a doctor. Upon his return to the Macaulley house, he found it locked. He charged the door until the lock finally gave way, and he stumbled into the parlor where he found Ida sobbing.

"Where is my revolver?" she asked Chapin. "I heard him groaning just now. He is not dead. I'm sure he is not dead. Give me my revolver, and let me kill him. O, let me kill him! I tell you he must not live. I must kill him."

Chapin then proceeded into the room where William lay. He described the scene to his readers the next morning. Chicagoans returning from Christmas services—such as the one held at the Cathedral of Saints Peter and Paul, filled with the voices of fifty white-robed young choir members singing "Adeste Fideles"— read in the *Tribune*: "The position of the murdered man was unchanged, but the blood and brains that oozed from the bullet-hole had formed quite a pool around his head. Bending over the almost lifeless form of his papa was baby Willie, his chubby hands smeared with blood. In his childish prattle he was asking his papa what made such a funny noise."

Ida continued to scream about wanting to finish the job and suddenly rushed to the kitchen. Divining her purpose, Chapin followed her and struggled to keep her from obtaining a knife, and forced her back to the parlor. At last subdued, Ida poured out her woes to Chapin, detailing the story of her marriage of three years, her husband's infidelity, and how she had purchased the pistol at a pawnshop. When she had confronted William, he told her that he planned to leave her for Mollie. He proposed she give him the eldest child, accept a sum of money, consent to a divorce, and leave town. The discussion had gotten no further because that was when Chapin had rung the bell.

While Chapin was interviewing Ida, the front door opened, and Harry and a constable arrived for the planned arrest. Chapin told them they had come too late.

"I'm glad you did it, sister," said Harry.

"Why don't you kill your wife?" replied Ida.

The doctor arrived next. After a quick examination of William, he concluded the man had not long to live. While the constable took custody of Ida, Chapin dashed to the flat where the pair of lovers had been meeting. There under guard of a policeman and in the company of a friend, he found Mollie, "a slight and quite pretty woman." He asked if she were willing to tell her side of the story. He played out his interrogation for his readers the next morning.

"I have nothing to say," was her reply.

"It is true, then, that you were living here as the mistress of your brother-in-law under the name of Williams?" She hung her head and made no reply.

"Mrs. Mackin, Mrs. Macaulley has just shot and killed her husband."

"O God! How horrible," she exclaimed.

"Can I see him?" she faltered.

"No."

"O, Please let me see him."

"It is impossible."

Harry Mackin and the constable had by now caught up with Chapin and prepared to take Mollie to jail. But the day's drama was not yet done. Chapin—witness, inquisitor, and chronicler— now took another role. Before they could leave, he took Harry aside and pleaded with him not to permit the jailing of his wife for the sake of the baby. Harry consented that he would offer himself as bond for his wife. Before they left, Harry took Mollie by her arm and led her to the crib in which their child lay.

"The little innocent looked up and smiled," wrote Chapin. "Pointing to the child Mackin dramatically exclaimed: 'Mollie, you never lied to me in your life. Tell me, is that my child?'

'As God is my judge it is.'"

Then the two constables escorted Mollie from the room. She was brought before the judge and released on bond. Chapin went to the Twelfth Street police station where he secured an interview with Ida Macaulley, who, three hours after the shooting, was much calmer. "I was afraid they were going to run away," she told Chapin. She had bought the revolver that morning with the intention of using it on herself. She had laid it on the mantel of the parlor upon her return to the house. When she saw Chapin and

Will go into the room together, she was seized with the thought that no other woman should ever have her husband.

"We were so happy before all this trouble, and O, I loved him so," said Ida. "Last Christmas we had such a nice time at our house, seventeen of our family and such a nice Christmas dinner, with Will carving and being so nice. O, my God! It's awful! I cannot bear it."

She was right. Although Ida was acquitted, Chapin said she gassed herself and her children a few years later.

7
At the Editor's Desk

Chapin's account of the Macaulley murder was certainly read in all of the city's newsrooms, but it was of greatest interest in one in particular. Just a few blocks from the *Tribune* building, James J. West and Clinton A. Snowden were confronting the fragile state of affairs at the *Chicago Times* when Chapin's prominent story gave them an idea. Since the death of Wilbur Storey, the editor who had been kind to a younger Chapin fifteen years earlier, the paper had fallen on hard times. On January 1, 1888, West, an investor with little newspaper experience, had gained control of the paper from the estate. In turn, he made Snowden, his brother-in-law, who had been city editor under Storey, editor-in-chief. "New brains, new blood, and new capital are to be infused into what, in its day, was one of the few great papers of the country," Henry M. Hunt optimistically predicted in the *Journalist*. On Saturday, January 7, 1888, West and Snowden sent Chapin a note, asking him to call on them "about a matter of personal interest." The invitation reached Chapin while he was writing a story on a major fire that engulfed the upper floors of a substantial building on Dearborn Street. A few printers, working late on a Saturday, had discovered a small blaze in a pile of rags in the steam shaft at 4:00 P.M., and sounded the alarm. "Three upper floors were soon a solid furnace of fire, and a whirlwind of sparks careened upward and drifted eastward," wrote Chapin. "Embers and pieces of blazing wood a foot long fell in showers into the street and upon neighboring buildings." Fire was, of course, a sensitive subject in Chicago, and Hall gave Chapin two columns of the front page.[1]

The story completed, Chapin took the short walk to the *Times* offices at the corner of Washington Street and Fifth Avenue. Though Chapin had only just turned twenty-nine, West and Snowden offered him the city editorship of the *Times*. Chapin accepted their offer on the sole condition that he would have full authority in the newsroom, and no one could be hired or fired except by him. They agreed, but insisted that Chapin begin work that very night. "I felt considerably embarrassed when I returned to the *Tribune* office to quit without notice for I recognized that I had been kindly treated during the years I had been there and I recognized that it was the training I had received under Mr. Hall that had made it possible for me to land a city editor job." Hall flew into a tirade and forbade Chapin to leave. Patterson, on the other hand, was more reasonable. In the end, he promised Chapin there would be a job for him at the *Tribune* if the editor's job did not turn out well.[2]

Chapin walked out of the *Tribune* building and returned to the *Times*. The entire staff had gathered, having gotten wind of the change at the city desk. Guy Magee, the city editor, gracefully surrendered the desk and departed. Chapin felt angst when he realized what his arrival meant to the old editor. "It is the fate of most newspaper men," Chapin wrote when he recalled the moment. "They give all that is in them to the service of their employers and when they are old and worn-out they are cast adrift, like battered wrecks."[3]

Within fifteen minutes of assuming his post, Chapin fired a reporter. It was the first of more than one hundred he would eventually fire as a city editor in Chicago, St. Louis, and New York. But like any first, Chapin could still recall the victim's name at the end of his life. W. Scott, a hotel reporter, had the misfortune to be overheard in an adjoining room commenting on the arrival of the new city editor. "When he coupled my name with the most objectionable epithet he could think of," said Chapin, "I stepped into the room and discharged him."

"If there are others who share Scott's opinion of me you may all ride down in the same elevator," said Chapin, who then returned to his desk.[4]

"Just as predicted last week," said Hunt at the *Journalist*, "the appointment of Charles E. Chapin to the city editorship of the *Times* has resulted in a number of changes in the reportorial corps of the paper." Several old-timers left, and Chapin hired a half-dozen new reporters. Among them was Finley Peter Dunne, whom Chapin had run into on his way to the office. He was young, just out of high school, and had worked for a while for the *Daily News*. An immensely talented reporter and writer, Dunne would later assume Chapin's post at the *Times* and, later still, become immensely famous as the author of the "Mr. Dooley" stories about a South Side tavern keeper, written in Irish dialect. "I hired hundreds of men afterwards, but Pete was always my special pet, both because I was fond of him and that in hiring him I was raised from reporter to boss."[5]

As Chapin settled into the editor's chair, his first task was to reinvigorate the paper that had once been the talk of the town. When Storey was publisher, the paper shocked and scandalized readers with its sensational tales of gory crime and explicit sex. Its headlines were known across the nation for their puns and alliteration, the most famous of which had been "Jerked to Jesus," used to crown a story of the hanging of four murderers who had found God just before their end. Chicagoans had responded in droves, and though it wasn't the favorite of advertisers, the *Times* regularly led the *Tribune* in circulation.[6]

But Storey was gone, and the paper had become dull and predictable. What gave Chapin the idea is unknown, but he seized upon a plan to reinvigorate the paper. In June, he hired Nell Cusak, a pretty young, brown-haired and brown-eyed woman who had been a schoolteacher. Women were rare in journalism at the time, and Chapin had no intention of changing that. Rather, he had another role in mind for her. Chapin directed Cusak to answer help-wanted advertisements for factory jobs and sweatshops, and report back on the working conditions she discovered. By the 1880s, a few forward-thinking reporters had begun to see the power of the press to highlight social inequities. Two years earlier, Helen Stuart Campbell had published a series on working conditions among women in the needle trade in the *New York Tribune*.

The first installment of Cusak's "City Slave Girls," written under the pen name "Nell Nelson," appeared on July 30, 1888, and it was an instant success.[7]

> Tuesday, July 10, according to instructions, I made up for the role of shop-girl, and with a list of factories in one hand, and gentle peace in the other, sailed down town under a brown baize veil as impenetrable as an iron mask.
>
> I did not realize the ignominious position of respectable poverty till I reached a cloak factory on Madison Street, where labor is bondage, the laborer a slave, and flesh and blood cheaper than needles and thread. Corporations are said to be without heart, but this concern is a commercial inquisition. It puts help on the plane of slavery, and nothing but civil law prevents the use of the lash.[8]

The following day the paper's editorial gloated that "the great demand for the *Times* of yesterday morning proved that the public is deeply interested in the exposure of factory life in Chicago, which this newspaper is now engaged in making." Additional press runs were ordered, and again readers flocked to the paper. The *Times* promised that Chicagoans would find much more to shock them in succeeding days. "Today's revelations will add to their amazement. Tomorrow they will probably be stunned." The series ran all summer. Cusak's, or "Nelson's," articles were eventually collected in two books, and she moved to New York where in September of 1888, the *New York World* commissioned her to write a New York "White Slave Girls" series.[9]

The series also impressed West, who came to Chapin with an idea for a similar series on abortion. "What he asked me to do," said Chapin, "was to send a man and a woman reporter to all the reputable physicians in the city, let them pretend they were sweethearts, that the girl was in trouble, and offer to pay liberally for an illegal operation." Chapin was outraged and called the idea the "'yellowest' suggestion ever made in a newspaper office." Snowden joined the conversation, and he had the same negative reaction. "Both of us flatly declared we would sever all connection with the paper before we would suffer our professional reputations to be linked with such indecency." Chapin and Snowden assumed that West dropped the idea. Circulation, after the boost from the slave-girl series, resumed its decline. Rumors began to spread about West's finances, putting his solvency in doubt. In the late fall, West sent Chapin a note requesting that he assign "a bright man and woman to report to him for instructions." Chapin didn't pay attention, nor did he when the reporter wanted to explain what West had in mind for the pair.[10]

On December 11, 1888, Chapin strolled into the composing room late at night as was his habit. There he discovered what West had done. He had assigned the pair to do the series on abortion, and the first installment was ready to go to press. Chapin dashed to Snowden's office, told him the news, then the two waited, stewing in anger, until West returned from a night at the theater. Indignantly, they confronted him and pleaded that the story be pulled. He refused. They both quit. Out of work, Snowden headed to the West. The *Journalist* said he went for the "benefit of his health." Chapin went back to the *Tribune* and collected on the promise Patterson had made, that "if I grew tired of the job, to remember there would always be a good one waiting for me in the *Tribune* office." He didn't come back alone. In tow were Finley Peter Dunne and another reporter.[11]

Back at the *Tribune*, Chapin agreed to take a long journey to write a coda to the story that first made him a star. McGarigle, the former police chief who had fled after being convicted on corruption charges, was said to be living contentedly in Banff, Canada. Chapin set off to do a northern-climate imitation of Henry Stanley's 1871 pursuit of Dr. Livingston, and seek out McGarigle. First he traveled west by train on Union Pacific's circuitous route to Seattle. From there he caught a steamship to Victoria, then another across the water to Vancouver, where he began another long rail journey to Banff. Crossing the Rocky Mountains by train was no easy task. Canada's transcontinental railroad was completed in 1886, seventeen years later than that which crossed the United States. In the rush to finish the line, the Canadians ran the tracks up and down the Rockies at such steep angles that trains had to shed wagons to reach the top, and table settings and food flew in all directions when the trains climbed or descended. To make matters worse, the train Chapin was on became trapped for several days by heavy snow. "I was the only passenger in the

Pullman, and the only white man on the train, except the train crew," said Chapin. "All the rest were Indians and Chinese."[12]

After almost two weeks of continuous travel, Chapin finally reached Banff. It was after midnight, but he found a sleigh waiting for him at the depot and in a few minutes was taken to the Sanitarium Hotel, adjacent to a sanitarium opened in 1886 by a pioneering doctor. "I was standing by the fire warming the tips of my fingers when McGarigle came tearing down the staircase, and lifting me bodily from the floor he gave an exhibition of his strength by twirling me around in the air and then hugging me until my ribs fairly cracked." The greeting surprised Chapin, who reminded McGarigle that he had failed to show at the Belchamber Hotel to finish his interview the morning after Chapin tracked him down two years earlier. McGarigle, laughing, explained that he had been tipped off that the police might arrest him and had pushed off on the first available train.[13]

Sore feelings soothed, the two headed for a plunge in one of the hot sulfur spring baths. The contrast between the air and the water was a novelty. Above water, it was so cold that icicles formed in one's hair, but they thawed as soon as one ducked under. Like kids, the two men played leap-frog and frolicked in the water for half an hour, at which point they went back into the hotel, opened a bottle of wine, and talked until six in the morning about old times in Chicago. Chapin noticed that McGarigle was in excellent health, a complete change from the pale, thin escapee he found on the Canadian shore of Lake Huron. At last, Chapin was shown to a bed, and he slept until noon.[14]

At lunch, McGarigle and Chapin were joined by two ministers and a member of the mounted police. The luncheon company was testimony to McGarigle's newfound status in Banff. His flight from the Illinois law seemed to have had no effect on the Canadians, according to Chapin. "He is the best known man in the Northwest Territory, is the honored guest at the Governor's house, and is even consulted about political affairs, and is the confidant of nearly every member of the Territorial Parliament." After lunch, the group bathed in sulfur spring baths in and around a cavern at the base of Mount Sulfur. For the evening's entertainment, McGarigle organized a sleigh party with nearly two dozen friends. Large sleighs were ordered, and at six, the group dashed off into the darkness, bundled in fur coats, hats, and buffalo pelts. "The moon never shone brighter and the clear sky seemed lighted by millions of electric lamps," Chapin told his readers. "Stars never looked so big to me before. They don't twinkle and blink up here, but even the smallest shine with lustrous brilliancy."[15]

They disembarked at Devil's Head Lake and took turns on McGarigle's ice boat, skimming across the twelve-mile-long lake at sixty miles an hour. Ravenous, the party descended on the Beach Hotel, where they devoured a feast that had been packed in the sleighs. After the tables were cleared, a banjo was produced, and each member of the party sang a song or danced. "At last McGarigle got up and said he wanted to sing one of the grandest songs ever written, and I detected a shade of sadness and a slight trembling in his rich voice as he sang: My country 'tis of thee, Sweet land of liberty, of thee I sing." What a scene it must have been: the convicted boodler, the hardened reporter, the ministers, the mounted policeman, and the assembled Canadians and Brits all singing. "Never was the dear old National hymn sung with greater fervor," said Chapin, who noted a tear in the corner of McGarigle's eye.

It was two o'clock in the morning when the party returned to the Sanitarium Hotel. "It had been a night of pleasure that I shall always remember," said Chapin, who wanted to head to bed. But McGarigle insisted he follow him to his room. There, after two days of partying, McGarigle finally gave Chapin the interview he had sought for two years. In it, McGarigle offered a lengthy explanation, filled with details of many financial transactions, that in the end, he said, proved his innocence. Chapin consented to publish the account. As morning approached, Chapin asked if McGarigle was content to remain in Canada. "You might as well ask if I would be content to be buried alive," he replied. Underneath the jollity and levity of the past two days, explained McGarigle, was sadness at his being separated from Chicago, his wife, and his children. "I have as yet formed no plans for the future, but if it could be arranged so that I could return to Chicago I think I could soon demonstrate to the people there that McGarigle is not so black as he has been painted."[16]

Chapin's story of the encounter with McGarigle appeared on

the front page of the January 31, 1889, *Tribune* and consumed almost an entire inside page. In an era of unsigned articles in which reporters referred to themselves in the third person, Chapin's account was remarkably personal. "I have often wondered," he began, "why McGarigle buried himself away up here on the summit of the Rocky Mountains, amid deep snow and everlasting glaciers." The story had a considerable effect on Chicagoans. Four months later, McGarigle's sentence was reduced to a $1,000 fine, and he returned home. He bought a saloon and never again entered public life. Chapin's status as a premier reporter also was confirmed by the appearance of his initials at the end of the piece, a rare practice in a news article.

In early February, back in Chicago, Chapin ran into James West on the street. He startled Chapin by asking him if he would come back to work for the *Chicago Times* as the paper's correspondent in the nation's capital. Despite his trepidation about his former publisher, Chapin had none about the allure of being a Washington correspondent. "I had a yearning for that sort of work and as there was no other opportunity within reach I smothered my feelings and accepted." Relations between West and others who quit also must have improved. About this time, Dunne reconciled himself with West and returned to the *Times* as its city editor.[17]

A few days later, Chapin replaced Frederick Powers, who had been the *Times*'s Washington correspondent for six years and was president of the Gridiron Club. The club was formed four years earlier by newspapermen in hopes of improving the worsening relations between reporters and members of Congress. Though it had become a popular dining club for the press and the political elite, it was not clear whether the club had met its goal. For example, just before Chapin arrived in Washington, Texas Representative William Harrison Martin was introduced to George Harris of the Washington *Evening Star* as he was leaving the floor of the House one afternoon: "You're the man that has been writing about me," said Martin, lowering his brow. The reporter conceded he had mentioned Martin from time to time in his articles, which was not entirely truthful. A few months back, Harris had poked fun at Martin for having blown out the gaslights in his rooms at the Willard in what was portrayed as contempt for "modern methods of illumination."

"I don't want to shake hands with you, sir," said Martin, who then walked off toward a cigar stand, one of many that lined the main hall of the Capitol in those days.

"You don't have to and I'm rather glad of it," replied Harris. "I would like to be excused from touching your hand until it has been washed." Words turned to blows before the two were eventually separated.[18]

Politics taken so seriously that they could turn to fisticuffs was not a new phenomenon for a Chicago reporter, but there were other ways in which Washington was vastly different from the Windy City. Physically, it was impressive. In the past decade, Washington had completed its transformation from a provincial town into a cosmopolitan capital. "Washington," observed Englishman James Bryce in 1888, "with its wide and beautifully graded avenues, and the glittering white of the stately Capitol, has become within the last twenty years a singularly handsome city." It also was far more leisurely than the fast-paced Chicago, which was propelled by the engines of commerce. "Compared with New York or Chicago, Washington, although it is full of commotion and energy, is a city of rest and peace," noted S. Reynolds Hole, an English minister touring the United States. "The inhabitants do not push onward as though they were late for the train or the post, or as though the dinner hour being past they were anxious to appease an irritable wife." This languid atmosphere, perhaps a Southern attribute of Washington, also existed on Capitol Hill, where Chapin would spend much of his time. Congress occasionally had more of an atmosphere of a barroom than that of a center of lawmaking. Members of the House could be found talking and laughing, their feet propped on desks, and shooting wads of spit toward the ubiquitous cuspidors.[19]

There was also a sense of temporalness to the city. Virtually no one, except for those who serviced the needs of the well-to-do, regarded Washington as *their* city, certainly not the politicians and the press. Only the wealthiest politicians purchased houses. Theodore Roosevelt, who also came to Washington that spring, confronted a real estate market that would far exceed his salary as Civil Service Commissioner. The approximately 150 correspondents resided mostly in boarding houses and hotels. They came and went with such frequency that the *Journalist* had a hard time keeping its readers up to date on who was reporting from Washington. It was as if the city were hosting a political convention that was never gaveled to a close. Chapin and Nellie found rooms on 17th Street about five blocks north of the White House, next door to Senator Charles Farwell of Illinois.[20]

A new administration was arriving in Washington at the same time as the Chapins. Grover Cleveland had won the popular vote in 1888 by more than 100,000 votes, but lost the electoral college to Benjamin Harrison. The *Chicago Times* had at least three reporters on hand for Harrison's inauguration on March 4, 1889. Chapin covered the parade and formal proceedings, which made sense, as he was hardly familiar with Washington politics. The dreary, rain-soaked day, however, left him to describe a diminished spectacle. "The sight, under a cloudless sky, would have been worthy of all the adjectives which are wasted upon ordinary scenes of a martial character," he wrote of the blocks of assembled processioners. "But today there was none of that burnished glory, none of that glistening armor, none of that steel field of bayonets, nor resplendence of swords. The atmosphere was as dreary as November."[21]

For the first time in fourteen years, Republicans controlled the presidency and Congress, and the spoils of victory lay at their feet. Although the Civil Service reform movement—which aimed to end patronage and have government jobs awarded on the basis of merit—had won a major victory six years earlier with the passage of the Pendleton Act, the law did not cover the vast majority of federal jobs—some 112,000 still lay beyond the oversight of Roosevelt in his new post. The filling of these jobs was the big story of the first months of the new administration, and correspondents scrambled to be first with the news of an appointment, especially if it was one from their home city. No post was too small to escape press attention. "There is one federal job in Chicago that most office-seekers seem to have overlooked," reported Chapin. "It is that of oleomargarine inspector, the income of which is about $2,500 a year." Most eyes, however, were on the plum jobs being distributed by John Wanamaker, the Philadelphia retailer whom President Harrison had appointed postmaster general as a reward for his munificent support in the election. Since Wanamaker's assumption of the post, Democratic postmasters were, by one count, being replaced at the rate of one every five minutes. According to Chapin, there were 40,000 postmaster positions to fill and "decapitation and appointment must of necessity be rapid."[22]

Chapin kept a careful watch on Chicago appointments. Being Senator Farwell's neighbor helped. "He directed me to drop in on him every evening, and he would stuff my notebook with news that would interest my readers," said Chapin. As for Shelby Cullom, the senior senator from Illinois, Chapin loosened his lips with a common correspondent's technique of writing a flattering profile that compared him to Lincoln. The biggest Chicago job waiting to be filled was that of postmaster, and both senators favored Colonel James A. Sexton, a stove manufacturer. On April 10, Chapin wired the *Times* that Cullom, in the company of Congressman Albert J. Hopkins, took their man's name directly to Wanamaker at the Post Office. New rules, however, would hold up their choice. President Harrison, according to Chapin, had found that the "helter-skelter way in which business was done around the White House during the first month of this administration nearly drove him wild." Now the president had set aside a day for each department, and the post office's day would not come until the following Tuesday. "So it will probably be a week before Mr. Sexton can begin bouncing the Democrats out of the Chicago Post Office."[23]

Chapin himself joined the patronage frenzy. Two friends of his were among the hundreds of newspapermen Harrison rewarded for their editorial support with jobs in the administration. The first was Wanamaker's assistant postmaster, James S. Clarkson. The other was E. W. Halford, who had been editor of the *Indianapolis Journal* before becoming Harrison's private secretary. 'Lije, as Chapin called Halford, wanted to bring one more colleague on board, and the trio conspired to make it happen. Halford's man was Frank E. Palmer, an editor with whom both he and Clarkson had worked. The job in question was the lucrative post of government printer. The salary was $4,500 a year, but apparently it was no state secret that the pay was only a small part of the remuneration. In April, Chapin explained to his readers in a matter-of-fact tone the potential rewards of the post. When a Captain Meredith had been rumored for the post, a businessman approached the potential nominee with a proposition to supply ink. "He said he could make contracts with the manufacturers and get a rebate of 25 per cent on all bills," wrote Chapin. "This he would divide with Capt. Meredith and they would make about $30,000 a year each."[24]

In early May, Chapin called on Halford at the White House to see how their campaign for Palmer was coming. He found 'Lije agitated. The Typographical Union in Philadelphia had its own candidate and was trying to blackball Palmer because his current paper employed nonunion printers, Halford told Chapin. "I explained to Halford that Palmer was working for a salary and had no more to do with employing printers than I had to do with hiring compositors on the paper I worked for." That night, a messenger from the White House reached Chapin. The President wanted to see him. "I obeyed the summons and was conducted into the President's private office, where he sat so sedate and dignified at his desk that one couldn't help wondering if he had ice water in his veins," said Chapin. The President asked Chapin to repeat what he had told Halford. Chapin did so. Then he asked if there was any way to determine if the Typographical Union in Chicago would complain about the appointment. "I replied that my brother was a member of the union and I could wire to him."[25]

"Do so tonight and send me the reply; I will wait up for it," said Harrison.

Unfortunately for Chapin, he was not sure he could count on Frank's reaction, especially as they had not always remained on friendly terms. So instead, he chose to fabricate an appropriate telegram. He dictated what he wanted to hear, sent it by wire to his Chicago office with instructions to send it back. Within half an hour, Chapin was on his way back to the White House with his brother's purported endorsement of Palmer. The message had its expected effect.[26]

Chapin returned to his office and filed his story. "Tonight the President sent a telegram to Chicago asking Frank Palmer if he would accept the office of public printer," he wrote. "When Mr. Palmer gets his telegram it will be the first official knowledge that he has ever received that he was being considered in connection with the printership, for at no time has he been a candidate in the sense of making personal application for the office." No one, in fact, in the Illinois congressional delegation knew anything about this appointment until they read about it in the *Times*, said a triumphant Chapin. Hinting at his role, Chapin said the idea was that of Halford, Clarkson, and "a few personal friends [who] helped the matter along by convincing the President that objections raised by other candidates were groundless."[27]

Their feat was complete. Palmer arrived in Washington on May 5. Clarkson brought him by Chapin's office, and the three went out to dinner. Two days later, Harrison signed his commission with a batch of appointments that included Roosevelt's. The inclusion of the two in the same raft of appointments was ironic. Palmer would oversee 2,500 employees and, said Chapin in his dispatch, "as the printing office does not come under the control of the civil service, every political boss in the country will besiege him for a share of the patronage." Among those who benefited was Chapin's brother Frank. That year, he obtained a job in the Government Printing Office and moved to Washington.[28]

A little more than three weeks later, on May 31, 1889, a privately maintained dam about 200 miles north of Washington, which sustained a lake for the weekend pleasure of Andrew Carnegie, Henry Clay Frick, and other wealthy Pittsburgh residents, gave way during an intense rain storm. A forty-foot wall of water burst forth and, traveling with the speed of a train, headed toward Johnstown, Pennsylvania, fourteen miles downstream. The ensuing flood killed 2,209 residents, and was the biggest news story since Lincoln's assassination. More than one hundred newspapers sent writers and illustrators to Johnstown. The tales they carried back to their readers—not all necessarily accurate—touched off the first large-scale private relief. Americans responded with money, clothing, food, building materials, and medicine. An incredible $3,742,818.78 was raised. This flood of charity swept up even Chapin. He joined three other reporters, including one from the rival *Tribune*, to solicit clothing for the victims. They spent two days at it. "They met with frequent rebuffs," reported the *Journalist*, "but they harvested a bountiful supply of old coats and trousers." Three weeks later, Chapin got a first-hand look at the disaster courtesy of the railroads.[29]

In the 1880s, the railroads had developed the habit of taking newspapermen on all-expenses-paid excursions. Their motives were transparent. The railroads, which had grown into one of the nation's largest and most profitable industries, had just acquiesced to a modest form of federal regulation with the passage of the Interstate Commerce Act two years earlier. Corporate chieftains now deemed keeping the national press happy almost as important as lining the pockets of politicians. The press certainly didn't object. Journalists had no stated aversion to enjoying corporate favors. In fact, the trade press reported on these junkets with not the slightest trace of misgivings. Thus, according to the *Journalist*, it was a jovial scene on Friday, June 26, 1889, at Washington's B&P Station, a Victorian-styled edifice made famous by President Garfield's assassination less than a decade earlier, as journalists and their families crowded on board a chartered train (known in those days as a "special") for a weekend junket to Cresson Springs, Pennsylvania. Among the throngs were Charles and Nellie. This kind of privilege was, in part, what attracted Chapin to newspapers. Since his days in Atchison, the press's access to those with power and money was infectious for Chapin.[30]

The Pennsylvania Railroad special that Friday night was fully loaded as it headed north from Washington. It was the best-attended junket since the railroad had begun these excursions. "Newspaper row was deserted," said O'Brien-Bain of the *Journalist*, "and the Washington columns of the daily papers throughout the country were wonderfully thin." The high point of the journey promised to be a visit to Johnstown. After lunch on Saturday, another specially provided train took the journalists from Cresson Springs into the flood-torn valley. Nellie retired to a private car belonging to one of the corporate officers, which had been given over to the ladies. Charles and the men climbed on the tender— the car behind the locomotive. Slowly the train traveled through the valley, which had been scoured by the rushing waters. "The scene was one of the most remarkable ever witnessed," said O'Brien-Bain. Following the tour of the destruction, the train returned to Cresson Springs where, at the expense of the railroad, Charles and Nellie and the group were entertained for the weekend with dances, lavish meals, musical entertainment, and nature walks. "Monday morning," said O'Brien-Bain, "the party left Cresson regretfully."[31]

Shortly after his return to Washington, Chapin heard unsettling news from Chicago about the financial state of the *Times*. He was certainly aware of the tenuous nature of his Washington posting, but what he heard was foreboding. One of his predecessors had returned to personally try to collect a large amount of back pay owed him. That was not a good sign. More ominous, however, was his publisher's visit to Washington. West's arrival was announced by a messenger who arrived at Chapin's house early one July morning with the news that "a crazy man in our hotel wants you to come as quick as you can." Chapin followed the boy. At the hotel, he found West in a high state of commotion, pacing his room like a caged animal. "He was almost hysterical," said Chapin. "I calmed him the best I could and after much urging got him to tell me what ailed him." According to Chapin, West confessed he had created duplicate stock certificates so as to secure a loan and that he was about to be found out. "He had brought a suitcase full of money to Washington and he wanted me to go to Europe with him," said Chapin. "I counseled him not to act like a madman, but to return to Chicago on the next train and try to adjust his tangled affairs before it was too late."[32]

There was considerable evidence of a crime. On Saturday, July 13, 1889, Pinkerton detectives swarmed the *Times* building. The elevator boy was told to cease running his lift, and staircases were guarded to prevent anyone from leaving with anything more than the clothes they wore. A criminal warrant was soon issued for West's arrest. The new management, appointed by West's previously silent partners, put Frank. H. Brooks, an old Chicago newspaper hand, in charge. Although he was apparently popular with the remainder of the *Times* staff, Chapin couldn't stand him. "It didn't take me long to telegraph my resignation and follow it by the first train." Among other casualties of the turmoil at the top was Dunne, who moved back to the *Tribune*.[33]

Chapin's return to Chicago heralded his only foray into politics. A wholesaler he knew gave Chapin's name to a Mormon banker who was in the East seeking to hire a campaign manager for a fierce municipal election in Salt Lake City. "The proposition appealed to me, for I had never been in Salt Lake City and this would afford me the best opportunity I might ever have to get a close-up view of Mormonism," said Chapin. "Besides, I needed the money." Chapin said he spent less than a month in Utah working for the Mormons in their efforts to ward off a growing Gentile challenge to their monopoly of political power in the August legislative and county elections. The fear that they could lose to the new Liberal Party, comprising Gentiles who had moved to Utah, drove the Mormons in Salt Lake City to recruit new Mormon voters from other parts of the state with jobs on public-works projects. Even then, Chapin did not see how they could win, and headed east before election day. He was right. On August 6, 1889, the *Salt Lake City Tribune* headline read, "Salt Lake City Goes Liberal; The Death Knell of Mormon Rule; The City is Gentile by Forty-one Votes."[34]

Unsuccessful in the task for which he was hired, Chapin nonetheless found that the journey to Utah solved part of a decade-old family mystery. While traveling, Chapin alighted from a train in Springfield, Missouri, and explored Public Square, then the main square of the town of 6,000. In passing Joseph Willeke Jeweler, Chapin peered in the window as the son of two generations of jewelers might when passing such a store. To his astonishment, he saw his missing father at work inside. Chapin entered and, according to Fannie, he found that "father appeared very glad to see him and inquired about the family but at the same time appeared remorseful. Charley said he demanded no explanation of Father concerning his conduct and asked no questions as to his whereabouts or what he had been doing and he left after a short interview." He apparently also kept this remarkable encounter from his mother.[35]

Back in Chicago, Chapin accepted an offer from Horatio Seymour to come to work for the *Chicago Herald.* He had become acquainted with Seymour during the past eight years as he made his way through the world of Chicago newspapers. Seymour was one of Chicago's best-known editors. His fame came in part from the famous "Jerked to Jesus" headline he crafted for the *Times.* Seymour possessed an almost complete store of knowledge in the running of every part of a newspaper. Chapin admired him greatly and relished the idea of working with him. "His brain was ever alert with ideas and with power to express himself as such possessed by few editors I ever came into contact with," he said. The *Journalist* had predicted correctly when Seymour took over the paper three years earlier that he would make a success of it. The *Herald's* circulation was now second only to the *Daily News*, and it had just moved into a spacious new building on Washing- ton Street, which Theodore Dreiser described as "one of those onyx and bronze affairs." The new post suited Chapin well. "In many respects the *Herald*," said Chapin, "was the pleasantest of- fice I ever worked in." The crew at the *Herald* certainly was excep- tional. Aside from recruiting Chapin, Seymour had already assembled some of Chicago's best young reporters. "In the vocab- ulary of the profession, they were all stars," said Chapin. Among them was his old friend Dunne, who had been hired to cover po- litical news, and Charles Seymour, the brother of the editor, and one of the era's best "specials" (someone who could handle any story). Charles Seymour had an eye for what made compelling reading. Once, for instance, he was assigned to cover one of Chi- cago's premier charity balls. He reported spotting two poor chil- dren being chased away by a police officer from a doorway where they had huddled for warmth. "Get along with you," the police- man said to the kids. "Don't you know this is the charity ball."[36]

At first, Chapin served as the paper's drama and music critic, a post for half of which his background as an actor served him well. Years later, he admitted he knew as little about music as he knew about "holy Sanskrit." But by the summer of 1890, music lovers could breathe a sigh of relief, as Chapin was installed as city edi- tor. Controlling the youthful but talented gaggle of reporters he was given was not easy. Dunne and Charles Seymour, and others on the staff, were members of the infamous Whitechapel Club. Seymour was one of its founders. A bohemian club of sorts, lo- cated in the back room of Koster's saloon in an alley behind the *Herald*, the club took its name from Jack the Ripper's London neighborhood. Seymour decorated the place with Indian skulls. Others donated pistols and knives that had been used as murder weapons, and even a set of photographs of Chinese pirates before and after decapitation. *Herald* reporter Brand Whitlock contrib- uted a signed portrait of Buffalo Bill Cody, and Wallace Rice, another *Herald* reporter, concocted a special punch for guests.[37]

The club was an outlet for reporters who worked six, often seven days a week covering the rawest aspects of city life. The morgue humor, drinks, and camaraderie offered an escape.

Chapin did not appreciate it. "Stories came to my ears that made me apprehensive that some of my youngsters were in danger of becoming demoralized," he said. He posted a notice that anyone who was a member of the Whitechapel Club could not be employed at the *Herald*. As a result, all his best reporters quit, leaving him only a few cubs. Chapin claims they all came back after reading the diminished *Herald* and asked for forgiveness. As they all remained active members of the club, especially Dunne and Seymour, it's more likely they simply ignored Chapin's edict.[38]

Though Chapin had a talented staff, perhaps the best in the city, he came close that year to having the opportunity to hire a reporter who would become one of America's greatest novelists. Like Chapin, Theodore Dreiser had been drawn to Chicago and the idea of becoming a reporter. To him, newspapers always were dealing with great events, tragedies, and pleasures. It was a brilliant world "that I imagined if I could once get in it—if such a thing were possible—that I would be the happiest person imaginable," wrote Dreiser. In December of 1890, he answered a help-wanted advertisement in the *Herald* for young men to assist the paper in a Christmas holiday-gift bureau for poor Chicagoans. Dreiser responded to the ad in hopes that the work might lead to a chance to be a reporter. "Well," replied the business manager, "this is as good a way to begin as any other. When this is over I may be able to introduce you to our city editor." Despite several visits Dreiser made to the newsroom that winter, the introduction to Chapin never occurred. Their paths would, however, cross again.[39]

All the while, Chapin was too involved in the charity project to worry much about hiring more reporters. In February, an extended and severe cold front descended on Chicago. Chapin sent out his reporters to learn how the poor and destitute were coping. What they uncovered he put on page one with the headline "Dying in Bitter Cold: Thousands of Persons Literally Starving and Freezing to Death, While Other Thousands are Rolling in All the Luxury of Wealth." Although in New York Pulitzer's *World* was publishing similar accounts, the *Herald*'s piece was ahead of its time for Chicago. It was certainly the product of many reporters, but it clearly showed the mark of Chapin's hand in its choice of adjectives, scene setting, and the dramatic anecdote that was its lead. A Mrs. Goodyear, who lived in a Fulton Street tenement, had left her bare room in pursuit of a few pieces of coal the night before "when the cold was most intense, and a keen wind cutting into the face like thistle points." She got only as far as the home of her neighbor Julius Selke, where she fell faint to the floor. In vintage Chapinesque prose, readers learned how she avoided her end. "And death from freezing in a city of great riches and great plenty would most certainly have been her fate had Mr. Selke not responded promptly with aid and without waiting for the slower processes of charity organizations." He carried her back to her room and restarted the fire with bushels of his own coal while neighbors fetched food.[40]

"Old Mrs. Goodyear was but one among thousands whom yesterday's cold cut and stung with the keenness and cruelty of a knife," continued the article, which then detailed sad case after case. By the next day, it was clear the *Herald*'s readers had been moved by the account of misery. "Though they were but a few out of the thousands of similar cases, the recital of the suffering touched the hearts of many people," the paper explained in another front-page story. Henry C. Levi of the Hub Clothing Company offered 100 tons of coal. Using this contribution as a nucleus, the *Herald* decided to launch a relief effort. It would be headquartered in the old *Evening Post* building just down the street from the *Herald*. "Within two days we had a building full of willing workers for a headquarters and the merchants sorted their stock and sent around dray loads of goods of every description while the well-to-do reduced their wardrobes to contribute to the poor."[41]

Chapin threw himself into the enterprise. He ordered story after story, detailing more needy cases, listing the donors, and describing how the *Herald*'s efforts were paying off. Typical was the tale of Mary Frohmiller, an aged German widow who lived in the basement at 480 Fifth Avenue. "When a reporter from the *Herald* knocked for admittance, Mrs. Frohmiller was lying on the bed and unable to open the door. 'Herein,' she cried out in a feeble voice and the visitor went in." Hardly able to rise from her bed, she explained to the reporter that her husband had died without leaving even enough money to pay for his burial. Her daughter had supported her until she had died nine months earlier. Since

then, Frohmiller had gone to bed cold and hungry. But, no
longer, said the *Herald*. She was given $5 to relieve her immediate
needs, and half a ton of coal was ordered. "Any one having extra
bed clothing can cheer a deserving old lady by giving the same to
Mrs. Mary Frohmiller."[42]

The campaign continued until February 21, 1891. Day after day,
the *Herald* published lengthy stories intended to tug on the heart-
strings of its readers and generate support for the relief effort. All
told, more than $2,300 were raised and distributed. Tons of coal
had been dispatched to heat homes, and an endless procession of
carts delivered clothing and food to thousands. "The bitter cry of
extreme destitution has been changed to a song of joy and grati-
tude in the many homes that have been lightened of their cares
by the relief corp," said the *Herald* in its final installment. Again,
in prose that reveals Chapin's hand, the paper congratulated itself
on its efforts.

> Where the black shadow of the bailiff was thrown
> across the threshold of a destitute family at the bidding
> of a landlord who wanted his rent or his house, report-
> ers gave peace and comfort. Where empty stomachs
> pined for food, barrels of provisions were brought,
> enough to last the household two weeks. At the bed-
> side of the sick, who tried hopelessly and helplessly not
> only to fight against disease, but against the noxious
> vapors of their dank and darksome homes, aid was
> brought, and the invalids were helped to a stronger and
> healthier plane of existence. Home, no matter where it
> is, is home to the poor, though the wretched dwelling
> may not be fit for human beings to live in. They cling
> to their dark tenements, fearful that, if they change
> their location, they may fall into more terrible depths
> of poverty and destitution. The known danger is
> fought against or borne with a patience born of de-
> spair. What lies outside—to change from a grasping
> landlord to one who may be still worse—is what is
> feared mostly by the poor who burrow in strange dens
> in the heart of a great city. Toward the alleviation of
> this misery the *Herald* has done much.

After a decade in Chicago, Chapin had achieved what he first hungered for as a young fourteen-year-old in Atchison. He was a newspaperman. He was in charge of one of the city's best papers. He was respected, feared, and even held in awe by some reporters. His income was finally sufficient to live as he wanted. Instead of a boarding house, the luxurious six-story Richelieu Hotel was now where he and Nellie lived. But, just as happened in Atchison when everything seemed right, Chapin fell ill and left the *Herald* at the beginning of the summer.

Park Row

On July 18, 1891, Chapin resurfaced. "After my health was re-stored, or partly so," said Chapin, "I went to New York from the seashore, drifted down to Park Row and was attracted by the gilded dome of the World building." He, and Nellie who accom-panied him, were not the only ones drawn to the site. The new building erected by Joseph Pulitzer to house his prodigiously suc-cessful *New York World* drew thousands of sightseers. One count placed the number of daily visitors at 2,000. Opened only eight months before the Chapins reached New York, the World build-ing was the tallest office building in existence anywhere. Standing at 309 feet—345 feet if one included the flagstaff—it reached higher into the sky than even the torch of the Statue of Liberty. In fact, its 850,000-pound shimmering dome was the first glint of the new world seen by immigrants on the decks of ocean liners coasting by the statue each day on their way to Castle Garden or the soon-to-open Ellis Island.[1]

Situated at the north end of Park Row—America's Fleet Street—and directly across from City Hall, the sixteen-story, Re-naissance-style building was the latest work of George Brown Post, considered the father of the tall building in New York. The cavernous vaulted entrance of Corsehill stone, rising three stories up into the building, tugged at the flow of pedestrian traffic like an eddy on a fast-moving stream. Above the entrance stood a quartet of bronze female torch-bearers, representing Art, Litera-ture, Science, and Invention. The next ten floors above continued

the grand scale of the design. Each story was coupled vertically with tall, Palladian-style windows, and banded horizontally by a stone ledge, giving the effect that the building was an opulant pal-
ace of industry, and effectively disguising its utilitarian content of 149 suites that Pulitzer leased to insurance salesmen, stockbrokers, lawyers, and other professionals. Stacked above this hive of commerce, the remaining few floors were distinguished by concave corners and four sculpted black copper figures representing the four races—"Caucasian, Indian, Mongolian, and Negro"— supporting a large pediment as if a Greek temple were part of the upper structure. And, above it all, was a tall, narrow, barrel-like edifice, containing the offices of Pulitzer and his lieutenants, capped with the gilded dome.[2]

Just as Pulitzer's building had altered the New York skyline and pointed toward a new future, his touch had transformed the drab world of newspapers and laid the foundation for the modern mass media. It had been less than a decade since the Hungarian-born publisher arrived on Park Row, but already historians of the press were dating the epoch of new journalism to his purchase of the *World* from Jay Gould in 1883. Building on the success of his *St. Louis Post-Dispatch*, Pulitzer combined all the converging elements of entertainment, technology, business, and demographics to revive the moribund *World* and build it into the largest circulating newspaper in America. He adopted the techniques of mass entertainment made popular on Coney Island and Broadway, filling each day's paper with human-interest stories and sensationalism. He created the first separate sports department. He stole the graphic advertising designs of the emerging retail industry and used them to adorn stories with large, colorful headlines and illustrations on page one when other newspapers devoutly continued with their placid single-column headlines. In comparison, it seemed as if the front page of the *World* screamed. He admonished his staff to write in a buoyant, colloquial style comprising simple nouns, bright verbs, and short, punchy sentences to attract readers from the ranks of the working class and immigrants who arrived daily in New York. Moreover, he took on their cause. The moneyed class learned to pick up the *World* with trepidation. Each day brought a fresh assault on privilege and another revelation of the squalor and oppression under which the new members of the laboring class toiled. Lastly, he offered this wonder for two cents, a price almost anyone could afford and less than all the other papers, and he shrunk the paper's page size so it could be read on the trains and omnibuses that ferried workers.

The towering *World* building made it clear to all on Park Row that Pulitzer's brand of journalism was not a passing fad. Pulitzer was the midwife at the birth of the modern mass media that would simultaneously elevate the common man and take his spare change to fuel corporate profits. By the end of Pulitzer's first year at the helm, the *World's* circulation had quadrupled, and other papers were forced to slash prices. The *Herald* came down from three cents and the *Times* from four. By the time Chapin reached Park Row, the *World's* daily circulation had topped 300,000, and the *Evening World's* was on its way to exceeding that number.[3]

Acting on an impulse, Chapin decided to go inside. Even though it was a Saturday, the building was teeming with activity, the day still being a workday for most New Yorkers and certainly for journalists. Chapin followed the crowd through the entrance arch into the main vestibule. If a visitor doubted that one could make money from newsprint, the vestibule was intended to erase any uncertainty. In every direction Chapin looked, he saw marble. The floor was white marble, and to his right, an iron and marble staircase rose, winding upward and turning at forty-five-degree angles to form a triangular shaft reaching to the twelfth floor. Chapin walked past the information desk, where visitors could talk to editors on house phones or send up a business card via pneumatic tubes, and approached a bank of four Otis elevators. The lifts were considered "the highest perfection of the vertical railway and hydraulic engineering," capable of safely hoisting twelve to fifteen people in seconds to the floor of their choice. Nervous passengers were reassured by operators who explained that because of the hydraulic system, which had been thoroughly tested, "a wild elevator in the Pulitzer building can practically run into only a soft water cushion."[4]

Chapin selected the elevator reserved for editors and reporters and requested the first floor of the dome, rehearsing what he might say when he reached his destination. There, however, he found the way to the editor-in-chief's office unobstructed. He simply walked in. Ballard Smith had been in the post for less than

a month. Pulitzer had been unhappy with the conduct of affairs at the paper while he had been on a trip to Europe and had stopped in New York for a week to reorganize the staff. He had
orchestrated the shake-up entirely from his 55th Street mansion, not having even once entered his new building. He had removed his long-time right-hand man and made Smith acting editor. For Smith, the promotion had its downside. He was acrophobic and did not dare look out his new windows with their unobstructed view of the city below.[5]

Chapin introduced himself to Smith and began to tell him about his newspaper work in Chicago. Smith interrupted him, said he knew of him, and asked if he would come to work for the *World*. "I had been told that one needed a jimmy to break into the organization of a New York newspaper, but here was an editor offering me a job before I even had time to apply," said Chapin. "Would I join the staff of the *New York World*? I would have bartered ten years of my life for the chance."[6]

Nellie and Charles found accommodations for the night, and the following morning he reported for work. In his years in Chicago journalism, Chapin had never seen a city room like the one he entered. From its windows, reporters could look beyond the East River, across to Brooklyn, even out to sea. All Manhattan was visible, noted one observer, and it gave *World* reporters a cocky sense of power. Stretching out one hundred or so feet, the room was awash in crisp white light from electric ceiling and desk lamps. Eighty-four desks of antique ash, three feet long by two feet wide, each with mail slots for the reporters, were crammed into the expanse, lining the walls, standing back to back, side to side, and creating a maze of aisles. At each, shirt-sleeved men, sometimes sitting two at a desk, were composing stories by pencil or on a few "typewriters," some with two sets of keys—one with capital letters and the other containing lower-case letters. Almost like the hillside view of a mill town, smoke streamed upward from each cluster of desks like small factories, as the men puffed on an endless succession of cigarettes and cigars. Above this scene, pasted on the walls and columns, were large printed cards that read: *Accuracy, Accuracy!*; *Who? What? Where? When? How?*; and *The facts—the color—the facts!* Another, newer set of cards exhorted the staff to *Promptness, Courtesy, Geniality.* Everywhere copy boys dashed back and forth, responding to the cries of "Coppee!" heard over the din of voices and telegraph keys clicking out news from distant points. At the end of the room was a platform upon which several men at desks overlooked the floor. This was the perch of the city editor. In his various tours as city editor in Chicago, Chapin had never experienced the power that this plan conveyed. But for now, he would have to be content with being a reporter once again. Into the fracas he walked.[7]

The fellowship Chapin entered was a small one. By one estimate there were only 500 reporters working for the nearly three dozen major papers in New York, many of which had morning and evening editions. Nearly all the reporters were young men, and almost all, like Chapin, came from out of town. On the staff of one newspaper, fewer than four of the forty reporters were from New York. Only a handful of Park Row journalists were college graduates; most had matriculated from newspapers elsewhere. Unlike Chapin, however, many of his new colleagues did not plan on remaining in the news business for long. Most stayed on the job for five to seven years at best. Rather, they saw it as a stepping-stone to a career in law, politics, or business, often through the contacts they made as reporters. The turnover was tremendous. "If a man should to-day be selected from the staff to represent his paper in London, and should return in six or seven years hence, he would find that the majority of the reporters were men he had never seen," wrote a columnist for the *Journalist*.[8]

Chapin had been at the *World* for a few uneventful weeks when the Dolly Varden local ran into the Albany express at Spuyten Duyvil Station, the same rail juncture where a terrible train wreck had taken scores of lives nine years earlier. The station, only five stops north of Grand Central, took its name from the raucous waterway the Dutch called the "Devil's Spate" that separated the northern tip of Manhattan and the Bronx mainland. But neither the devil nor God would get any new souls that day because, fortunately for the passengers, this wreck took no lives. Unfortunately for Chapin, to whom the story was assigned, this meant the accident would certainly not be front-page material. That was unless he could turn it into something more than a routine story.

Working in Chapin's favor was the fact that newspaper writing, in its quality, tone, and style, had changed greatly in the past two decades. In part, this was because the reporter's desk had become the training ground of aspiring writers. "The daily newspaper sustains the same relationship to the young writer as the hospital to the medical student," said George Horace Lorimer, who as editor of the *Saturday Evening Post* would hire widely in the coming years from the ranks of New York papers. A more important factor leading to this change in writing style, though, was the fierce competition for readers, who now made the paper a part of their daily routine. Editors at the *World*, in particular, craved human-interest stories written in a heart-tugging style. They wanted New Yorkers to ask each other, "Did you read the article in the *World* about . . ." Every day, the editors endeavored to offer front-page fare with that goal in mind. So Chapin set out to spin a front-page story from a train wreck that in the hands of another would, at best, merit a few column inches tucked deep inside the paper.[9]

He abandoned the inverted pyramid style, which was then becoming the norm in papers because of the widespread use of telegraph wires to transmit stories; reporters were forced to put all the important facts at the beginning of a story in case the transmission ended prematurely. Instead, Chapin began his tale slowly, introducing his readers to John Cummings, the engineer of the Dolly Varden, a suburban train that carried chiefly factory workers and other laborers on a loop from Manhattan through the lower Bronx and Harlem. The only complicated maneuver that Cummings had to exercise on this short hour-long run was at Spuyten Duyvil, the center point on the loop. There, the engineer had to switch his train to eastbound tracks and obey signals to keep his train clear of the one hundred express trains heading north and south. Cummings arrived at the spot at 6:32 P.M. with his one-engine train pulling three crowded coaches.

"When Cummings reached Spuyten Duyvil last night," wrote Chapin, "the signal for him to stop and await orders was conspicuously displayed. There was good reason, for the Albany express, under control of Tom Connors, engineer, due at Spuyten Duyvil at 6:32 . . . was thundering down the tracks from northward, and her headlight was already throwing a streak down the ties. . . . It is a fast train and last night it was flashing along at race-track speed."[10]

"Engineer Connor whistled his approval with a loud shriek and slackened speed to round the curves safely," wrote Chapin. "And then there was a sight to look upon and not forget in many a day. There was a crowd there to see it. They saw that the Dolly Varden, not heeding the signal set from the semaphore, was also moving rapidly toward the station. The crowd was amazed. No one could conjecture what John Cummings meant by coming ahead when the signal plainly told him that to do so meant a smash and that a smash might mean death. And yet Cummings sat complacent in his cab, with his hand on the throttle and gazing straight ahead."

The crowd remained transfixed. The trains charged toward each other. Cummings continued to stare out his window unaware that his hand on the throttle was pulling his train into the path of the express train. "The two trains were running almost at right angles. As they neared each other the spectators held their breath." The angled metal protrusion on the front part of Cummings's train, known as a cowcatcher, crossed the first rail of the main tracks. The express was a few inches away. "Daylight could scarcely be seen between the two puffing monsters," wrote Chapin. The crowd felt a nervousness that Chapin said was like that when one sees a "fellow being hanged." They continued to watch even though they knew the two ponderous engines were about to meet in a fatal embrace.

"They watched, and then they saw and heard the crashing, smashing, tearing, terrifying coming together. They heard a fearful grinding sound as the steel and iron monsters shocked together. Then came shrieking and hissing sounds of escaping steam, the cracking and splintering of timbers and the breaking of glass."

"Mingled with all the deafening noise rose the screams of terrified passengers." Cummings's engine was sent off its track by the force of the faster, larger oncoming express. Enough of its metal work continued to protrude that it raked each wagon and tore off all the steps as the express shuttered to a stop. "John Cummings, with his engine torn to pieces, with the roof of his cab falling in splinters upon his head, sat like a statue. . . . When the whole dreadful affair was over the only movement he made was to close the throttle and shut off life from his engine."

If the Dolly Varden had traveled a few more inches across the tracks, the slaughter of a decade earlier might have been repeated. As it was, workers at midnight were still trying to get Cummings's engine back onto the tracks and to a repair shop. "He was still seated among the wreckage of his cab. He was asked for an explanation, but his eyes did not turn and his lips did not move. He was as motionless as when he ran into the Albany express."

The piece made the center of the front page.

A week or so later, Chapin was summoned to Smith's office. The editor-in-chief said he wanted to read aloud from the heavy cable traffic between the Dome and Paris, where Pulitzer was currently staying. Though rarely in New York, Pulitzer still remained in constant contact, dispatching dozens of telegrams a day to New York and demanding a steady stream of reports on the affairs of his empire. Pulitzer wanted to know who had written the article about the wreck of the Dolly Varden. Smith said it was the work of Chapin, a new man on the staff. By return wire, Pulitzer instructed that Chapin be presented with his personal compliments and, as was his habit, a cash reward. Though he could certainly use the cash, more important to Chapin was the imprimatur the attention conveyed. Chapin's stock rose quickly in the city room.[11]

On the first weekend of October 1891, the city desk selected Chapin to catch a train to Kingston, New York, to follow up on a tip from an ambitious reporter at the *Kingston Leader* that the town's bank was collapsing because of a massive swindle. A state banking examiner had discovered more than $400,000 missing from the Ulster County Savings Institution's assets. When Chapin reached the small town, 100 miles north of the city, he found the bank locked up with a sign announcing its suspension of business. "The town went wild," wrote Chapin. "Through the streets to the bank rushed hundreds of excited men and women." The scene was extraordinary. Within a half-hour of the time the first early risers spotted the sign, a great crowd gathered at the door. "Men rushed about hatless and with faces inflamed with passion, wildly gesticulating and shaking their clenched fists at the closed doors." Chapin looked around at the women with tears streaming down their faces and the old men sitting on the curbstones exhausted from having dashed to the bank. "It was a pitiful spectacle, that procession of sad-hearted men and women, driven to desperation by the loss of their savings and swearing vengeance against the men they had trusted and who had betrayed them." The crowd tried storming the bank, but was repulsed by the police. When word spread that the police had arrested two officers of the bank in their homes, bags packed, ready to flee, the crowd turned toward the jail. There, the two bankers, who heard the rabble approach, begged the sheriff to strengthen his guard. He had already done so, and the crowd was turned away.[12]

That evening, Chapin returned to the jail in hopes of getting an interview with the accused embezzlers, Matthew Trumpbour and James Ostrander. The sheriff agreed to permit Chapin to see the men, but as they ascended the stairs, one of the attorneys representing the men caught up with the party. The interview was a bust, as both men offered only tame answers to Chapin's questions in the presence of the lawyer. Not one to give up easily, Chapin returned the following night with a promise from the sheriff to have two uninterrupted hours with his prisoners. He found the men excited and nervous. They had spent much of the day in court facing angry defrauded depositors whose threats unnerved them. Ostrander, who was ill and being tended by a private nurse, sat shaking in a chair, nursing a bottle of whiskey. Trumpbour was not much better off. He sat with his head in his hands, looking gray, with black rings around his eyes and traces of tears on his cheeks. They both perked up upon seeing Chapin and unleashed a barrage of questions about the crowd outside the jail and whether he saw any danger that the crowd would become violent.

Trumpbour became agitated again and burst into tears. Chapin took him down the corridor and almost out of earshot of Ostrander. There, Trumpbour put most of the blame on his partner. It was Ostrander, he said, who got most of the missing $513,000. Armed with this accusation, Chapin retired for the night. The following morning, he returned, again without the knowledge of the attorneys. He found the prisoners even more despondent, not having slept, and Trumpbour more willing to tell his tale. From his cell, the accused Ostrander "frequently made interruptions in order to criminate the other, though when he realized how much

Trumpbour was telling he tried repeatedly to silence the tell-tale tongue of his fellow-prisoner," said Chapin.

Chapin again had a front-page story, this time the result of his own enterprise. "M. T. Trumpbour, the handsome white-haired bank-wrecker, made a full confession of his crime to the *World* representative today," began Chapin's piece. "He talked fully and freely, giving in detail the manner in which he and Treasurer Ostrander plundered the Ulster County Savings Institution and covered up their operations for more than twenty years." Not only did Chapin's jailhouse interview scoop the rest of the New York press, but it also precipitated an attack on him. The local reporter who had tipped off the *World,* and was miffed that Chapin had gained the glory for himself, charged him with faking the Trumpbour interview. But, concluded the *Journalist,* Chapin "has a good many friends among newspaper men who declare that the confession was genuine, and that the people of Kingston will stand by Chapin if the charges are pressed." They weren't, and the Kingston episode added another set of laurels to Chapin's nascent New York career.[13]

Being in New York City offered Chapin another potential dividend. It brought him in close—and what he hoped would eventually become beneficial—proximity with Russell Sage, his great-uncle and the richest man in America. With an estimated $100 million fortune, Sage was frequently the talk of the town. For instance, at the same time as Chapin joined the *World,* the paper published an illustrated feature on how Wall Street tycoons would look if they followed Sage's newest custom of a whiskerless face. "If the 'shaving' fad instituted by Deacon Russell Sage should find followers among the acknowledged leaders of finance in Wall Street, the possibilities would be fearful to contemplate," read the article. "Just to show what might be, *The World* artist has endeavored to picture Deacon Sage as he is, and the other gentlemen as they would be if they chanced to follow the pernicious example set by the giant of the 'put and call' market."[14]

Like Chapin, Russell Sage had begun life in Madison County in upstate New York, and, as Chapin had done, Sage left home at an early age. Before he was even a teenager, he moved to Troy to work in his brother's modest grocery store for $4 a month. Within a few years he owned the store and was operating a sloop, moving dry goods and vegetables up and down the Hudson River at a considerable profit. In 1837, he returned triumphantly to Durhamville for a family Thanksgiving reunion at which he paid off the farm's mortgage. All of his siblings were in attendance, including Chapin's grandparents Fannie and Samuel, and their five-year-old son Earl, Charles's father.

In his twenties and thirties Sage continued his storied success and was soon a prosperous member of the Troy business community and, for a while, a politician, serving first as alderman and then in Congress for four years. In 1863, Sage moved to New York, where in partnership with Jay Gould, he played a key role in organizing the nation's railroads and telegraph systems. He accrued a fortune in the process. In the 1870s he inaugurated a new stock-trading practice called "put and calls," a kind of sophisticated option to buy or sell stock at a set price within a given time. It was, at best, a form of high-stakes wagering, and Sage's success in this mysterious financial sport spawned a thousand legends.

One could hardly meet someone from New York's financial world who did not have a story to tell about Russell Sage. Shortly after Chapin arrived in the city, the *New York Times* wrote, "no man in the history of Wall Street has been such a peculiar character in its doings as Russell Sage." He stood five feet nine inches, but most concluded he was taller from his erect posture. His clothes were well worn for one so rich, and many described him as wearing tattered and frayed garments. He did nothing to diminish the tales. In fact, his parsimonious nature required shoes with a piece of wrought iron in the heel to extend their life. As he walked to work, sparks would occasionally fly from under his shoes when he traversed flagstone and rough concrete. In his great-uncle Chapin saw his chance at fortune. "I had expectations of inheriting great wealth," said Chapin. "I had visions of a mansion on the Avenue, a home in the country, a yacht, a garage full of cars, a closet all of my own to hang my clothes in and a pair of suspenders for each pair of trousers."[15]

On Friday, December 4, 1891, Sage, following his usual routine, was in his office in the old Arcade Building at 71 Broadway. Across the street, A. M. Leopold, a stockbroker, stood at the window of his second-story office. Suddenly, he felt the floor tremble. "Then I saw a sheet of flame and a puff of smoke shoot out from

a window of the office occupied by Mr. Sage and almost at the same instant I saw a man's body thrown out and fall headlong to the street," Leopold said. "The explosion was deafening and it is
a wonder to me that the wall of that old building survived the shock." An extortionist, unable to get what he wanted from Sage, had pulled a dynamite bomb from a satchel and detonated it, blowing himself to bits, destroying the office, sending one employee out the window, and causing bedlam in New York's financial center.

On Monday, Chapin obtained an audience with Sage. No newspaper reporter had yet spoken directly with the money king since the explosion. The press accounts of the events had been based on those of eyewitnesses and the police. Sage had remained cloistered in his Fifth Avenue mansion, across from the 42nd Street Reservoir. The only information concerning Sage's condition had come through Inspector Thomas Byrnes and Sage's brother-in-law Colonel J. J. Slocum. It was known, though, that he had identified his assailant, or, more properly, what little was left of him—the police had brought the man's head in a basket to Sage's bedroom on Friday night. But his version of the events was still untold.

That evening when Chapin was admitted to the mansion, he found his great-uncle lying on a lounge upstairs. Chapin was surprised by his appearance. His face was clean-shaven and showed almost no marks of the glass cuts from the explosion. "Here was the face of an old man, hearty and robust, tenacious of life and good for many years yet," wrote Chapin. Clueing his readers to his intimacy with Sage, Chapin said he was startled to see him looking so well. He was even more astonished when Sage rose to greet him. In the most purple of prose he would file later than night, Chapin wrote, "He was like a warrior after battle: a warrior who has come from the thick of fight, covered with the dust of conflict, yet without a hurt to body or limbs."[16]

Sage then proceeded to recount the events of Friday with, as Chapin saw it, astonishing calmness and little emotion. He began with his return to the office following a meeting with bank directors. Norton, one of his clerks, came into his private office with the news that a man who claimed to have been sent by Mr. Rockefeller was in the front office and wanting to see him. "Well, what does he want," Sage said he asked. Norton replied he didn't know.

"I went out," Sage told Chapin, "and, looking through the little window in the partition, I saw a young man sitting on the bench. He had a dark beard somewhat pointed. I did not know him but the head that Inspector Byrnes brought here . . . was that of the man who was waiting for me."

"I don't know why but I felt instinctively a distrust of the man," continued Sage. "Still I said to him 'Do you want to see me?'"

When the stranger replied that he did, Sage said he asked him what he desired. "He simply handed me a card on which was written H. D. Wilson and said he was from Mr. Rockefeller. All this while I was on the inner side of the partition and he stood outside looking intently at me. After I glanced at the card, he thrust in a typewritten paper. I took it and read it. The first words strengthened the first feeling of distrust I had felt." Sage then struggled to remember the exact text of the note, telling Chapin that it contained a demand for $1.2 million and the information that his bag held ten pounds of dynamite, "sufficient to blow this building and all its occupants to instant death."

"All sorts of thoughts came to me. The chief was that I had a dangerous person to deal with. I knew at once he was a lunatic, because any sane man knows that no man, however wealthy, has a million dollars about him." Sage then explained he resolved to gain time. "That was the point," said Sage. "If I could parley with him I might save myself and all the others in the building, for I knew there were many others around."

"I looked at the man, trying not to betray my emotions." There was a detective in the hallway, and Sage told Chapin he counted on the blackmailer permitting him to retreat into his private office from which he could slip out into the hall. "So I looked at the man and began reading the paper again. I read it through once more and said, 'I have an appointment here to meet a gentleman that I made yesterday. It will not take more than two minutes for me to attend to it. If you will wait until then . . .'"

Before he could finish his sentence, Sage said the man, whose name was Henry Norcross, interrupted, "I understand then that you refuse." Then he raised the valise with his right hand. "The pose of the man was dramatic," said Sage. "His arm was raised with a gesture of threat. He held the bag up as if he would drop it that instant. It was a terrible moment and he made it more awful by saying 'I have but to throw down this valise to kill every- one in the building.'"

Sage continued to plead with Norcross. At that moment William R. Laidlaw Jr., a cashier who worked for financier John Bloodgood, came into the room. His business regularly brought him to Sage's office, and Sage said he opened the door in the partition for Laidlaw to enter. "Right behind him crowded in the madman. It was a relief to have Mr. Laidlaw come. But his presence did not do any good. The crank stood on the threshold. He was glaring at me. I had just finished my last sentence when the man raised the bag and dropped it."

The blast was tremendous. Sage and Laidlaw were thrown back violently. They came to rest on the floor, unconscious but alive. The doctors believed that the detonation created two currents of air that prevented the debris hurled by the explosion from striking the pair of men. "A few seconds and I recovered consciousness," Sage said. "Mr. Laidlaw was lying across my knees." The two struggled to their feet. "I suppose it was a few seconds after I recovered my senses that we rose, for I remember seeing in the meantime poor Norton being flung out of the window. Perhaps, though, that was before I became unconscious."

As Sage recounted the events, Margaret Olivia Sage, Russell's wife, sat listening with great interest, even though she had heard the story numerous times and had supplied Chapin with similar details that Friday afternoon. Before Chapin rose to take his leave, he asked Sage when he might go back to work. Sage rubbed his chin, clenched his jaw, and then said, "Say I'll be down to business at the usual hour tomorrow."

With this interview, Chapin's stock at the *World* continued its rise. The pattern of Chapin's success in Chicago journalism seemed to be repeating itself in New York—that is until his health failed him again, as it had in Chicago. This time, the Chapins headed west to Colorado for a cure and a job on the Missouri Pacific Railroad, on whose corporate board served great-uncle Sage.[17]

St. Louis

On May 23, 1894, a legion of bedraggled unemployed workers, making their way across the country to petition Congress, set up camp on a small wooded strip of land known as Goose Island in the Mississippi River, near Quincy, Illinois. Led by self-styled General Charles Thomas Kelley, a typographer from the *San Francisco Chronicle*, the 1,200 men had left California two months earlier as one of the divisions in an army of unemployed industrial workers known as Coxey's Army. They were marching in protest on Washington after losing their jobs in the 1893 depression. The Goose Island contingent, the largest group, had been renamed Kelley's Navy since taking to the river in rafts after railroad officials had barred them from reboarding trains in Des Moines. The flotilla of leaky rafts, built from donated supplies, had barely made it this far, according to writer Jack London, who was a teenager among their ranks. "Here the raft idea was abandoned, the boats being joined together in groups of four and decked over," he wrote. Quincy citizens generously donated clothes and money. The rebuilt fleet, now with masts holding great white sails, was soon ready to continue its journey.[1]

Needless to say, the prospect of this fleet descending on gentile St. Louis down river was not going unnoticed. The editors of the *St. Louis Post-Dispatch* had already published one dispatch from the front and now decided to send a reporter to probe the intent of the navy. On hand for the assignment was Chapin. He had just resurfaced in the world of journalism after convalescing for more than a year in Colorado. Having recovered from his second bout with his "tubercular throat," Chapin was returning to the East in 1894, when he stopped off in St. Louis and encountered Florence White, who had been with Pulitzer since 1879 and was now manager of the *Post-Dispatch*. The paper was, of course, the birthplace of Pulitzer's publishing fortunes. In 1878, having already earned his stripes as a reporter, elected official, and publisher, Pulitzer bought the *Dispatch* at a sheriff's sale and merged it with the *Evening Post*, whose owner wisely decided that merging was better than competing with the aggressive young newcomer. At first, the newspaper was delivered by wheelbarrow to a few hundred readers. Soon, however, its owner's indomitable crusading editorial spirit and the paper's revealing exposés on prostitution, gambling, monopoly practices, and mud streets made the *Post-Dispatch* the city's dominant newspaper and one of the nation's best known. "The *Post-Dispatch* is a marvel of journalistic success and may be justly regarded as one of the best evening papers in the country," concluded historian Thomas Scharf in 1883. An evangelist of "new journalism," Pulitzer gave his editors free reign to offer readers a daily array of the city's best tales of sex, murder, violence, and lynchings. Within a few years, his presses might well have been printing money, considering the profit they generated, and Pulitzer left to invade New York, where his St. Louis formula worked like alchemy with the moribund *World* he bought in a fire sale from Jay Gould.[2]

White knew of Chapin—the staffs of the *World* and the *Post-Dispatch* were keenly aware of each other, and reporters often moved from one paper to the other—and he offered Chapin a position. It would be different from any previous job, thought Chapin. He had always worked for morning papers, which demanded long night hours and eliminated any semblance of home life. "To one recovering from a long spell of sickness it looked attractive," said Chapin, "so I hung my coat on a peg and went to work."[3]

Even though he was new to the *Post-Dispatch*, Chapin was a natural choice to go north to report on the protesters. He was probably more familiar with Kelley's group than anyone else on the staff. A few months prior they had traversed Colorado and had several run-ins with railroad authorities. On the other hand,

Chapin's tour of duty with the Missouri Pacific Railroad line apparently did not prejudice him against the protesters.

Chapin arrived at the Goose Island encampment the morning after the army reached it. Kelley was not there. Instead Chapin found him at the courthouse, where he was endeavoring to spring one of his men, who was accused of pawning a stolen watch. Chapin caught up with the peripatetic commander as he left the police station. Chapin explained he was there to learn about the group's mission, talk to Kelley's followers, find out about them, and learn their motives for crossing the entire continent. "I am glad you have come and I can assure you that every facility will be given to get at the exact facts," replied Kelley. "We have so far been badly misrepresented by most of the newspapermen who have written about us. They seem to think we are a lot of worthless vagrants, and few of them have taken the trouble to find out we are not."[4]

Chapin followed Kelley down to the riverfront and onto the ferry heading to the island. The boat was jammed with Quincy residents coming to see the gathering that was "almost as attractive as the first circus of the season," quipped Chapin. So many onlookers crowded around Kelley, trying to shake his hand and talk with him, that the two had to find a secluded spot on the deck to converse. They were soon interrupted again by the ferryman with a business proposition to keep the army on the island for a week so as to milk the tourist trade. Kelley declined and turned back to Chapin, telling him that wherever they had gone, people had sought to turn the army into a sideshow and make a profit from it. At last, they alighted on the island and shortly thereafter reached the tent in which the commanders were busy issuing orders, handling recruits, and worrying about the logistics of feeding and housing more than one thousand people on a river voyage. Most pressing was the need to find lumber for the 185-boat fleet, in sore need of repair and being reconfigured into larger crafts. Chapin was given permission to join the aquatic caravan. To provide him with complete access to the camp, Kelley made him a staff officer, with the rank of colonel, in the "United States Industrial Army" and presented him with a signed card testifying to his new status. Thus equipped, Chapin wandered among the men.

He found the camp was carefully laid out, military style. Each company had an enclosed area with a large tent around which men congregated. Barbers were busily trimming hair and shaving

the men. "In fact," reported Chapin, "the men presented a far better appearance than one might reasonably expect, considering the vicissitudes of their toilsome journey." Good hygiene was high on the list of requirements placed on the men. At night, they all stripped, bathed in the river, and washed their underwear, which they left to dry on the bushes while they slept. As Chapin strolled about the camp, he found many of the men resting under the shelter of trees reading "not cheap novels, but daily newspapers and monthly magazines" (a sight bound to please any reporter). He talked with at least 100 recruits and told his readers, "he was favorably impressed with them."

The next morning, repairs concluded, the men took again to the Mississippi with Chapin on board. "The men [were] singing and hurrahing as they moved down the river and [were] apparently unmindful of the fact that the commissary was almost exhausted and that there would be no supper for them unless it was donated by the citizens of Hannibal," said Chapin. Seated in the stern of the flagship, Chapin interviewed Kelley as they lazily drifted downstream. Kelley told Chapin his life story, including the fact that he had once lived in St. Louis, and described his plans for their arrival in Washington. "As soon as our forces are massed to their full strength we will march to the capital and petition Congress to take some action on our behalf," said Kelley.

"Coxey has already done this and made a miserable failure," interjected Chapin, referring to how Coxey's effort to lead a peaceful protest had been broken up by the police in fifteen minutes. Coxey had been jailed, and within several days his army had disintegrated.

"True, but Coxey's indecent haste in forcing himself and a few stragglers to the front could not have resulted otherwise. Had he gone into camp and waited patiently for the coming of other forces Congress might have listened to him."

"Are you not afraid that you will be put in jail?"

"Not in the least. I shall avoid trouble instead of seeking it. My plan is to assemble our combined forces at the capital. A balloon will be sent up and fastened to the earth by wire ropes. From this elevation I intend to address Congress and the multitude. I shall tell them that we are honest workers who have been thrown out of employment through no fault of our own."

As the convoy drifted at a pace slower than walking, Kelley continued to expound on his hope that Congress would put his men to work digging irrigation ditches in the West, on how all the logistics for feeding his troops in Washington were under control, and that his security arrangements would keep the troops in line when they arrived at their destination. All day, as the two talked, small clusters of people gathered along the shore to see the passing show. "It is the oddest and most picturesque sight ever beheld on the broad bosom of the Mississippi," said Chapin. That night they camped in Hannibal. Young Jack London deserted the ranks and headed east on his own. Chapin's lengthy, illustrated, and sympathetic report on Kelley's Navy consumed an entire page of the Sunday edition. As the flotilla neared St. Louis, the *Post-Dispatch* published daily updates, and the day after it arrived, the paper surrendered more than half of the front page to Chapin.

The arrival of the troops in St. Louis on May 28, 1894, was a tumultuous affair as 12,000 citizens gathered at the river's edge to see the goings-on. "Barnum never drew a greater throng," said Chapin's first-person account. He told the citizens of St. Louis they had nothing to fear from the men camping on the levee. "I may be mistaken, but I have talked with more than one hundred of them and have, so far as possible, investigated their personal conduct and private character and the further I investigate the better I am impressed. Such is the rank and file of Kelley's Industrial Navy." The men were also thrilled with Chapin's coverage after months of bad press. When they arrived, Kelley mounted a moored scow and led the men in cheers for the benefactor, who, on Chapin's request, had brought them food. "Three more cheers for the press of St. Louis, and especially the *Post-Dispatch*, the honest, true friend of the working man," said Kelley. "Three rousers, boys, for the splendid and truthful story of our army that was published in the *Post-Dispatch* of last Sunday." Chapin said he had never heard such an "energetic lung chorus," except maybe at political conventions. "The boys cheered louder than ever, and then repeated the chorus until I felt more than repaid for the kind words I said of them last Sunday."[5]

The *Post-Dispatch*'s main rival, the *Globe-Democrat*, virtually ignored the arrival of Kelley's Navy, consigning its coverage to page five. However, Chapin's expansive front-page coverage, filled with memorable personal narratives, got him noticed by St. Louis readers and other reporters, and ensconced him safely at the *Post-Dispatch*. It had been the pattern in Chicago, it was repeated in New York, and now it was happening again in St. Louis. He had proven his worth, and the choicest assignments were his. Within a week, for instance, he was off to Kansas to write a profile of Mary Ellen Lease, an agrarian Mother Jones who had won considerable notice with her call to farmers "to raise less corn and more hell."

"I went to Kansas to see this woman of commanding power, partly to learn more about her and partly to investigate the conflicting stories in regards to her health," Chapin told his readers. His account of his journey and the subsequent interview was written in what had now become his recognizable first-person style, filled with anecdotes about pursuing the story. For instance, Chapin described what happened when the cab, which he got at the train station, dropped him in front of the house where Lease was staying. He approached a man leaving the stout brick building and asked where he could find Lease. "He didn't reply. I got in front of him and asked again. He placed his fingers to his lips and shook his head. A little further up the graveled walk was a pretty girl. She smiled when I lifted my hat, but when I began to speak the smile died from her lips and the pathetic expression of her eyes told me that she was also deaf and dumb." Chapin then discovered the sign above the door announcing he had arrived at the State Deaf and Dumb Asylum. "Surely this ought to be a good place for one suffering from nervous prostration," he thought as he pressed the button. The bell rang, but no one answered the door. He rang again—loud enough to wake the dead, he said—but still no one came. At last, as the door was not locked, Chapin went in and took a seat in the parlor. Shortly, a trim, bespectacled woman wearing a linen gown entered and gazed inquiringly at the seated visitor. Chapin took out paper and pencil and wrote, "Is Mrs. Lease here?" The woman burst out laughing when he handed her the note.

"I'm not a mute," she said. "I am Dr. Haviland, Mrs. Lease's private secretary."

Chapin was ushered in to spend a good part of the day with Lease, and soon St. Louis readers received a lengthy account of his journey, the condition of Lease's health (recovering from exhaustion), her looks (endowed with womanly grace), her contrary ways (her husband does the household chores), and lots of copy on her politics.[6]

In subsequent months, the Sunday paper was Chapin's province. For weeks, he wrote an exciting series of police stories that he garnered from St. Louis police chief Larry Harrigan, whom he befriended in the process of developing sources. Chapin frequently used the reporter's technique he first used in Washington of writing a flattering story of one who could later prove useful. Typical of the ploy was the profile piece of Henry Samuel Priest, who had been appointed federal judge by President Cleveland in September. As usual, Chapin himself intruded in the piece. "The afternoon that I spent with him in his library at home he seemed to take pride in showing me his books," Chapin wrote. "I should think any man would be proud of such a library as he possesses, and the character of the books indicated the character of the man. They include many of the choicest gems of literature, and there is not an unclean, impure work in the entire collection."[7]

By winter, Chapin's success had paid off. He was made assistant city editor. Meanwhile in New York, changes were brewing that also played out in his favor. Pulitzer had dispatched his cantankerous editor Colonel Charles H. Jones, who had been a disaster at the *World*, to St. Louis to look at ways to revive the *Post-Dispatch*, which had lost some of its luster in the intervening years since Pulitzer left St. Louis. Upon his return to New York, Jones proposed that Pulitzer give him "absolute control" and majority ownership of the paper. The latter idea died in the ensuing negotiations, but the former somehow survived in the final agreement, to Pulitzer's later chagrin. In February 1895, Jones was in place in St. Louis, and he immediately cleaned house, sending Pulitzer loyalists packing, including White. Chapin, on the other hand, benefited from the turmoil. By spring 1895, Jones had made him city editor.[8]

"It wasn't long," recalled reporter Francis A. Behymer, "until he was sitting there at the city desk, square of jaw and baleful of eye, chewing a big black cigar or a gob of gum or a bite out of a plump reporter." Nor did it take much time for Chapin to resurrect his demanding ways as city editor, which he had learned at the feet of Fred Hall in Chicago. Chapin assigned Behymer to cover Belleville, the county seat of St. Clair County, Illinois, across the Mississippi from St. Louis. He demanded a decent news story a day about the quiet little town, whose industry consisted primarily of foundries producing nails and stoves, and material for a column called "Belleville Notes." One Saturday, Behymer failed to get the column on the evening train going to St. Louis because a heavy rainstorm delayed him. The 1890s were the golden age of bicycles, and Behymer was more concerned with calling in his coverage of that day's bike race. By the time he had dictated his story to the city desk, it became clear to Chapin that the "Belleville Notes" were missing. "Quite impersonally he blasted the daylights out of me and hung up with a bang," recalled Behymer. "I realized quite suddenly that no 'notes'—no job; storm or not; and that I would have to deliver them to the city room, even though there were no more trains that would get me there in time." So Behymer hired a horse and raced fourteen miles through pouring rain to place the inestimable "Notes" on Chapin's desk in time for the early Sunday edition. "Chapin offered no words of praise for this feat," said Behymer. "He expected it."[9]

Though the *Post-Dispatch* dominated the city, and was unrivaled in the afternoon, competition was still vigorous. The city supported four major dailies, and reporters were always looking over their shoulder when in pursuit of a story. Theodore Dreiser, who came to St. Louis shortly after Chapin left Chicago, learned this while at the *St. Louis Globe-Democrat*. Once, he was sent off to get details on a murder in the middle of night, at an hour when streetcars retire until morning. "The great fear on all these occasions was that the rival paper—the *Republic*—might have it, whereas we wouldn't," said Dreiser.[10]

Chapin drummed up readers for the *Post-Dispatch* by combining what he learned in Chicago with the Pulitzer method of giving readers stories they would talk about. "St. Louis, just at this time, appeared to love turgid color—the daring, bizarre, rather loose and colorful style of newspaper descriptions in vogue there," said Dreiser. And Chapin delivered. "Exaggeration was a grace—or vice—that he encouraged reporters to cultivate in the interest of bigger and better stories," said Behymer, who believed that Chapin would even tolerate fakery. It was, in fact, a Chapinesque story that rescued Behymer from the torment of covering Belleville. The reporter received a tip that a woman was going to go after a businessman with a whip on the public square for having made a derogatory remark about her. He told Chapin and suggested the police should be told. "We won't tell the police because I don't believe a damn word of it, but you take Carlisle Martin and go over there—just in case," said Chapin. The whipping occurred. Behymer brought in the exclusive and Martin the illustrations. "Chapin beamed his satisfaction, and he could beam with the best of them when he wanted to," said Behymer, who did his own beaming when he learned that Chapin was promoting him. On the other hand, the fear that Chapin created permeated the city room. On the slightest provocation, he fired reporters, often rehiring them the following week. But they put up with it because his was the best newsroom in town. "I feared and hated—and loved—the sonofagun. He made a reporter of me—if I am one," said Behymer.[11]

Chapin was in his element, and he thrived. He and Nellie rented a small house west of downtown and hired a black servant named Old Moses. Everything was perfect about St. Louis and the job, except for one thing. He had to put up with—in his own words—the "pompous little man with bristling white whiskers." Colonel Jones's five-year contract to run the *Post-Dispatch* was only in its first year, and he frequently made life intolerable. Once, for instance, the *Post-Dispatch* was scooped on a mid-afternoon fire in East St. Louis. Jones had gone home, and Chapin hoped he wouldn't see the competition's late afternoon edition. He did. The next morning Jones "came into the local room with whiskers flying and tore into Chapin with all the naughty words he could think of in the presence of all the reporters who hadn't gone out on their runs," according to Behymer. At the end of his haranguing, Jones let loose one final volley and told Chapin that as a city editor, he was a second-rate office boy. "And," said Behymer, "Chapin the Terrible had to sit there and take it." Worse, in many respects, was that Jones seemed intent on driving the

paper into the ground by alienating all St. Louis businesses and ferociously campaigning for free silver, a movement that advocated silver currency to restore the economy. "It was said of him
that he used vitriol when writing editorials," said Chapin. "He was volcanic and turgescent." In fact, Jones's conduct almost cost Chapin his life.[12]

In late December, Jones ordered that the paper publish an article critical of Frederick W. Brockman, president of the school board. Two days later, Brockman sued the *Post-Dispatch*. When a warrant was issued for alleged criminal libel, Jones was conveniently out of town, and the warrant was sworn out against the city editor. The warrant did not charge that Chapin had written the article or even inspired it. Rather, his post with the paper simply made him liable. A "city editor of a newspaper is responsible for everything that goes into its columns," alleged the complaint. A trial date of January 17, 1896, was set, and, accompanied by attorney Charles Napton, Chapin appeared in court before Judge David Murphy, a cantankerous and notorious jurist. Chapin and Napton knew Murphy would be trouble. Just weeks before, an article questioning his Civil War heroism had appeared in the *Post-Dispatch*. Immediately, Chapin's attorney filed a motion for a change of venue. Murphy said he would hear testimony on the motion after lunch. When court reconvened, Napton said it would not be necessary to offer any testimony. He would instead rely on the affidavits he had filed. "Then," said Murphy, "I will hear the testimony of this party who signed the application. Is Charles E. Chapin here?"[13]

"Yes, your honor," replied Chapin.

Napton objected, but Chapin was sworn in and placed on the witness stand.

"Krum, examine this witness in this matter," said Murphy to the plaintiff's attorney.

"Yes, sir," he replied.

As Chester Krum approached Chapin, the judge's connivance became clear. Murphy had given Krum a copy of the article that had so offended him, and together they planned to seek revenge by crucifying Chapin on the stand. Krum began by asking Chapin what proof he had to offer that Murphy was hostile to the *Post-Dispatch* as alleged in the motion. Chapin replied with tales of several instances in which he thought Murphy had betrayed his sentiments, including one case where the judge had left the bench, approached a 13-year old *Post-Dispatch* messenger boy, and asked if he was a reporter. When the boy said he was not, Murphy said, "To judge from the articles I have read in the *Post-Dispatch* about this court, I thought possibly you were."

"What articles criticizing the judge has the *Post-Dispatch* published?" asked Krum.

"Well, I would not pretend to enumerate them now from memory," replied Chapin, adding that there was, of course, the one about his war record.

Krum reached into his pocket, drew out the article, and began to read from it. Then he asked, "Who wrote it?"

Judge Murphy now leaned over and glared at Chapin.

"I object to that testimony," interjected Napton.

"Objection overruled."

Then it became clear to Chapin that Murphy wanted to know who was the reporter. As Chapin refused to answer, Murphy became angry. Krum and Murphy both warned Chapin that he could only decline to answer the question if doing so would incriminate him.

"What is the answer?" Krum demanded.

"I refuse to answer," said Chapin.

"On what grounds?"

"The grounds you suggested."

"That it would incriminate yourself?"

Before Chapin could answer, Krum launched into a defense of Murphy's honor as a Civil War veteran, saying that he himself had witnessed his heroism. When he was done, the courtroom was silent. Murphy was white with anger.

"Where did you get the information on which you based that publication?" Krum persisted.

Napton again tried to object but was overruled, and Krum pressed Chapin.

"You are assuming, Mr. Krum, that I am responsible for the publication of that article," said Chapin.

"Well, I know you are."

The two went back and forth until Chapin finally relented.

"I will not answer that question," he said.

"On what grounds?" said Krum, nearing victory.

"Well, I will say, then, on the ground that it might incriminate myself."

Then Krum and Murphy pressed forward with their attack, trying to get Chapin to change the word "might" to "would."

Finally Krum withdrew, and Murphy pronounced himself satisfied that Chapin had proved himself to be a "character that would malign any citizen."

"I object to that statement from the court," piped up Napton, who had been silent during the last part of the battle. Murphy then let loose a long biographical and pompous speech comparing his life to an open book that anyone could read. "And," he continued, "to say that there is a man in this city that would through the columns of a newspaper denounce him as a coward in war, when he knows nothing about it, I must confess that man is such a malicious liar that I could not give him a fair trial." Then he turned and faced Chapin. "I am personally responsible to you for anything I say here if you have got any manhood in you."

No one in the courtroom misunderstood Murphy. He had just challenged Chapin to a duel. "Every one thought there would be a tragedy," reported the *Post-Dispatch*. "They knew that if the witness lost control of his temper and attempted to resent the insults Judge Murphy was heaping upon him he would be shot. The witness did not move."

Murphy then ordered a recess and Chapin regained his seat next to Napton. Then Murphy slowly descended from the bench and came over to where Chapin sat, surrounded by several reporters from his staff.

"Court is not in session now, and I am a private citizen," said Murphy glaring at Chapin. "You can talk to me just as you please. If you have anything to say I am personally responsible for everything I said on the bench, and for everything I say here. I consider you a malicious characteristic liar and coward, and if you have a spark of manhood in you, you will take it up."

Chapin did not move or even glance up at Murphy. He sat motionless, though turning pale. Finally with a snort, Murphy turned and sped into his private office. When he returned a few minutes later, he announced that another judge would hear the case and adjourned the court. As Napton and Chapin gathered their belongings, they found themselves again face to face with Murphy, who now stood with his fists raised. "You can take this up for your client, Mr. Napton; you can take it up now."

"I am in the habit of fighting my cases before the court and not with the judge," replied Napton, as the crowd surged forward in anticipation of a fight. Murphy glared. "And any other son of a bitch that wants to take it up for him can do so. The dirty, lying, scoundrelly pack of bastards dare to attack me on the bench, when I have no chance to fight back but cringe like curs when I meet them on actual footing as a private citizen. This will show if I am a fighter or not. Why don't you jump on me now and see whether I will fight?"[14]

When no one took him up on the offer, he turned and once again retreated to his office, this time followed by a volley of laughter from the crowd. Chapin repaired to police chief Harrigan's office. Murphy's regular attacks on the police had caused him to be despised by law officers almost as much as the city's press corp. Harrigan lent Chapin a pistol and told him not to hesitate to use it should Murphy assault him.

Reporters from rival papers rushed to get comments from Chapin. He was rather taciturn, declining entirely to make any comment to the *Globe-Democrat* and telling the *Republic* that Murphy was armed, had armed sheriffs at his disposal, and took advantage of the situation to "vilify me in a manner that is a disgrace to him, to his court and to any man." Late that afternoon, Chapin said, Murphy appeared drunk on the street outside the *Post-Dispatch*, shaking his fist and cursing, but nothing came of it.

A week later, however, Chapin was walking down Olive Street on a quiet Sunday morning when he spotted Murphy approaching from the opposite direction. There was no one else on the street and no place to go. Chapin put his hand in his pocket and grasped Harrigan's pistol. The two came closer. Murphy reached into his jacket's breast pocket. "Neither of us slackened paced and we were soon so close that we could have touched each other," said Chapin. "Judge Murphy averted his eyes from me and I was just as polite to him, though I am positive that both of us were cautiously squinting out of the corner of an eye." The two passed, and the confrontation faded into the lore of St. Louis journalism.

In February, the case went to trial under another judge and was soon dismissed. The winter gave way to spring. Relief from Jones seemed possible because Pulitzer had launched a court fight to regain control of the paper and break the contract. It turned out to be stronger than Pulitzer's best lawyers, and the Jones regime endured. So did Chapin.

Shortly after lunch on May 27, 1896, Chapin put the paper to bed as usual. It had been a good day. Aside from the usual free silver articles that Jones insisted on running, Chapin's reporters had brought in two front-page stories that were bound to be conversation kick-starters that night. The first, which Chapin topped with the headline "Rats Gnawed Him While He Slept," concerned a drunken homeless man on whom rats had begun to feast and whose life was saved only by the intervention of some good Samaritans. The other city tale was about a wronged wife who chased her husband across the city, on and off streetcars, with a pursuing crowd of spectators. She caught up with him as he tried to dodge into a saloon and, in her moment of triumph, pelted him with a sack of red pepper. This one Chapin named "Red Pepper for a Husband's Eye." At the end of the droll account, the reporter dryly noted that the temporarily blinded man said he would sue for divorce. The weather forecast on the front page predicted that several thunderstorms were possible that evening. H. C. Frankenfield from the St. Louis Weather Bureau, whose predictions the paper used each day, stopped in. Chapin and Frankenfield had known each other when the weatherman worked in Chicago in the 1880s. He had been transferred to St. Louis the same year Chapin arrived. Frankenfield suggested that Chapin consider heading home because the darkening skies and the falling barometer made the predicted thunderstorms more likely.[15]

"Cyclone?" asked Chapin.

"No, not so bad as that. We never have cyclones in cities, but I think it will be a nasty storm and I would advise you to hit the trail."

The advice was good. By the time Chapin reached his home at 1316 N. King's Highway, five miles west of the *Post-Dispatch* building, a storm had indeed begun. Old Moses helped him secure the windows. "When this was done I watched the storm wrench branches from trees and carry them over the tops of houses. I saw my chicken house topple over and the prize rose-bushes I had nursed so tenderly torn up by the roots," said Chapin. This was the price he paid for living outside the city, thought Chapin, who ate the dinner Old Moses served him and Nellie and afterward went to bed a grump.[16]

It was a vastly different scene in the city. At the time that Chapin's roses became airborne, Frankenfield and Martin Green, a 26-year-old reporter for the *Republic,* were standing at the window of the Weather Service offices. Below them they could see people crowding onto streetcars and seeking shelter from the rain in doorways. The wind was picking up. Signs were swinging wildly, and, strangest of all, Green spotted blue balls racing along the telegraph and trolley wires.

"It's a bad thunderstorm," said Frankenfield, who began to move back to his desk.

"My God!" yelled an assistant. "Look out there in the West!"

The pair turned and incredulously watched as a sausage-shaped cloud descended from the storm onto the city, its approach illuminated by bright orange lighting bolts. The wind indicator in the office read 70, then 80 miles an hour. Buggies on the streets flipped over, awnings rolled up like scrolls, and bricks and timber flew through the air, shattering windows as men and women shrieked in the darkness. In less than twenty minutes, the second-worst tornado in U.S. history retreated back into the sky. Rescue crews worked through the night. By dawn, it was clear that at least 200 people had perished, and hundreds of homes, businesses, and worse, even the city hospital, lay in ruins.

In the morning, Chapin rose as usual at five so as to reach his office by seven. The morning paper had not been delivered, and the streetcar he normally took was not running. "More penalties for living in the suburbs," he thought to himself, "more annoyances to start one off to business in bad humor." Four blocks away, he found a streetcar that was running and boarded it. Halfway to the office, Chapin watched a passenger board with a newspaper. He hungrily eyed it. The man opened it, and Chapin saw the headline. "Hundreds killed; thousands of homes in ruins! And I was grieving over uprooted rosebushes and a wrecked chicken house," said Chapin. When, at last, he reached the office, he found his staff had worked through the night. An extra was already on the street. But even as Chapin prepared the additional editions they would run that day, it was clear the story belonged to Green. His account had an immediacy that was unmatched by any other that night.[17]

"St. Louis was a city of darkness and desolation last night; a stricken city," read Green's lead. "Wind and rain and fire combined yesterday afternoon in a mission of destruction; hundreds were killed, thousands were wounded and there is no telling what the dawning of the day may bring forth." In carefully crafted prose, Green detailed the destruction, alternately recounting what he and Frankenfield witnessed from their perch above the city. At the end of the onslaught, Green described the return of the rain, which had been held in abeyance during the tornado. "It was a wonderful rain, a steady, pounding, penetrating rain that seemed to gather strength as it fell. Amid the horror and the wild rumors of countless fatalities the rain came down harder and stronger, gloomily sounding a knell." Dark clouds gathered again, and it looked as if another assault was being prepared. "The sky was green and the clouds were wicked. But the wind did not gain the strength necessary to do damage. Nothing came but rain; a rain that beat long and pitilessly on the helpless city." Chapin would not forget who wrote the account.[18]

In the fall, Chapin invigorated the *Post-Dispatch*'s circulation with a stunt he had used so successfully in Chicago. Readers picking up their copies of the paper on Thanksgiving week found the front pages dominated with a new series: "Factory Girls in a Big City." Chapin's introduction explained that the paper "proposes to place before its readers a plain story of the struggles, the hardships, the difficulties, the hopes, the joy and fears that go to make up the life of one girl who came to the city of St. Louis to earn her living." To write the series, Chapin had engaged Lucy Hosmer, who had left a comfortable life in a small town because of a reversal of fortunes. "Another helpless girl," said Chapin, "cast upon the world to battle for her daily bread, with no better equipment for the struggle than two willing hands, a stout heart and a deep-rooted purpose to earn an honest living, no matter how hard the work, how long and dreary the way." The series ran for nearly two weeks as Hosmer went from working in a shoe factory to a tobacco plant to a candy manufacturer, and Chapin put each installment on the front page.[19]

Even better news than the success of the series was the announcement that the Jones era had come to an end. Though Pulitzer had lost in court, he finally persuaded Jones to give back control of the paper for a considerable payment. With Jones gone and many of the Pulitzer regulars back, Chapin's position as city editor seem a sinecure. The paper was thriving, and there was little reason to think that Pulitzer would want to alter the winning formula that Jones had left behind with Chapin in charge. But change of another sort—which would alter American journalism—was in the air.

In January of 1897, there were nearly forty U.S. war correspondents in Key West, though there was no war. Both Hearst and Pulitzer had their best men on the scene trying to get any scrap of information about the Cuban insurrection against Spain. Their coverage, especially of alleged Spanish atrocities, increased anti-Spanish sentiment in the United States and did wonders for circulation. By year's end, war with Spain was a common topic of conversation, though the new president was opposed to any kind of military intervention. Then in February 1898, the *U.S.S. Maine* exploded while in Havana's harbor, killing 226 sailors. President McKinley converted his reluctance for war to the hope that it would be short and with the least bloodshed possible.

In March, Chapin was discussing the possibility of war over lunch with Alf Ringling, one of five Wisconsin brothers who had launched a traveling circus fifteen years earlier. In two years the show had become so popular in the Midwest, it took four trains to haul it from town to town. A messenger boy from the *Post-Dispatch* cut the pair's conversation short. In his hands was a telegram from Pulitzer. In Pulitzer's usual imperious style, he directed Chapin to leave for New York that night, if possible, and come prepared to remain. "A few hours later I sat in the end of an observation car and watched the twinkling lights of St. Louis fade into nothing," wrote Chapin. "My newspaper career in that city was at an end and I was glad of it."[20]

New York to Stay

The urgency of Pulitzer's summons became clear when Chapin reached New York. Pulitzer was in desperate need of an editor. Ernest Chamberlain, a prized recruit from the *Sun* five years earlier, had become a Park Row casualty of sorts in the impending war. It seemed that Chamberlain, a thin, pasty, 38-year-old man with an oversized mustache, who was the managing editor of the *Evening World*, had dispatched telegrams summoning every member of his staff to the office late one night toward the end of February 1898. Though dramatic, the telegrams fit the heightened sense of expectation among the press corps in New York. Since February 15, when the *U.S.S. Maine* was blown up in Havana's harbor, it had been assumed in certain quarters of Park Row that war was coming. The two major press lords were certainly doing all they could to fan the flames. Hearst's *Journal* added American flags to a front page already packed daily with incendiary headlines about Spain's culpability. The *World* splashed an artist's rendering of the explosion across all seven columns of its front page and promised that the guilty would soon be identified. "The World Has Sent a Special Tug, With Submarine Divers, To Find Out," proclaimed its headline two days after the detonation. War fever on Park Row was infectious and, best of all, it was good for business. In the week following the sinking of the *Maine*, the *World* sold five million copies, permitting it to call itself "the largest circulation of any newspaper printed in any language in any country."[1]

Chamberlain, who sent out the call to the staff that night, had caught a full-blown case of the fever. A glutton for work, he was reputed to stay at his desk for such long shifts that reporters returning to work the following morning would find him at the same post where they had bade him goodnight. Remarkably, he seemed to sustain his pace solely on a diet of crackers and milk served in a quart bowl from Hesse & Loeb, a restaurant three floors above, open twenty-four hours a day.[2]

"When we arrived, one after another, we were greeted by Chamberlain with the terse announcement that the war was on," recalled Albert Terhune, a reporter who had joined the *Evening World* in 1894. "The war has begun, boys," said Chamberlain. The "extra" he ordered was spread out before the astonished staff. Only the world "WAR!" was above the fold. What little copy there was on the page below the headline gave no reason for such a conclusion. The night crew rapidly explained that after all the other editors and reporters had left for the night, Chamberlain had suddenly risen from his desk and ordered the special run of the *Evening World*. An alert newsboy brought a copy to the morning staff, at work in the newsroom upstairs. "Chamberlain was taken to task for it by the *Morning World* bosses," said Terhune, who watched the spectacle, still only half awake. "They guessed his condition after a few minutes' talk and sent two men home with him." An order went out to retrieve "as many copies of the warless war extra as possible." Chamberlain was taken home in a cab and, not long afterward, died of pneumonia.[3]

Upon arriving in New York, Chapin repaired immediately to the *World* building. Almost seven years had passed since he had first ventured into the building. It was no longer the tallest in the city, but it remained unquestionably the apogee of journalism. Chapin was no longer a reporter looking for work, but Pulitzer's designee for the city editor's desk at the *Evening World*. Life under the dome had changed greatly in Chapin's absence. Three years earlier, when Pulitzer's journalistic empire enjoyed a virtual monopoly on success, it had been challenged by an upstart from California with an immense financial reserve in the form of a check-writing heiress and mother of the publisher. William Randolph Hearst had followed the Pulitzer game plan better than the master himself. He had purchased the poorly managed *Journal* and overnight turned it into a bright, lively, sensationalistic paper that was an easy sale for the newsboys on the street. He "dawned on New York's journalistic horizon—if a thunderbolt can be said to dawn," said Terhune. Stunt after stunt brought in readers by the droves.

For instance, Hearst hired novelist Richard Harding Davis to cover the Yale-Princeton game and hinted to readers that he paid $500—an unheard-of sum—for the famed writer's services. Not content with famous freelancers for his covey of writers, Hearst raided the *World* itself. "He was willing to pay good wages for especially good work," said Terhune. "While the *World* stared helplessly aghast, he took from it a goodly number of its stars." At one point, he lured away the *entire* Sunday staff. Pulitzer ordered his adjutant to get the staff back at any cost. He succeeded, but twenty-four hours later they marched back to Hearst, and before long, even the adjutant himself jumped ship. The competition was certainly good for newspapermen, as salaries rose rapidly. "The days are passing when a newspaperman can be recognized by the shabbiness of his attire and the dandruff on his coat collar," noted the *Journalist*. For Chapin, the competition secured him an unheard-of $100 a week. With cocktails selling for a dime, and a porterhouse-steak dinner, complete with French fries and a saucer of piccalilli, for fifty cents, it was a handsome take.[4]

Nothing seemed to slow Hearst's assault on the *World*'s dominance. Readers loved the spectacle of the two papers battling it out. There soon ensued one of the greatest competitions in American journalism history. When a story broke in a distant part of the city, reporters would pour from their Park Row citadels and grab bicycles, carriages, and anything else that moved in a race to be first on the scene. When the news was in a distant land, cable bills of thousands of dollars became routine. The war turned the competition into a twenty-four-hour-a-day affair, creating what reporters called the "Lobster Trick," a shift of reporters and editors who worked from 1:00 A.M. until they were relieved by the day staff in order to get out an earlier-than-noon evening paper. "An epoch of delirious journalism began," said Chapin, "the likes of which newspaper readers had never known." With rival editors feeling no compunction about appropriating each other's stories for their next edition, a scoop was an ephemeral victory. In fact, the habit of stealing stories became so commonplace that several months after Chapin's return, the *Journal* published a phony report about the war heroics of a "Colonel Reflipe W. Thenuz," who was fatally wounded. After the *World* published its account of the good colonel's deed, lifted entirely from the *Journal*, it was gleefully announced at Hearst's headquarters that the colonel's name was an anagram for "We pilfer the news."⁵

Soon, every flank of Pulitzer's empire was challenged, even his technique of making the paper affordable to the masses. Pulitzer had been forced to cut the price of the *World* to one cent to match the *Journal*'s price. Now every man or woman in New York with a spare penny was a potential reader to be fought over. The war over that penny was fierce, driving each paper to frequently abandon reason and publish stories so extreme, so "newsworthy," so outrageous that they weren't to be believed. Often they weren't.

Nowhere was this cutthroat competition more exacting than in the afternoon. The public had developed a voracious appetite for news, and electric lights made reading the newspaper an evening pastime. "The evening paper is the paper which goes into the home, it is the one read by every member of the family," explained the *Journalist*. Men tended to abscond with the morning paper and throw it aside when they reached their workplace. "With the evening paper the case is different; its reader delves into its pages after the work of the day is done, he sits by the fire and digests it and discusses it with his wife and family." Rather than publishing a single edition, the evening papers were seemingly in constant production all afternoon. "Editions of evening newspapers made their appearance before six in the morning and almost every hour afterward until midnight," said Chapin. The *Evening World* would produce as many as forty "extras." In fact, the *Evening World* was printing so many editions that it often ended up competing on the street with the morning edition of the paper. Editions were numbered in a bewildering fashion, and even printed on different colored paper, in order to gain a competitive edge over Hearst's evening *Journal*, which seemed a master of this practice. "Does anyone know at what hour the first six editions of the New York *Evening Journal* are issued?" asked a writer in the *Journalist*. "I get up too late in the morning—half past six—even to get a really early copy of this paper, the best I can do being to

get the 'seventh edition, latest afternoon,' in Jersey City at about
9 A.M." First editions were numbered ninth, sometimes four-
teenth. By supper, the 127th edition had hit the streets. The *Jour-*
nal offered cash rewards for some of the "missing" editions, but
none were ever claimed.[6]

With Chamberlain gone, Pulitzer reorganized. Foster Coates
took over as managing editor. Though he was—in Chapin's
words—"the perfection of affable gentleness," Coates was the
only member of Pulitzer's staff who could rival the boss's use of
profanity. Pulitzer, who had acquired his English while serving as
a mercenary in the Civil War, regularly reconstructed the language's vocabulary by inserting a profane word in the middle of
another word. "Inde-goddamn-pendent," for instance, was the
most famous of his lexicon. "Profanity with him was more an art
than a vice," said Chapin. Curser Coates, as he was nicknamed,
could do just as well. Once when he was told to do something,
Coates replied that he was under no "obli-goddamn-gation" to
do so. "There was no word in blasphemous vocabulary that wasn't
on the tip of his tongue," recalled Chapin. "He ripped out oaths
that fairly made the windows rattle, but it was habit more than
temper, for otherwise he was almost without faults and to me was
ever generous, warm-hearted, and kindly."[7]

Frederick Duneka, Coates's assistant, was told to hold down
the city desk until Chapin arrived. He was entirely different from
Coates. Whereas Coates was excitable, Duneka was calm.
Whereas Coates was coarse, Duneka was refined. "He was gor-
geously good company and the most considerate boss in the
newspaper business," said Terhune. Prior to his post on the *Eve-*
ning World, Duneka had served Pulitzer as one of his many private
secretaries and as London correspondent for the *World,* a post for
which the publisher usually hand picked the reporters. Duneka
welcomed Chapin on his arrival from St. Louis and graciously
turned over the desk to him. From the start, Chapin, Coates, and
Duneka worked well together and had considerable affection for
each other. "In all my newspaper experience I do not recall two
more delightful men," said Chapin.[8]

Despite their warm sentiments toward each other, the three
also knew that their first loyalty lay with the increasingly absent
publisher. This was an inescapable part of the work culture at the

World. Pulitzer would have it no other way. Though he was gone most of the time, sailing the world in his yacht in an obsessive
pursuit of silence, Pulitzer relinquished no control. The idea of managing such a complicated and competitive institution as a newspaper from the far reaches of the globe seemed foolhardy to anyone who knew the business. Pulitzer, however, pulled it off. He required that all his top men send him daily reports on their doings and the doings of others. In a sense, that made Pulitzer's presence felt even more strongly than if he had been in the building. Everyone worked knowing full well that whatever they did eventually would become known to Pulitzer. Each day, his private secretaries read these voluminous reports to Pulitzer, who was growing blind. He would then dispatch dozens of instructions by telegram. To retain secrecy—telegraph operators were not known for their discretion—Pulitzer developed a 250-page codebook, containing an estimated 20,000 coded names and terms. The morning *World* was known as "Senior," the evening *World* was "Junior." "Grandam" was the term for city editor, and Pulitzer ("Andes") christened Chapin with the moniker "Pinch." The telegrams all were signed with the word "Sedentary," code for an immediate reply is required. The preferred reply was "Semaphore," which meant that the order was received, understood, and would be carried out.[9]

The central task for the Chapin-Coates-Duneka team was to compete with Arthur Brisbane. Brisbane had been among Pulitzer's best editors and had revived the fortunes of the *Evening World* in 1897 after it lost money. Now, however, he was working his magic next door for Hearst at the *Evening Journal*. His skill and the war were creating record newspaper sales. In the three days following the sinking of the *U.S.S. Maine*, the *Evening Journal* sold more than three million copies. By the time war was officially declared on April 25, 1898, the *World* and *Evening World* had caught up. But the competition between the afternoon papers was not restricted solely to circulation. Both seemed intent on outdoing each other in creating astonishing headlines. Coates, at the *Evening World*, would not concede a point of lead to Brisbane. Headlines grew to the point where they often consumed the entire front page like a poster instead of a newspaper. "Coates defended his poster type headlines by likening the front page of a newspaper to the show window of a department store," said Chapin. "One must display his wares attractively, he argued, or the other fellow would reap the largest sales." And, when size was not enough, Coates took to decorating the type with stars and stripes.[10]

There was almost no type size large enough when news of victory in Manila came on May 7, 1898, from correspondent Edward Harden who had left the Philippines for Hong Kong as soon as the smoke of battle cleared. He paid the highest cable rate, and his dispatch reached the United States before the government's own official report. Early that Saturday morning, by the time Chapin reached work, the Lobster shift had put out an extra of the Senior but sold only a few by the Brooklyn Bridge. The scoop would belong to the evening edition. Chapin selected the largest type in the composing room. Then he ordered his staff to churn out copy to fit the historic moment. In flowed stories on Manila Bay, why the Spanish fleet was there, how Dewey caught it unprepared, profiles of key officers, and anything else Chapin's bleary-eyed reporters could crank out. "By the time the press crews had reported, the extra was ready for them," said Chapin. "Every press in the great battery was soon in motion and was kept going throughout the day and far into the night, stopping only long enough to change some of the pages as additional details came from cable and telegraph wires."[11]

The last battle at an end, Pulitzer sought to restore a more measured tone to the offspring of his more serious morning *World*. He had tolerated the headline war between the *Evening World* and the *Evening Journal* for the duration of the fighting, but now he moved to bring it to an end. He ordered that all the large type in the composing room be melted. The foreman carried out the edict, but the *Evening Journal*'s Brisbane, no longer covered by a Pulitzer edict, kept using them to great effect, especially when it came to sales. Pulitzer's effort to suppress large heads was thus soon doomed. The evening press was solidly wedded to their use, and eventually Chapin would be employing the screaming headlines again.[12]

With the shooting war at an end, Chapin collapsed. Since his return to New York, he had kept a grueling schedule of reaching his desk by 4:00 A.M. and not leaving for home until after dark.

Meals were taken at his desk, or, sometimes while supervising the pasting up of an edition in the composing room. Like Chamberlain before him, Chapin contracted pneumonia and was confined to bed. Each day, Duneka would send a messenger boy uptown to 16 East 22nd Street, where Charles and Nellie had found quarters, to obtain a report on Chapin's condition. The report would then be posted on the office bulletin board. At night, when he finished work, Duneka would come by and sit with Chapin, filling him in on the doings at the *Evening World*. Unlike Chamberlain, Chapin recovered and was soon back at work.[13]

At ten o'clock Saturday, July 2, 1898, Chapin went to wish a *bon voyage* to friends who were sailing to Europe on *La Bourgoyne*. Cross-Atlantic ship travel was becoming increasingly commonplace, but it was still customary for the ships to be sent off by large flag-waving crowds and bands playing gay tunes. No less than a dozen ocean liners from all the major European ports were docked that week. Built in 1886, *La Bourgoyne* was the third largest ship in the French line and was only exceeded in speed by her sister ship *La Touraine*. Chapin, along with many others, boarded the ship to say his good-byes. While on board, he picked up a passenger list and put it in his pocket before heading back to the office. As he left the pier, he ran into Judge John F. Dillon, whom he had met at his great-uncle Russell Sage's house. A former Iowa judge of considerable repute, Dillon had come to New York in 1879 to teach law and serve as an attorney for Jay Gould, Sage's frequent partner. Dillon was sending off his youngest daughter and wife, and he and Chapin walked together to Dillon's carriage in the scorching heat. Dillon returned to his office and caught a 3:50 P.M. train home to New Jersey.[14]

On Wednesday morning while at his usual post on the city desk, Chapin was handed a telegram from the Canadian city of Halifax. An enterprising stringer there, J. Watson Fraser, had heard that a steamer was approaching the harbor, towing the *Cromartyshire*, a British sailing vessel. It was said that the ship's bow was smashed in, parts of its foremast were missing, and, ominously, it was flying its flag at half-mast. "This plainly told to me," said Fraser, "that a sea tragedy of some kind had happened, and in order to get the news first, if possible, for the *Evening World* I mounted my bicycle and rode at top speed to Mount

Pleasant, to the ferry, to get suitable craft to go to meet the vessels." His bicycle trip gave him a head start on other newspapermen who instead boarded slower boats. Fraser reached the
Cromartyshire first. A strong wind was blowing, and his small craft struck the larger vessel, almost capsizing, before he managed to scramble up the side. On board, he discovered that two days before, in a thick early morning fog, the *Cromartyshire* had run head on into *La Bourgoyne,* sending the latter to the bottom with 571 of its 600 passengers. The few survivors were now on board the crippled sailing ship. Fraser rushed back to shore with his story and met up with three Canadian Pacific telegraph messengers on bicycles, whom he had asked to wait for him. He then composed his bulletins and dispatched them to Chapin by bicycle relay.[15]

"In ten minutes his message of disaster and death was before me," said Chapin. "I rushed it to the composing room to be put into type and telephoned the mechanical forces to get ready for an important 'extra.'" He topped the page with a headline "Panic and Death" in type more than three-and-a-half inches tall. Suddenly, Chapin was thunderstruck. The passenger list. He had one. He had brought it back to the office after seeing the ship sail off. In less than fifteen minutes, the story, the list, and his Chapinesque headline were in the hands of the composers. The press hardly paused that day as extra after extra went to the street. The other papers played catch up all day and night. By the final edition of the night, Chapin couldn't resist boasting. "The *Evening World* as usual gets all the news first," he splashed on page three, under an illustration of the ill-fated liner. "It never fakes the news or fools people. It is first in everything. It is the leader now as it has always been in rapid journalism. Its motto is: 'Get there first.'"[16]

"As the extra went to press," said Chapin, "I thought of poor Judge Dillon and what the sinking of *La Bourgoyne* meant to him." He lifted the telephone at his desk and reached Dillon in Far Hills, New Jersey. After breaking the news to the judge, the phone went dead. Chapin asked the operator to reconnect the call, but she told him the receiver was off the hook. The sad episode soon passed from Chapin's mind as his insatiable appetite for work returned, and there was no shortage of news to keep him occupied. Over the coming year, the Spanish-American war drew to an official close, the "Affaire Dreyfus" put France in turmoil, and Marconi sent the first press message across the English Channel to France by means of his recently invented wireless at a rate of fifteen words a minute. Besides, it was out of character for a hardened city editor to give more than a moment's pause to the tragedies with which he filled the pages of his paper.

As the summer's news became more routine, Chapin once again brought out his tried and true series of the reporter exploring the underside of urban life. He had done this with great success in Chicago with his "White Slave Girls" series and in St. Louis with his "Factory Girls in a Big City" series. This time, he dispatched reporters Charles Garrett and Catherine King separately to pose as young people in search of work. The installments were introduced with the usual melodrama, describing how the reporter endured genuine deprivation to bring the story to the reader. "The *Evening World* regards the story as a remarkable disclosure of the inner life of this great metropolis and presents it for its singularly interested information in that direction," wrote Chapin in his introduction to Garrett's story, which he followed two weeks later with King's trials and tribulations.[17]

All in all, management was pleased with the direction of the *Evening World*. In the six months since Chapin had assumed the city desk, the *Evening World* had acquitted itself admirably under the pressure of the war, gained several peacetime scoops, and produced stories worth reading when news was absent. Business manager Carlos Seitz sent Pulitzer a glowing report on Chapin's work, though he, too, noted the darker side of Chapin's character. "He is a keen, hard master and drives the men rather too hard I think although his ability is in the line of the thing at hand, I mean he is swift at grabbing stories and pushing them in as they come along." Pulitzer rewarded Chapin, Coates, and Duneka with alternating Saturdays off so that each editor had every third Saturday free unless an emergency occurred.[18]

On Thanksgiving 1899, Charles and Nellie Chapin were supping at the Hotel Savoy. At the time, the Savoy, along with Delmonico's, Rector's on Broadway, and Sherry's were among the few restaurants that catered to the rich and powerful of New York. The dining room was packed that night, and the air was stifling.

It was too much for Nellie, and she began to faint. Charles caught her before she slipped from her chair. The commotion attracted attention, and with the help of two waiters Charles lifted Nellie
in a chair and carried her from the room. Suzanne Warriner rose from a nearby table and accompanied the procession, insisting that Nellie be taken to her room in the hotel. There she was put in a bed, and cold compresses were applied. "While we waited for my wife to recover," said Chapin, "she told me that she was in mourning for her mother and sister who were lost on *La Bourgoyne*." Chapin, recognizing this was the elder daughter of Judge John F. Dillon, immediately told her how he had been the one to call her father after the sinking. Warriner filled him in on what had happened, explaining that the judge had collapsed after speaking with Chapin. The two talked into the night, long past midnight. Warriner insisted that Nellie stay for the remainder of the night and brought her back to Chapin the next day. After that, the Warriners became frequent dinner companions of the Chapins until Suzanne died in 1904.[19]

The year 1900 brought major changes in the *World* building, the first since the turmoil caused by Chamberlain's departure two years earlier. Several of Pulitzer's prized editors decided to leave. One joined the *New York Times*, another left for the *Chicago Tribune*, and Duneka resigned to join Harper & Row. William Van Benthuysen, editor of the Sunday *World*, was also ready to jump ship, but Pulitzer stemmed his departure with a long, all-expenses-paid vacation in California and a bonus. Before leaving on his trip, Van Benthuysen recommended that Chapin be given Duneka's position as managing editor of the *Evening World*. "He has both the general knowledge and preeminently the city capacity so that he would look after both the news ends faithfully and well."[20]

After two weeks of silence, Chapin couldn't take the wait any longer, and he went to see Coates. Chapin told Coates he should have the job. He had worked hard, coming in at 3:00 A.M. for the past year and a half, and it was only fair that he should be next in line for a promotion. Coates reminded him that Pulitzer had already given him a $10-a-week raise and that, certainly, his work was appreciated. Coates was honest about the latter point. "I am more convinced day by day that Chapin is a very valuable man," he wrote to Pulitzer after Chapin left his office. Pulitzer, however, selected Joseph Eakins, a sports editor, to fill Duneka's spot, and brought Florence White back from St. Louis to replenish his stable of trusted aides. Chapin showed his disappointment, but Van Benthuysen told Pulitzer, "he has taken it with fair philosophy."[21]

Money was certainly on Pulitzer's mind at this time. Profits had been falling, no doubt thanks to Hearst, and Pulitzer ordered his business manager, John Norris, to cut expenses. Several days later, Pulitzer had Chapin in for breakfast. The two had breakfasted before when Chapin had been selected to read the paper to the publisher. "I felt a keen delight while reading newspapers to him, he grasped everything so quickly and with such perfect understanding," said Chapin. "No matter what the topic might be, blind as he was, nothing need be elaborated or explained. He instinctively knew." On this occasion, Pulitzer asked what was new at the office. Chapin told him that he had fired a dozen reporters.

"Were there no good ones among them?" asked Pulitzer.

"Some very promising and in time might have developed into first-class men," said Chapin.

"Then, why fire them?"

"I was ordered to by Norris."

"But why fire men you considered worth keeping."

"What could I do but obey the order from Norris?"

Pulitzer frowned and compressed his lips, as he did on occasions when he was irritated.

"I know what I would have done had I been in your place," he said.

Chapin needed no further explanation. The next time Norris came by his shop ordering staffing cuts, Chapin refused. "Norris fumed and fussed and ripped and snorted, and even threatened, but I stood pat," said Chapin.[22]

Though he gave Chapin *carte blanche* to run the city desk of the *Evening World* as he saw fit, Pulitzer remained reluctant to give Chapin a higher management position. It was not, however, a reflection of either Pulitzer's or the office staff's appreciation of Chapin. Quite the contrary, the editors continued to report on Chapin's prodigious talent. Bradford Merrill, an editorial executive, wrote to Pulitzer that "Chapin is twice as valuable on city features, and half the ideas that Chapin gets he executes himself.

If a big story is being handled, by telephone, for instance, he is very apt to take it himself, write it, put a head on it, while another man would be summoning a reporter or shorthand man to the telephone." Several days after this memo, Chapin demonstrated his willingness to do just that. A report reached the paper that a man had shot himself and fallen over Niagara Falls because of his love for Lillian Russell, a famous English singer and actress who had made her home in New York and was frequently seen in the company of Diamond Jim Brady. Chapin immediately turned to his telephone, and in two minutes was interviewing Lillian Russell.[23]

"Poor fellow, perhaps he is better off," Russell told Chapin over the phone. She had never met the man, but explained he had been mailing her letters in French, regularly professing his undying love for her. "He called me his grand goddess and other such foolish titles and said that he continually saw my soul in a vision." Russell concluded that the letters, while odd, were harmless, but abruptly, just before Christmas, they stopped coming. Chapin thanked Russell and composed an inside-page story for that day's edition in his inimical style, deftly satirizing—almost cruelly—the spurned lover. "In the dawn of the world," wrote Chapin, "their souls had mingled like blended drops of dew. Through dim and forgotten cycles they had met and loved. And so it would continue until the world had ceased to be and eternal night had snuffed out the lamps of heaven."[24]

Coates, who watched Chapin carefully, was so impressed he sat down and wrote a memo to Pulitzer describing Chapin's willingness to descend from the dais on such a moment. "I mention this just to show his news instinct and brain activity," wrote Coates. "My admiration for his news sense and news abilities increase daily." The reports from Merrill, Coates, and Van Benthuysen all had the same effect on Pulitzer. Ironically, like a typecast actor, Chapin found that his unmatched skill as city editor, so well suited for the unusual demands of an evening paper, predestined him to be passed over for the plum jobs.[25]

Being back in New York, however, did have another reward. It afforded Chapin a chance to work on what he thought was his fiscally promising relationship with his great-uncle Sage. Certainly, Chapin made sure the *Evening World* took a new interest in the old financier. But it would take more than a few flattering mentions in the press to restore his standing with Sage. During the years Chapin had been away from New York, Sage had been the center of a series of highly publicized trials resulting from the bombing of his office, in which Chapin had unwittingly played a key role. William Laidlaw, the cashier whose unfortunate timing had brought him to Sage's office at the very moment Sage was holding the bomber Norcross at bay, was crippled by the blast. Sage had done nothing for the man. Sage was convicted in the court of public opinion and subsequently had to defend himself in a court of law for allegedly having used Laidlaw as a human shield. The former cashier sought, in the words of the *New York Times*, "to extract from the fat wallet of the aged financier the damage which he believes Mr. Sage should pay him." The trials, four in all, were heavily publicized, well-attended, embarrassing affairs, and taxing on the septuagenarian. Sage's life was made miserable in particular by Laidlaw's artful attorney, Joseph H. Choate, who also found time between these trials to persuade the U.S. Supreme Court to declare the nation's income tax unconstitutional.[26]

For Chapin, the trials would not be a subject he would dare bring up with his great-uncle. The famed exclusive interview he obtained with Sage following the bombing had been repeatedly used in court, and to Sage's distinct disadvantage. When brandished by Choate in court, the reporter for the *New York Times* said, Sage "eyed it as a defendant in a breach of promise suit might regard a gushing letter." It was a damning piece of evidence in Choate's capable hands. For two days in the 1894 trial, for instance, Choate used the article to go after Sage. He began by asking whether Sage had been interviewed by a *World* reporter.[27]

"Yes. The man who wrote it was a relative of mine—a grand-nephew," replied Sage.

"Did not the reporter call and find you on the lounge?"

"I don't remember where I was," said Sage.

"Then the article says: 'He looked as vigorous as ever.' Were you as vigorous as ever?"

"No, indeed."

"Then the reporter says: 'His face was clean-shaven. In fact, he had risen and shaved himself yesterday.' Didn't you tell the reporter you had shaved yourself?"

"I don't remember."[28]

The tussle continued between the men, but every memory lapse diminished Sage's defense. Going over the interview sentence by sentence, Choate forced Sage to retract his claims that he was injured by the blast, that he never took his eyes off the bomber, and other critical aspects of his prior testimony. Worse for Sage, Choate introduced the idea that Chapin was put on the payroll of the Missouri Pacific in order to keep him out of town. Cumulatively, the questions Choate proffered on the basis of the article, even one as to whether he had read the article, impugned Sage's veracity. "Mr. Sage said that it was true and wasn't true and that he had read it and hadn't read it," said the *New York Times.* "He at one time said that, when it was written, his hands were useless, while the story said that the day after the explosion Mr. Sage shaved himself." This constrained Mr. Choate to ask:

"How do you shave yourself, Mr. Sage—with your feet?"[29]

On that note, the court adjourned until the following day when "Mr. Chapin's unfortunate but ambitious interview with his uncle was taken up, and Mr. Sage fidgeted in his chair while the interrogator read about his keeping his eye on Norcross and vice versa." Once again, Choate hammered at Sage's inconsistencies about where each party stood in the office and about whether Sage knew that Norcross was mad and might detonate a bomb. "The next half-dozen questions based on the grand-nephew's interview, made Mr. Sage desperate in his endeavor to shirk all responsibility for it by inspiration or otherwise."

"I demand a categorical answer, just as Norcross did—'Yes' or 'No'—did you think you had a desperate man to deal with?" continued Choate. The judge ordered Sage to give a categorical answer.

"Yes, I did," said Sage.

"Now Mr. Sage, I am trying to read your secret thoughts, as your grand-nephew did. Didn't you think Norcross was insane enough to think you could satisfy his demand for $1,200,000?"

"I didn't think of it that way," said Sage. Frustrated, Choate tried another approach.

Once again quoting from Chapin's article, Choate reminded

Sage he had called Norcross a "lunatic" and "madman." He further pushed Sage to explain his sentiments when Laidlaw appeared.

"It was a relief to have Mr. Laidlaw come in?"

"I didn't say so."

"Was it a relief?

"Well, if Mr. Laidlaw had not come in, he would have been standing close to Norcross and would have been blown to pieces."

"So you consider Mr. Laidlaw is indebted to you for saving his life, instead of your being obliged to him in this respect."

"I certainly do—most decidedly."

At which point a loud "whew" was emitted by the audience, the judge's gavel rang out for order, and Choate said, "Well, that makes a pretty plain case of it."[30]

This was not an experience Sage would soon forget, likewise the role that his grand-nephew had played. But Sage had no children, and Chapin was eager to play the doting relative. "He liked to go about with me, for I had passes to everything that was worth while and it pleased him we could sit in a box at the opera or at any of the theaters and not have to pay," said Chapin of his notoriously penurious great-uncle. As Chapin's own fortune rose, he continued to entertain Sage. "Sometimes he would drive with me behind my team of fast horses, sometimes I drove with him behind his, and often we would meet out at the speedway and he would race his team against mine," said Chapin. "I took him for his first automobile ride. It tickled him so much that I think he would have been tempted to buy a car if my chauffeur hadn't told him how much gasoline was consumed in a drive of twenty-five miles."[31]

During their times together, Sage told Chapin, "You'll be a rich man some day." Once, when he repeated this remark several times, Chapin thought the old great-uncle was expecting a reply. "I said I hoped I would get more enjoyment out of riches than he did."

"I hope," said Sage, "you will get as much pleasure out of spending my money as I have had in accumulating it."[32]

A New Century

Chapin and the *Evening World* greeted the arrival of the twentieth century with a publicity stunt. Precisely at midnight on January 1, 1901, New York's acting mayor Randolph Guggenheimer gave the signal from his office across the street, and the monstrous presses in the *World* building roared to life, drawing miles of newsprint through their swirling cylinders. Within seconds they were spewing out copies of the *Evening World* embossed with the claim of being the first paper published on the American continent in the new century. A clean copy was carefully selected and handed to an awaiting messenger who jumped into a cab, dashed for a ferry that carried him across the Hudson River, and boarded a Washington-bound train. Six hours later (the train ran one-and-a-half hours late), he arrived in the nation's capital, where a reporter from the *World*'s Washington bureau escorted him and his precious cargo to the White House. Soon, it was hoped, President McKinley would sit at his breakfast table and read the first newspaper published in this new century, and it would be a copy of the *Evening World*. That was, as long as Randolph Hearst did not have his way. A copy of the *Evening Journal* with the headline "The Journal, The First Newspaper of this Century—McKinley" was encased in a beautiful silver box on the lap of Landgon Smith, who was already at the White House. He had beaten the *World* staffers by traveling on a train chartered by Hearst. Though he had reached the White House first, Smith had not made it past the anteroom to the executive offices. It seemed that McKinley's

staff was in no rush to deliver to the president a copy of a paper that made it a daily practice to criticize their boss. In fact, the
World men walked right past Smith and were cordially greeted by the doorkeeper, who had been instructed by the president's private secretary to let them in as soon as they arrived. The secretary took the paper, and within minutes it was with the president as he sat for breakfast. "When the *World* men left the White House," reported Van Benthuysen to Pulitzer the next day, "Mr. Langdon Smith still sat in solitary grandeur in the corridor, the rays of the morning sun lighting up the silver box upon his knees."[1]

The victory in the race was sweet, but pyrrhic because Hearst was winning where it counted the most. "The *Evening Journal* beat us at almost every point," said reporter Terhune. "Its circulation soared. Ours did not." A few days after the *Evening World*'s celebration of its New Year's caper, White reported to Pulitzer that the *Evening Journal* was now selling 425,000 copies a day, thirty-three percent more than the *Evening World*'s 324,200 circulation. "Nothing especially encouraging can be mentioned regarding the Evening Edition," he said. Nor was the Hearst assault showing any signs of letting up. Coates, the master of the oversized headline, had been stolen away and was now seen driving about in a $1,700 automobile. Pulitzer warned his top editors to keep an eye open for another raid. Watch Chapin, said Pulitzer as he left for Europe to buy paintings and tapestries for his new house. "Especially Chapin because I heard before I left that Grasp [Coates] was cultivating him and wanted him; I know and you know he put a very high value on C's ability, and with good reason."[2]

The fact that the staffs of both newspapers thought the president would be keen to receive newly minted copies of a New York newspaper was a reflection of Park Row's belief that it was the center of a universe of great importance. Indeed, these were intoxicating times for its inhabitants. The combined circulation of Senior and Junior now regularly topped a million copies a day. Every three months, the enterprise consumed a spruce forest as large as Central Park to supply the necessary paper and used enough lead type to set the New Testament 17,383 times. Technological advances were speeding the delivery of news, and photographs were adding to its immediacy. "Those of us newspaper

reporters in New York of the 1900s who were unwitting Bohemi-
ans lived in a sort of ecstasy of unreality, a sort of blissful dream,"
said *World* reporter Donald Henderson Clarke. "It was the Land
of Our Dreams, a fairyland of romance and high promise."[3]

The euphoria of the new century was also being celebrated in
Buffalo, New York, where the Pan-American Exposition opened
on May 1. Though it had been intended solely to recognize the
achievements of industry and culture in the Americas, it quickly
became a celebration of the twentieth century and its marvels.
President McKinley, unable to attend the opening because of his
wife's illness, finally made it in September. On September 5, 1901,
before an enthusiastic crowd of 50,000 fair goers, he extolled the
virtues of American prosperity and the technology on display at
the fair. "Out of this city may come not only greater commerce
and trade for us all," he said, "but more essential than these, relations of mutual respect, confidence and friendship, which will
deepen and endure." Some 300 miles away, Chapin squeezed Mc-
Kinley's speech into the corner of the last page of an edition
whose main story was about how baseball's New York Giants
were outclassed in the first game of a series with the Pittsburgh
Pirates at the Polo Grounds.

The next day, a Friday, Chapin decided to leave the office early
and enjoy one of that afternoon's doubleheader games between
the Giants and the Pirates. The Giants were last in their division.
The prospects that their pitching would hold off the Pirates's hitting remained slim. And it was hot. So Chapin changed his mind
on his way to the ballpark, which was at 157th Street, and instead
disembarked at the Hotel Majestic at 71st Street and Central Park
West, where he and Nellie had taken up residence. Escaping the
heat in his room, Chapin was soon fast asleep. When he awoke,
he found several notes had been slipped under the door saying
that the *Evening World* had called. The hotel did not yet have
telephones in the rooms, so he went downstairs to call the office.

The operator rang the number for the *Evening World* for
twenty minutes with no success.

"Busy," said the operator each time.

"Anything happened?" Chapin at last asked.

She shifted the gum in her mouth and with a languid drawl,
replied, "McKinley's shot."

Chapin was aghast. "The nation pulsating with horror and an editor sleeping his wits away because the day was warm!" he said. The operator finally got through to the *World* offices. An extra had already gone to press with an illustration of the assassin felling McKinley, and a monstrous-sized headline. There was nothing left to do, thought Chapin, except to have dinner, smoke a cigar, read the papers, and go to bed. "And that is what I did."[4]

Though Chapin's hotel did not have telephones in its rooms, which would have saved him the embarrassment of sleeping through McKinley's assassination, the new device was making itself regularly heard in the city room. At first, wood-encased phones labeled 1, 2, 3, and 4 were hung on the newsroom wall. Phones then were added to the city desk and eventually to those of reporters. Heralded by a ringing sound, news could instantly travel from any part of the five boroughs to Chapin's desk. Prior to the installation of the telephones, an editor had to await the arrival of copy boys delivering the first takes on a breaking story, and until a reporter had gathered all the facts, completed all the interviews, then traveled back to Park Row for the remainder. Sometimes, just when an editor signed off on the front page of an edition, a reporter would come running in, out of breath, with a breaking story. For a morning paper, this was not a major problem because its news stories usually developed over the course of the previous day, and the staff had the evening to assemble the paper. But, for an evening paper, publishing half a dozen editions, keeping up with the day's events could be a minute-by-minute affair. The cry of a newsie on the street hawking a breaking story ahead of the competition frequently generated an enormous spike in circulation.[5]

Before telephones, the story usually came into the newsroom as a fait accompli. The telephone gave Chapin greater command of the men in the field and, more importantly, greater power over shaping the paper's coverage. Although many newsmen considered the telephone a crutch for the lazy reporter, Chapin put this new technology to full use and, in so doing, created a new way to gather and write the news. He took the city map, drew a checkerboard pattern on it, and stationed a reporter in each of the squares, much like a police beat. "Each reporter," said Chapin, "was held responsible for all the news happening in the square to which he was assigned, and he was required to keep in communication with the office by telephone." Instead of wasting precious time traveling, the reporter would now call in all the details of the story, and a member of the office staff would write the story. To accomplish the latter, Chapin created a team of writers who remained in the office at all times. Soon these rewrite men, as they came to be called, were the new stars of Park Row and the heart of Chapin's news machine. It took Chapin five years to put together the right combination. When he did, it was unrivaled.[6]

The first of those who would eventually become part of the team was Martin Green, who had single-handedly beaten Chapin's crew in St. Louis during the tornado of 1896. In fact, his tornado story had caught the attention of a *Journal* editor, who brought Green to New York in August 1897, a year before Chapin himself was called back. Like Chapin, Green was intoxicated when he first saw Park Row. "The intangible odor of printers' ink, beer, whiskey, and delivery horses was overpowering and pleasant. The cries of newsboys were as music to my ears," Green recalled. "I was sure I had found the spot where I was to spend the rest of my life." Since taking over the city desk, Chapin had worked on Green and finally, in 1902, lured him onto the staff of the *Evening World*. Others had wanted Green. Within a few months, the *Herald* tried to grab him, and Chapin had to raise his salary to $60 a week to weaken the allure of the *Herald*'s $75 offer. In justifying the increase, Bradford Merrill told Pulitzer that Green was "said to be one of the best writers on the staff." Although Pulitzer might have agreed with everyone's estimation of Green's talent, he remained unconvinced of Chapin's approach. But as Junior continued to contribute more than its share to the combined profits of the papers, Chapin's authority to build his staff was unchecked.[7]

Around this time, an office boy began bringing Chapin a list of story ideas submitted by a young woman who came to the *World* building every day. Twenty-seven-year-old Zona Gale had left her native Wisconsin with aspirations of landing a newspaper job on Park Row. With some limited experience on a Milwaukee newspaper, Gale pitched Chapin ideas such as interviewing an old industrialist on how he earned his first 100 dollars, or a great lawyer on his first case. She hoped Chapin would check off a story that appealed to him and let her have a chance at writing it. Though the *Evening World* was a man's world, Chapin suc-

cumbed to Gale's approach. Soon he was smitten with his new "general reporter." Gale could weave a good story from any assignment he gave her, including the *Evening World*'s most valuable fare—crime stories. In February 1901, for instance, Chapin dispatched Gale to Arlington, New Jersey, three days after the town's Episcopal minister was gunned down in the streets by a parish member who thought his wife had paid the good reverend some inappropriate attention. The town was swarming with reporters and detectives. Gale had to conduct her research while betraying as little as possible that she was connected with a newspaper. She put her first dispatch—seventeen pages long—on the morning train to New York, addressing the envelope only with Chapin's name and the office address, purposely leaving off "Evening World." Gale went on working, "scared to death," she said, "for fear they couldn't use a word I had done and overwhelmed with the responsibility of living up to the $25 they have given me for expenses." At three-thirty in the afternoon, she went to a newsstand and picked up a copy of the *Evening World*. Chapin had splashed her story across the front page. "Secrets Laid Bare, First story of the Arlington case. *Evening World*'s special staff correspondent, who has been for several days studying the case from sources of undoubted authority, sends report of true state of affairs." Gale was ecstatic. "I tore across to the station—the only safe place to be seen with a paper—and read it, and whooped with glee."[8]

Chapin hired other women, but none would be as much favored as Gale. Even at the height of his dictatorial powers, he admitted, he could never be harsh with her. She had a habit of coming in late, even though everyone knew of Chapin's reputation for keeping an eye on the clock. "I scolded her one morning, but the next morning she came much later. I asked her the reason and she began to cry. 'Run along, child,' I said to her, 'they don't pay me enough salary to make girls cry.'"[9]

The telephones that permitted Chapin to re-deploy his staff in his new beat system also made it possible for readers to call in with news tips. From bank presidents to florists, city dwellers within reach of a phone began developing the habit of calling the newspaper when they witnessed a newsworthy occurrence, or even when it wasn't so newsworthy. Chapin got calls about runaway carriages, fatal automobile crashes on Riverside Drive, and the death of a financier (the household was buying flowers). He even received a call from a prominent corporate attorney who saw a man leap from the skyscraper across the street from his office. Shortly before 9:00 A.M. on January 8, 1902, for instance, H. N. Cary, a former *Evening World* reporter and now an editor with *Appletons' Journal*, reached Chapin by phone. He had just crawled out of a train wreck in a tunnel leading to Grand Central Station and had rushed to the phone to alert Chapin of the disaster. Chapin's crew lived for moments such as this. He dispatched whatever reporters he had on hand, and his rewrite crew prepared for the onslaught. Soon his men in the field were reporting the horror. Passengers were trapped under the engine, and some were being roasted by escaping steam. The rewrite men cranked out the story in staccato bursts of fact-packed, almost telegraphic prose, a signature style of the *Evening World* in such moments. "In the forward coaches a fire started. The passengers frightened past understanding, streamed into the tunnel and stood calling for help. . . . Down the sides of the tunnel the firemen let ladders and streams of hose. The fire was extinguished and the work of rescue begun. It was sickeningly slow."[10]

The *Evening Journal* was caught flatfooted. Manager Seitz gleefully wrote Pulitzer the next morning that Hearst was left with a "dozen lines in fudge" while the *Evening World* led with a double-column story. "Evening people—Eakins and Chapin—did extremely well on the railway accident. I think their story was better than that in today's morning paper." As usual, the pleasure of success was also financial. Chapin received a $5-a-week raise. But Chapin's winning method still did not sit well with Pulitzer. He told White, who had been brought back from St. Louis to replace business manager John Norris, of his displeasure. "He remarked we do not need high-priced writers to take stories from the telephone and re-write them. That is unnecessary and even wrong; for every embellishment added by the writer is likely to be a liberty taken with the facts."[11]

In March 1902, Nellie left for Bermuda. Charles joined her in late April. That summer, they fled the heat of the city for the

Thousand Islands in northern New York after July 4. Nellie, who was in her late forties, had been in poor health, and this concerned Charles. At the end of the summer, he took it up with Merrill, who had Pulitzer's ear. Chapin explained that she was "passing through a critical period of life and again had to be sent South." He asked Merrill if he could have an advance on his December bonus. Two years earlier, a similar request had been turned down, but this time management's attitude was different. "It seemed to me wise to seize the opportunity to renew his contract with him for another year," Merrill wrote Pulitzer. He accomplished this by adding $10 a week to Chapin's pay and $100 to his annual bonus. Both Seitz and White were in agreement about Chapin's worth. "Indeed, everyone who has had anything to do with Junior has expressed the same opinion about his extraordinary news instinct, industry, and nervous energy. He is the only high-priced man needed on the paper except the editor." They also were keenly aware that Junior was back in the black with a $200,000 profit that year. Aside from using bonuses to retain Chapin, Pulitzer also dangled them in front of him as motivation, at one point promising a $10,000 bonus should Junior's circulation increase by 100,000. For Chapin, these bonuses were becoming increasingly important because of his growing propensity to live beyond his means.[12]

In April 1903, Chapin made another attempt to increase his power. The occasion was the departure of Eakins, the sports editor who had taken over Duneka's job. Chapin went to White and told him, in no uncertain terms, that he ought to "be given a show," that he would not submit to any more "lunkheads" being forced on him, that he was ready to quit and go to the opposition. "I disputed the fact with him that he had suffered from any serious interference from the men who had come in there," said White. But Chapin insisted he be given a chance to talk directly to Pulitzer. White then wrote to Pulitzer saying that he ought to grant him an interview, adding, "He said he was afraid that if he saw Mr. Andes [Pulitzer], he would get a lot of assurances that everything was all right, get patted on the back, but that nothing 'would happen.'" Pulitzer agreed to talk with Chapin. White prepped Pulitzer for the interview. "Here are some facts with which to allay any persecution mania that might develop in Saturday's interview with Pinch [Chapin]," he wrote to Pulitzer. First, Chapin does not work as many hours as he claims. Second, if one considers his sicknesses, out-of-town trips, and vacations, he has

been away from the office on full pay more than anyone else on the eleventh floor. Third, his salary now stands at $111.50 a week, and he has received four raises in three years. Fourth, unlike all other city editors, he reserves for himself all the perks of the office, such as free theater tickets. Fifth, the staff he surrounds himself with is entirely handpicked by him and retained with lavish salaries. "I mention these facts as answer to any dissatisfaction that Pinch might express," concluded White. "His present position and swing is unduplicated in any office in New York, a fact that I think he really recognizes." But at the end of his indictment-like memo, White begrudgingly admitted, "His energy along the line of the spontaneous news, and the fact that he sticks at his desk with unrelaxed energy throughout the day, constitute his capital."[13]

On April 10, 1903, Pulitzer's fifty-sixth birthday, White had a present for the publisher. He could scratch the interview with Chapin off his calendar. Instead, they would suggest that Chapin put his new ideas for managing the paper to the test while Van Benthuysen—who was taking Eakins's place—was on vacation. Not to be put off easily, Chapin began his campaign by writing to Pulitzer. "I simply ask that you do not, for a time at least, assign a managing editor to the *Evening World*," Chapin wrote. "Let me run the shop with our organization to the best of my ability until I demonstrate to your entire satisfaction that I am either capable of getting along without a superior editor's guidance or interference—or—that I am unfit except under the supervision of a more masterly mind." Chapin was not seeking Eakins's job; instead, he wanted to run the *Evening World* from the city desk. He would agree to remain under White and receive Pulitzer's instructions through White. The only other change he would seek would be a few more "moderately priced" reporters.[14]

In the ensuing days, Pulitzer received several other reports from Chapin about his management of the *Evening World*, the hours he kept, the minor news items he cultivated into bell-ringing stories, such as the two-line police report on a woman and her children fighting off a rabid dog in their apartment, or major stories, such as the "Man in Barrel Was Tortured then Murdered" article, complete with photographs of the dead man, the instruments of his torment, and his crucifix. "With the exception of the editorial and magazine pages—with which I am told I have nothing to do—there is not an illustration nor an article, excepting minor news, that I did not personally direct." Chapin assumed he would not get his interview with Pulitzer and told Seitz as much. Chapin also asked if Pulitzer had been "put out" by his letters. "I said that I knew Mr. Andes appreciated Pinch's work but that the request that Pinch had made was doubtless troublesome, as it practically meant ousting Van Ben." Chapin, in a rare act of consideration, told Seitz that if "his ambition meant a displacement of Van Ben, he would withdraw the request for the interview and also the letter he had written." Chapin's campaign ended.[15]

Thwarted, Chapin returned to the duties of his desk. He published an interview with his great-aunt Olivia Sage, who was pleased that a smoking parlor and tearoom for women had been closed. "I am glad," said Sage. "I had heard some comment when the *Evening World* published the story of the start of the place that the publication would only increase its popularity, and the remark was made that the place would die if let alone. But I think the paper did a good act in making the facts public. That's what killed it."[16]

He found time to renew old Windy City acquaintances. In April 1904, members of the New York press corps who had once worked in Chicago gathered for dinner at the Republican Club. Chapin was not alone among the Chicago alumni to have met with considerable success. Melville Stone, whom Chapin had beaten in the chase after McGarigle in 1887, was now general manager of the Associated Press. He presided over the evening's festivities. Robert C. Clowry was now manager of Western Union, and Charles S. Diehl was preparing to buy a newspaper in San Antonio, Texas.[17]

Time for frivolity, however, was short-lived. Like most editors, Chapin was soon preoccupied with a raft of scandalous, tragic, and generally first-rate news stories. Early in the morning of June 4, 1904, a bookie named "Caesar" Young was found dead in a hansom cab on West Broadway. Sitting in the cab was the beautiful, petite Nan Patterson, considered a *Floradora* girl for having had a role in the newest theatrical sensation in New York. The gun that had slain Young was in his jacket pocket, still warm. Patterson

claimed Young had committed suicide. When reporters learned that she was Young's mistress, that he was preparing to set sail for Europe with his wife when he died, and that he had spent evenings with Patterson in Turkish baths, the story seemed to be an inexhaustible source of reader-grabbing copy. To Patterson's defense came Abraham Levy, one of the city's most noted criminal lawyers, whose offices, conveniently enough, were in the *World* building. No lawyer could ignore the court of public opinion now shaped by the press lords of Park Row. Abe Levy, as the newspapers preferred to call him, was a favorite of reporters. "The mighty Abe Levy," said the normally truculent Alexander Woolcott at the *Times*, is "the most adroit and zestful practitioner of the criminal law in the country." The century's first great murder trial was off to a great start.[18]

Eleven days later, on the morning of Wednesday, June 15, 1904, the telephone on Martin Green's desk rang, the wall phones having been exchanged for desk models. "There is a boat burning up here on the East River," said the caller.

"Where are you?" asked Green

"In an office overlooking the river at 137th. The boat is downstream from me at about 125th Street, coming north."

Green cupped the mouthpiece and yelled across the room to Chapin. "There's a boat burning in the East River, at about 125th Street."

Removing his hand from the phone, Green went back to his caller.

"What's her name?" he asked.

"I can't make it out . . . She's a sidewheeler. I can see women and children running madly about the upper and lower decks."

"Try to make out her name. It should be forward on the pilot house. Watch for it," pleaded Green.

"I will, but the smoke is getting thicker. Wait a minute; the breeze is shifting. I got it. The first word is G E N. . . ." The smoke, however, blocked the remainder of the name. The caller was getting more frantic. "Good God! Flames are bursting from the upper cabins. Women and children are climbing on deck chairs and beckoning to the shore. . . . A woman with her child in her arms has just jumped overboard. . . . A girl in a blue dress struck the hood of the paddle wheel, slipped off and has gone under the blade." As Green wrote everything down furiously, it became clear to everyone in the city room that the carnage was unmatched by any other New York disaster.

"Slocum, General Slocum," yelled the caller. "S L O C U M. That's her name."

Again, Green cupped his phone and shouted the name to Chapin. A check of listings of marine vessels revealed the *Slocum* to be an excursion boat. It had been loaded that day, they soon learned, with 1,700 parishioners of St. Mark's Lutheran Church on the Lower East Side. The group, almost entirely women and children, as the men were at work, was heading to its annual picnic at Locust Grove on Long Island. Chapin dispatched two reporters to St. Marks and anyone else in the room uptown toward the burning wreck. One reporter, at Chapin's suggestion, called Eugene F. Moran, who owned the Moran Towing Corporation. When the reporter got through, Moran already knew about the blazing ship. "Can you get us up there in a tug?" asked the reporter.

"Take the El, it's faster," replied Moran.

Green, meanwhile, remained on the phone with his caller.

"Why doesn't the captain put her ashore?" Green yelled.

"God knows. He is still holding to midstream. . . . Women and children are now going over the rail by the dozens. . . . The ship is veering toward the Bronx shore in the 130s. She is going in. . . . Smoke and flames envelop her. God, man, I can't stand any more. I'm sick at the stomach. You'll have to get along now without me. I'm all in. Goodbye."[19]

The line went dead. Within minutes, Green was back on the phone as the legmen Chapin had dispatched called in their reports. For hours, Green sat transforming the dispatches into copy that Chapin then rushed to composition. It wasn't long before the first of a stream of extras was on the street. One person who picked up a copy was William Henry Irwin, a reporter arriving for his first day of work on the *Sun*. He was lunching in the dining car of a train coming in from Chicago when a boy came into the car, calling an extra. Upon getting off the train, Irwin quickly

made his way to the *Sun*'s dingy newsroom adjacent to the *World*. "This seems like a very big story and I thought you might be needing me; so I've come straight from the train," Irwin said to
Chester A. Lord, the managing editor.

"In other words the war horse smells the battle from afar," replied Lord. "Thank you for reporting. But Denison is handling this," referring to Lindsey Denison, who was Green's rival at the *Sun*. He said a little more about the paper's plans, and then his voice choked up. "This was the only disaster I ever covered where hard-boiled newspapermen burst into tears on the job," said Irwin. The city editor, George Mallon, told him he could stick around if he wished. Something might come up for which he would be needed. At six o'clock, Denison returned. He recognized Irwin, whom he had met out West, and after a few words went to work assembling the story.

Although all the papers were reporting the *Slocum* disaster after the *Evening World* broke the story, the day remained a triumph for Chapin late into the night. He paced the newsroom humming a tune and gloating over every new fact, vignette, or statistic that came in by phone. His staff, with its head start on the rest of Park Row, had the story first and tenaciously built its lead into the best coverage. As the twelfth edition went to press at 7:30 P.M., it was clear that the *Evening World* had scored one of Park Row's best scoops. The next morning, Merrill wrote to Pulitzer that not only did Junior beat Geranium [Hearst's *Journal*], but also Senior, whose coverage lacked "unity, pathos, and wholeness."[20]

The *Slocum* was a victory for Chapin, for his new methods, and for his hand-picked staff. Over time, Chapin had found ways to rid himself of the reporters who had been at the *Evening World* when he arrived and replace them with ones from outside, including many from St. Louis. "Nearly all of them [were] crackerjack reporters and rewrite men," said Terhune. But, for an old hand like Terhune, these changes created a cultural void in the city room. "They were good fellows. They were civil to me, as was I to them. But I let them alone, outside office hours." Part of what differentiated Chapin's men from others was their tolerance of his cruelty, tempered only by an occasional kindness. "He drove his men, mercilessly, in true Simon Legree fashion," said Terhune. "They hated him. But he got tremendous work out of them. He knew they detested him, and he seemed to glory in his power to earn their hatred." But they invariably stayed, even when Hearst dangled better money before them. They may have hated Chapin, but they loved working for him.

Terhune hated Chapin, too, and had avoided both being fired and being under his rule for seven years by moving into the editorial department. But in February 1905, an office reorganization put him back in the city room. Oddly, Chapin treated him kindly, even when Terhune committed the unforgivable crime of being late to work. After three months, Terhune was rescued and sent back to the editorial staff.

"Going back to your old desk, hey?" said Chapin when Terhune approached his dais. "I'm glad, for your sake. I know you haven't been happy out here. But I've tried to make it as pleasant for you as I knew how. Your job with me is waiting for you, any time you want it again."

"I don't know what the game is," said a bewildered Terhune. "But you've played it better than I have, whatever it may be. You've been after my scalp for six years. Then when you got it, you left it on my head. What's the idea? You don't like me any more than I like you. Yet you've given me something better than a square deal this past three months. You've had plenty of chances to fire me. Why didn't you?"

Chapin paused and grinned cryptically. "Don't talk nonsense. I like you and I like your work. I always did."

"That was all I could get out of him, though both of us knew he was lying," said Terhune later.[21]

Chapin was now firmly ensconced at the *Evening World*, which was to his benefit. But it worried Pulitzer that the paper's current success, especially the financial one, would end if Chapin left. To thwart that possibility, the publisher offered Chapin a contract for $6,760, the same pay as Frank I. Cobb, Pulitzer's golden boy who wrote the morning editorials. In return, Chapin had to agree not to work for any other New York newspaper until after 1907. The contract was checked by Pulitzer's legal team, which believed the non-compete clause would "hold him" should he leave the paper. The money, however, was not all that held Chapin to his desk. He knew that Coates was earning three times as much as Chapin working for Hearst and that he, too, could profit from a move. But Chapin had chosen his side on Park Row. He loved both Pulitzer and the fiefdom he was given. Even if given the chance, he wouldn't renounce either.[22]

His staff, and thus its conductor, was beginning to be noticed. Large posters were plastered throughout the boroughs of Manhattan and Brooklyn proclaiming that Green's articles appeared exclusively in the *Evening World.* The staff's fame made it easier for Chapin to recruit. "What inducement the *Evening World* management offered to 'Billy' Willis to induce him to leave the *Sun* where for years he was a star man, is one of the things which causes newspaper men on Park Row to ponder over, when they have nothing else to do," said the *Journalist* in reporting Chapin's latest hire.[23]

And, as if there were no such thing as too much of a good idea, in February 1905, Chapin again trotted out his series featuring the newspaper reporter exploring the economic underside of metropolitan life. This time, the idea was easily summed up in the headline, "Where Can a Girl Alone in New York Find Assistance." Chapin assigned reporter Emmeline Pendennis to assume the role of a stranger in New York. She was to take the name "Helen King" and begin her investigation by asking women at Grand Central Station for help, claiming that her bags and purse, containing all her money, had been lost, and that she knew no one in the city. Her reports, which ran for nearly two weeks, detailed at great length the kinds of services and shelters that were open to single women in New York and invited other women to tell the *Evening World* of their similar experiences. This was the third time Chapin had used a newspaper to explore this theme of female destitution. It was, obviously, a subject close to home. He had seen what happened to his mother when his father left home. "A man in a similar situation can get along almost any way; but a girl, for whom one demands a certain standard of environment, what is she to do?" he asked.[24]

In late spring 1905, Charles and Nellie set off on a grand tour of Europe by motorcar. The hundreds of steamships now routinely crossing the ocean made the centuries-old habit of English aristocrats the new passion of Americans of means. In particular, the automobile was inaugurating a new era of travel. In fact, that same year, a ride called "Touring Europe by Automobile" replaced the "Fall of Pompeii" on the west promenade of Coney Island's Dreamland. Americans arriving by the droves on the continent jumped into rented Panhards, Peugeots, and Renaults and rushed about the countryside in a whirlwind of culturally edifying tourism. "The motor-car has restored the romance of travel," declared novelist Edith Wharton, who passed down many of the same roads as the Chapins a year later in her own Panhard. "Freeing us from all the compulsions and contacts of the railway," she wrote of car travel, "the bondage to fixed hours and the beaten track, the approach to each town through the area of ugliness and desolation created by the railway itself, it has given us back the wonder, the adventure and the novelty which enlivened the way of our posting grandparents."[25]

The Chapins knocked about from chateau to chateau in the Loire Valley and lingered so long on the Riviera that they abandoned their plans of going to Italy. France of this period—known as "la belle époque"—was immensely welcoming and fascinating to Americans. Chapin recalled "making the trip so slowly and with such frequent stops that I missed nothing and enjoyed it all as I have never enjoyed a similar outing." His long absence was, however, undermining his claim of indispensability in New York. The paper was getting along fine without him, a fact that did not escape White's attention. "McLaughlin and Randall have done good work during Pinch's absence, and have in fact shown that his loss would not be as great as we had previously estimated," White told Pulitzer. Further, Seitz had settled two libel suits brought against the *Evening World* for $500. Eager to please Pulitzer with his own work, Seitz told him, "These two suits due to one of Chapin's reckless mistakes might easily have cost $10,000 if allowed to go on." On the other hand, Chapin was traveling with the confidence that any chatter among the editors in New York could not void the two-year contract he had signed before departing on his European *séjour*.[26]

In late June, the Chapins alighted in London after completing a similar motoring trip around the British countryside and its lavish estates. They spent a Sunday with Edith Helena, a famed opera singer who was performing at the Grand Opera at Covent Gardens and who was married to a former *World* staffer. Then they packed and readied for their return to New York. Shortly before midnight, on the eve of their departure, Pulitzer arrived in London from Carlsbad, Germany. Told that Chapin was still in London, he immediately sent word for him to cancel his passage home and come to lunch the next day. Chapin, of course, complied.[27]

Pulitzer had come to London to pose for John Singer Sargent, whose portraits were becoming a prized commodity among the rich and famous. By the end of Sargent's career, other prominent Americans, such as Woodrow Wilson, Theodore Roosevelt, John D. Rockefeller, and Henry James, also would be immortalized by Sargent. Over lunch, Chapin told Pulitzer all about his trip in France and England, and the publisher insisted that he stay in London at least another week. He urged Chapin to visit the House of Commons and the National Portrait Gallery. Again, there would be no thought of disobeying an edict from Andes. Chapin headed off to be a tourist, and Pulitzer to pose at Sargent's studio on Tite Street, an enclave of American painters and writers. At the studio, Pulitzer asked Sargent how he would proceed. "I paint what I see," said Sargent to the now virtually blind publisher. "Sometimes it makes a good portrait; so much the better for the sitter. Sometimes it does not; so much the worse for the both of us. But I don't dig beneath the surface for things that don't appear before my eyes." Over the next days, Pulitzer rose each morning and went for a horseback ride through Hyde Park with his secretary before going to Sargent's studio, and Chapin continued his explorations of London.[28]

On the third day, Chapin joined Pulitzer on a carriage ride through the park and reported on what he had seen. "What interested him most was the description I gave of the wonderful paintings in the portrait gallery," said Chapin. He had spent almost an entire day in the famous museum, roaming from room to room, examining the portraits of the nation's royalty and historic figures. "When I finished tears were flowing down his cheeks," said Chapin.

"What wouldn't I give to see what you saw," Pulitzer blurted out, then sank back in silence into the cushions of the carriage.

A few days later, Charles and Nellie boarded the *Lucania*, a luxurious Cunard steamship with a knife-like bow that had plied the Liverpool–New York run for a dozen years, and set off for

New York. They reached the city on July 8, 1905, and Chapin returned to work.

Scanning the newspapers, Chapin found that Nan Patterson's second trial had ended in another hung jury, and she would go free, another considerable victory for his old friend Levy. The remaining news that summer continued to be dominated by the peace conference in Portsmouth, New Hampshire, to which President Theodore Roosevelt had brought negotiators from Russia and Japan in hopes of ending their war and preserving his open-door policy toward China. The conference had promised to be a great press event during a slow summer, and most of the papers had sent their heavy-hitters to New Hampshire. Chapin's *Evening World* selected Samuel Blythe, its Washington correspondent, for the job. The negotiators, however, remained aloof from the gaggle of reporters, and the editors were struggling to find any copy worth printing in the dispatches from their expensive pool of writers. That was, except for Chapin's competitor, the *Evening Sun*. It was running an immensely popular daily column, "Making Peace at Portsmouth" by Irvin Cobb, a low-paid neophyte reporter whose drawl betrayed his recent emigration from Paducah, Kentucky. Cobb, who knew he couldn't compete with the famous correspondents, stayed clear of covering what was—or was not—happening in the negotiating rooms and instead took to describing the sartorial styles of the delegates and the prodigious efforts at feeding these out-of-place foreigners. It all made for terrific reading. "All of us Washington correspondents rushed up there, but we could not find an earthly thing to write about," said the *Evening World*'s Blythe. "But that made no difference to the Paducah boy; he wrote it anyway. He scooped the life out of all of us."[29]

The coup did not escape the attention of Chapin, and upon Cobb's return to New York, he found one of Chapin's famous "come around and talk" letters among the stack of job offers. Ironically, Cobb had called on the *Evening World* first when he arrived in New York the year before. An editor had sent a recommendation to an old friend on the staff before Cobb arrived, but there were no vacancies. It was the same tale at each paper. His success in Kentucky and Ohio seemed to matter little in New York, which regarded such places as backwaters. At last, ready to give up, he mailed all the Park Row editors a flippant letter threatening that this would be their last chance to hire him. If you don't hire me, he wrote, "your whole life hereafter will be one vast surging regret." The next day when he called on the *Evening Sun,* the editor, waiving the letter in the air, told Cobb, "If you've got half as much ability as you have gall, consider yourself hired."[30] Now, following his triumph in Portsmouth, Cobb had five or six offers from the editors who were feeling the regret he had promised in his fatuous letter.

At the *Evening World,* Cobb this time found himself being wooed by its city editor. Chapin prevailed over Cobb's other suitors by promising to double his salary to $60 a week. Money aside, the two also found they had much in common in their reporting pasts. They shared, among other things, journalism experience outside the insular world of Park Row and encounters with the celebrated Joseph Medill of Chicago. From their first meeting, Chapin took a liking to Cobb and considered him "one of the cleverest [men] I ever knew." As a newspaperman, Chapin quipped, Cobb was "worth his weight in gold, and he weighs something under a ton."[31]

A Grand Life

In April 1906, the same month that an earthquake devastated San Francisco, Chapin became enmeshed in disaster relief of a different sort involving the Pulitzer family. Pulitzer had "yanked" his son, Joseph, out of Harvard University after learning he had cut classes thirty-seven times. He decided that Joe's lessons would be better learned in a newsroom and that his new teacher would be none other than Chapin. Word of Chapin's new duties came to him by telephone. For the minions of the Pulitzer empire, the new technology now meant that "Andes's" orders no longer arrived solely in the form of a cryptically coded telegram. "I am sailing for Europe in the morning, and I am sending Joe down to work under you," announced Pulitzer when he reached Chapin. The boss's son underfoot would be a challenge Chapin had never before faced. In fact, over the years, Chapin had increasingly been given free reign to rule his roost almost without any meddling from the publisher. "He never troubled himself about the Evening," said Chapin. Instead, the publisher centered his attention on the morning edition. "The Morning was Pulitzer's pet."[1]

Though many considered the *Evening World* the black sheep of the Pulitzer papers, Pulitzer was not condemning his son to purgatory. Quite the contrary. He was at his wit's end with Joe and thought time spent with Chapin, whom he held in high esteem, might be the answer. Joe was smart and talented when it came to writing, and he loved journalism. But he had been a failure at St. Mark's School, an exclusive boarding school in New

England, and now at Harvard. "I know you know how to handle young men," said the elder Pulitzer to Chapin, "and I wish you to do the same with him that you do with them."

"Treat him exactly as you would any other beginner and don't hesitate to discipline him should he need it," he urged. "There is to be no partiality shown because he is my son. Do you quite understand?"

"I think so," replied Chapin.

"Promise me you will do as I ask."

"Your instructions will be carried out."[2]

Chapin's nervous reticence reflected his veneration of Pulitzer. "To me he was always kind, courteous, generous, and indulgent, mild in criticizing, and almost prodigal when praising my efforts," said Chapin. "I loved Joseph Pulitzer."[3]

Young Joe arrived in the city room early one morning in late April. "He appeared to be enthusiastic and eager," said Chapin. From the other side of the desk, however, Joe saw the same fearful vision that appeared before most reporters when they stood before the dais on which the city desk was perched. The eyes that stared back at him were like disks of polished flint, deeply set in a gray, stern face. His expressionless mouth was more like a slash set beneath a close-clipped, gray mustache. Grayness permeated all of Chapin's features. His skin, observed Cobb, possessed "the color of wet wood ashes, as though overlain by some strange patina." But then, almost as if he were one of the hand-tinted tintypes of the era, the portrait in gray was spattered by a stroke of color from the bright crimson or purple tie projecting from the narrow opening of his starched high collar. In his hand, invariably, was a mangled, soggy, smoking cigar. Meeting Chapin was not an inconsequential affair.[4]

By this time, Chapin's reputation preceded any encounter. He was certainly the most-talked-about editor in New York. "Chapin was an unequaled city editor," said Terhune. His management style was notoriously harsh, and his frequent dismissals of reporters spawned tales of the glee he took in sending packing those who didn't live up to his expectations. There was never any question regarding one's standing with Chapin. He was not one to cushion the blow. One reporter, departing on vacation, stopped by the city desk, assuming he would be told to have a good time.

"You're leaving on your own vacation?"

"Yes, Mr. Chapin."

"Well, I just want to tell you that if, on your return, your work doesn't materially improve, the *Evening World* will have to dispense with your services. That's all. . . . Have a good time."

In fact, for some reporters, the only option was to beat Chapin to the punch by resigning before the ax fell. Veteran Clarke remembered how, one day, a reporter (whose name he had forgotten) picked up a chair and smashed it to bits against a steel column in the city room. Chapin looked up from his desk as the reporter destroyed a second chair in the same manner.

"'Just what do you think you're doing, Mr. So-and-so?' Chapin asked in his peculiar voice—a blend of snarl, whine, and nasal modulation.

'Resigning, God damn it, resigning,' Chair Wrecker replied, shattering a third chair."[5]

One reporter, who feuded with Chapin continuously, obtained a literary revenge against his taskmaster. John Henry Goldfrap, a talented member of the staff, wrote juvenile dime novels on the side. Chapin frequently suspended Goldfrap without pay for playing hooky or arriving to work on a schedule of his own making. The reporter, however, got even as a novelist, concocting a secret, horrible-smelling poisonous compound named "Chapinite" that he included in his books.[6]

The only kindness Chapin ever displayed toward any weakness in a staff member was when it involved drinking. For instance, one reporter he brought to New York in 1903 from the *Post-Dispatch* was sent on an out-of-town assignment that he failed to write because he fell into a week-long drinking binge. Chapin reinstated him a few weeks later. This leniency may have been because he recognized the same weakness in himself. From every account, Chapin was a ceaseless consumer of pies, ice cream, cakes, doughnuts, sticky nut bars, pickled cherries, canned peaches, and intensely sweet coffee, the not-too-infrequent diet of a recovered alcoholic. In fact, Chapin confided once to a friend that he had been a heavy drinker when a barnstorming actor in the 1870s and a reporter in Chicago, and hinted to another friend that he had renounced drinking in St. Louis. He further told Terhune, "If I can leave it alone, you fellows can. God knows I want it just as bad as you do."[7]

This must have created a singular tension in Chapin, because drinking was so much a part of the news culture that it was done openly at desks. "When I went to work on the *Evening World*, practically every man there drank more or less; many more," said Terhune. "Copyreaders drank beer or highballs—and sometimes champagne—as they edited stories and wrote headlines," said Clarke. "Newspaper reporters often sent up to the *World* restaurant in the dome of the building for liquid inspiration—as I did later myself." For those on the night shift who preferred ale, one could pick up a lidded tin pail holding 64 ounces at Hesse's All Night Saloon before coming on duty. Reporters also gathered continuously at Perry's Hole in the Wall on the left side of the lobby. It was a small three-sided room, lined with shelves. The shelves contained an endless variety of whiskeys. Old Doc, as the barman was known, would pour a customer a shot and then, when the glass was drained, refill it from a large bottle of orange juice. "To the writer that is a hallowed spot. Or was," recalled reporter Barry Faris. "Real truths came out there after a couple of 'shots' with an orange juice chaser." By the time young Joe Pulitzer appeared at the *Evening World*, Chapin had curtailed most of the visible drinking.[8]

At first, Chapin assigned Joe to work with Bob Wilkes, a veteran reporter who covered the criminal courts. For two consecutive mornings, all seemed well. On the third morning, Joe arrived more than an hour late. "The butler neglected to call me," he said by way of explanation. Chapin, displaying uncommon restraint, explained that reporters don't usually depend on butlers to be roused in the morning, and suggested that purchasing an alarm clock might advance his career. "The alarm clock did the business and Joe got down on time for almost a week," said Chapin. Then he didn't show up at all. This time, the culprit was a dentist appointment and an afternoon baseball game. Chapin's patience—if he could be said to have any—was being severely tested. Normally, he would have fired without compunction a reporter who did this. But this was Pulitzer's son. So, instead, Chapin tried another tack. "We had a serious talk about it and I tried to impress upon his youthful mind that every member of the staff was expected to obey the rules of the office, one of the rules being that no one should be absent from duty unless he were ill or had been excused," he said. Alfred Butes, a longtime private secretary to Pulitzer, reported the conversation to Joe's father. "Chapin gave him a vigorous calling down, concluding with the remark that Joe was going to be held to his work and his hours 'even though it costs me your friendship and my place.'" For a while, Joe watched the clock more carefully and was assigned to work with Peter Barlow, another reporter with considerable experience. "Chapin tells me the boy has developed more in a few weeks than could be expected from an ordinary young reporter, just from college, with the spur of necessity behind him, in as many months," Butes reported to the elder Pulitzer. "His power of observation and writing have both improved." Barlow gave Joe a tip that he had heard a song called "Damn, Damn, Damn the Filipinos" had become a popular ditty down at the Navy Yard (from which the ill-fated U.S.S. Maine had been launched), and it might make a good story. Joe followed up on the idea and published a story on the back page of the Evening World.[9]

Despite his improvements, Joe had a hard time behaving like just one of the frightened cubs working under Chapin. Soon, the scion began asking Chapin for time off to meet a girlfriend at the train, to spend the weekend with her family, to attend a party. The special days off mounted, and sometimes they included a day that had not been granted but taken anyway. When Chapin scolded him, Joe "was as penitent as an heir to millions might be expected to be and he made lots of promises that I think he sincerely intended to keep." But soon he disappeared for an entire week without permission. When he returned, Chapin was back to his natural self. He fired Joe on the spot. "The office gasped with astonishment when it got noised about that I had discharged 'Prince Joe,' as they called him, but Joe good-naturedly treated it as a joke and took the night train to Bar Harbor, where he fitted out his yacht and sailed it in all the regattas there that summer, or until his father returned from Europe and sent him out to St. Louis."[10]

That crisis over, Chapin returned to the business at hand. Hearst's Evening Journal continued to eat away at the Evening World's circulation. From a financial point of view, Chapin's paper remained very profitable, generating more than sixty percent of the morning and evening papers's combined profits, yet costing less than half to publish. But Hearst was winning the circulation war. Back in February, Pulitzer's right-hand man Seitz had called all the principals together to ask why they thought the *Evening Journal* had a circulation that at times was twice that of the *Evening World*. None had a convincing answer. All Chapin could offer was that Hearst devoted more energy to promoting his papers, a veiled suggestion that Pulitzer was cheap on that front, and that Coates, who had switched sides, brought in readers with headlines he used to compose when he was with the *Evening World*. "As a newspaper it is not in our class, its features are inferior to ours," said Chapin. "But as Coates said to me—I do not give a damn for the news, all I want is to spring that headline, without regards to facts." Pulitzer turned to Merrill and asked him to spend several days trying to figure out why Hearst had gained the upper hand in the afternoon. The *Evening Journal*, Merrill told Pulitzer after dissecting several days' worth of issues, is designed to appeal to the passions, prejudices, and hatreds of the masses. It "is full of love and the devil, as Goethe says. It comforts the afflicted and at the same time makes it its business to afflict the rich and comfortable." In the end, no one had a solution. Instead, as it often did, city life would provide one.[11]

On the evening of June 25, 1906, Terhune was at the Madison Square Roof Garden to review the opening of "Mam'zelle Champagne" for the *Evening World*. A few minutes before 11:00 P.M., the musical was approaching its final act.

"Here is the spot where the hero slays the villain!" bellowed E. Fowler, who played a rich plumber.

"We will fight with pistols," replied comedian Harry Short, who began singing "I Could Love a Million Girls," the refrain of which was soon taken up by a chorus of dancing girls that trooped onto the stage. While this number ran its course, a young man in an overcoat approached the table where architect Stanford White was dining, and drew a revolver from his jacket. Calmly, Harry K. Thaw pointed the gun at White and pulled the trigger three times. Watching the whole episode from two tables away was Green. There was no mistaking that the shots had accomplished their deadly mission. White lay immobile in a pool of blood on the gray floor. "As the gaze of hundreds rested on Thaw after he had fired the shots he straightened up and extending his right arm, elevated the muzzle of the revolver in the air after the manner of one who has made a good shot and is waiting for the judgement of the referee," said Green. Thaw walked away slowly and was apprehended. "A waiter threw a white cloth over the body and somebody picked up a straw hat and placed it on the table alongside the partially consumed drink that Harry Thaw had interrupted." Terhune commandeered a phone booth being used by a young man and called in the story. While fighting off the offended man and a companion who had come to his aide, Terhune dictated an account that led the morning edition of the *World*. It was lost on none in the *World* building that Junior's men were doing Senior's work.[12]

Thaw had done the deed, he claimed from his prison cell, because White had had an affair with his wife, Evelyn. He further claimed that White was ruining other young girls, and tales were soon circulating of debaucherous stag parties where naked young girls were served up as sexual favors for powerful men of New York's elite society. The murder was like an elixir that revived both Senior and Junior. Within a week, both papers were selling an extra 100,000 copies a day. Seitz excitedly reported to Pulitzer that they were beating Geranium (the *Journal*) "edition after edition, day after day, on new things. Doubtless no little credit is due to Chapin. His marvelous quickness and splendid news instinct in a story of this kind are almost matchless."[13]

The crime exposed the seamy underside of New York's upper crust. But Chapin was no longer merely an ambitious reporter outside looking in on the inner circles of metropolitan life, as was the case twenty years earlier when he stayed at the Union Club as a guest of William Howard. Rather, he and Nellie now regularly joined the elite at the best theaters, shows, and exhibits using the complimentary tickets that Chapin kept for himself, contrary to *World* policy. If he didn't use the tickets himself, Chapin was notorious for making sure no one else did. Walter Marshall, a copy boy, would eye the tickets that sat on Chapin's desk all day. Then he would watch desultorily as Chapin would pick up the tickets and begin to tear them. "He never tore them neatly in two, so that any could be retrieved and pasted together," said Marshall.

"He tore them into tiny bits, then let them fall like snow—not into the wastebasket, but into the spittoon he used all day."[14]

In April, Charles and Nellie sat among the Vanderbilts and other leading New York families at the annual spring horse show at the Durland Riding Academy, near Columbus Circle. "The world of sport, society, and fashion again made a brilliant showing, the boxes all being filled, while there was not a vacant seat in the galleries," said the *New York Times*. In addition to hobnobbing in New York and vacationing in spots such as Bermuda and other preserves of the well-to-do, the Chapins were eyeing a new residence. At Central Park South and Fifth Avenue, construction was underway on an eighteen-story hotel on the site of the fifteen-year-old Plaza Hotel. Though Chapin's position at the *Evening World* gave him considerable access, the real source of Chapin's entrée and wealth remained his anticipated inheritance from his great-uncle Sage. He had parlayed this expected windfall into extensions of credit from those who thought lending money to a powerful city editor might be a prudent investment.[15]

On Sunday, July 22, 1906, Russell Sage was resting on his bed with a view of the ocean in his summer retreat in the Village of Lawrence, twenty miles from New York. Nearing his ninetieth birthday, Sage had been seriously ill for a month, and just that Friday, his doctors had thought the end had come. But by Sunday morning, he seemed quite revived, told his wife he was in splendid humor, and pointed out to her a ship, with all sails set, on the horizon. By nightfall, he was dead.

Monday morning at his post in the city room, Chapin was "all in a dither," said Cobb, who was given the job of writing the page-one obituary. The morning papers offered no clue as to the disposition of the Sage fortune. The *New York Times* said that Sage had made a new will several years ago, "but not the faintest hint of its provisions is known even among his friends."[16]

"Cobb," said Chapin who darted up to his side, "do a new introduction, quick as you can. Play up the fact that in spite of his age, Uncle Russell had one of the keenest brains of any man in Wall Street—clear as a bell up to the last moment—knew exactly what he was doing and saying—everyone who saw him marveled at his grasp on things." Chuckling, Cobb then proceeded to craft, as he called it, "a bill of mental health for the deceased." He had just put the finishing touches on this version when Chapin emerged from one of the telephone booths along the newsroom wall. He was trembling as he rushed back to Cobb's side. "I think he would have cried except that rage was choking back the sobs," said Cobb.

"Throw away that new introduction," Chapin ordered. "I've just heard—well, something has come up that changes the whole aspect of this sanity business. I was wrong. Why, Cobb, there isn't any doubt about it, that miserable old ingrate was doddering, senile—in no shape to dispose of his affairs—putty in the hands of any unscrupulous scoundrels who wanted to enrich themselves at the expense of those who are really entitled to a suitable share in his fortune."

"So, write another lead," Chapin continued, "bringing out this fact. And intimate pretty strongly that already a number of the surviving relatives are taking preliminary steps to fight in the courts for justice and what's rightfully coming to them." Once again, Cobb went to work. As Cobb prepared the new version, Chapin engaged in more frenzied telephone calling. Soon he was back at Cobb's side, telling him to once again scrap the newest version. "The original lead," said Cobb, "the one which so fulsomely praised Sage's testamentary capacity, was hurriedly rescued from the wastepaper basket and printed as written."[17]

Comparing what New Yorkers read about Sage's death in the various papers that Monday, Chapin's hand was clearly evident in the *Evening World*'s account. "He had prepared, as a prudent business man, for the end of his life, and that his preparations were wise and proper was evidenced by the slight ripple his removal from the field of active finance created upon the surface of the market," said Cobb's article. Further, the article quoted Sage himself in a remark said to have been told to "an intimate friend," who one supposes was Chapin. "Everybody will be much surprised to learn what I have done with my money. But they will never learn until I am dead."[18]

But as the *Evening World* article itself speculated, the surprise might be an unpleasant one for Chapin. "Rumors that the bulk of the great fortune of Russell Sage, estimated at between $80,000,000 and $100,000,000, will go to charity were so persistently circulated in Wall Street to-day that they were looked upon as having basis in fact," wrote Cobb. The truth of the matter was still several days away. The waiting must have been excruciating for Chapin. He was convinced that Sage's death would make him a rich man. He had not kept his anticipation a secret. "For years and years," said Cobb, "Chapin had played attendant coyote to Sage's gray wolf, for he was by way of being the octogenarian's nephew and, as all of us knew, had been encouraged to believe that services rendered in print and elsewhere, the old man meant to leave him a considerable fortune, at least a half a million, according to the account."[19]

No one had a clue about Sage's plans. "Mrs. Sage in Ignorance of Husband's Will," read Chapin's headline in the next day's *Evening World*. Relatives, however, were not waiting; they hired an attorney. Meanwhile, preparations for Sage's funeral and burial continued as scheduled. Sage's body was brought to his home on Fifth Avenue. Early the next morning, Chapin and Nellie were among a few invited to the house for a short service after which Olivia Sage, the Chapins, and a small coterie of friends and family servants, set out in five horse-drawn coaches for Grand Central Station. There they boarded the Saratoga and Montreal Special, departing at 9:45 A.M., bound for Troy, New York, where Sage was to be buried. A special car, owned by the Kensico Cemetery, was attached. Dark, with heavy drapes and thick upholstered chairs, it held three compartments: one for the body, one for a dozen members of the immediate family, and one for thirty friends and relatives. "For absolute privacy of a funeral party, leaving the Grand Central Station, it is so arranged that the round trip can be made without the slightest contact with the traveling public," promised the operators. To be sure the party was undisturbed, policemen from the East 51st Street Station were dispatched, and a half-dozen Pinkerton detectives boarded the train.[20]

Privacy was not the sole concern of the funeral party. High on their minds was a remarkable grave robbing years earlier, in which the body of Alexander T. Stewart, one of New York's richest merchants, was dug up and held for ransom. The body was said to have been taken by a gang led by "Gypsy Larry," cut up into pieces for easier shipping, and sometimes re-stolen by differing gangs. Negotiations were carried out for weeks while the robbers

threatened to destroy the body in lime if they were not paid. No one would say if the body was ever recovered or if the crypt still
lay empty at St. Mark's Church on Second Avenue. To prevent any such fate for Sage, the estate was planning on placing the copper-lined mahogany coffin into a six-ton steel case, the lid of which featured a self-locking mechanism, clamping down at twenty different points and leaving not the slightest gap for the insertion of a wedge, according to the *Evening World.* "The steel casing is so hard that it would take expert safe-openers a full day to break the outer shell, and then only by the employment of specially constructed tools."[21]

The funeral party reached Troy at 1:30 P.M. Following a simple grave-site ceremony, the casket was lowered into the specially prepared grave in front of the Sage monument, with the inscription "I have done the best that I could by the light of the day." In his funeral address, the Reverend Dr. Hagemen hinted that Sage's immense wealth may better serve for the improvement of mankind than if it were distributed in smaller ways. To Chapin, such words had an ominous sound. He and Nellie stepped forward, peered into the grave, and then turned away. The party reboarded the train at 5:05 P.M. and arrived back in New York by nine o'clock. Once again, Chapin continued his anxious wake, awaiting the reading of the will. The next morning, the clues continued to be frustrating. None of the morning press had any idea how Sage planned to dispose of his fortune.[22]

Finally, Chapin got word. Aside from a small bequest to Chapin's grandmother, Sage's sister Fannie Chapin, the will was going to leave the entire estate to his wife Olivia Sage. Chapin rushed the news into print. "The exclusive publication in the [*Evening*] *World* today of the chief provisions of the will amazed the relatives of Mr. Sage, who are entirely overlooked. Already some of these have prepared for a contest of the will." For years, said the article (which one presumes was closely edited if not written mostly by Chapin), relatives have been waiting for the distribution of the millions of dollars from their "penurious" relative. "Up to today they believed he had provided for all his kin in a will made years ago." Each expected one million dollars, which would still leave half the fortune for Sage's wife. The grounds for a challenge, explained the *Evening World*, was that Sage had not been mentally competent to draw up the newer will, and that he was under the undue influence of his dominating second wife.[23]

The next morning, the reading of the will essentially confirmed Chapin's story. All $75 to $80 million would go to Olivia Sage, and each "blood nephew and niece" would receive $25,000. If such relatives had predeceased Sage, the $25,000 would be divided among the nephew's or niece's children. Earl, Chapin's father, was still alive, so the $25,000 was slated for him. This was a bitter pill for Chapin, considering how Earl had abandoned the family and not seen Sage in decades, while his son had been the great-uncle's frequent companion in his last years.

Chapin and the other relatives prepared to fight. "Sage Heirs Get Busy on Plans to Break Will," read Chapin's headline three days later. But most observers knew such an effort would be futile. Colonel Slocum, Olivia Sage's brother and confidant, told the press the will would be hard to break. "Personally," Slocum said, "I feel that Mr. Sage has been most magnanimous in the distribution of his money. He gives to each of his nephews and nieces—good, bad and indifferent—$25,000, when many of them do not deserve 25 cents." Chapin's hopes continued to be on display in the *Evening World,* which published articles on the effort long after other papers lost interest. As late as August, Chapin published an allegation that the will was altered, claiming that the dates had been erased, solidifying the claims of the disgruntled relatives. Legal reality and Olivia's offer to double the inheritance if the suit was ended brought the matter to a close by the end of summer. If Chapin were to get any money, it would have to be through his father, who was now to inherit $50,000, enough for a person to live comfortably for a decade or more.[24]

In September, Chapin received word that his father was dying. He had not seen him since their chance encounter in Springfield, Missouri, twenty-two years earlier, but the Sage money caused Chapin to take a renewed interest in his father. He immediately wrote to his sister Fannie and asked her to meet in him in Chicago and accompany him to Milwaukee. On Saturday, September 22, the pair reached their destination. Charles went first by himself to see their estranged father. To reach the Soldier's Home, where Earl was convalescing, he passed the numerous saloons that lined its entrance to satiate the thirst of veterans and visitors,

and ascended the wide carriage drive by the man-made lakes. The home was one of ten such facilities built around the nation to care
for veterans of the Civil War. Constructed after the war, the complex consisted of an elaborate set of stone Victorian buildings dominated by a tall tower that soon became a Milwaukee landmark.

Once inside, Chapin found his father vastly diminished from the tall, lean, brown-haired figure of his memory. Since Earl's admission to the home in 1902, his health had steadily declined. His vision was cloudy at best, his teeth were mostly gone, and he complained of the pains and stiffness of old age. The liver cancer and chronic diarrhea were more serious. They had taken their toll. It was clear the doctor's prognosis was reasonable. What the son and father said to each other at this reunion is not known. Chapin left no record. In part, that may be because Chapin's purpose was not entirely charitable. He had asked the court in Milwaukee to appoint a guardian for his father. Clearly his ruse was to gain the upper hand in planning the distribution of the $50,000 Sage inheritance that Earl was set to receive. Judge Carpenter of the city's probate court came to the home that evening to evaluate Earl. Although he discovered that Earl was infirm, Carpenter ruled that his mental abilities were fine. Charles's motion was denied.[25]

Before Charles left the Soldier's Home that Saturday, his father asked him to send Fannie. Earl knew he didn't have long to live, and for the first time in almost a quarter of a century, he was reaching out to his family, though maybe not yet willing to share entirely how he had spent his time since leaving them. Fannie came the next morning and spent Sunday with him. "In talking with him the day I saw him last," said Fannie, "I said to him that I did not wish to discuss the past, but that there was one question I wanted him to answer and that was why he left us as he did." Earl replied that it was too long a story to tell, but offered a hint at what might have happened. He said that, "for four years after leaving us he was not himself, that when he came to a realizing sense of his condition, it was too late for him to return." Fannie accepted this answer and questioned him no further because, she said, "he was at this time in a dying condition and was very much overcome with emotion."[26]

Earl had been apart from his family for twenty-six years, the equal to his years of living with Chapin's mother Cecelia. After his stay in Springfield, Missouri, where Charles had met with him, Earl moved to Oshkosh with Mary McCoy and their son Edward Gwynne. Everyone there assumed they were husband and wife. "Mr. Chapin always spoke of the woman who joined him here as his wife," recalled Louisa Harrison, who lived near the jeweler for whom Earl worked. Mary and he had another child in August 1892, whom they named Edna Marjorie. The May–December match did not fare well. Two years after Edna's birth, the couple broke up. This time it was Mary who left Earl. Their relationship was not always peaceful, according to those who knew them. "Mr. Chapin was ugly to Mary and didn't seem to provide for her and they had trouble that way," recalled Harrison. Mary's sister laid similar blame at Earl's feet. "I think the cause of the separation of my sister and Mr. Chapin was that he was jealous of her and then he did not treat her well," said Sarah Ramaker.[27]

Eventually, Mary left the children with Earl and married another Oshkosh man. Earl pursued a variety of jobs, from making watches to violins, and tried to raise the children. Gwynne was soon able to support himself, but Edna posed a different problem. Now approaching his seventies, Earl found it impossible to care for himself, let alone his nine-year-old daughter. In June 1902, he placed her with the Children's Home Society in Milwaukee, and in August he won admission to the Soldier's Home. During the next two years, while Earl was cared for as a Civil War pensioner, Edna lived either in the Children's Home itself or with one of various families that took in children. Earl visited Edna and found her well cared for. "I have inquired several times and was always told that the child was happy and contented and wanted for nothing," he wrote. In 1904, after a dispute with the Children's Home over redirecting some of his $12 a month pension to their expenses, Earl regained custody of Edna.[28]

Now as he talked with Fannie, Edna was much on his mind, and he spoke of her with fondness. "You children," he said to Fannie, "had a mother, a beautiful mother, but she has no mother." As two residents of the home witnessed and Fannie watched, Earl then dictated his final will and testament. The fate of Sage's $50,000 would now be decided. Cecelia, whom he called his "wife," would receive $15,000, and Fannie would also get $15,000. Then Earl directed that $15,000 be given to his "daughter" Edna Marjorie Chapin, along with a $1,200 bank deposit. Franklin, his son by Cecelia, and Gwynne, his son by Mary, were to split $5,000 between them. No money was to be left for Charles. In Earl's mind, there was no reason to leave anything for him: Charles was the successful one, who lived the life of luxury in New York. The other members of the family were paupers in comparison. His esteem for Charles was reflected in the fact that he made Charles and Fannie executors of the estate and joint guardians of his last important possession, his daughter Edna. Earl died that Tuesday morning, and the following day his body was shipped to Oneida, New York, for burial with his family. Charles took Edna to Washington, D.C., to be with Cecelia and his sister Marion. Edna remained there for a few months and then was sent to school in Virginia. Eventually, she came to live with Fannie in Elgin, Illinois. Fannie, who had married William Skinner, a crockery merchant, and had a daughter by him, raised Edna until she graduated from high school in 1913. Fannie died shortly thereafter in 1915.[29]

Chapin was soon back at his desk in New York. "When I tumbled from the dream clouds and realized that the millions I had expected to get had faded into a single cipher that hadn't even a rim, I accepted the situation philosophically," he said. "I had been successful with speculation in Wall Street and had salted away in a safe-deposit vault securities that apparently insured me a competence as long as I might live." One day, he let Cobb, with whom he had grown friendly, have a peek at his wealth. "Chapin took from a locked drawer in his desk six deposit books and showed me he had opened comparatively recent savings-bank accounts aggregating $150,000," said Cobb. When Chapin saw Cobb's expression, he hurriedly explained that the money was the product of his thrift. Cobb thought otherwise, believing that much of the money may have been paid to Chapin by the Sage relatives in hopes of sustaining their attack on the will in the press.[30]

The fall and winter of 1906 also looked promising. The city was abuzz with talk about the upcoming Thaw trial. Chapin knew the trial would be a boon to afternoon papers, as the public would not be willing to wait until morning to get the latest installment on the saga. Equally important, Chapin went yacht shopping. Though he already possessed a pair of horses he kept in Central Park, an expense beyond the income of most newspapermen, Chapin purchased a twelve-year-old, thirteen-ton, fifty-five-foot-long yacht, a sale sufficiently significant to be listed in the *New York Times* summary of yacht sales that winter. In addition to spending at least one or two thousand dollars on buying *Eidolon*, Chapin became a member of the Columbia Yacht Club, the Brooklyn Yacht Club, and the more prestigious Atlantic Yacht Club, among whose members were many prominent New York families. For one who had not grown up around water, Chapin became enamored of yachting. He became an active member of the fifty-year-old Atlantic Yacht Club, situated in a handsome building and harbor in Sea Gate on Coney Island, where he served on a variety of committees. He outfitted *Eidolon*, whose name came from a Walt Whitman poem, with a private signal flag consisting of a red "C" set on a white background trimmed by a blue border with stars, and he regularly participated in regattas, though not always with great success. In one, for instance, Chapin ran aground in a near dead calm that made maneuvering the bulky yacht almost impossible. But because he obtained the help of a powerboat to get back to the starting line, the regatta committee later disqualified him. As with anything in which Chapin became interested, the *Evening World* followed along. Though it was hardly the paper of choice to the yacht club set, the paper announced that it would be making a feature of yachting news and urged boatmen to submit items of "interest to others and thereby aid in making the season on the water the best in years."[31]

On January 23, 1907, Thaw's trial for the murder of Stanford White began. The new century was only seven years old, but the case was already being called "The Trial of the Century." Chapin took Cobb off the rewrite desk and assigned him to the trial. Though other papers assigned whole teams of reporters, Chapin and Cobb's plan was to give their coverage the distinctive voice of a single writer. Cobb had honed his skills in recording trial testimony and churning out copy on deadline from his notes six years earlier while covering nine trials related to the assassination of Kentucky Governor William Goebel, a Huey Long-style politician who was gunned down in the state Capitol. The first few days of the Thaw trial made the Goebel affair seem simple. The media attention was unlike any trial America had seen. The event was "being reported to the ends of the civilized globe," according to the *New York Times*.

"Why is there so much interest taken in the Thaw case?" asked the *Evening World*. The interest is so enormous, said the paper, that the spectators could fill Madison Square Garden if the trial were held there. If Thaw's beautiful wife, Evelyn Nesbit, merely sat on the stage, the gate receipts alone would pay Thaw's attorney fees. The reason was not the murder by revolver, which was commonplace in New York. Rather, said the *Evening World*, the extraordinary interest in the affair could be attributed to Thaw being like thousands of young men brought up by a father who failed to attend to his child-rearing duties. "Instead of training his children, he trained his bank account."[32]

Telegraph cables poured down into the courthouse through its central skylight. Western Union opened an office in the main hall. And the crush of reporters and lawyers meant there would be no room for the general public. Hearst confounded Chapin's plans slightly. He assigned three women to cover the trial, forcing Chapin to add Nixola Greeley-Smith to his team. She joined the Hearst women at a special table set up in front of the courtroom. She, however, was assigned only to provide color, especially the woman's perspective, as the headline on her first report revealed—"Thaws in Court as Seen by a Woman." Reporting the trial would still be up to Cobb, who enlarged the journalism lexicon by promptly nicknaming the four women the "sob sisters" for their maudlin copy.[33]

After a few false starts, Cobb and Chapin devised a system to make their plan work. Two copy boys were assigned to stand behind Cobb. One kept him supplied with freshly sharpened pencils. Each time he completed a sheet of copy the other boy was to run it downstairs to a basement corridor, where a reporter, Johnny Gavin, would read it over a private telephone line to a stenographer in the *Evening World* city room. Not more than five minutes passed before his story was in type, giving the paper the freshest copy in town.

Cobb's prodigious output included long, detailed accounts of that day's goings-on in court and sidebars on the courtroom cast of characters. Typical of the latter was a "pen picture" of Thaw. "As Thaw sat studying the end of his fingers and occasionally shooting one of those peculiarly angled glances out from under his frowning brows," wrote Cobb, "he did not fit the picture of the fast young man of the Tenderloin, although the newspapers have word-painted him as such a thousand times. For, be it contested, Harry Thaw would look more at place on Tenth Avenue than on Fifth." The plan functioned flawlessly, and soon readers were hooked on Cobb's voluminous daily accounts, sometimes exceeding twelve thousand words. And, as if he were showing off, he never failed to file his regular humor column. By the end of the trial, Cobb was being called Chapin's star reporter, and he soon signed a three-year, $7,500-annual contract with the *Evening World*.[34]

In April 1907, Joseph Pulitzer turned sixty and ordered his St. Louis and New York staffs to celebrate the event, even though he was thousands of miles away in southern France. Chapin joined fifty-nine other select members of the *World* staff at Delmonico's, while sixty members of the *Post-Dispatch* staff gathered simultaneously at the Planter's Hotel in St. Louis, on the evening of April 10. The *New York Times* called the dinners "practically family affairs" because the only outsider admitted to any of the gatherings was a banker who also was an officer of the Pulitzer corporation. At the appointed hour, a long-distance telephone line was opened between New York and St. Louis so that greetings could be exchanged. The evening concluded with a raft of congratulatory telegrams being read aloud, each with a toast, and then wired to "J. P."[35]

The telegrams reached Pulitzer in Menton, France, a secluded Mediterranean village a few miles from the Italian border, where he was resting after a fatiguing cruise and awaiting the arrival of Auguste Rodin, the sculptor, who had been summoned from Paris to execute a bronze-and-marble bust of the publisher. Several weeks' worth of the *World* and the *Post-Dispatch* newspapers had piled up while he was on his cruise, and his secretary Samuel

Williams brought them in to read to Pulitzer, who by this time was quite blind. First, he read the copies of the *World* and then turned to the *Post-Dispatch*. Williams read the St. Louis paper so poorly that Pulitzer grew angry and asked him what was wrong.[36]

"The damned paper is so rottenly printed it is almost unreadable. The type is bad, the ink is pale and dauby, the quality of the paper is inferior and the presswork is worse than the rest," Williams explained in his defense.

"Dear me, is it really so bad as all that?" asked Pulitzer. "From the way you described it I think they must have substituted shoe pegs for type and tar for ink. Send a cable to Chapin to go out and take charge for a month and put it in shape."[37]

Chapin had made one of these inspection-and-repair trips to St. Louis before, in 1905, but he found that much had changed since he last visited—and not all for the better. True, Oliver K. Bovard, who took over the city editor's desk on the third floor of 513 Olive Street after Chapin's departure eight years earlier, seemed to be cut from the same cloth as Chapin. He had built up a highly disciplined news staff on fear, intimidation, and ceaseless demands for stories that made readers talk. But the paper looked shabby, and even the good stories were so poorly edited they lost their bell-ringer quality by the time they reached readers. In his first week, Chapin ordered all new type for the paper and re-worked the layout and headlines. The next week, he took over the copy desk to retrain the copy editors, whom he thought were the paper's great weakness.[38]

Among those in St. Louis watching Chapin's every move was young Joe Pulitzer, who had settled comfortably into his new life at the *Post-Dispatch* and was happy to see his former mentor. The two immediately began spending considerable time together, often going to the park for walks. Pulitzer gave Chapin a couple of ideas, which Chapin told him to work up into news stories. But in keeping with the culture of the Pulitzer kingdom, as Chapin should have known, Joe also reported to his father on Chapin's work. "Reached the office at 7:28," Pulitzer wrote to his father in a typical dispatch on May 9. "Chapin as usual had been down since 7. Chapin is a wonder in his energy, persistence and positiveness. He is much less tyrannical here than in New York. Here he is actually kindly, makes pleasant remarks to everyone and makes a point of congratulating a man whenever he writes a good story or makes a good suggestion."[39]

Chapin remained in St. Louis for six weeks, battling a bad cold and hiring new staff. Toward the end of his tour, Chapin read that the *Chicago Chronicle* was closing. The news caught his attention because Horatio Seymour, who had been editor of the *Chicago Herald* when Chapin was its city editor, was now the newspaper's publisher. Seymour's backer had been sent to prison for fraud, which killed the *Chronicle*. Chapin immediately wired New York for the authority to hire Seymour. Ralph Pulitzer, Joseph Pulitzer's son, responded by asking if Chapin could ascertain the state of Seymour's health, as he was certainly no longer a young man. Chapin vouched for the man's vigor. By return wire, Ralph approved, saying that Chapin could go as high as $9,000 a year to lure Seymour to St. Louis. Pulitzer had twice before tried to get Seymour, but the editor had declined out of loyalty to his current publisher. "Bear in mind in whole negotiation that our real need is on Grasping [the *Post-Dispatch*], using Genuine [the morning, evening and Sunday *Worlds*] only as extra inducement," Ralph Pulitzer wired using his father's codes. "Don't grudge a few extra days possible absence from New York on this. If you succeed will please Andes tremendously." The older Pulitzer, never one to leave all business decisions to his children, obtained his own intelligence about Seymour. "Mr. Seymour," wrote Pulitzer's Chicago informant, "has the head of an intellectual giant; the neck of a bull; the jaw of a Croaker; the face of a fighter, and the body of an ordinary man of short stature."[40]

"I located Mr. Seymour amid the ruins by long-distance telephone," said Chapin, "and made an engagement to meet him in Chicago the next morning. In the disconsolate mess I found him in it didn't require much persuasion to induce him to accept the editorship of the *Post-Dispatch* at a liberal salary and with a contract that insured permanency." Chapin, as one might have expected, offered his old friend the full $9,000 and further agreed that he could switch to New York after six months in St. Louis if things did not work out as expected. His job done, Chapin returned to New York. Either his cold got worse, or he caught a new one on the sleeper, but he went straight to bed upon his arrival. Pulitzer, back from Europe, called Chapin at home to tell him how pleased he was with the result of his efforts in St. Louis, then instructed that his salary be raised by $500. "Sorry I could not be on my feet to welcome you home," Chapin wrote Pulitzer from his room in the Hotel Majestic. "I welcome you in my heart." Although the money was appreciated (to put it mildly), Chapin also was pleased to have saved his old Chicago mentor, Seymour. Back at his desk a week later, he took out a piece of *Evening World* stationery and sent his best wishes to Seymour, "hoping you will soon get the troublesome affairs of the *Chronicle* adjusted and that shift to the new field in St. Louis will bring peace and happiness, which I am sure it will, believe me."[41]

In the fall of 1907, Chapin completed his conquest of Manhattan. Nearly a quarter of a century after ogling the rich and famous as a guest of the Union League Club, Chapin would now live with them. "He dearly loved money," said Cobb, "not for the sake of hoarding it but for what it could bring him in luxury and display." In late September, he and Nellie moved into the Plaza Hotel at Fifth Avenue and 59th Street. Designed by Henry J. Hardenbergh, the Plaza was built for the unheard-of cost of $12 million and promised to be *the* residence for New York's most eminent families. It was an aesthetic and technological marvel, appealing at once to both lovers of French Renaissance architecture and American can-do engineering. Devoted to the style of Louis XV and XVI, Hardenbergh selected the finest French marble for walls, bronze for elevator doors, and tapestry for furniture coverings, all of which was lighted at night by 17,000 incandescent bulbs, powered by a four-engine, 1,100-kilowatt generating plant, heated in the winter by nine coal-fired boilers, and cleaned by day by a building-wide vacuum system whose two steam-driven pumps sucked dust and dirt down hundreds of feet of pipes. When the hotel opened, promised the *New York Times*, "one more institution will have been added to New York's variegated social life. The city will have gained another show place, the tourists on the rubber neck automobiles will have an additional kink put in their necks, and a few more descriptive paragraphs will have to be crowded into the all-around-the-city travelogues of the megaphone cicerone." The hotel was not yet officially opened when the Chapins moved in. The marble tiling, for instance, was not finished when they began taking their meals in the dining room reserved for the sole use of permanent guests. Though they were among the first guests, the privilege of being the first to register when the hotel opened on October 1, 1907, was accorded to others with considerably more status, such as Alfred Gwynne Vanderbilt, son of Cornelius Vanderbilt. The night before it opened, the hotel gave a gala dinner to which it invited newspaper editors, advertising managers, and real estate writers. Chapin never missed such dinners.[42]

Chapin's private pursuit of the life he had coveted for so long was at its zenith. "He reveled in luxury as a cat would, rolling in a catnip bed," said Cobb. He was reputed to earn one of the highest salaries of any city editor. His residence, his horses, his yacht, his acquaintances all bespoke of his success. In the morning, he could invariably been seen taking a canter through Central Park, and in the afternoons racing his trotters. His clothes were now tailor made. When he appeared at work, he cut a striking figure. "He was vain of his compact, straight figure," said Cobb, "so he walked all reared back, with his heels coming down like drumsticks on a snare drum."[43]

On Park Row, Chapin's professional pursuit of a dream staff was complete. By outspending other editors, he had secured many of the best writers and legmen of New York. At Cobb's urging, for instance, Chapin brought Max Fischel over from the *Sun*. Fischel was the ultimate legman of the era. Born in Prague in 1863, he came to the United States when he was four. His family found a home in a tenement near the police headquarters on Mulberry Street, where, at age nine, he obtained work as a copy boy for police reporters. There he met Jacob Riis, who trained him to do the early morning rounds of the city and return with all the facts about the night's fires, arrests, crimes, and accidents, which Riis then would write up. Later, Riis credited Fischel with providing him with some of the most moving stories contained in his famous book *How the Other Half Lives*. After Riis, Fischel did leg work for Lincoln Steffens and countless other reporters, including Cobb when he was at the *Sun*. Without ever touching the keys of a typewriter, Fischel had brought forth many of New York's best news stories but had remained in the background, unknown to all except inhabitants of Park Row.[44]

Money alone did not retain the kind of talent that Chapin had gathered at the *Evening World*. Rather, despite his fearsome reputation, Chapin offered reporters something they couldn't easily find elsewhere: tremendous freedom and support. Once he assigned a story to a reporter, Chapin resisted all temptation to interfere in any way, and when the story came in, he did not hover nervously around the rewrite team awaiting the first copy. It was as if once he assigned a task, Chapin presumed displaying any concern about its success would reflect a lack of faith in his own judgment, said Cobb. "There might be brutal rebukes for whosoever failed in his share of the consolidated operations. But that would come after the battle was ended." Chapin also was unstinting in defense of his staff. Whether they were accused of misdeed by an irate reader or an important politician, Chapin always presumed innocence. "He gave the accused the benefit of every reasonable doubt, standing by the guns until conclusive guilt had been shown or vindication was offered," said Cobb. "This gave us confidence because a reporter's business is other people's business." Chapin pushed his staff hard, and behind his back they cursed, but they never quit. "Because if he never spared them," said Cobb, "this taskmaster of theirs never spared himself, either. And he stood loyally behind his men so long as they kept the faith with him."[45]

At the heart of Chapin's news-gathering operation remained his prized rewrite team. Barton Currie was his star. "He could take a bare handful of semi-statistical notes and turn them, on demand, either into a tensely dramatic or roaringly funny column story," said Terhune. The last to join the group, which now consisted of Cobb, Green, and Currie, was Lindsey Denison, the dark, handsome writer from the *Sun* who, despite the reputation that preceded him, was modest. "He could write rings around the rest of us when he chose to," said Terhune. As a team, they were the only members of Chapin's staff who, because they were so indispensable, gave Chapin as good as he gave them. One exchange gave birth to one of the most-often-told legends about Chapin. One day Chapin sent word that he was ill and would not be in to work. "Dear me," said Cobb without looking up from his typewriter, "let us hope it's nothing trivial." The affection was palpable. "To me they were always wonderful," said Chapin. "I watched them day after day through a long stretch of years and marveled at what they accomplished."[46]

There was an undeniable sense that Chapin had put together for the *Evening World* a team of writers that, if journalism were an athletic endeavor, would be long remembered, much like the Highlanders playing at the time on the Polo Grounds would be after changing their name to the "Yankees." "In olden newspaper days there was a legend of the greatest staff ever assembled under one editor, the staff of the *Evening Sun* at some period during the 1880s," said Terhune. "I believe our *Evening World* staff, off and on, between 1911 and 1916, was infinitely more scintillant, and that it was the premier staff in newspaper history."[47]

On Senior's Desk

Over the years, the *World* and its crusades for the common man had frequently earned it the enmity of those in power, but in 1908, Pulitzer faced the full wrath of the nation's number-one citizen, outgoing President Theodore Roosevelt. The *World* had accused the president of lying about the Panamanian revolution and raised pointed questions about the possibility that the $40 million payment used to purchase the New Panama Canal Company may have ended up lining the pockets of some Americans with the president's complicity. Roosevelt's reaction was rapid and rabid. He sought to have the U.S. attorney in New York invoke charges of criminal libel and told Congress, "It should not be left to private citizens to sue Mr. Pulitzer. He should be prosecuted for that by the governmental authorities." As days stretched to weeks, the direction from which the first legal assault would come remained unknown. High among the possibilities was that William T. Jerome, the district attorney for New York, would arrest the publisher and try him under state law. Jerome, no fan of Pulitzer, relished the ninth circle of hell in which Pulitzer found himself. For four weeks, he remained silent regarding his intentions.[1]

One morning in the middle of January 1909, Cobb arrived in the city room as usual at 9:00 A.M. But before he could even check in with Chapin, John Tennant, the managing editor, intercepted him and said he was wanted immediately in the business office. There Cobb found Seitz, White, and Merrill.

"Mr. Cobb," said Seitz, "we have just heard that you are a close friend of District Attorney Jerome. Is that correct?"

"Well, sir," replied Cobb, "I wouldn't go that far."

The truth was that the two had come to know each other pretty well when Cobb virtually lived in the courtroom where Jerome prosecuted the famous Thaw case. In fact, Jerome had been the source of several off-the-record tips, and they both liked each other. Now privy to this connection between the two, the triumvirate wanted Cobb to use his friendship with Jerome to determine the prosecutor's intentions.

"To put it baldly," said Seitz, "we've exhausted practically every expedient, every available resource we could think of—we and our lawyers and our other representatives—and without success. A grave emergency exists. Mr. Pulitzer is in a very depressed, very harassed state. The possible consequences to his health are dangerous—most dangerous. So as a last resort we are asking your cooperation. Can we count on you—for immediate action?"

Cobb consented to help. He was told he could have the assistance of anyone on staff and an unlimited expense account for this project. Cobb demurely declined help, left the room, and hopped on a trolley to the Criminal Courts building. He caught up with Jerome at Pontin's Restaurant, a hangout for legal types and select members of the fourth estate. The place was quite empty, as it was still early in the morning, but Jerome was there having a drink. Cobb decided to forgo any ruse. Instead, he would simply ask Jerome point-blank about his intentions. "I'm sure it was Chapin who first showed me the value of such a tactic," said Cobb. In the summer of 1906, an ex-policeman had been prosecuted on corruption charges. Cobb was sent to interview the prisoner on the day before he was being sent to Sing Sing. "It's the psychological moment for that boy to talk," Chapin advised Cobb. "Don't fool around with him. Shoot when he shows the whites of his eyes. Tell him we'll give him a fair deal if he'll come clean. And my guess is he'll break down." Chapin was right, and Cobb forever adopted the direct approach as his only method. It didn't hurt, however, that Cobb had a Kentucky drawl and a backwoods "ah, shucks" charm.

After concluding his cocktail-laced interview, Cobb caught

another trolley back to the *World* building and was back in the business office within two hours of receiving his assignment. To the astonishment of the three men, Cobb announced that Jerome had no intention of prosecuting Pulitzer. Cobb was immediately put on the telephone to Pulitzer's house, and he repeated the good news to Norman Thwaites, the chief's personal secretary.

"Cobb," said Thwaites, "Mr. Pulitzer is sitting here beside me. He has just asked me to express his deep appreciation for the service. . . . Mr. Pulitzer is desirous of knowing how this most gratifying result was accomplished so speedily?"

"Well, it's like this," said Cobb, who then recounted how he grabbed a trolley to the courthouse and simply asked Jerome.

"Well, I wish I might be God-dammed," said Pulitzer loudly enough to be heard over the telephone when Thwaites repeated Cobb's explanation. Cobb turned in his expense report of ten cents for the two trolley rides and went back to work in the city room.[2]

Unfortunately for Pulitzer, Roosevelt was not easily put off, and a federal case proceeded. In the midst of this turmoil, Pulitzer left the country for the entire year, but, as usual, distance did not dissuade him from reorganizing the staff from afar, directing them like marionettes on a string. Before February was over Chapin found himself on the city desk of the *World*. "Chapin had been making a wonderful success as city editor of the *Evening World*," said James Barrett, who would later serve as city editor of the *World* himself. "Pulitzer saw no reason why those remarkable talents should not be just as effective on the morning paper, not knowing that city editors cannot be transplanted—at least not as a rule."[3]

Even if there were an exception to Barrett's rule, there was an enormous difference in the culture of the two papers that would work against anyone making the transition. For Pulitzer, the *World* had always meant Senior. This was an appraisal not lost on those who worked in the *World* building. "The *Evening World* and the *Sunday World* were incidental side-shows so far as we of the morning staff were concerned," remembered Barrett. The content, style, work pace, and attitudes that permeated Senior were vastly at odds with those of Junior. Whereas the *Evening World* was managed at a frenetic pace, trying to gather every breaking morsel of news to feed a ravenous stream of extras, the *World* had the luxury of night to produce a more carefully tailored rendering of the day's events.[4]

"JP's idea was to give Chapin plenary authority over the staff and full powers to get the news, no matter if he had to invade the territory of the telegraph-cable news editor and the managing editor," said Barrett. Chapin took full use of his new power and immediately began remaking the city desk in his image. First, he eliminated day and night city editors and instead opted for day and night assistants. If he were going to be the city editor, then there would be only *one* city editor. He eliminated the space-rate plan whereby writers were paid by the printed inch, and put writers who pleased him on salary. Third, he went on a hiring binge. His strategy was not to build a larger staff, but to create, as he had on the *Evening World*, a small, tight cadre. "I would rather have fifteen high-class men at $70 to $80 a week than forty men of $40 and $50 class," Chapin told Pulitzer. In addition, he wanted to hire young beginners at $15 and $20 a week to assist his high-paid reporters and be trained by Chapin. "What we need is systematic organization, energetic, concentrated effort and esprit d'corps." But in this endeavor, he found resistance to his job offers unlike when he was at the *Evening World*. It turned out reporters at other papers were reluctant to make the move, he wrote to Pulitzer, "because they understood I was only temporarily on the Morning *World*, and would soon return to the Evening, and that any man I brought into the organization would be a shining mark for decapitation after I was gone." Upon receiving this note, Thwaites underlined the word "temporarily" and wrote down, in the margins, the response Pulitzer dictated.[5]

"I would like you to be honest and frank as to what your position is," said Pulitzer's message to Chapin the next day. "I had always been positively assured that nothing would take you away from the Evening paper permanently or I would have put you on the Morning long ago. Would you like to stay? There is certainly more honor in it and a bigger field."[6]

Most any editor in New York at the time would not have hesitated. To be offered the city desk of the *World*, whose daily circulation and power were unmatched, was to win the fourth estate's keys to the kingdom. But Chapin, as Pulitzer wisely surmised, was a different breed of journalist, or, as he insisted on calling himself, newspaperman. For eleven years, Chapin had held the reins of the *Evening World*, more than half the life span of the paper itself. "I have a deeper affection for that paper than for anything else except my wife."

"You want me to be honest and frank about myself," said Chapin in his reply. "Here goes."

"Would I like to stay on the Morning *World*? From choice— not if you doubled my salary!" Chapin carefully spelled out his reasons. First, the *Evening World* has a harmonious staff built entirely of men of his choosing. "Every man pulls together. There are no politics, no bickering, no jealousies, no Black Hand." Second, his staff is loyal beyond that of any newspaper staff. "There is not one man among them would not work twenty-four hours on a stretch if I asked him and thank me for the privilege." Third, they are the best reporters and writers that any afternoon paper ever had. "I had hoped to remain with them so long as I might prove useful."

Earlier, when Pulitzer asked him to take over Senior, Chapin had interpreted the request as a command. "I understood that you worried about the lack of organization here; that you thought I could make the organization what it should be; so I came gladly and I will stay here as long as you desire." After eighteen years in Pulitzer's service, Chapin said there was nothing he would not do cheerfully for the publisher. But if it were to be running Senior, then Chapin would have his price. "If I remain on the Morning *World*," said Chapin, "I wish to have absolute control of the organization so far as the reporters and copy editors are concerned, just as I expect to be under the absolute control and direction of whomever you place in editorial charge." The latter was his trump card because Pulitzer was leaning toward Chapin's old friend Seymour. "If he is to be in charge, I would, if you wish me to, remain here as long as you desire, although it means practically destruction of home life and the associations I have been accustomed to the last fifteen years."[7]

His play for control was immediately opposed by some of the old hands, who felt their power was being eroded. Caleb Van Hamm told Pulitzer that he disagreed with any move to put the copy editors under the control of the city desk. "You retain all powers over the staff," came Pulitzer's reply. But he added, with snappish tone, "You alone (and not Chapin) as managing editor are going to be held responsible for that paper although I hope you will have sense enough to appreciate Chapin's value and ferocious energy." Van Hamm quickly reassured the chief that he recognized Chapin's virtues, but did so in a manner to bolster his case against extending more responsibility to the city editor. "As to the change in city editors, I wish to be emphatic in my appreciation of the untiring energy of Mr. Chapin," Van Hamm told Pulitzer. "I think he if anything overworks every day, which is bad for himself as well as for the paper."[8]

On March 17, 1909, Pulitzer slipped into town and stayed briefly at his 73rd Street mansion. Chapin met with him, one assumes with considerable nervousness. Indeed, a face-to-face meeting with "Andes" was a rare privilege for any member of the *World* staff. In all, Pulitzer had visited his offices only three times since the *World* building had opened. Chapin had mostly communicated with Pulitzer on paper and, in recent years, by telephone. The longest spell of time Chapin had spent with him was during his stay in London four years earlier. Once, he had breakfasted with Pulitzer and, as many others experienced on such occasions, had been asked to read the morning newspapers to him. While Chapin opened the bundle of papers the butler brought, Pulitzer lit a cigar and prepared to hear the news. After Chapin had read for a few minutes, Pulitzer interrupted to ask if his cigar was still lit. As he asked, he blew a choking cloud of smoke into Chapin's face. "I have thought of this incident many times and I have closed my eyes while smoking to try and realize the sensation that comes to a blind man when he is unable to tell if his cigar is lit," said Chapin. "I have read of the enjoyment of blind men for tobacco, but I don't believe it."[9]

On the day of the meeting, Pulitzer was immensely distracted. He was eager to regain the tranquility of his yacht *Liberty*. Anything might seem more peaceful than the scene that greeted him in New York: a grand jury was meeting to consider the government's libel case against him; he was embroiled in another struggle with his son Joe; and the squabbling under the dome threatened the paper, especially with Hearst's relentless pressure. Pulitzer and Chapin discussed how the *Evening World* was getting along under Chapin's assistant, who had taken over during his absence. They agreed Chapin would stay on Senior until either Pulitzer changed his mind or Chapin wanted to return to Junior. As long as he was on Senior's city desk, he would have full control and would report only to Van Hamm. If he disagreed with Van Hamm, he could appeal to Seymour. Chapin promised he would be more careful in hiring, Pulitzer being ever mindful of keeping the newspaper business a moneymaking operation, and would clear financial decisions with White. Lastly, Chapin promised to shorten his hours as soon he felt comfortable to do so.[10]

Chapin's performance on the morning *World* continued to show considerable promise. Samuel Williams, a *World* writer and Pulitzer confidant, reported to the chief that the paper was doing a better job covering the news and getting more scoops over other newspapers than before. The credit was due to Chapin. It was true. From his years of covering breaking news, Chapin brought a greater sense of urgency to Senior. One night, for instance, Chapin joined reporters on the front lines of a story. Nellie had called about five minutes till midnight to report that a seven-story apartment building adjacent to the Plaza Hotel was on fire, and she could hear women and children shrieking. Charles, however, had already left for home. When he approached the hotel, he found fire engines and hundreds of spectators. All the guests of the Plaza, including Nellie, were gathered outside with their valuables. The hotel was filled with smoke, and in the café, doctors tended to twenty-one injured persons. Chapin immediately found two reporters and worked with them until 2:00 A.M. when they filed their story. "We had the best story in two—about two and a half columns, with names, incidents, and interviews," he said. A few hours later, when he woke from a shortened night's sleep, he went to the hotel newsstand to read his handiwork. He was steamed to find only the early edition for sale. He immediately told them to destroy it and had later editions rushed to the hotel.[11]

Despite the kick-in-the-pants attitude Chapin employed to invigorate the morning staff, Barrett's forecast proved true. Chapin was a square peg in a round hole. "He was bound to some extent by the tradition of the evening paper, no doubt, and it will take time to open up to him the larger field of the morning but that he will grasp it, is grasping it, I do not doubt," Seymour told Pulitzer. Chapin faced resistance on two fronts: existing reporters were unwilling to change their ways, and entrenched managers such as Van Hamm felt threatened. Seymour, who was, as one might imagine, a strong supporter of Chapin, had a clear sense of the problem. "For some weeks he was badly handicapped by what amounted to a rebellion in his staff, but that spirit has now been defeated and I would have beaten it as he did, if every man on the floor had to go," reported Seymour. "With a better disposed staff and with the idea he is at the city desk only temporarily pretty thoroughly exploded, there is no reason why he should not do the best work of his life." In the end, Seymour counseled Pulitzer to keep Chapin at the desk.[12]

Over the summer, Seymour, Van Hamm, and Seitz each sent a stream of reports to Pulitzer in Europe on the harmony in the office. The very fact they were all writing about it revealed to Pulitzer the growing conflict under the dome. Pulitzer had begun to fret openly that his plan was not working. He wrote a private letter to his son Ralph, admitting that Chapin may have too much power. "The Chapin–Van Hamm friction ought to be settled by the committee," he said, dictating notes to his secretary while in Germany. "It does not seem possible that these two will ever get along permanently or that Chapin will want to stay permanently."[13]

Finally in the fall of 1909, in the words of Barrett, Pulitzer "threw up his hands" and gave up on keeping Chapin on Senior. He was considerate enough, however, to try to make the change in a manner least damaging to Chapin. Seymour agreed to the plan while Chapin was convalescing at the Plaza from illness brought on by exhaustion. "Your decision that Chapin's transfer to the evening should be made on his return to the office is, in my opinion, wise and can be carried out with no humiliation to him or unnecessary comment," he wrote Pulitzer in November. The needed changes he brought to the *World* had been completed, and "in view of the effects on his health, recently noted," Seymour wrote, "I doubt if he could stand the strain much longer anyway." Thus, after nine months at the helm of Senior, Chapin was back at the *Evening World*.[14]

Most of the news in 1910 related to the city's new mayor,

William J. Gaynor. A former reporter and former member of the Christian Brothers Order, Gaynor had been elected with the support of Tammany Hall—the corrupt Democratic-party machine—though he had a reputation as an honest reformer. The values of the latter prevailed when he took office, to the disappointment of the Tammany stalwarts. His inauguration was the talk of the town. It was Gaynor's first-ever visit to city hall, and he marked it by walking from his home in Brooklyn. His style, freshness, and his willingness to appoint qualified people to city posts gave reporters endless copy.

On August 6, Chapin sent a reporter to Gaynor's Brooklyn home for an interview before the mayor departed on a vacation to Europe. Chapin thought he might get a better interview at the house than at the pier. The reporter checked in with the city desk after completing the interview, and Chapin instructed him to accompany the mayor to Hoboken, where the ship was docked and where William Warnecke, a *World* photographer, was to meet him. Warnecke was delayed, and by the time he reached the pier, the other photographers had gone. Nonetheless, he set up his camera and took some photographs of the mayor having farewell conversations with some aides. As he loaded his last batch of film into the camera, a disgruntled city employee drew a pistol and aimed it directly at Gaynor's head. The first shot misfired, but the would-be assassin got off two more shots, one of them hitting the mayor in the neck. All this time Warnecke was himself shooting, too, capturing the horror on film. He rushed back to the *World* and brought the negatives to the city room where an amazed group of reporters and editors stared at the image of Gaynor collapsing into the arms of "Big Bill" Edwards. "What a beautiful thing," said Chapin. "Look—blood all over him! And exclusive too!"[15]

Gaynor survived the attempt on his life, though doctors were unable to remove the bullet. He died suddenly, however, three years later from complications resulting from the shooting. Unlike with President McKinley's death in 1901, the yellow press could not be blamed this time. The would-be assassin was a reader of the staid *New York Times*.[16]

On Sunday, October 29, 1911, Pulitzer was on his yacht, anchored in Charleston, South Carolina. He had slept poorly the night before, waking Alleyene Ireland, his secretary, at 3:00 A.M. so that he could be read to. Later in the day, when the chief seemed to be resting comfortably, Ireland lunched with Thwaites and another shipboard companion. Abruptly, the head butler entered through the door at the front end of the saloon and said "Mr. Pulitzer is dead."[17]

Pulitzer's body was brought back to New York. On November 1, Chapin joined 300 of Pulitzer's other employees who, along with hundreds of politicians, financiers, and other dignitaries, filled St. Thomas Episcopal Church at Fifth Avenue and 53rd Street. A huge crowd of more than 2,000 blocked traffic on the street outside the church. Many of these were alumni of Pulitzer papers who, not having seen each other in years, added an odd touch of merriment to the somber proceedings inside the church. When the voices of the choir sang "Abide with me, fast falls the eventide," the presses at the *World* and the *Post-Dispatch* fell silent. The lights were turned off. The telegraph and telephone lines were disconnected, and for five minutes the staffs of the two papers remained silent and cut off from the world.

That afternoon, a small group of editors accompanied the family and the casket on a special train to Woodlawn Cemetery in the Bronx, where Pulitzer was interred just before dusk. He was buried next to the grave of Lucille Irma Pulitzer, his daughter who had died in 1898. He lay in his casket, his right arm across his chest, clasping a copy of the *World*. The iron grip, however, was now gone. It would be up to the sons, Joe in St. Louis and Ralph in New York, to carry on. Most knew, however, that it would never be the same. "I watched them lower his body into the grave," said Chapin, "and I felt as if my spirit was being buried with him."[18]

A Titanic Scoop

On the morning of Wednesday, April 10, 1912, Carlos F. Hurd, a slender, professionally dressed man in his thirties, made his way through the thick crowd of men who milled around Park Row each day. The brims of a thousand hats registered an identical backward tilt as their proprietors gazed upward to read the headlines posted on tall blackboards hanging from the second story of Pulitzer's *World* and Hearst's *Journal* buildings. There, racing back and forth on balconies, men from the newspapers tried to offer up the latest news, one step ahead of each other. During the past four decades, as the telegraph and telephone revolutionized the transmission of news, reading the bulletins had become a fashionable New York pastime. One of the earliest such gatherings had occurred twenty-six years before when the *World* erected a tableau across the front of its building depicting an ocean scene, complete with a lighthouse, and raced two miniature yachts across the panorama as each dispatch arrived from the America's Cup race between the *Mayflower* and the *Gallatea* taking place in England. Seven years later, 25,000 people filled Park Row and City Hall Park to "watch" the heavyweight championship of the world being fought 2,000 miles away in Carson City, Nevada. The *World* had built a reproduction of the boxing ring on a platform outside its building, seeking to outdo its competitors' bulletin boards. To the joy of boxing fans, four-foot-tall string puppets reenacted the blows in the fourteen-round bout from telegraphic reports. At the end of the match, the Tills, renowned marionette operators, even provided an encore of the final round.[1]

As Hurd passed through the crowd, just as Chapin had two decades earlier when he had arrived from Chicago, he approached the gold-domed *World* building like a pilgrim would a holy shrine. Time had robbed the remarkable building of its claim as the tallest structure in New York, and certainly diminished its status as the most idiosyncratic. Within a year, that prize would be incontestably snatched away and retained for the next two decades by the 792-foot, Gothic-style Woolworth building rising across the park. But for an out-of-town reporter like Hurd, the *World* remained Gotham's most recognizable building.

The stars at the *World* were well known to Hurd. Copy from the best of them ran frequently in the *St. Louis Post-Dispatch*, where he had worked since 1900. The son of a congregational minister, Hurd was born in Cherokee, Iowa, in 1877 and began his journalism career at the *Springfield Leader* in 1897 after graduating from Drury College in Springfield, Missouri. The next year, he moved to St. Louis, then the nation's fourth-largest city, and soon thereafter joined the Pulitzer empire. Hurd had come to New York after securing a two-month leave from the paper to take a long-awaited tour of Europe. He and his wife Kathleen had sent their two children to stay with their grandmother and had arrived by train the night before. Emerging from the crowd, Hurd entered the *World* building. His goal was to see Chapin. All reporters knew of Chapin, but those from St. Louis were often weaned on Chapin stories dating from his years there. In any case, Hurd had worked under Chapin for a brief time in 1906.[2]

As usual, alas, Chapin had little time or patience for such callers as Hurd. "I was so busy that I could spare but a few minutes to chat with him," said Chapin. The audience was over as soon as it started. Hurd scarcely had time to tell the irascible editor anything beyond the fact that he was in New York to catch the *R.M.S. Carpathia* of the British Cunard Line. Shoptalk would have to wait for another meeting. Disappointed, Hurd exited the city room and presumably toured the pressroom before leaving. No one came to the *World* without seeing its presses, a string of Hoe & Company machines, any one of which could run off the entire circulation of a small city newspaper in an hour. When running at full tilt, their rhythmic beat could be felt 300 feet above in the noise-proofed sanctum Pulitzer had built under the cupola at the very top of the twenty-story building. The smell of ink, the sound of the bell announcing the first turns of a press, the ensuing locomotive-like thumping cadence building to a deafening level, and the procession of cut, folded, and gathered pages pouring out with increasing speed was an irresistible sight to most members of the fourth estate. For a reporter in the early 1900s, the power of the press was a figurative *and* literal idea.[3]

The following night, Carlos and Kathleen Hurd sailed from New York in a second-class cabin on board the *Carpathia*, bound for Italy and the traditional grand tour from Naples to Liverpool. Originally, they had sought to make their crossing on the new, faster German ocean liner the *S.S. Berlin*, but it had been chartered. The *Berlin* was only one of many new ocean liners from which a traveler could choose. In fact, the copy of the *World* in Hurd's stateroom carried extensive coverage from Southampton, England, of the newest liner to set sail. "The new White Star Line *Titanic* started on her maiden voyage from this port today with 350 first class passengers for New York," read the story. "She had a great sendoff, crowds coming from London to examine the luxurious accommodations in this the latest thing in floating comfort."[4]

Chapin's encounter with Hurd was certainly not on his mind three days later when he worked at his desk. It was the end of the week for Chapin. The *Evening World* didn't publish on Sundays, and he was in the habit of using the quiet of the evening to catch up on desk work and get a measure of the week ahead. The news was dull. By the time he headed home to the Plaza that night, the only items of interest were a couple of murders in Brooklyn and Greenwich Village and a church-roof collapse in New Jersey that sent two parishioners to meet their maker. The items would be stale by the time he published Monday's *Evening World*. Maybe the morning would bring something newsworthy.

The scene was the same at other papers around the city. At the *New York Times*, which had followed the building trend northward and left Park Row for midtown a decade earlier, editors were drifting lethargically around the city room of the Tower as the first editions of the morning paper rolled off the presses seventeen floors below. By 1:00 A.M., the copy boys sat with nothing to do. A rewrite man organized a pile of notes on his desk. Their common challenge was to stay awake. Suddenly, the rope that guided the dumbwaiter down from the telegraph and cable room on the floor above banged noisily against the metal walls of the shaft, the signal of an incoming bulletin. A copy boy shook off his drowsiness and rushed to the box that had been lowered. He retrieved the sheaf of paper that lay in it and carried it rapidly to Jack Paine, the night telegraph editor. The Associated Press dispatch was from Cape Race, Newfoundland.[5]

> At 10:25 o'clock tonight the White Star Line steamship Titanic called "C.Q.D." [code for distress] to the Marconi station here, and reported having struck an iceberg. The steamer said that immediate assistance was required.
>
> Half an hour afterward another message came, reporting that they were sinking by the head and that women were being put off in the lifeboats.[6]

The bulletin reached the other newsrooms simultaneously. Not since the explosion of the *U.S.S. Maine* fourteen years earlier had a news flash hit the city press corps with such force. Editors roused correspondents from their sleep along the East Coast from New York to Halifax. The wire service ordered staffers from Washington and Cleveland and other bureaus to catch the first train to New York or Boston. The race was on to cover the disaster that couldn't happen.

On board the *Carpathia*, a few hours later at 5:40 A.M., Hurd awoke with the sun in his face. After three days at sea, he knew this signaled that the ship had drastically changed course. Further, the ship's throbbing engines were silent. "I realized the startling fact that the ship was standing still." With the instincts of a newspaperman, Hurd dressed hurriedly and ran out into the hall. "There came," he said, "the sound of wailing, deep and prolonged, from the other side of the ship, the port side." He immediately encountered a stewardess, slowly leading two weeping, disheveled women down the hall. "The *Titanic* has gone down," she said to Hurd without pausing to answer his questions. "We are taking on her passengers." Hurd ran back to his cabin, where he found that Kathleen had also been awakened by the noise. "The *Titanic* has gone down, and we are taking on its passengers," Hurd said, repeating the stewardess's words. He went over to the shelf on the wall of the cabin and grabbed Thursday's edition of the *World*. From it he tore the article about the *Titanic* with the names of prominent passengers. He stuffed it and pencil and paper into a pocket and raced off again. In her nightgown, Kathleen rose, hastened to her porthole and looked out onto a field of ice that extended for miles, punctuated by tall icebergs. "The brilliant glare almost blinded me for a moment. Then I gazed below me and saw two overturned lifeboats. That was my first realization of the great tragedy." Kathleen then dressed and went onto the deck in pursuit of her husband.[7]

Although the Hurds knew the *Titanic* had sunk, confusion reigned in New York. On Monday morning, when Chapin was putting together that day's *Evening World*, all the morning papers had already run specials. Scanning the papers, he could see that no one paper had any exclusive news. They all were reporting the same news based on the one Associated Press bulletin that had come in during the night. The *Times* headline read: "New Liner Titanic Hits Iceberg; Sinking by Bow at Midnight; Women Put Off in Life Boats; Last Wireless at 12:27 A.M. Blurred." Senior took the same slant. "Titanic Strikes an Iceberg, Begins to Sink at Head," read its headline.

By midday, New Yorkers were anxiously awaiting the evening papers. Chapin—as all other editors in town—had no reliable new information to offer his readers. The incoming bulletins were based on intercepted wireless messages, the credibility of which was unknown. Some claimed that all the passengers on the *Titanic* had been transferred to another ship. The *New York Sun*, in a burst of optimism, took the bait and proclaimed "All Saved From Titanic After Collision." Other messages described the *Titanic* being towed into the shallow waters near Cape Race in hopes of beaching her.

Chapin dispatched a reporter to the offices of the White Star Line down the street on Broadway. There he found a confused scene. Outside, relatives of passengers were besieging the place, demanding information, and no one was prepared to help them. Inside, the reporter found Phillip Franklin, the highest-ranking White Star official on that side of the Atlantic. Upon his return to the city room, the reporter told Chapin that there was no news from the *Titanic*. Franklin said wireless messages were not being received, either because of the atmospheric conditions or because the *Titanic* was too busy communicating with other ships. More important, the reporter told Chapin, the company claims that nobody needs to fear that the ship will go down. "I am free to say that no matter how bad the collision with an iceberg, the *Titanic* would float. She is an unsinkable ship," Franklin had told the reporter.[8]

The time had come to put the front page together. Chapin could put it off no longer. He took all he had, the conflicting bulletins and official pronouncements, and created a hodgepodge for his readers. With each edition, it was clear he could not make up his mind. By the time he put the final edition to bed, Chapin's take on the event remained of two minds. "Disabled Ship Under Tow After Hitting Big Iceberg," read his main head on the front page where, above the masthead, in larger type, was the headline "Liners Take Off Passengers; Titanic is Reported Sinking." At the bottom of the page, Chapin placed his reporter's account of the White Star official's optimism and, for good measure, added a dispatch from Belfast, where the ship's builders asserted the ship would survive.

Minutes after newsboys began hawking Chapin's final edition, it became embarrassingly clear that the ship's owners were at least correct on one account. All day they had asserted that news about the *Titanic* was based solely on rumors transmitted by amateurs via the new wireless. They were proved right—but not in the manner they hoped. At 6:15 P.M. the first official account reached New York. The *Titanic* had gone to the bottom at 2:20 A.M. with more than 1,500 passengers still on board. Survivors who had been rescued were on the *Carpathia*, heading to New York. In part because it didn't publish an afternoon paper, the *New York Times'* morning coverage looked prescient, having implied doom for the *Titanic*. For the editors who had kept the ship afloat all afternoon, the only consolation was the company of their rivals. They had, without exception, all gone the same route. For Chapin, however, the news also held special significance. When he saw the name "*Carpathia*," he realized he had "a reporter on the spot where all hell broke loose." His St. Louis caller of five days earlier, Carlos Hurd, was on board![9]

Hurd, of course, already knew the enormity of the story. The only survivors from one of the century's largest disasters were on his liner, and no other members of the press were anywhere to be seen. From the minute the survivors boarded the *Carpathia*, Hurd was able to interview them. This proved a lucky stroke because, in their current state, they were very willing to talk to anyone about their ordeal. "After that first morning, this ceased to be true in regards to many of the wealthier survivors," said Hurd. "As they regained their composure, they regained also their reserve, which some of them did not again break."[10]

Hurd's wandering around the *Carpathia* brought him to the tiny wireless shack installed atop the second-class smoking room. By 1912, almost every ocean-going vessel possessed Guglielmo Marconi's remarkable invention. There Hurd first learned from Harold Cottam, the young English wireless operator, of the happenings of the night before. Cottam told Hurd he had been preparing to retire for the night around 12:35 A.M. Just seconds before removing his headphones—thus cutting off the ship's only communication with the outside world—he received the *Titanic*'s famous call. "Come at once. We have struck a berg. It's a CQD OM [old man]."

Leaving Cottam and his Marconi equipment, Hurd ran into Captain Arthur Rostron. In only his third month as captain of the 13,000-ton ship, Rostron was an unusual seaman. He did not smoke, drink, or use profanity. Because of his boundless energy, Rostron inspired considerable loyalty among his crew, and because of his willingness to render a quick decision, he had acquired a reputation as a no-nonsense officer. Hurd explained how he was a newspaperman and said that it was his duty to send a story as soon as possible to the *New York World*. "There was no hesitation about the British captain's answer," said Hurd. "He meant to see to it that the rescued persons in his care were not annoyed by press men." There would be no further entry into the wireless room, and certainly no messages would be sent to New York. "The captain's no-wireless ruling was a jolt in the jaw, to put it very mildly," said Hurd. The restriction had no effect at first because the *Carpathia*'s wireless was too weak to reach another ship or shore and would not likely succeed for another twenty-four hours. "But when we should get within range of communications," said Hurd, "I knew that every paper in New York would besiege the operator with queries and offers and I could hardly imagine that some of them would not get a reply from him."

At the first chance he had, Hurd approached Cottam when he was away from the wireless room. He promised him cash and additional payment from the *World* if he would get even a short message to Chapin. Cottam refused. "His reply showed that the captain's thorough discipline extended to the Marconi service and that messages not expressly authorized by the captain had no chance to go." Rostron wanted to wrap the victims in a blanket of protection. "I could not allow the passengers to be interviewed," the captain said later. He told the survivors on board not to wire anything beyond the basics. "That's it, that is it," Rostron said. "There is a news freeze."[11]

Undeterred, Hurd persuaded his wife to help him. The pair began systematically interviewing the rescued. In doing so, they became the very first to piece together the story of what had happened Sunday night. As luck would have it, among the first survivors Hurd met was Spencer V. Silverthorne, a buyer for a St. Louis department store, who was eager to help. Silverthorne gave Hurd a copy of the *Titanic* passenger list, the only thing he took with him when he left the sinking boat, aside from the clothes he wore. The deck of the *Carpathia* was in turmoil as the lifeboats were emptied of their cargo. The rigid class distinctions of steamer travel were gone. The disaster was the great leveler. Women with cheap shawls stood touching women draped in fur. "Disheveled women, who the night before could have drawn thousands from their husband's letters of credit or from the *Titanic*'s safe, stood penniless before the *Carpathia*'s purser asking that messages be forwarded—collect," wrote Hurd.[12]

By the end of the day, the bedlam of the morning had subsided. "Wailing and sobbing of the day were hushed as widows and orphans slept," said Hurd. On Tuesday, the survivors met together in one of the *Carpathia*'s large halls to organize themselves, take stock, and express thanks to the *Carpathia* crew. Hurd recorded it all. But Rostron continued to add to the difficulty of his work. By his orders, Hurd was cut off from all stationery supplies. The Hurds had to resort to using whatever scraps of paper they could come by, including toilet paper. Even keeping control over what notes he had became a challenge as they discovered that their cabin was being searched. To protect their notes, Kathleen sat on them when stewards came in. No one in their right mind would touch a lady.[13]

Hurd found that, with the two French children from the *Titanic* who had been placed in his cabin, and the overcrowding of the ship's salons, the only time he could write was at night. "It seemed to me that, beside and ahead of the individual experiences of the survivors, the story of the disaster itself should be told." Monday and Tuesday, as the *Carpathia* retraced its path toward New York, Hurd worked late into the night writing and revising in longhand the tale as he pieced it together. "The endeavor to fit such a story together showed how fragmentary was the knowledge of individuals. One would mention an incident that could be confirmed or completed only by another. In the search for the other, new suggestions and new complications would arise." Worse was that, despite all his efforts, Hurd was still unable to get his copy into print. He hadn't even been able to get word to Chapin that he was working on the story. Rostron was intransigent. Even Marconi himself, in New York at the time, couldn't persuade the captain to lighten his censorship by sending a wireless to the *Carpathia* inquiring about her silence. "The Captain posted Marconi's message on the bulletin board and beside it a bulletin stating that no press message, except a bulletin to the Associated Press, had been sent," said Hurd. "The implication was that none would be sent, and the most urgent and respectful appeals failed to change his determination, which, he seemed convinced was in the best interest of the survivors and their friends." New York would be reached Thursday afternoon or evening. "The *Carpathia*, making 13 knots an hour, was taking us in with the story for which the world was waiting," wrote Hurd. "Continued attempts to get use of the wireless, all of which were futile, took much time and nerve force." Instead, he turned his remaining energy Wednesday night to making the final revisions to the story he had written, now more than 5,000 words long.[14]

In New York, Chapin—and other editors—were apoplectic. Hurd's copy, if it existed at all, was with the survivors and was not going to beat them back to New York. There seemed to be nothing Chapin could do to break the seafaring embargo. A United Press correspondent on another ship, the *Olympic*, was even barred from filing his copy. There simply was no hard news to be had since the disclosure that the ship had sunk. At first, Chapin had recovered from his botched run of paper on Monday by leading his Tuesday afternoon editions with the angle that the fault lay with the ship's captain. "Titanic Was Warned of Ice Ahead 48 Hours Before Crash Killed 1,410," read his headline. That morning, the *World* had skewered Franklin and White Star's Monday performance. Junior simply continued the assault, in the *World*'s typical style of exposé journalism, blaming the officials for having led the ship to its doom. Chapin made no mention of Monday's coverage. Rather, he now focused on the lack of information, perhaps intimating that the *Evening World* should not be responsible for its earlier gaff. Until *Carpathia*'s silence ends, read Chapin's front-page story, "the stupendous story of the most disastrous ocean tragedy in history is shut off from the knowledge of the outside world."[15]

Wednesday brought no news. The *Carpathia* had even turned a deaf ear to President Taft's calls, which came from the *U.S.S. Chester*, dispatched expressly by the president to get within wireless range of the *Carpathia*. A few private messages from some survivors on the *Carpathia* to relatives in the United States served as the basis of Chapin's afternoon press run. "Heroes of Titanic Died Amid Work of Rescue, Says First Wreck Story," read his lead story based on "an absolutely well authenticated source." In the end, three days after the first bulletin, the only news Chapin could offer his readers was speculation. He became so desperate, he ran a story titled "What Probably Happened on the Titanic," based entirely on an interview with a captain whose ship arrived in port that week after traversing the ice field that sunk the *Titanic*.[16]

Unwilling to wait any longer, the newspapers began chartering their own boats. The first to set out was a tug chartered by Hearst out of Newport, Rhode Island. It carried reporters and photographers and, typical of the enterprising publisher, an added ingredient of drama for *Journal* readers—Jack Binns, the telegraph operator who three years earlier had been the first to use the wireless for a distress call at sea. His messages were credited with saving the entire crew and passengers of the sinking *Republic*, in the largest-ever open-water rescue effort. Hearst's tug, however, cruised into a blanket of fog and never made contact with the *Carpathia*. It did, however, intercept the famous "Yamsi" telegram in which J. Bruce Ismay, director of the White Star Line, tried to send a coded message to his company in hopes of escaping the investigators waiting in New York. A tug carrying Louis Seibold of the *World* and a gaggle of other reporters left from Providence, Rhode Island. Ill-equipped and without sufficient provisions for a large contingent of reporters and photographers, the tug captain soon faced a mutiny. Only the promise of *World* money to pay overtime kept the crew at work long enough for the reporters to gain a view of the *Carpathia*'s stern as she steamed toward New York.

As the hour of the *Carpathia*'s return drew closer, New York papers planned their final assault. The *New York Times* had won the initial battle. Its coverage had been the most accurate and complete, and it had been rewarded with a spike in its circulation. But none of the New York papers was going to concede defeat, especially now that the return of the *Carpathia* could level the playing field. At the *Tribune*, publisher Ogden Reid—a sailor himself—directed the paper's coverage. They would take to the sea in two tugboats in hopes of boarding the *Carpathia*. On shore, a corps of reporters would await the ship at the pier. Carr V. Van Anda at the *New York Times* planned to keep his forces on land, choosing instead to send a crew of sixteen to meet the *Carpathia* at the pier. They would be the best equipped. *New York Times* city editor Arthur Greaves put rewrite men in the Strand Hotel on West 14th Street, blocks from the *Carpathia*'s pier, with four telephone lines left open with the city room. Greaves also arranged for a set of backup phones further uptown and hired cars and chauffeurs to transport the reporters. "I'm sending sixteen of you down to the pier, even though we have only these four passes," Greaves told his staff. "Men without passes will have to try to get through to survivors—crew and passengers—on their police cards. If that can't be done they will work as close in as they can and get survivors leaving the pier in cabs."[17]

Chapin, on the other hand, took a different tack. Ever since the 1880s, when he had singled-handedly pursued a crooked Chicago police chief by boat across Lake Michigan and also gained his exclusive on the sinking of the *Vernon*, Chapin had gone for the long shot when it came to stories on the water. He was betting that tonight, Hurd would be his trump card. He would leave it to Senior to cover the return at the dock. He would take to the high seas. After the last edition on Wednesday, Chapin sat down with publisher Ralph Pulitzer and explained his plan. Rather than wait for the story to reach New York of its own accord, when all the survivors would be open game, Chapin told his boss that he planned to intercept the *Carpathia*. Pulitzer gave the okay to the plan and its associated costs. At 9:10 P.M., he wired Hurd.

NEW YORK APRIL 17TH
CARLOS HURD, CARPATHIA, NY.

CHAPIN IS ON TUG DALZELLINE. WILL MEET CARPATHIA BETWEEN NEW YORK AND FIRE ISLAND THURSDAY. BE ON LOOKOUT AND DELIVER TO CHAPIN TUG YOUR FULL REPORT OF THE WRECK WITH ALL INTERVIEWS OBTAINABLE.

RALPH PULITZER[18]

Pulitzer and Chapin weren't the only ones trying to reach Hurd. The *New York Sun* hoped to get Hurd to jump ship, so to speak. It wired Hurd, "Sun will pay handsomely for wireless dispatches Titanic and exclusive story when you land." The *Post-Dispatch* city editor, working with Chapin, aimed to keep the story as their exclusive by wiring Hurd to ignore any requests from the Associated Press and give it only to the *World*. "World steamer will meet Carpathia have completed story ready throw them," wrote Bovard, *St. Louis Post-Dispatch* city editor. None of the messages, however, were delivered because the *Carpathia* continued to maintain a radio silence. Instead, they were all put in a bin to be processed for refunds as "non-transmitted" messages.[19]

Thursday morning, the waters between the permanently moored *Ambrose* light ship and Sandy Hook were churning as

more than fifty boats of all sorts and sizes cruised back and forth like sentinel ships of a blockade. A strong east wind was blowing, and the waters were rough and choppy. The Associated Press, the *Herald*, the *Tribune*, and the *American* each had its own tug, and each was decorated with a massive banner visible a half-mile away. Not to be outdone, the *Sun* had procured a tug with a powerful searchlight. The greyhound of the fleet, however, had been grabbed by the *Evening World*. On board Captain Augustin Keene's *Dalzelline* were Lindsay Denison, from the rewrite desk, and reporters Rosswin Whytock, Samuel Eiseler, Harry Stowe, and Herman Robbins. In command was Chapin.

Authorities were also preparing for the rescue ship's return to New York. The Treasury Department issued orders that no newspapermen were to board the ship at an area called Quarantine. Mayor Gaynor revoked pier privileges to all but a handful of photographers and reporters. No one from the press would have easy access to the survivors. "Extraordinary Precautions Taken to Prevent Newspaper Men Reaching Them," declared the *World*.[20]

On the *Carpathia*, Hurd readied himself as well. Pulitzer's telegram had been intercepted, but Hurd believed that the infamous editor would not fail him. In fact, he was convinced that Chapin would meet the ship at Sandy Hook. Late Thursday, with help from Silverthorne—the St. Louis merchant from the *Titanic*—Hurd worked on a way to protect his story should the chance come that he could engineer a transfer to Chapin. He obtained some waterproof white canvas, placed the story and his notes at the center, and rolled it up tightly like a furled sail. It looked like "a package about the size of an unabridged dictionary," said Silverthorne. "Knowing that the matter might have to be tossed over the ship's side," said Hurd, "others advised me to attach some sort of buoy or ballast as the bundle might fall into the water." A cigar box was found and tied to the bundle with a cord. The bartender contributed a bunch of champagne corks that were also made fast for additional flotation. At last, the job was complete. With his book-sized bundle, cigar box, and dangling champagne corks, Hurd looked for a place to position himself.[21]

Miles to the south, the *Dalzelline*, her boilers stoked, docked

at Sandy Point at the bottom of the bay where Chapin waited in the tower of the tug's wireless station. The wireless reports from the *World* offices continuously updated Chapin on the *Carpathia*'s
progress. Unbeknownst to him, the reports were inaccurate. Hoping to catch the press flotilla unprepared, the *Carpathia* had been broadcasting false reports of her position. Each wireless message masked her approach, claiming she was forty miles away when she had less than twenty to travel.

A little after 6:00 P.M., a tug named *New York*, carrying a harbor pilot—which was required to steer a liner to its berth—began to steam out from New York. The tug had been working her wireless under "low tension" all day, a technique that hid messages from others, and thus had successfully received a secret signal from the *Carpathia* to meet her. The press boats ignored the *New York*'s move, continuing to be misled by the wireless reports they heard. "It can't be the *Carpathia*," insisted the captain of the *Sun*'s tug. The sun was now rapidly falling. By 6:38 it would be gone. In the distance, a pall of smoke was spotted. It was a liner for sure, but which one? It could be the *Mauretania* or any other of several expected in that night. In the dusk, it raced past the assembled press boats. The *Sun*'s powerful searchlight painted the hull and lit up the stern of the swiftly moving ship. It read *Carpathia*.[22]

The ship moved swiftly into the Ambrose Channel, the faster and preferred path from the open sea into the New York harbor, marked by the light ship *Ambrose*. Captain Keene had anticipated Rostron's move. He had pumped all the water out of the bilge in the bow, permitting his tug to hydroplane, making it faster and more nimble than the other press boats. In fact, the *Dalzelline* moved so quickly that Chapin and his crew found themselves in the channel ahead of the *Carpathia*. Behind the ship lay a long procession of tugs desperately trying to catch up. Keene, fearing he would outrun his prey, but wanting to keep his head of steam up, spun his wheel, carving a wide turn and bringing the *Dalzelline* to the stern of the speeding *Carpathia*.

It was now 7:35 P.M., and the steamship entered the lower bay followed by a swarm of tugs. The pursuing press was convinced that its chance to board the ship would come when it slowed to pick up a required medical team at Quarantine. The tugs raced each other to be in position. The *Dalzelline* used her speed to zigzag and slow up Hearst's tug, its closest rival. Under no conditions would Chapin permit a Hearst reporter to beat him. After being cut off three or four times, the Hearst tug took a chance and tried to break through. The move failed, and it violently crashed into the *Dalzelline*. Reporters were willing to risk another seagoing accident to get the edge on this story. Only the strength of the tugs kept them from sustaining crippling damage.

At last, the *Carpathia* slowed. Hurd had positioned himself in the *Carpathia*'s hold by the lower doors, which were opened to take on the doctors approaching on a small launch. He figured Chapin might try to board through the doors. On deck, Rostron felt his fear of the press come to life as he looked to his stern and saw the bevy of tugs chugging their way toward his ship. "Naturally, I did not care to have any of the passengers harassed by reporters seeking information; so I decided not to allow anyone on board the *Carpathia*." He ordered his crew to prevent any boarding by the press and prevent any contact between the press and his passengers. The weather rallied to his cause. A strong rain began to come down in torrents, lightning competed with the magnesium flashes from the photographers, and rolling thunder drowned out the questions being called up from the bobbing boats. "It was a scene never to be effaced from one's memory," said Rostron.[23]

In the ensuing chaos, reporters did try to board the ship and all were repelled, except for one who was confined to the bridge. As this battle ensued, Hurd vainly tried to spot the *World*'s tug. The *Carpathia*'s screws began to churn the water. At that instant, through the open door, Hurd saw Chapin. It was too late. The *Carpathia* was underway, and the doors were closing. Hurd rushed topside. Denison, meanwhile, had grabbed a megaphone and began calling loudly for Hurd, as did reporters on the other tugs. "As I got back to the upper deck, my name was being called through megaphones," said Hurd. "Not only the *World*, but the others, called for me in tones suggesting the summons of judgment day."[24]

It was now 7:50 P.M. The *Carpathia* glided past the Statue of Liberty and would soon approach the Battery at the tip of Manhattan. Gaynor and other city officials saw the ship from their large tug and let off a blast of its steam whistle. All the other boats in the harbor followed suit, creating a din of bells, whistles, and sirens that signaled to the city, and the 30,000 standing in the cold rain on the Cunard pier, that the wait was over. From the shore, said a witness, *Carpathia*'s "dim outline would be thrown momentarily into bold relief by a monster flashlight exploded on shore by photographers, who sought early pictures of the incoming rescue ship."[25]

Chapin would have one last chance to effect a ship-to-ship transfer of Hurd's precious cargo before the *Carpathia* docked and all reporters would have access to the survivors, who had been until now the exclusive property of Hurd. The opportunity came in the vicinity of the Cunard pier when the *Carpathia* came to a surprise stop off the White Star pier to unload the *Titanic* lifeboats. The press boats were hardly able to stop. In fact, two of them crashed into the stern of the liner. By this time, Hurd had successfully gained the rail of the deck. He climbed up, by a stanchion, and yelled, "Here I am. Ready." Rival newspapers again began to call for him. Hurd was not fooled by the impostors and clutched his canvas bundle. Below, Captain Keene maneuvered the *Dalzelline* alongside, actually bumping into the *Carpathia*. Hurd looked down, and for the second time that night, in the illumination of the magnesium flashes, spotted Chapin. The moment had come. Chapin stood, feet apart, arms extended, on the open deck of the tug. Hurd took his bundle and flung it into the darkness. The package and its cigar box, trailed by its string of champagne corks, flew through the air. Then it stopped midflight. Its train of flotsam had become tangled in the supporting rope of one of the *Titanic* lifeboats hanging off the deck below. There the exclusive story—swaddled in its canvas—swayed back and forth, just out of reach. Once again, all seemed lost. Suddenly, a barefooted sailor on the lower deck leaped up onto the rail and, looping the cord around his foot, caused the canvas pack to swing back over onto the deck. An officer, loyal to Rostron, ordered that the bundle be brought to him. "Throw it," cried a dozen passengers. The sailor hesitated for an instant, then turned to the rail and, in a single motion, pitched the package into Chapin's outstretched arms. The passengers let off a loud cheer. Keene responded with a blast of the *Dalzelline*'s whistle. Then he threw open the throttle, and the tug surged forward toward shore.[26]

Keene maneuvered the *Dalzelline* to an abandoned dock at 12th Street and let off Chapin, Denison, and the others. Two blocks to the north, the *Carpathia* was beginning to move again, having dropped off the lifeboats. Chapin and his crew looked around. They were not home free. Between them and the street was a shuttered warehouse. In the darkness, they entered it and battered their way out the other side. Then they caught an elevated train and rode it to the station just above Park Row. Hurd's story, an extract of it marked up with Chapin's typesetting instructions, was then given to a reporter, who sprinted the last half-mile to the *World* offices.

Back at Pier 54, the *Carpathia* was beginning her final approach. It was 9:10 P.M. The only sound came from the ship's engines and the agitated water behind her propellers. The crowd stood in anxious silence. Several minutes later and a few blocks away, shrieking newsboys poured out of the *World* building. In their arms were bundles of extras, the ink still wet. "Titanic Boilers Blew Up, Breaking her In Two After Striking Berg," read the massive headline. "Ship Was Going 23 Knots an Hour After Warning of the Icebergs." They were hawking the first eyewitness accounts of the sinking of the *Titanic*. A full twenty minutes before any other reporter, including Van Anda's army of *Times* reporters, even had a chance to talk to a survivor, Chapin's *Evening World* had Hurd's story in print—John Astor's refusal to board a lifeboat, Mrs. Isidor Straus's choice to die with her husband, and the band's playing of "Nearer My God to Thee"; it was all there.[27]

The *Carpathia* edged closer to the dock and began to warp in. At 9:35 P.M., her gangplanks were lowered, and the procession began. The *Times* reporters and those of other papers with passes descended upon the survivors. But it would be another three hours before the *Times*' presses would begin rolling out its extra. One could read all about it only in the *Evening World*. Even Hurd, who had participated in the remarkable transfer, was amazed when a newsboy sold him a copy of the *Evening World* as he approached the nearby "L" station. But soon the city was littered with "extras" from every newspaper. "Probably not in the history of American journalism has there been a demand for newspapers equaling that of Thursday night," commented the *Fourth Estate* the next week.[28]

Carlos and Kathleen Hurd made their way to the *World* building. This time when Hurd entered, his anonymity was a thing of the past. The *World* staff was building the entire morning issue around Hurd's exclusive account. The Associated Press was transmitting all 5,000 words to St. Louis, where the *Post-Dispatch* was preparing an extra. In his joy, Ralph Pulitzer grabbed a scrap of paper and a grease pencil and wrote, "A bonus of $1,000 and an extra vacation of three weeks have been awarded to Mr. Hurd."[29]

"For the little I did towards securing the beat," said Chapin, "he rewarded me almost as generously."[30]

The Crisis

By this time a Pulitzer bonus check was like chump change to Chapin. The $1,000 could have bought him a year's rent for his rooms in the Plaza. But within days, it would be gone to meet past obligations. Chapin was like the *Titanic*, seemingly unsinkable to all around him, but going down fast. There were no financial life rafts in sight, such as the potential inheritance from Sage six years earlier. Time was simply running out.[1]

His last hope was the stock market. Still mostly unregulated, it remained a place where a fortune could be made. "The number of speculators who buy and sell stocks in Wall Street since this became the greatest speculative mart in Christendom is now four times as great as ten years ago," Van Benthuysen wrote Pulitzer a few years earlier. At the Plaza, where Charles and Nellie lived, there were a half-dozen brokerage offices. But it was certainly risky. One of the most common get-rich-quick schemes of the era often left the investor holding the bag. "Bucket shops," the name given to fly-by-night investment dealers, would encourage small investors to purchase stock at a small fraction of its price— what is called buying "on margin." The dealer would then place the order simultaneously with his own, thereby driving up the stock's price. As long as the price rose, the strategy worked. If the price fell, then the investor would be called on to make good on the balance of the stock at its former price. For stockbrokers, and the occasional lucky investor, the scheme provided a short-term killing. For the bulk of investors, though, it left them poorer than when they started. Chapin, like many speculators, also bought on margin. But inside information he acquired as a powerful editor had rewarded him handsomely. A man with inside information using a common scheme could turn a 450-percent profit as companies "surprisingly" merged, and inexpensive shares were exchanged for highly valued shares in the new combination. Chapin was not alone in prospering from the market's fortunes. Since the panic of 1907, stocks had climbed steadily in value, and the market's leading index now stood forty percent higher, a fact his paper reported each night.[2]

In December 1912, the Chapins traveled to Washington, D.C., to be with Charles's mother, who was gravely ill. For the past eight years, Cecelia Chapin had lived in a three-story brownstone at 30 Rhode Island Avenue, in northeast Washington, with her daughter Marion and her other son Frank. On December 10, at seventy-six years old, Cecelia died. Chapin walked five blocks to Glenwood Cemetery and secured a family plot. Two days later, they buried her. The woman whose portrait Chapin had fallen in love with as a child, the woman into whose arms he had run after his first foray into the world, was gone.[3]

Upon returning to New York, Chapin threw himself back into his work. There was plenty of news to fill the pages of the *Evening World*. Woodrow Wilson was soon to take office in Washington, the first Democratic president in twenty years, and many in Chapin's circle were hoping to land a patronage job. Much of the press, including the *World*, was swept up in the enthusiasm for the college-president-turned-governor-turned-president. Delaware's legislature gave the final necessary nod for the ratification of the sixteenth amendment, and there was talk of letting citizens directly elect their U.S. senators. The rarified air of politics also was evident in theater, music, and the visual arts. In February, the famed New York Armory Show opened. On April 26, 1913, the *Evening World* gang came together at Delmonico's to roast Martin Green. By now, Green was the best-known member of Chapin's crack rewrite team. Irvin Cobb presided, and speakers included the lieutenant governor of New York, a former district attorney, and a smattering of politicians and lawyers. One friend, who posed as Green's Boswell, read a humorous biography marked by Green's arrival at the "halfway house to the grave," and then the gang presented him with a silver chest.[4]

In late spring, Chapin's health failed. Just as they had twenty years earlier, doctors ordered him to go West to rest what they diagnosed as a "tubercular throat." He consolidated all the investments under his control, including the $15,000 his father had entrusted to him for his step-sister Edna until she turned twenty-one later that year. "In the hurry of getting away my only thought was to leave with my brokers more than sufficient collateral to protect my account in any emergency that might arise while I was away." But unbeknownst to Chapin, his investments, like his health, were beginning to take a turn for the worse. To fight his real or imagined bacillus, he extended his stay in the West, even taking a three-month journey to Hawaii. To make good on the money he borrowed to finance his faltering stock purchases, his brokers began selling the collateral. "For three months I didn't see a market quotation," he recalled. "On my return to California I found that all my supposed profits had been swept away and that many of the securities I had deposited as margin had gone with them." He placed a transcontinental call to his broker. "A reassuring reply came back that the worst was over and the tendency of the market was now upward. . . . I had been scorched a bit but was far from consumed."[5]

While in San Francisco, Chapin had occasion to lunch at a club with a banker and a group of financiers. They all spoke optimistically about their investments. Chapin confided to the banker about his losses. Buy sugar, he said, and all will be well. That night, Chapin wired his broker. A San Francisco throat specialist offered him more practical advice. Chapin should wait for the warm weather to set in before returning to the East. Thus, the Chapins set off to visit a friend in Colorado and put off returning for another month. "On the way I read the newspapers and sugar looked to be sweetest quotation in the market report," said Chapin. If it held its course, he would wipe out his losses and even pay for his trip. "I decided to act on the advice of the banker and not sell until sugar reached a point that he had jotted on the back of his visiting card."[6]

Colorado was wonderful, a complete escape from his troubles. Chapin hunted and fished with cowboys on his friend's ranch, situated 6,000 feet up on the western slope of the Rocky Mountains. Though now fifty-four years old, he even found enough vigor to join a round-up. "It was the best fun I ever experienced and all the while I knew that the tubercular germs in my throat were being killed and that sugar was going to bring me greater riches than I had ever known." The pleasure and escape from worry ended with the delivery of a telegram. The sugar market had collapsed and with it everything Chapin owned. The pair returned home. "I found that my imagination hadn't pictured the situation any worse than I found it." Practically all his investments, including Edna's inheritance, had been swept away. His only remaining asset was his salary, now more than $250 a week, and frequent bonuses, and he went right back to work so as to collect on it. He had been in financial straits before, but he had kept debtors at bay through his wiles, his imperious conduct at the *World*, and his visible associations with his great-uncle Russell Sage and Joseph Pulitzer. Creditors often believed the rumors of his high salary, and that he was listed in the wills of the two magnates, an impression Chapin did nothing to discourage. With these two men dead, however, his means of deception were diminished. He bought what time he could by painfully selling *Eidolon* and his automobile.[7]

Chapin carried his burden by himself. He decided not to tell anyone, including Nellie, of his troubles. Panic seized him. "I believed that if it became known to others that I was in financial difficulties, my newspaper position would be jeopardized and my creditors would get me by the throat and prevent me from doing anything to rehabilitate myself." He had ruled his newsroom with terror, and he had built his reputation into a legend. If he were to reveal his clay feet, his world would collapse. Certainly, he remembered how the *Chicago Times* city editor he had replaced had been cast aside like an old worn-out, battered wreck. His only hope was that his past luck with the market might again provide an escape. "There had been many times in recent years when speculative ventures yielded astonishing results with almost no effort or wisdom on my part," said Chapin, "but now that I had reached the brink of a precipice and knew that it would take but a little push to send me over, luck forsook me." No matter whose tip he followed, no matter how sure the investment seemed, his situation grew more hopeless. The stock market had begun a precipitous slide similar to that of five years earlier, and it was taking Chapin's last borrowed dollars with it. The ticker in his office convinced him that soon his financial woes would become public. But as much as he feared that day, there was yet another, greater problem terrifying him.[8]

He knew that his debts eventually could be paid by garnishing his wages, as embarrassing as such a course might be. The growing nightmare was the missing investments from Edna's trust that were swept away along with his own stocks and bonds. She would turn twenty-one soon, and he would have to produce this investment in court as part of a final accounting of the trusteeship. He had to replace the bonds, or else he would be exposed as an embezzler. But like a spiteful lover, the market continued its cruelty. Several times, his newest investments would rise promisingly, then fall again. "Fear took possession of me and fairly choked me into submission."[9]

Each day and night brought a new terror. Chapin's imagination ran wild. He would jump when the phone rang at night in his hotel suite. He would tremble and change his route when he saw a policeman in the street. "Often when I went to the *World* office in the early morning, I felt certain that the policeman near the entrance was waiting for me with a warrant, and my heart would thump wildly against my ribs until I had passed him and was at my desk." The court date neared, and Chapin still did not have the money. He won a short respite by telegraphing the lawyers that he was detained on business. They were, of course, without suspicion, and an extension was routinely granted.[10]

Chapin considered his position. All his life he had defined himself by his possessions. His address at the Plaza, his yacht, his horses, his automobile, his access to New York society—or at least that part that would have him—comprised the elixir that transformed the baseness of life. Nothing Chapin had ever accumulated was for its own sake. He rode a horse to be *seen* riding a horse. Permanence and the future were not part of his ethos. After all, in thirty-three years of marriage, the only home he had provided Nellie was a hotel suite. The loss of all of this would mean a descent into the city's inferno that he portrayed each day from his desk. He would become nothing more than the tragic subject of a headline, just like countless others about whom Chapin had constructed catchy headlines. He had once told Cobb that he liked a certain murderess because she had a short name, one that would fit almost any headline. Now another editor would get the same joy out of "Chapin." His importance would be measured in type point size, his significance in position on the page, his legacy in the number of subsequent editions in which his fate would be discussed.[11]

Others could turn to their friends in such a moment, but Chapin could not. He believed he had no confidants among his few friends and certainly none among his many acquaintances. "I had greater affection for my horses than for the multitude of men who courted me," he said. The handful of colleagues at work who had sought his friendship had been kept at bay, even the irrepressible Cobb. "I never saw or spoke to a member of the staff outside of the office, or talked with them in the office about anything except the business of the minute," said Chapin. "I gave no confidences, I invited none." Chapin's sole intimacy was his marriage.[12]

Only once in his six years at work by Chapin's side had Cobb witnessed a crack in the irascible editor's veneer of emotionlessness. Chapin was preparing to fire a reporter. "Red" McLaughlin, a copy editor who was teased by the staff for his softness regarding the sad lives he read about daily, tried to intercede. After vainly arguing with Chapin, McLaughlin returned angrily to his desk. As he did, Chapin said, in a loud voice for all to hear, "Red, you're too mushy-hearted, too sentimental for your own good. You'll never get ahead in this game, never get an inch past where you are now. And when you die, you won't leave a red cent to bury you with."

"True for you, Chapin!" responded McLaughlin. "But when I die, there'll be a hell of lot of people who will come to the funeral."

It was as if he had been physically hit, said Cobb. "We saw Chapin wince and get white as a flour mask. For an hour he sat there, staring at nothing and chewing the dead stub of a cigar to sodden pulp, a shriveled and blighted shape."

With the advantage of hindsight, Cobb later reflected on this scene. "With that sixth sense of his I think perhaps he was tearing apart the veil of the future, no longer beholding himself in the flattering mirror which he usually held before his deluded eyes but in an honester light. I think he saw a man being slowly stripped naked of power and perquisites."[13]

Now, years later, Chapin was convinced he was facing just such a day of reckoning. "I knew I was at the end of my rope and rather than suffer disgrace and imprisonment, I resolved then to do the only thing that was left to me." He picked up his telephone and called an old friend, Rhinelander Waldo, who was now Mayor Gaynor's police commissioner. He was not in to take the call. Instead, as would be Chapin's luck, he was put through to Waldo's chief of staff, Winfield Sheehan, a former *World* reporter who had just been hired away from the newspaper. Chapin explained that he was in need of a revolver. It had been only a year since the state had begun to require gun permits, a law that was enforced only against hoodlums, and a request from a noted citizen for such a weapon was not considered remarkable. Just as the police in St. Louis had obligingly armed Chapin twenty years earlier, the New York police department was ready to help. Sheehan promised that a revolver would be waiting for him in the office. Within an hour, Chapin walked the few blocks from his office to the elegant gray stone police headquarters at 240 Centre Street. A police officer was provisioned to show Chapin how to use the weapon.[14]

Late that evening, Chapin returned to his office. He left a note that he would be absent for several days and destroyed what personal papers he had in his desk. He told Nellie he had business in Washington, and she gladly consented to accompany him. At midnight, they boarded a train for the capital at Pennsylvania Station. On the train, he continued his destruction of private papers and tore up his bankbooks. "I would never see New York again, for I was going away to die, to die like a coward and leave her to bear all the poverty and disgrace that was sure to follow, leave her this way after a lifetime of affectionate devotion. I cried all night, sickened with the thought of it." By the time they reached their destination, Chapin had also come down with the flu, and upon arriving he went right to bed in the Rhode Island Avenue house where his two siblings continued to live.[15]

The first day that Chapin felt well enough to leave the house, he walked the few blocks to Glenwood Cemetery. There he re-

flected on his plans to soon join his mother. Up until now, he had
thought only of putting an end to himself. But as he considered
his fate that day, he began to worry about what would happen to
Nellie. She had no family, and they had no children. "She was so
fragile and delicate it was impossible that she could ever do for
herself," thought Chapin. He continued to ponder his situation
with a walk in some quiet woods near his family's house. "When
I returned I had made up my mind to do the most dreadful deed
that my distorted brain could conceive," he said. "It was hideous,
but there was no other way." To be sure, Chapin asked Marion
and Frank if they would look after Nellie if anything happened to
him. The frigid silence and the stony stare that greeted his question made it clear to him there was no hope of sparing Nellie's
life. The following morning, he selected a large block of granite
at a tombstone maker and gave directions for it to be installed on
the plot with his and his wife's name.[16]

Outwardly, nothing had changed for Nellie. During the day
they took long automobile rides, and at night they enjoyed Washington theater. On their anniversary, Chapin took her to dinner
at the New Willard. Opened in 1901 on the site of the original
Willard, the new hotel consisted of what looked like several
buildings, each taller than the other, stacked one against the
other, and topped with a story of decorative, carved stone. It was
designed by Henry Hardenbergh, the same architect who had designed the Plaza in New York. The interior was sumptuous, with
plush carpeting and beautiful mosaics, appropriate considering
the Willard's historic role as temporary residence of presidents
and potentates, neatly positioned across the street from the tem-
ple-styled Treasury building. "The day after that dinner was to be
our last day on earth," Chapin thought. "Could anything be more
horrible?"[17]

In the morning, Chapin presented himself at the *World*'s
Washington office at 1403 F Street, a block from the Treasury
building behind the Willard, to write several farewell letters.
When he completed them, Harry Dunlop, the paper's Washington correspondent, asked Chapin to come with him to a press
conference at the White House. In a new twist on Washington
presidential politics, Woodrow Wilson had consented to meet
regularly with reporters since his ascent to the presidency in

March. The supposition was that Wilson would talk about the political turmoil in Mexico. Chapin was reluctant, but the newspaperman in him consented. The press conferences were held in the East Room of the White House. About two hundred correspondents attended them, and, so far, the new approach was not serving the president well. "He came into the room suspicious, reserved, and a little resentful—no thought of frankness and open door and cordiality and that sort of thing," recalled reporter R. S. Baker. "It was a silly thing to do. He could not be as frank as he could have been with one; and he was embarrassed and had this rankling feeling, and he utterly failed to get across to those men anything except that this was very distasteful to him."[18]

Wilson said little that was newsworthy that day, but engaged in enough saber rattling to provide some copy for the reporters trying to file stories about developments in Mexico. As the president was concluding his remarks, Joe Tumulty spotted Chapin. Tumulty, a former northern New Jersey politician, had been Wilson's secretary since his election as governor of New Jersey in 1910. Unlike his boss, Tumulty understood newspapermen and liked their company. He came over and greeted Chapin and asked him to stay behind and meet the president. For fifteen minutes, Chapin and Wilson, who was far more pleasant in smaller encounters with the press, chatted about politics after the room emptied. "I felt grateful that he could not read my thoughts or know that the hand he grasped so cordially would soon press the trigger of the revolver that was concealed in my pocket."[19]

As Chapin departed, a Secret Service agent approached him. Would he, asked the agent, accompany him to his chief's office? The gun in the pocket was not the cause of the invitation. No one knew of its existence yet. White House security was still a rather casual affair, and the current chief of the Secret Service was William Flynn, whom Chapin had known when he was deputy police commissioner in New York. Flynn had heard that Chapin was in the White House, and he wanted to take his old acquaintance to lunch at the Willard. After lunch, Chapin was finally free to continue working on his plans. He went to a writing table in the hotel and wrote an additional note for Flynn, to be delivered with the others he had already prepared in the morning, after his body was found.

That evening, Charles and Nellie resumed their theatrical excursions by attending the Zeigfeld Follies, now an annual review that seemed to be on continuous tour since its original success a half-dozen years earlier. It was nearly midnight when they settled in for the night in the room that had once been his mother's, in the bed in which she had died. After they turned off the light, Charles lay awake in the darkness, his revolver under his pillow, trembling in anticipation. The regular cadence of Nellie's breathing was the signal the time had come.[20]

Charles drew the revolver in one hand and raised himself on his elbow. As he prepared to fire, his eyes were drawn to the side of the bed behind Nellie. There stood his mother. "Not the white-haired old woman wasted with disease, that I had come to see a few days before she died, but the beautiful mother I had idolized when I was a child," said Chapin. "She looked at me with the same sweet smile and gently shook her head, just as she had done in childhood days when reproving me for something I shouldn't have done. Then she faded away." Chapin thrust the revolver under his pillow and took Nellie in his arms. Instead of a bullet, he planted a kiss and said a silent prayer that she was still alive. "I have thought of it often since," Chapin later wrote, "and have wondered if it really was my mother's spirit I saw, or if my fevered brain imagined it. I know it all seemed real at the time."[21]

In the morning, Chapin was reminded that his woes were not figments of an overactive imagination. A telegram arrived at 30 Rhode Island Avenue demanding that he appear in court with no further delay for the accounting of the trust. This time the message included a threat of bond forfeiture if he failed to show. Once again, Chapin rekindled his plot. To combat the real or fantasized spirits, Chapin resolved to leave the family house and carry out the deed elsewhere. That evening, the Chapins sailed down the Potomac to Old Point Comfort. Finding no lodging there, they then traveled by train to Richmond. Nellie noticed a change in Charles, but attributed it to a weakened condition from his recent bout with the flu. She was accustomed to leaving everything to her husband, and he had trained himself to mask his thoughts even to one so devoted to him. "It is the worst thing a husband can do and brutally unfair to the wife," conceded Chapin, "but I had always gone on the principle that the husband should bear all the burdens and that he owed to his wife to share only his joys and pleasures. What blind idiots some of us are."[22]

In Richmond, the Chapins obtained a suite of rooms. They spent the afternoon driving about the city and visited the site of the Libby Prison, in which Nellie's late brother had been confined during the Civil War. After dinner, Chapin once again prepared a set of letters providing instructions to the hotel staff and coroner. When he rejoined his wife, he found her in the company of an old friend who had seen their name in the evening paper. The pleasure of the evening left Chapin without the will to carry out the murder. The next day, they returned to Washington. Chapin found he had acquired some breathing room. The telegram he sent to the New York court had resulted in a one-week extension. They began their return to New York, stopping overnight in Baltimore where they took in a performance of George M. Cohan in *Broadway Jones*. Chapin's mood now rose and fell with each hour. The play was a tonic. In it, Jackson Jones inherits a rural factory that he immediately plans to sell, but he is talked out of it by a secretary whom, at the end, he marries. "I don't remember enjoying a play so much in all my life," he said. "The comedy of it caused me to forget myself completely, and the horror was suspended above my head."[23]

The fears returned with the morning. When Chapin and Nellie left the hotel for a walk, Chapin was sure he spotted two men, with slouched hats drawn down over their eyes, watching their every move. He began to shake and could hardly continue his walk. He led Nellie to a bench in a small park. He could no longer see the pair but suspected they were hiding behind a bush. The agony was too much to bear.

"Those two men who just passed us are detectives, and they will arrest me," he said to his stupefied wife.

"Arrest you! Arrest you for what?" she frantically asked.

Chapin then confessed. He told her about his losses in the stock market, about the bonds, and about his plans to commit suicide. He did not, pointedly, mention that he had plotted to take her with him to his death. When he finished, Nellie took his hand in hers and soothingly told him that his mind had gotten the best of him; it was unlikely anyone knew or cared about his troubles. "You have worried so much over it that you have magni-

fied your troubles and lost control. Try to pull yourself together."
As they sat, Nellie advised Chapin that they should return to New
York immediately and turn to one of their lawyer friends.[24]

The pair boarded a train that night. In the days that followed,
Chapin visited two friends who were lawyers. The first counseled
him to tell the bonding company what he had done and propose
a payment scheme to replace the missing funds. Then he called
on Benjamin Duke, the tobacco and textile entrepreneur whom
he had befriended in recent years. Duke interrupted Chapin at
the start of this tale of woe. "I don't care how you got into trouble,
just tell me what I have got to do to get you out of it," he said.
Within hours, Chapin was on the way to the court with sufficient
funds to replace the missing investments. The court approved the
final accounting of his duty as trustee of Edna's money and released him from his purgatory. "Only my wife, the lawyer who
counseled me, and the friend who aided me, ever knew of the
peril I was in," said Chapin.[25]

The immediate danger past, Chapin's life regained some normalcy. He enjoyed new and enhanced access to New York's inner
circles now that John Purroy Mitchel, a man he knew well, held
the mayor's office. Chapin had, like many newspapermen, come
to know Mitchel when his investigations as the city's Commissioner of Accounts uncovered corruption in the police department
and elsewhere, at one point forcing the ouster of three borough
presidents. A friendship with the "Boy Mayor," as he was called
because of his young age, certainly had its benefits. For instance,
it earned Chapin a seat at a Lotos Club dinner for which the new
mayor was the guest of honor. Founded in 1870, the Lotos Club
was a retreat of the elite, housed in a five-story, red brick town-
house at 110 West 57th Street, that had been originally conceived
as a literary club and included among its earliest members Mark
Twain, who called it the "Ace of Clubs." The dinner was one of
the largest the club had ever given, and many of the city's most
famous had turned out for the soiree, including Andrew Carnegie, who mistakenly referred to Mitchel as "Mr. Wilson" several
times. A month later, Chapin was among those at the head table
for the annual dinner of the Association of City Hall Reporters
at the Astor Hotel. On other occasions, Chapin dined alone with
Mitchel. One such night, the mayor was angry about the press

coverage he had been getting. "I tell you, Chapin," he said, banging his fist on the table, "that the worst iniquity in this city today

is yellow journalism." Chapin disputed the mayor's assessment of the press, but they remained friends. In May 1914, the mayor appointed Chapin to a committee to represent the citizens of New York upon the return of the remains of seventeen sailors killed during the American occupation of Vera Cruz.[26]

Although Charles and Nellie were able to take a two-week cruise to Costa Rica in June, creditors began to hound him again. He was able to keep them at bay and ward off further legal troubles, though. His old sailing buddy Harry Stimpson helped ease the pressure by letting the Chapins move into the Cumberland Hotel, which he managed, leaving behind the more expensive Plaza and a $2,000 unpaid bill. Chapin also stayed clear of the market. But his resolve broke when he received what he was certain was a solid tip. He plunged every dollar he had and could borrow into it, and, at long last, he had success. Part of his winnings went to his creditors, but Chapin plowed the remainder back into the market with continued success. Then on July 31, the market collapsed as Germany went to war. At 9:56 the next morning, officials closed the exchange for the remainder of the year. This time, the financial bottom Chapin hit was even worse than the first one. Like a bad dream, Chapin entered a four-year period in which he kept only one step ahead of disaster. "Creditors harassed me day and night, and there was no way of satisfying them." He borrowed from one friend to repay the other. To satisfy an impatient Duke, who had saved Chapin from his court troubles, he pawned Nellie's diamonds for $6,500. However, they spent Thanksgiving at the Greenbrier, an elegant resort in White Sulfur Springs, West Virginia, where other New Yorkers such as the families of Jacob H. Schiff and Cornelius Vanderbilt also vacationed.[27]

Though the European war had hurt Chapin financially, it propelled his old friend Cobb to fame. The prodigious scribe of the Thaw trial was sent overseas by the *Saturday Evening Post*, where he had gone after leaving the *Evening World* in 1912. His reports from the front, including an interview with British Secretary of War Horatio H. Kitchener, were a sensation in the States, and upon his return he embarked on a three-month lecture tour. In the spring of 1915, Chapin caught up with Cobb. Chapin and 112 other editors, writers, and entertainers organized a massive dinner in Cobb's honor that reflected how far up in the world Chapin's former star had risen. On April 25, 650 men gathered in the Waldorf-Astoria ballroom. In keeping with the custom of these dinners, women were permitted to watch the speeches and entertainment from balconies. On the floor below them milled a veritable "who's who" of New York entertainment, including, among others, Douglas Fairbanks Sr., George S. Kaufman, George M. Cohan, and Irving Berlin. After creole gumbo, roasted filet, squab, corn bread, and biscuits, and a dessert of Savannah au rhum, and after a long array of speeches, the lights were dimmed and a comic, biographical film with a cast of 200, made solely for the occasion, was shown.[28]

In the spring of 1917, the nation abandoned its isolationist posture, and President Wilson obtained a declaration of war from Congress. A month later, New York City gave a jubilant welcome to visiting French and English dignitaries who had come to rally Americans to the cause. Among the events planned for French Marshal Joseph Joffre and British Foreign Secretary Arthur Balfour was an elaborate dinner at the Waldorf-Astoria on May 11. More than 5,500 people applied to be among the 1,000 invitees whose selection would mark them as "the best there is in all walks of life in New York—official, financial, professional, and commercial," according to the *Evening World*. It was copy that would certainly pass muster at the city desk, especially as Chapin managed, through his friendship with Mayor Mitchel, to be among the select elite. The soiree was exactly the kind of evening that Chapin coveted. The luminaries ranged from society patriarchs such as the Vanderbilts and Choates to former presidents William Taft and Theodore Roosevelt, who was wildly cheered by the guests with cries of, "Let Teddy go," when speakers called for aid to the Allies. The *New York Times* called the soiree "a gathering distinguished as even New York has rarely seen before."

Chapin shared a table with Bartow S. Weeks, a supreme court justice—the title given in New York City to those judges who try criminal cases. Weeks knew Chapin through his membership in the city's yacht clubs and had frequently sailed with him on the *Eidolon* before Chapin had been forced to sell it. Over a five-course meal of what was described as "American dishes," the two reminisced and talked of the war, which was already altering life. To set an example of the kinds of necessary wartime economies, the dinner committee had selected what they thought would be appropriate fare, the simplest ever served at a Waldorf public function of this sort. Cherrystone clams would be followed by pepper pot, Delaware planked shad, squash, chicken roasted with sweet potatoes, and for dessert, strawberry ice cream and petits fours. When the evening came to an end, Weeks and Chapin rose and shook hands. "I hope we'll meet again soon," said Weeks. They would, but in circumstances neither would have predicted.[29]

About this time, Chapin's friendship with another judge took him to an unusual dinner. In July 1915, Mitchel had appointed Henry W. Herbert to the Court of Special Sessions. Chapin had lobbied for his selection, and the mayor had consented. Herbert was an unusually caring jurist. As a magistrate, he had worked assiduously for the creation of a night court for women. "The night court is really a rescue institution of the best kind," he said. "You can't save a girl by arguing with her on the streets." One day, after gaining his new post, Herbert invited Chapin to come with him to visit John S. Kennedy, a former court officer who was now warden of Sing Sing. They had dinner in the warden's residence. Joining them was Father William Cashin, a young Catholic priest who had been appointed prison chaplain only a few years earlier. After dinner, the prison keeper took the party for a tour through the prison. Chapin felt horror when he saw the cells in which the inmates were confined. "It seemed incredible that human beings could live in such dank and smelly cells and not go mad or waste away with disease," he said.[30]

As 1918 opened, Chapin was again plotting suicide. On June 1, he again cleared his desk of personal papers and went to stay with Seitz at his summerhouse in Maine. His newest plan called for him to "accidentally drown," leaving his woes behind and his wife the beneficiary of life insurance policies. But before a stormy day presented such an opportunity, Chapin reconsidered his course. "The more I thought about it, the less plausible it seemed. If I were drowned while bathing, it might at first be reported as an accident, but my experience with such matters convinced me that my plan was impossible, for the insurance investigators would be certain to find out how hopelessly involved I was and there would be sufficient grounds to contest payments of my policies." He returned to New York.

In Europe, the tide of war had turned against the Germans after the second battle of the Marne. In New York, the Yankees were headed for a second-place finish, and tenant organizations were flexing their muscles against New York landlords. On September 12, 1918, reporter Emmet Crozier spotted Chapin back in the office and walked up to his desk with a carefully rehearsed speech. Crozier had received an offer from the *Globe* to work on its rewrite desk for $10 more a week than he was getting at the *Evening World*. He told Chapin how much he hoped to continue working for him and that he hoped that the *Evening World* would match the *Globe*'s offer. Chapin listened quietly.

"How much did they say they'll pay you?" Chapin finally asked.

"Fifty dollars a week. But I'd rather stay on the *World*," replied Crozier.

"Um-mm. Well, that's a good salary for a young man. If I were you, I'd take it."

That afternoon, Crozier cleaned out his desk.[31]

Life in the *Evening World*'s newsroom was comforting. For nearly forty years, the rhythm of producing a daily paper had provided Chapin with a sense of normalcy. Even now, as his life was falling apart, it continued to do so. But events outside the newsroom were intruding even on this, his last refuge. His creditors had come to the limit of their patience "I had exhausted every expedient I could think of and knew that I could no longer stave off legal proceedings," he said. "Lawsuits and exposure meant the loss of my position. I was against a stone wall." On September 14, the mailman delivered an ominous packet of letters to the Cumberland Hotel. A bank refused to renew his note, and another notified him he was overdrawn. Two creditors sent word that his checks had bounced, and another said he would garnish Chapin's wages.

"The following day was Sunday. It meant a respite of twenty-four hours. After that abysmal ruin. Nothing could save me."[32]

The Deed

In the morning, the exceptional stillness that reigned in midtown Manhattan caused Chapin's financial maelstrom to recede for a few precious moments. For a New Yorker wanting to flee the complications of modern life, Sunday, September 15, 1918, held remarkable promise. It was the third "gas-less Sunday" proclaimed by the Federal Fuel Administration, during which the use of an automobile for pleasure was prohibited to conserve fuel for the war effort. For a day, New York sounded as it did when Chapin first arrived from Chicago twenty-seven years before.

Nothing else had so dramatically transformed the city as did the automobile. At first, only a few custom-made cars appeared on the streets. They were solely the playthings of the rich. But the car's promise of speed brought rapid change. In 1900, hordes of New Yorkers descended on the nation's first automobile show, held in Madison Square Garden. Within a few years, thousands of them were steering their own unmuffled, roaring, gasoline-powered contraptions through the ill-paved streets, belching smoke and fumes, causing delicate women to raise handkerchiefs to their mouths and noses, and backfiring, frightening those few work horses still plying their trade. Over time, the ruckus from the jammed streets became even worse as New Yorkers discovered the horn.

By 1918, there were more than five million automobiles in the United States, and on certain days it seemed as if all of them were in New York. But not today. On the main thoroughfares, the only traffic comprised the occasional motor bus filled with passengers enjoying the crisp fall weather. Among the fleet were steel-gray double-deckers put into service only the day before, the first to be made in the United States with a roof to protect the passengers riding in the open-air seats up top. Deserted side streets traveled only by horse buggies and dog carts, said a *New York Times* reporter, "made New York look strangely like the days before the automobile was in use."[1]

On this Sunday, New Yorkers were complying in record numbers with the gasoline restrictions. Patrolman James Kennedy of the East 51st Street Station reported only two violators on his beat. The first was a motorcycle with American flags hanging from the handlebars. Kennedy gave the rider a lecture about his obligation to the government and sent him home. The second was a car transporting an entire family with a sign marked "DOCTOR" in the window. The driver admitted to Kennedy that he was just "taking the folks out for a little ride."[2]

When Charles and Nellie emerged from the Cumberland Hotel, they, too, were ready to take full advantage of the holiday-like atmosphere. The morning sun reaching 54th Street was warming the air slowly, and with no clouds in sight, it was assumed the temperature would reach the mid-seventies by lunchtime. Perhaps it was a bit cool for the seashore, but going to Brighton Beach in Brooklyn was a favorite excursion of Nellie's. She was not alone in her preference. During the past three decades, doctors, lawyers, white-collar office workers, and other New York professionals had come to favor it over the more garish Coney Island. Brighton's enormous, mansard-style hotel and four-hundred-foot-wide, two-story bathing pavilion certainly fashioned a more refined landscape than the Coney Island pavilions. Although Charles felt both places were beneath him, he would go willingly in order to indulge Nellie. His affection for her made him the antithesis of the demon of the city room. "In her presence," said Cobb, "his voice softened, his manner changed. Toward her he was gentle, considerate, mindful of the small graces which mean so much to any woman and notably to a woman who is no longer young." But before the pair had walked two blocks down Broadway toward the subway, an old woman accosted them. She wore a faded black dress, and her face was a portrait of deprivation and suffering. She stretched out a trembling hand toward Charles. He dropped a coin into it, simultaneously rewarding and repulsing the intrusion.[3]

"Oh, God!" exclaimed Nellie. "I wonder if I will ever come to that?"

The comment was intended solely as fodder for conversation during a stroll. She could know nothing of his current troubles, thought Charles. Nonetheless, the words burned in his brain like acid, stripping the Sunday morning of its promised deliverance. "What she said cut into my heart like a knife stab. I knew that within a few hours she would be almost as friendless and helpless as that poor creature." Three times Chapin, as city editor, had commissioned articles on the fate of penniless women in cities. Now Chapin, as a husband, considered the potential fate of his wife. Once again, he could not shake the terror. "If I were alive on Monday morning, there would be a pack of sheriff's officers and process servers waiting at my office," said Charles. "I would be turned out of my hotel and all my belongings would be seized. Probably I would be arrested for overdrawing my account."[4]

Release from his fear was now impossible, even for a few hours. The agony surfaced again, coming on like a migraine that returns only when the suffering has eased just long enough to let one discern what life can be like without it. The torment would not let up the entire ride on the subway and the above-ground Brooklyn, Flatbush, and Coney Island Railroad running from Prospect Park to Brighton. The beach became an extension of his nightmare. As he sat on the sand with Nellie, surrounded by a cacophony of joyous sounds emanating from the children in the water below and the happy crowds jamming the boardwalk behind them, Charles could think only of the sad old lady from the city streets. In his thoughts, her face would become indistinct and in its place he would see Nellie's. It was Nellie's hand that reached out.[5]

In the late afternoon, the Chapins re-boarded the BF&CI Railroad, which was packed with other returning beach-goers. Nothing in the attire of the travelers betrayed how they had spent their day, except for the bags into which they had stuffed their bathing accouterments. New Yorkers were still not entirely comfortable with the idea of flesh, water, and sand. The train ride was part of the journey back to sartorial normalcy. When they reached

OUR COMPLIMENTS.

PUBLISHED MONTHLY.]   *Ne Cede Mallis.*   [BY CHARLIE CHAPIN.

VOL. 1.   FREEPORT. ILLINOIS, MAY, 1875.   No. 4.

Written for Our Compliments.

That New Boy

By "PHIL STANLEY."

NE day after school, while at play, the usher brought him out and told us he was a new scholar; he was about sixteen years old, rather thin and muscular, fair complexion, black hair and eyes, and looked French, as he was from head to foot.

"Fellow, what's your name and who are you?" asked Dick Harris the big bully of the school, as he looked him in the face.

"My name isn't fellow, its Louis Montey, who I am is none of your business," said the irate boy.

"Be careful how you use that tongue of yours, you frog-eating Frenchman, or you will be sorry for it," said the bully.

"Whisper in my ear when I'm sad," said Montey.

The appearance of the principal M. C. put a stop to future parley and the boys returned to their play. After they were all gone I went up to the new comer and spoke to him.

"Louis," said I, "my name is Stanley, Phil Stanley, and I will be your friend, I see you are like myself a stranger here, I have been here but a few weeks."

"Thank you Phil," he said "I am glad to have you for a friend," and he extended his hand which I shook heartily.

Shortly after the bell for evening prayer, called us in and after prayers we studied an hour, and retired at nine.

The long dormitory in which we slept was divided by a long, narrow hall, on each side were small rooms, to accommodate two boys each.

Louis Montey was assigned a bed with me, as I was the latest arrival and still alone.

After we had gone to our room, I told my companion that it was a custom among the boys, to "haze" every new comer and that Dick Harris was always leader in the affair, and that they would come for him that night.

He took it very quietly and said he had "been there before. We went to bed, but not to sleep. Montey to be on the lookout and I staid awake to see what they, and he would do.

It was a clear, bright, moonlight night and the moon shone through our little window and made it look almost as bright as day.

We had not been in bed long, it was probably about eleven o'clock, when our door was soft-

---

During the 1870s, Chapin joined a nationwide do-it-yourself printing craze that had captured the imagination of just about every teenage boy in the nation, including the president's son. With his press, Chapin established a monthly magazine, *Our Compliments*, when he was just sixteen. Its Latin motto "Ne Cede Malis"—misspelled on the masthead—means "Do not yield to misfortunes." *(Courtesy: Collection of American Private Press Association Library, Stayton, Ore.)*

In December 1887, Chapin went to interview an alleged philanderer. While Chapin was conducting the interview, the betrayed wife took matters into her own and shot her husband dead. *(Courtesy:* Chicago Tribune, *December 25, 1887.)*

In 1886, the *New York World* mounted moveable miniature yachts on a track across the first floor of its building to illustrate the race between the *Mayflower* and the *Galatea* yachts. As dispatches arrived by telegram every ten minutes, the yachts were drawn across the painted scene by hidden strings. The crowds were so large that all traffic was blocked from Park Row from 11 A.M. until evening. (The Journalist, *September 11, 1886.*)

The World Building was the epicenter of American Journalism when Chapin arrived there in July 1891. The tallest building on the globe, its gleaming gold dome could be seen from miles away by immigrants on ships bound for New York. *(Courtesy: Library of Congress, Prints and Photographs Division, Detroit Publishing Company Collection.)*

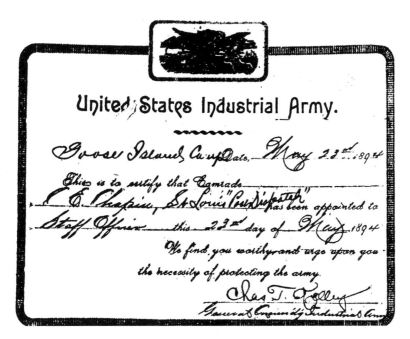

United States Industrial Army.

Goose Island Camp Date, May 23rd 1894

This is to certify that Comrade

C. E. Chapin, St Louis "Post Dispatch" has been appointed to

Staff Officer this 23rd day of May 1894

We find you worthy and urge upon you the necessity of protecting the army.

Chas. T. Kelley

General Commanding Industrial Army

In May 1894, Chapin covered the advance of the Kelley Navy, part of Coxey's Army, a rag-tag group of unemployed workers marching across the nation to seek relief from Congress for the ravages of unemployment. Chapin was made an honorary member of this army. *(Courtesy:* St. Louis Post-Dispatch, *May 24, 1894.)*

Arrival of the Flotilla.

Chapin traveled with Kelley's Navy for two days, and assured his St. Louis readers they had nothing to fear from these protesters who were floating down the Mississippi River. *(Courtesy:* St. Louis Post-Dispatch, *May 24, 1894.)*

In the early 1900s with financial success as one of Joe Pulitzer's leading
New York editors, Chapin indulged himself with horses and a yacht. Seen
here is his yacht *Eidolon*, which he purchased in 1906. *(Courtesy: Library
of Congress.)*

The closest Chapin came to having a friend in the newsroom was Irvin Cobb, who went on to become a famous humorist. He is seen here, on the left, with author Charles Norris, and Ray Long, editor of *Cosmopolitan* magazine. It was Long who sent Cobb to Sing Sing in 1924 to write an article about Chapin. *(© Bettmann/CORBIS.)*

In 1896, St. Louis Judge David Murphy's anger toward the *St. Louis Post-Dispatch* prompted him to challenge Chapin to a duel. "I consider you a malicious, characteristic liar and coward and if you have a spark of manhood in you, you will take it up," Murphy said after issuing the demand for a duel from his bench. *(Courtesy:* St. Louis Republic, *January 18, 1895.)*

Holding his ever-present cigar in one hand and news copy in the other, Chapin is clearly the centerpiece in this scene of the *New York Evening World* city room captured by a turn-of-the-century photographer. *(Courtesy: Brown Brothers.)*

As the *Carpathia* returned to New York in 1912 with the survivors from the *Titanic* on board, reporter Carlos Hurd, also on board the *Carpathia*, tossed his exclusive story to Chapin, who was on a tug that had come out of New York harbor to meet the returning ocean liner. *Courtesy: Publisher's Guide, October 1912.)*

TOSSED IT OVER THE RAIL

As these formal photographs taken between 1910 and 1918 reveal, Chapin had no trouble looking like a stern taskmaster. *(Left: Reprinted from Chapin, The Uncensored Letters of Charles Chapin, 1931; right: Reprinted from Chapin, Story, 1920.)*

When he was appointed warden of Sing Sing, Lewis Lawes befriended Chapin and, over time, freed him from most of the restrictions of prison life. "Men have done heroic work within these walls,"
said Lawes, "but few of them have left a lasting impress on the spirit of
the prison. Chapin accomplished just that." *(Reprinted from Lawes,*
Twenty Thousand Years in Sing Sing, 1932.)

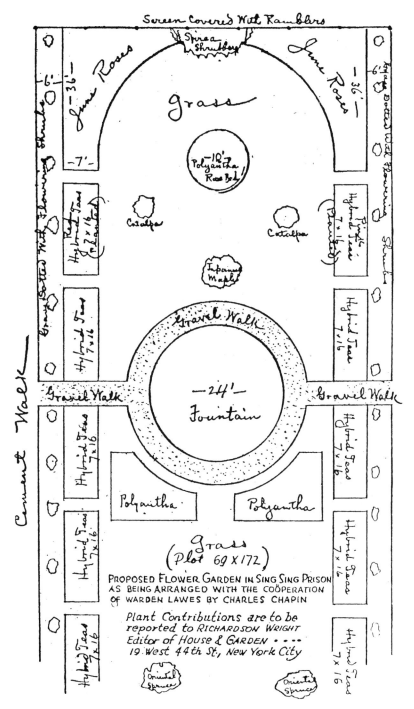

Screen Covered With Ramblers

Spirea Shrubbery

June Roses — June Roses

Grass bottes with Flowering Shrubs — Grass bottes with Flowering Shrubs

-6'- -36'- -6'-

-7'-

grass

-10'-
Polyantha
Rose Bed

Catalpa — Catalpa

Japanese Maple

Gravel Walk

-24'-
Fountain

Hybrid Teas (7 x 16) Standard — Pink Hybrid Teas (7 x 16) (Plants)

Hybrid Teas 7 x 16 — Hybrid Teas 7 x 16

Gravel Walk — Gravel Walk — Gravel Walk

Cement Walk

Hybrid Teas 7 x 16 — Hybrid Teas 7 x 16

Hybrid Teas 7 x 16 — Hybrid Teas 7 x 16

Polyantha — Polyantha

Grass
(Plot 69 x 172)

PROPOSED FLOWER GARDEN IN SING SING PRISON
AS BEING ARRANGED WITH THE COÖPERATION
OF WARDEN LAWES BY CHARLES CHAPIN

Plant Contributions are to be
reported to RICHARDSON WRIGHT
Editor of House & GARDEN · · · ·
19 West 44th St, New York City

Hybrid Teas 7 x 16 — Hybrid Teas 7 x 16

Oriental Spruce — Oriental Spruce

In 1923, the American Rose Society published Chapin's ambitious
plans for a rose garden, urging growers to send plants care of
Richardson Wright, editor of *House & Garden*. *(Reprinted with permission, American Rose Annual, 1923, courtesy American Rose Society.)*

In 1924, *House & Garden* commissioned Mattie Hewitt, one of the most successful landscape photographers of the time, to take the photographs of Chapin's young gardens. *(Mattie Hewitt / © House and Garden, Condé Nast Publications Inc.)*

Viola Cooper, seen here, center, was the first of two women who became romantically involved with Chapin after his confinement to Sing Sing Prison. Cooper, however, was no wallflower; she ceased visiting Chapin when she set sail, literally, on one of the last windjammers to traverse the Pacific. *(Reprinted from Cooper,* Windjamming to Fiji, *1929.)*

Chapin's relationship with Constance Nelson became his longest and most serious besides his thirty-nine-year marriage. Nelson was an anomaly among women in the 1920s: aside from having the fortitude to maintain a relationship with a convict, an old one at that, she pursued a career as a professional in the Federal Reserve System. *(Courtesy: Federal Reserve Bank, Cleveland, OH.)*

Sing Sing warden Lewis Lawes granted Chapin remarkable prison privileges, as evidenced by this photo of Chapin reading and relaxing on the warden's porch. *(Reprinted from Chapin,* The Constance Letters of Charles Chapin, *1931.)*

The Chapins' mostly untended grave in Washington, D.C., offers no hint as to the way the interred couple met their deaths.

Manhattan, Charles left Nellie at the Cumberland and headed downtown to Park Row. After all these years, Nellie was accustomed to being abandoned on Sunday evenings and supping alone in their suite.

Like the eery silence of the streets of New York, spawned that day by the absence of cars, Chapin confronted a city room on the seventh floor of the *World* building possessed of a peculiar quiet from the absence of his staff. Chapin's editors, reporters, rewrite men, and copy boys would not re-assemble until morning, unlike Senior's staff on the twelfth floor who were scurrying to get their copy ready for Monday morning's paper. He made his way across the cavernous room, like a captain crossing an empty bridge, his path illuminated only by the handful of bare electric bulbs the parsimonious accountants would permit to remain on at night. Traversing the shadowy expanse, he reached his post on the dais at the end of the empty newsroom. For several hours, Chapin tried to occupy himself with correspondence and other duties at his desk. He had kept such irregular hours this summer that the work had piled up. As the clock approached midnight and *World* reporters could be heard drifting out into the night, Chapin ceased his work and reached into a desk drawer. From it he extracted the 32-caliber pistol given to him by Sheehan in Commissioner Waldo's office. It was just where he had left it after his return from Maine. No one at the *World* would have dared go into one of Chapin's desk drawers, or even touch his desk, for that matter. He pocketed the pistol, closed the drawer, and left the city room he had ruled for two decades.

The night air was cool, and Park Row was empty. City Hall, across the street, was dark. The only light descending on City Hall Park came from the second-floor pressroom of the *World*, the windows of an elevated subway station leading to the base of the Brooklyn Bridge at the right, and the few new streetlights. Monday's daylight would transform everything. In a few hours, the sidewalks would be so full of men and women that anyone in a hurry would be forced to dodge automobiles and trolley cars on the street. From Chapin's office at midday, Park Row looked like an undulating sea bearing a flotsam of hats and bonnets. If this were daytime, Chapin's presence would be acknowledged by murmurs of recognition. But at this hour, Chapin had the sidewalk to himself.

A twenty-minute subway ride brought Chapin back to the Cumberland. He crossed the tranquil lobby, engaged the elevator operator for a ride to the eleventh floor, and quietly entered his suite. He negotiated his way across the dark parlor. The dim shapes of dinner plates from Nellie's last supper were visible on the dining room table, along with the bags of beach clothing left in the corner for Katie to unpack and wash in the morning. Charles slipped into the bedroom where Nellie slept peacefully; she had loved their day at the beach. He went to the closet near his bed, removed the cargo from his pocket and placed it on a shelf adjacent to the spot he had hidden a revolver that he had previously found to be defective years earlier. He changed into his pajamas, retrieved Waldo's pistol, and got under the covers of his bed, separated from Nellie's by a small bedside stand. From here, Charles began his vigil. He watched and waited. Nellie lay in her bed facing him. He watched and waited. The balance of her life now hung on her somnolent moves. As dawn arrived, Nellie finally rolled over. With the pistol in his hand, Charles pushed back his covers. He stood up and stepped forward to the edge of Nellie's bed. She didn't move. The only sounds competing with her breathing were those of the awakening city rising up from the streets below. Charles placed the barrel of the pistol just behind her right ear, inches from her scalp. This time his mother did not intercede.

The gun recoiled in his hand. The discharge reverberated off the thick plaster walls, but was heard by no one outside the room. Nellie's body convulsed beneath him. After four years of waiting, the revolver had finally done its deed, but it also had failed to immediately dispatch Nellie. Unconscious, unaware of what had been done to her, and unsuspecting of who was responsible, Nellie was close to death but still alive. Charles could not bring himself to fire again, nor could he turn the gun on himself. "Had I killed myself while she were yet alive and she had survived, all that I sacrificed to save her from penury and want would have been in vain." Instead, Charles dropped to his knees, held Nellie's hand, and prayed. "Thou, Oh God, understands what was in my heart, that my heart was full of love for my wife when I killed her, and that what I have done I did for her protection to keep her from starvation and want." After half an hour—for Charles it seems like two hours—Nellie's labored breathing ceased. "When her life fluttered and went out, there came to me a strange exalta-

tion and with it all the worries that had been tormenting me faded into nothingness. I had nothing to worry about. No harm could ever befall her."[6]

Charles drew the covers over his wife's now still body and left the bedroom. In the parlor, the morning light reflected off the piano near the windows. Sheets of music lay on the keys, just as Nellie had left them the night before. The piano had been played almost every night since Charles had bought it for Nellie. The music had always been a remembrance of their theater days together so long ago.

Punctually at eight o'clock, the hall boy knocked. Chapin took the morning papers and ice from him at the door and gave him an unusually large tip. As was his habit, Chapin spread the papers on the floor before his chair. Leaning over, he studied the headlines. In Europe, the Austrians were making a peace offering, and in New York City, gubernatorial candidate Al A. Smith was said to be ahead in a straw poll. Within a few minutes, Chapin was interrupted by Mary Saulter, one of the chambermaids, opening the door. He headed her off and forestalled her entrance into the suite. "Mrs. Chapin and I do not wish to be disturbed until after luncheon," Chapin told her, keeping a hand on the door. "She retired very late and didn't sleep well at all."[7]

With the two intrusions repelled, Chapin sat at the desk in the parlor and wrote the first of two letters. "Dear Harry," he began. "I have been suffering pain which I have not mentioned to my wife, but my sufferings are leading rapidly to a complete nervous breakdown and I am on the verge of collapse. I cannot look forward to spending the rest of my life in a sanitarium. My wife has known nothing of this. I concealed my condition from her and withheld from her my fear of impending insanity."

"Please forgive me," Chapin wrote on. "I could not help doing what illness has forced upon me. She has no relatives and is so dependent upon me to live on when I have gone. She died in her sleep and never knew. We have been chums and I could not go and leave her to face the world alone."

"For a long time I have been unable to sleep. My nerves are

unstrung. I am tortured with pain. My wife died this morning. In a few minutes I also shall be dead. I have been ill for a long time,

fighting with all my might against it and to prevent a breakdown. I can fight no longer the pains that have been racking me for months. Good-bye and forgive me." He signed the letter formally "Charles E. Chapin," folded it, placed it in an envelope, and addressed it simply "Harry Stimpson."[8]

Next, he wrote to Seitz. He repeated his tale of torture and pain. "I know how wrong it is, but I cannot go on suffering as I have for months. It takes greater courage than I possess. I have tried to think out what is best to do, and cannot bear the thought of leaving my wife to face the world alone, so I have resolved to take her with me."

"When you get this letter I will be dead. My wife has been such a good pal. I cannot leave her alone in the world." Then in a most business-like fashion, Chapin concluded the letter with instructions that he and his wife be interred in the plots he had purchased at Glenwood Cemetery in Washington, D.C. Along with the letter, he placed some cash to pay for the burial costs in an envelope and addressed it to "Don Seitz, *The World*, Park Row, New York City."[9]

His correspondence concluded, Charles rose, crossed the room, and reentered the bedroom. From his closet, just feet from Nellie's corpse, he drew a light gray summer suit from among the two dozen hanging before him, and a cravat she had recently bought him. He selected a colorful, braided silk ribbon to run from the hoop in the right-hand rim of his tortoise-shell pince-nez glasses to a button of his suit. He took a derby hat off the shelf to complete his dapper look. His trim, elegant lines were spoiled only by his final gesture. He placed both Waldo's revolver and the broken one in his jacket pockets.

Dressed for the day, Charles returned to the parlor. There he picked up another piece of Cumberland Hotel stationery and, using an editor's blue pencil, wrote "Don't Disturb" in block letters. He placed the letter for Simpson at the center of the table and walked over to the fake mantelpiece, certainly a visible symbol of his descent, for the Plaza had real ones. On the mantelpiece, he located one of Nellie's hatpins. Then he moved to the door of the apartment. He listened for hall traffic. When he heard none, he slipped into the passageway. He took the hatpin, attached his crudely made sign to the door, and quietly closed it.

At the elevator, Chapin ran into Frank Caruthers from the

Morning World's business staff, who lived on the same floor. The Chapins had known Caruthers for years, and recently they had seen each other more frequently now that they were neighbors. The two greeted each other, and Caruthers, who knew that Chapin had been on extensive leave from work, asked Chapin how he was. Much improved, he said, adding that he would be back at his desk now if Nellie had not been feeling badly this morning. They went swimming yesterday, explained Chapin, and he thought maybe she had caught a cold.[10]

The door opened and the pair disembarked in the lobby. Chapin went directly to the desk and spoke to the clerk. "Please have the telephone connection to my room unplugged," he said, citing Mrs. Chapin's illness. He handed the clerk a check for $30, knowing very well that it would bounce, like the one for $75 he had cashed at the desk Sunday before heading to the beach and the one for $100 he had cashed Saturday at the cigar stand in the foyer of the *World*. Money in hand, he went next to the hotel's barbershop for his daily shave.[11]

By 9:15, when Chapin exited the Cumberland, the day was becoming overcast, and the noise of the city streets was jarring after the idyllic Sunday. He lifted his derby to his head, turned right, walked the few feet to Broadway, turned right again, and fell into the stream of pedestrians heading downtown. After three blocks, he turned left on 51st Street and stopped at the post office, where he dispatched Seitz's letter. Having now set into motion a literary time bomb, he walked the several remaining blocks to Central Park, where he planned to complete the double suicide. "Then came the delusions," said Chapin. "It seemed to me that, no matter where I went, there were hundreds of outstretched hands waiting to snatch my weapon and prevent me from carrying out my purpose." Thwarted, Chapin instead wandered aimlessly through the park. He certainly knew it well from his years of horse riding when he had lived in the Plaza overlooking the park. A well-dressed gentleman leisurely strolling in the park would have attracted no attention.[12]

Meanwhile, his letter to Seitz began its journey. It was postmarked at 9:30 A.M. at Station G. In an era when it was possible to request someone's company for dinner that night by posting an invitation in the morning, the letter arrived at the *World* at 3:45 that afternoon. Upon opening it a few minutes later, Seitz immediately dialed the Cumberland. He reached Paul Ullman, the manager, and told him about the letter. Ullman called the police.

A few minutes before four o'clock, Ullman and Patrolman Gross of the West 47th Street station opened the door to Chapin's suite with a passkey. As they entered the parlor, cool air and echoes of street noise greeted them from the open window overlooking Broadway. They saw the envelope containing Stimpson's letter on the table. They peered into the adjacent dining room where the supper plates were still untouched. In the bedroom, they found Nellie. Gross picked up the telephone. Shortly thereafter, Captain Arthur Carey of the Homicide Bureau arrived. Dr. J. R. Inglass, of 256 West 57th, three blocks uptown, was summoned to examine the body. He placed his hand on the inside of her arm, just below her armpit. It was cold and clammy. She had been killed in the early morning, Dr. Inglass concluded. The county physician was called, and he gave permission to have the body removed to an undertaker's fifteen blocks uptown, to be held until her only family, Chapin's brother and sister, Frank and Marion, made funeral arrangements.

Meanwhile, Gross's and Carey's inquiries of the neighbors turned up no one who had heard the shot through the thick walls. Nor could they find the murder weapon. Convinced from the letters that Chapin, if still alive, was armed and deranged, Carey put out a general alarm. Chapin was wanted for murder. Detectives fanned out to all of Chapin's known haunts. Some stopped in at the Plaza, knowing he had once lived there. Others visited the Manhattan Beach Bathing Pool where Chapin had a dressing room. It was also verified that the *Eidolon* was still in its berth in Gravesend Bay, though the police were unaware he no longer owned the yacht. In Washington, D.C., where Marion and Frank Chapin lived, police were told to be on the lookout upon receiving a tip that Charles might be heading their way.

At Rebel Ridge, in Ossining, Cobb picked up a ringing phone. A *World* staffer had the presence of mind to call him with the news. Cobb had been at his farmhouse since returning from the warfront in June. Hoping not to fall ill from exhaustion and frayed nerves, as had happened after his first trip to the war, Cobb had spent the summer growing vegetables and tending his horses, cows, and chickens after dumping off reams of copy at the *Saturday Evening Post*. It was the kind of life Chapin would have teased him about mercilessly. Cobb took the first train into the city and joined his former colleagues in the *World* newsroom monitoring reports from the citywide manhunt. Frank Chapin called from Washington. He told reporters that he had no word from Charles, but he admitted it would be unlikely because the two were not on good terms, having recently quarreled over property. The staff prepared a piece for the morning edition. Knowing what a field day the Hearst papers would have, they sought to protect their own the best they could, calling the homicide charge "technical" and explaining that "Chapin had been under the care of his physician for many months, and had been in a highly nervous state during this period." It would be a long night.[13]

By the time Cobb arrived at Park Row, Chapin had reached Prospect Park in Brooklyn. He was still confused and delusional. He sat in the park and waited for the evening crowds to thin out and leave him alone. "It was nearly midnight when I decided to fire the bullet into myself," Chapin said. "I took out the Waldo revolver and was about to shoot when I saw a policeman walking toward me. It was dark. He did not see me. I was terrified. I slipped the revolver into my jacket and left the park."[14]

"No thought of arrest for what I had done came to me. I thought only that an encounter with a policeman would result in the loss of my two revolvers and that I should then be without the means of destroying my life."

His fears drove him under ground. With a nickel, he purchased refuge in the subway. Fourteen years earlier, Chapin missed no detail in his *Evening World*'s coverage of the inaugural subway ride, when Mayor George B. McClellan Jr. and other dignitaries from City Hall rode all the way to 145th Street. Now he was oblivious to all things as he sat, crouched on a hard wooden seat at the end of a car, riding the same rails from end to end through the night. "I fancied myself dead and that it was the shell of what once was me that sat so silent and still in a subway train. It was as if I were in a trance. My hands were like lumps of ice. The blood in my body seemed frozen. For hours I couldn't even think. I had no sensation of thirst or hunger. I just rode on and on like a dead man might."

In the early hours of morning, Chapin disembarked at the Times Square station to use a bathroom. A newspaper boy was opening a bundle of *New York Times* papers, fresh from the press. "I bought one and got on a train to go to my office, just as I had done every morning." He read the war news on the front—the United States was spurning the Austrian peace offering—and then he turned to the inside pages. He reached page seven and froze.[15]

WIFE OF EDITOR
SHOT DEAD IN BED

C. E. Chapin of Evening World
Sought by Police—Disap-
peared After Leaving Notes.

HE THREATENED SUICIDE[16]

He began the article. Soon, he was reading his own words. The *Times* had reprinted his letter to Harry in its entirety. "Then it all came back. I wasn't dead; I was alive and was wanted by the police for murder! How many headlines like that I had written in my forty years as a newspaper man! And now it was me who was wanted for murder." For several more hours, Chapin vacillated between killing himself and turning himself in. At six o'clock, he made his decision in an irrevocable fashion. He walked into the West 68th Street Police Station.[17]

"I want to see Captain Tierney," Chapin said to the officer behind the desk. "Tell him it's important." The officer, Lieutenant Hamill, had no idea who the elegantly dressed man standing before him was. He said Tierney was asleep and couldn't be disturbed.[18]

"I'm Mr. Chapin of the New York *Evening World*, and I have just killed my wife."

"What did you kill her with?" asked the officer.

"This," said Chapin, who brought out the 32-caliber revolver with a single empty chamber. Then he placed the unused pistol on the desk before the astonished desk officer. Word of Chapin's apprehension was sent to police headquarters. The city's finest had not found Chapin; rather, he had found them.[19]

Within an hour, Chapin was led out of the station. On the street, waiting to transport him to police headquarters on Mulberry Street, was an eleven-foot-long, windowless black paddy wagon. The truck had the look of a carriage, though the police had given up horse-drawn wagons by 1918, with a long roof overhanging the front and a bench-like front seat. The back door, with the gold-starred N.Y.P.D. logo, was opened, and Chapin was lifted into the hot, stuffy, and dark interior. Down Broadway, the paddy wagon rapidly retraced Chapin's daily route. This time, however, instead of going to Park Row, where he had feasted on criminal news emanating from police headquarters, Chapin was heading to Mulberry Street, where *he* would be the news. Hearst's *Evening Journal* got wind of Chapin's surrender in time to run a boxed update, "Sought for Killing, Goes to Headquarters," adjacent to its long front-page story, "Search for Chapin Fails," set into type earlier in the day and too late to pull. His capture even made the *London Times*. Within twenty minutes, the wagon pulled up to headquarters. Most police reporters were unaware that Chapin was in police custody, so none were present, saving that awkward confrontation for a later time. The ever-present *Evening World* legman Max Fischel, however, spotted Chapin. Familiar to all police officers, no one held Fischel back when he approached Chapin. "You can't do anything for me, Max," said Chapin as they shook hands.[20]

The police placed Chapin in an interrogation room, where he was joined by District Attorney Edward Swann, Assistant District Attorney James Magee, both of whom he knew, and Captain Carey. While waiting for the questioning to begin, Chapin sat silently with his head in his hands.

"Have you any statement to make?" asked Magee.

"Yes, I have," replied Chapin. But before he spoke, they all warned him that anything he said might be used against him in court.

"I don't care," he replied. "I have no defense and am ready to receive whatever punishment the law demands."[21]

"I love my wife. That's why I killed her," he began. "I couldn't kill myself and leave her friendless, penniless and alone to live like a pauper and die to be buried in Potter's Field."

"I idolized my wife; she was the only thing I lived for. We lived together thirty-nine years. For the last twenty years she had been in a very delicate health. I loved her the more for that. She was my life, my religion and the only thing I lived for. It was because of this that I killed her, that I intended killing myself—to keep her from knowing the man I am."

Then without any further prompting, Chapin began his tale, continually rubbing his forehead and the back of his head. He admitted he had borrowed extensively, representing himself as a high-salaried editor and heir to the Sage and even Pulitzer fortunes. "I had borrowed money from everybody. I was being hounded by friends, and I was afraid she would learn," he said. "Ruin stared me in the face. I couldn't bear to let her know."

"I brooded over my troubles. And I decided the best thing to do was for me to kill myself." Chapin detailed his five years of hell, several times breaking down and openly weeping before the trio of investigators. He delineated his various failures, from his first attempt at murder in Washington, D.C., where he had bought their cemetery plots and headstones, to his last attempt at suicide in June in Maine. Then he turned to the main event.

"Two weeks ago I took another vacation. My head hurt. I couldn't sleep. My troubles were ever present." Step by step, Chapin led the investigators through the day he and Nellie spent at the beach, his retrieval of the pistol from the office, his vigil, how he shot Nellie, and his nighttime wanderings through the city. To Swann, Magee, and Carey, it seemed a complete and honest rendition of the crime and the events leading up to the crime. Chapin, however, had made no mention of the old lady on Broadway, the hands that rushed to steal his weapons, or the vision of his late mother.

Then he was done. He sighed. Nellie was gone and, with her, his fears. He looked at the three men. "And this is the first happy day I have spent in five years; it was worry, worry, worry, and no end of it. I know now—I am satisfied that I took the only honorable course in killing her. For four nights I have not slept. I will sleep tonight."[22]

He was wrong.

A Date in Court

While Chapin completed his confession before the three investigators, word that he was in police custody reached the city rooms of Park Row a few blocks away. The news confirmed everyone's suspicions about Nellie's death. A murder made perfect sense to those who thought of Chapin as a Simon Legree. "Few of the sweated oarsmen who manned Chapin's galleys were surprised," said Cobb. And for the competing evening papers, it made one hell of a story. Reporters swarmed police headquarters, where they caught up with District Attorney Swann. He promised to provide them with a copy of Chapin's confession later in the day. "There is no doubt that Chapin was mentally deranged," said Swann. "I saw him last about six months ago, and seeing him now one could easily detect the decided change in him. His face is drawn, and he seems highly nervous and depressed." Cobb and others at the *Evening World* asked Swann to see if Chapin needed anything or if there was anything they could do. "Nothing, thank you," was the message that Swann brought back. In fact, Swann said, Chapin asked that no one be permitted to see him. He was especially anxious to avoid seeing "his associates in New York journalism."[1]

After lunch, Chapin was brought before a magistrate in the West Side Court. The room was filled with reporters. Among them was Emmet Crozier, whom Chapin had let go the week before. He had just arrived for his first day of work at the *Globe* when his new editor told him to go out and cover his old boss's arraignment. Joseph E. Keating, an attorney for the *World*, informed the court that he would represent Chapin. The magistrate

ordered that Chapin be held without bail until the grand jury met to consider his case. Chapin turned to the table to his right and asked Swann if he would permit him to attend Nellie's funeral. In return, he promised, he would wave his right to a trial and submit himself for execution. Swann declined the offer. As Chapin was led from the courtroom, he suddenly collapsed and had to be lifted into the waiting taxicab, which conveyed him and the sheriff deputies to the Tombs.[2]

Chapin knew the place well. The Tombs were, after all, the holding spot for Harry K. Thaw and many other members of the *Evening World*'s rogue gallery. Opened in 1902, the jail took its unusual name from the one that had previously stood on the site. Competing stories are told as to the origins of the odd nickname. The most common legend is that the jail's original design included Egyptian motifs such as sun-god reliefs and trapezoidal windows, resembling those of an Egyptian tomb.

Upon his arrival, Chapin was put under the care of a doctor, and an extra watch was assigned. His cell, on murderers' row, was brightly lit, and he had about as much privacy as a bear in the new Bronx Zoo. He entered the cell without saying anything and sat on the six-foot bench. Two *Evening World* reporters asked if he needed anything. He said no, then changed his mind and asked for cigars. The anticipated rest was not to be had. He remained awake until 11:00 P.M. when he finally dozed off for a couple of hours. By 1:00 A.M., he was awake again. He sat for a while, his head in his hands, smoking a black cigar, then went back to sleep. At 4:00 A.M., he rose for the day and asked the guards for the morning papers, which they delivered to him. He read each one and studied the stories about him. "Chapin Defends Killing of his Wife," read the *New York Journal*; "Chapin Tells How and Why he Shot Wife," read the *New York American*; "Chapin Confesses he Planned Murder," said the *New York Times*; "Chapin led by Financial Ruin to Slay Wife," claimed the *New York Herald*; "Debt Drove Editor to Kill his Wife," announced the *New York World*.[3]

The papers read, Chapin asked the guards for a razor and warm water. The request was denied, but a barber was procured.

The journey from the barber's chair at the Cumberland to the one at the Tombs had taken only forty-eight hours. But Chapin was quickly learning what a distance he had traveled. He asked for breakfast. The guards explained he could have what came from the kitchen, or he could purchase breakfast from the prison's private restaurant. With the six dollars he had left, Chapin ordered fruit, rolls, and coffee from the restaurant. As he ate, he read the papers again. By late morning, several reporters sent in word that they wanted to interview him. Chapin declined, telling the various messengers that he had said all he cared to say about the case to the district attorney. "You can tell them, however," he added, "that, as well as I know newspaper reporters, I can't understand how they ever managed to distort what I said to Assistant District Attorney Magee as much as they did." In fact, they hadn't distorted his confession, and the irony of his complaint was lost on him.[4]

Eventually, Chapin did permit some colleagues from the *World* and *Evening World* to visit him in his cell. Cobb was not among them; he had returned to Rebel Ridge. Chapin told them he was feeling better than he had in years and was very content. He became agitated again, however, when the subject of his wife's funeral was raised. Guards told him that services were scheduled for Thursday evening. He pleaded with them to be able to attend "under any kind of restrictions."[5]

The grand jury convened in the afternoon. Five witnesses were brought before it: Captain Tierney, to whom Chapin had surrendered; Paul Ullman and Mary Saulter from the Cumberland; Dr. Otto Schultze, the medical examiner; and Reginald Birchall, the stenographer who had recorded Chapin's confession. Following the testimony of the five, the panel rendered an indictment for first-degree murder.

On Thursday, editors in their morning planning meetings were unclear as to what assignment to give their court reporters. The *New York Journal* was reporting that Chapin would not be formally arraigned that morning. Instead, it said that his defense attorney Keating would ask a justice of the New York Supreme Court to appoint a lunacy commission. "I do not intend to have Mr. Chapin placed on trial for murder," Keating told the paper. "He is not in his right mind and I look for him to collapse at any moment." However, at eleven o'clock, sheriffs escorted Chapin across the "bridge of sighs," as the above-street passageway connecting the Tombs and the Court of General Sessions was known. Cleanly shaved and well groomed, wearing a dark suit and dark tie and carrying a derby hat, Chapin looked as if he were on his way to work. He stood in conspicuous contrast to the five other prisoners—among them highway robbers, an army deserter, and a murderer—facing arraignment in the large, high-ceilinged, wood-paneled courtroom. Chapin appeared cool and collected and engaged in whispered conversations with Keating and Magee. He even greeted E. R. Rand, Sage's old personal secretary and now chairman of the New York County Grand Jury, who must have wondered how fate could have brought the two together in such a scene.[6]

After Judge William H. Wadhams read the indictment, Keating entered a plea of not guilty and requested a period of ten days to file motions. Wadhams recorded the plea, granted the request, and remanded Chapin to the Tombs. After Chapin was removed from the courtroom, Keating again brought up the subject of Chapin's wish to attend Nellie's funeral. Wadhams said he would take the request under advisement. A few minutes later, Swann announced outside the courtroom the request had been denied. Trying to head off any plans by the defense to invoke an insanity plea, Swann's assistant Magee told reporters that the district attorney's office would oppose any effort to lay a foundation for a defense like that offered by Harry Thaw a decade earlier. When he first interviewed Chapin, Magee said, he had thought the editor was insane, but he had since become convinced that his first impression was wrong. Look, he said to the reporters, Chapin himself insists he was sane. Coming into court that morning, Chapin was overheard saying to McGee, "I want to go to the electric chair—I am perfectly sane and want no sanity commission appointed. I want to pay the price." Pushed by one insistent representative of the *Herald*, Magee conceded, "It may be, nevertheless, that he is suffering from mental aberrations akin to Harry Thaw's condition."[7]

Magee also announced he would lead an investigation into Chapin's life to ascertain his motives. He made a public plea that all creditors to whom Chapin owed money contact his office. So

far, Magee had found that Chapin owed $860.10 to the Cumberland and a four-year-old debt of $2,000 to the Plaza. A search of Chapin's quarters had uncovered no useful financial records. They
had found, however, more they fifty portraits made by a *World* photographer of Chapin. In all of them, Chapin wore a severe scowl, said Magee. The checks Chapin had cashed over the weekend had all been returned as unpaid. The police had no explanation as to where Chapin had spent the cash. Perhaps, suggested Magee, Chapin had spent it in a way that caused Mrs. Chapin to be jealous, hinting at another possible motive for the murder. Hearst's *American* was ready with a similar accusation, claiming Chapin's "latest inamorata, according to the gossip of Newspaper Row, lived in an apartment on East 46th Street." Then Magee—in the words of the *Sun*—"burst a Park Row bubble" and revealed that Chapin's salary during the past two decades had never been higher than $150 a week or $7,800 a year. The rival press accepted the figure unquestioningly. It was, however, false. By this time, Chapin's salary approached $400 a week, and if one added in bonuses, he was earning approximately $30,000 a year in an era when the per-capita income of most New Yorkers did not exceed $1,000. If circulating this misinformation was part of the prosecutor's strategy, it was never revealed.[8]

In his cell that afternoon, Chapin was visited by a colleague from the *Evening World*, who arrived in the company of Abe Levy, one of New York's most famous criminal attorneys whom Chapin had known for nearly twenty years. Levy was not the typical, well-bred attorney of the era. English by birth, he had more in common with many of his hardened defendants than his colleagues, having obtained his education while living in poverty and doing menial work. In 1890, Levy had gained the attention of the city when he saved "Frenchy the Algerian" from a certain death sentence by persuading the court his client had been insane when he killed an underground figure called "Mother Shakespeare." Since then, Levy had become a favorite of many facing impossible courtroom odds, including Nan Patterson, who went free after two hung juries failed to convict her of murdering Caesar Young.

In the past, Chapin and Levy had frequently sparred over what the *Evening World* had printed about his clients. Now Levy had come to see Chapin as a would-be client. Chapin said he had no need for Levy's services; that he intended to call no witnesses nor offer any defense.[9]

"And then what," asked Levy.

"The judge will sentence me, and my troubles will soon be over," replied Chapin.

"And do you think there is a judge in our criminal courts who would permit you to do such a thing?" said Levy.

Levy then explained that he had been asked by Chapin's friends to represent him, and he planned to do so for no fee. "I look upon it as a sacred duty to save you from yourself."[10]

At 8:30 that night, the Reverend Dr. F. H. Miller, the assistant rector at St. Stephen's Episcopal Church, led a sparsely attended service for Nellie at the Campbell Funeral Church on Broadway and 67th Street. There were more onlookers outside the church than mourners inside. Most of those who attended the service were members of the *Evening World* staff, though Katie, Nellie's devoted maid, was among them. The following morning, Nellie's casket was loaded onto a train for Washington to be buried in the plot that Charles had selected for them four years earlier.[11]

Priests of various orders also visited Chapin in the Tombs, but he had little time for them. The last prayer Chapin had said was at Nellie's side. He decided now he would no longer pray, "because there was nothing left for me to pray for. I could not ask God to kill me." After several nights, he changed his mind again. He felt that, in the end, God would understand "that I did only what I had to do for the protection of Nellie," and in his new prayers he entreated that he be reunited with her when his turn came.[12]

On September 26, before the ten-day deadline expired and with Chapin's reluctant consent, Levy went to General Sessions Court to amend Chapin's plea to "not guilty on the ground that the defendant was insane at the time of the commission of the crime." Surprisingly, Alfred J. Talley, who represented the district attorney in court that day, announced he would neither oppose nor approve the new plea and would leave the motion to the discretion of the court. The district attorney's action, or lack of it, encouraged Levy, who was convinced Chapin's case might be winnable.[13]

Having laid the groundwork, Levy filed a motion seeking the

appointment of a lunacy commission to evaluate Chapin's sanity. "Mr. Chapin was mentally irresponsible at the time of the commission of the crime," said Levy. The district attorney's office belatedly opposed this move, but Judge Malone, to whom the case was now assigned, was swayed by Levy. On October 18, Malone signed an order appointing a commission comprising three prominent New Yorkers: George Wickersham, who had served as the attorney general under President Taft; Lamar Hardy, who had been corporation counsel during Mayor Mitchel's administration; and Dr. Smith Ely Jelliffe, the famous psychiatrist who had been a star in the Thaw trial. They were to "report to this Court with all convenient speed as to [Chapin's] sanity at the time of the commission of the alleged crime and also whether he is in a state of idiocy, imbecility, lunacy or insanity so as to be incapable of understanding the proceedings or making his defense on the trial of said indictment."[14]

Malone's order followed what had recently become a widely accepted legal principle stemming from a British criminal case sixty years earlier. Known as the M'Naughten Rule, it was the principle that a defendant could be declared insane and thus not culpable for his crime if he were deemed not to appreciate the nature of what he had done, nor appreciate that the act was wrong. In the United States, this line of defense had passed the ultimate legal test in the Thaw case, where the facts of the murder had never been in doubt. The study of criminal insanity, however, was in its infancy. Its best-known student at the time was Dr. Jelliffe, who had played a key role in the Thaw defense. Born in New York in 1866, Jelliffe had earned both a medical and a doctoral degree by the time he was thirty. While working at the Binghamton State Hospital, he decided to become a psychiatrist, or what was then popularly called an "alienist." Jelliffe then pursued his studies in Europe, including under Sigmund Freud himself.[15]

Europe was far ahead of the United States in its appreciation of the psyche. In 1912, when Chapin's trouble began, Hans W. Maier, a well-known Swiss psychiatrist, introduced the idea that logical thinking and psychological homeostasis can be overwhelmed by the emotional side of a person in connection with a delusional set of ideas. He called this syndrome *catathymia*—a term derived from Greek to mean "in accordance with emotions"—and contrasted it with other delusions, such as intoxication, which were connected to brain dysfunction rather than from psychiatric origin. By 1918, when Chapin's mental health was being evaluated, Sigmund Freud had just completed his much-talked-about lectures on psychoanalysis in the Vienna Psychiatric Clinic at the University of Vienna.[16]

Two decades later, American Freudian psychiatrist Frederic Wertham would extend and develop Maier's concept of the "catathymic crisis" to account for behavior, much like Chapin's, in which an individual commits an inexplicable act of violence on a victim with whom he has had a long-term relationship. In the catathymic crisis, a person with marked egocentricity is prompted by a traumatic experience, sometimes delusional, to acquire the idea that he must carry through a violent act—a homicide, suicide, or both—as the only way out. Extreme emotional tension culminates in the violent act, even though the victim may not be related in any way to the precipitating trauma. Immediately after the act, the person finds the tension lifted and regains calmness. However, at the time Chapin faced the lunacy commission, only Jelliffe among the three commissioners had any inkling as to the importance of the breakthroughs that were being made in the field of psychology.[17]

On November 1, the lunacy commission began its work in private. The district attorney's office vainly sought to have hearings open to the public. First among the witnesses was Rhinelander Waldo. He told the commission members, "Chapin was the last man in the world he would consider eccentric in any way." Chapin always seemed normal, said Waldo. Furthermore, he added, at frequent dinner parties with the Chapins, he had been impressed with the affection that seemed to exist between Charles and Nellie. John Tennant, managing editor of the *Evening World*, told the commission that he was "one of the most alert minds he had ever seen."[18]

To counter this impression of levelheadedness, Levy called disgruntled members of the *Evening World* staff, such as Clyde West and Samuel Williams. Chapin sat silently and watched the parade of witnesses. "Every little act of mine that could in any way be twisted into an indication of an insane mind was dug up and elaborated, until they got me to wondering whether I was a moral idiot, a paranoiac, or just an ordinary unclassified lunatic," said Chapin. One reporter went so far as to suggest that proof of Chapin's mental instability was the fact he had tossed piles of reporters' columns into the wastebasket by the city desk. Another said the proof lay in Chapin's constant darting into a telephone booth in the midst of conversation. Of course, unknown to the reporter, Chapin was using the phone booth to talk to his creditors without being overheard.[19]

The hearings dragged on for more than a month. From the traffic in the hall outside the hearing, one could tell that the subject of this investigation was unusually well connected. In addition to Waldo, Judge Herbert, who had taken Chapin on his Sing Sing visit, came by to testify on his behalf. Levy offered the testimony of Dr. Frank Ross Haviland of Fordham University, an authority on mental health, to provide a pathological reason for Chapin's recent erratic behavior. Haviland said he thought Chapin had contracted a disease that produced intermittent paralysis that caused him to be irrational and that might shorten his life. But under questioning, Haviland admitted that, at best, Chapin was in an early stage of "*dementia paralytica*" and still knew that he was killing his wife and that such an act was forbidden by law. Chapin was awakened from his trance-like observations of the hearing when Katie, Nellie's maid, arrived. She told the commission that in her eighteen years of tending Nellie, she had never heard Chapin utter a cross word. "He was her constant and devoted husband," she said, "more like a lover than a husband."[20]

At last, it was Chapin's turn to address the panel. During seven hours of testimony, Chapin led the commission step by step through his life story and the events leading to that September morning. The members of the panel were impressed by his memory, his attention to detail, and—in their words—how "he told his story with marked picturesqueness and sense of its dramatic quality." Chapin made no attempt to create an impression that he did not understand what he had done or that he was not responsible for his actions, even under questioning from his own counsel.[21]

"What you did was right?" asked Levy.

"That what I did, God understood why I did it," replied Chapin.

"And that it was right?"

"Right from my viewpoint, yes."

"According to your understanding and your light, is that right?" persisted Levy.

"I have tried to make myself perfectly clear."

"Well," continued Levy, "is my question clear to you?"

"Yes," said Chapin.

"Answer it please, did you think it was right according to your understanding?

"I certainly did, and I still think so, and always shall. Mind you . . ."

"In your judgment," interrupted Levy, "you set obedience to what you conceive to be the law of the Deity over your obligation to the laws of man, is that what you mean?"

"I say," answered Chapin, "that my duty to my wife took precedence over all the laws on the face of God's earth, and that law was not to be considered if I had to save my wife."[22]

Chapin was asked if he had no thoughts of the punishment that could be invoked for this crime.

"I haven't any thoughts of myself because I expected to die with her," said Chapin. "That is the only regret that remains. Now don't misunderstand me. Don't think that I could calmly kill my wife, that I could calmly decide to put an end to the sweetest little lady I knew without suffering the most intense agony. Please don't. But I gave no thought to anything beyond saving her, because I intended to die with her, and I had no fear of future punishment."[23]

Then Chapin delivered an unsolicited and impassioned soliloquy.

"Now I want to tell you all my relations with Mrs. Chapin," he said. "She was the dearest—she was the dearest, the sweetest, the bravest, the most loyal, the most loving, the most devoted little woman I have ever known or ever dreamed of."

"She loved me almost pathetically, and no matter what I have done, I adored Mrs. Chapin. I loved her with all my soul, and she did me. . . . She was my companion, my confidant, in most things," said Chapin, quickly adding the latter qualification, "my friend, my pal. Where I went she went."

"You never knew anyone so perfectly wrapped up in another as that dear little girl was in me," he continued. "And I killed her to save her, and I thank Almighty God that she is in heaven beyond the reach of . . ."

Words failed him. Chapin rested his case with, ". . . but was inevitable."

Wickersham then asked, "You believe in God and His watchful care and mercy. If you had killed yourself and not your wife, haven't you enough faith to believe that God would have looked after your wife and provided for her wants?"

Chapin had no answer.[24]

On December 14, the commission delivered its findings to Judge Malone. The massive 647-page report, written by Wickersham, covered all aspects of Levy's contention. It may be that Chapin was "afflicted with paresis in an incipient stage," said Wickersham, but there was no convincing evidence that Chapin did not know what he was doing, nor that he was, or is, "in a state of idiocy, imbecility, lunacy or insanity so as to be incapable of understanding the proceedings or making his defense on the trial of the said indictment."

It was unquestionable that at the time of the killing, Chapin and his wife "were living in relations which were singularly devoted," said the report. But Chapin did not murder his wife pursuant to a Divine command or anything else. He did what he did because he saw it as the only exit from the disgrace and ruin he foresaw. Although such thinking represents a false premise and defective moral reasoning, it is not cause to conclude that Chapin lacked a moral and legal responsibility for his actions. Judge Malone endorsed the report, writing on it that he agreed with its findings. Then before affixing his signature, he penned, "Let the defendant proceed to trial on the indictment." Trial was set for January 20, 1919, before Judge Bartow S. Weeks. Chapin spent Christmas in the Tombs. He refused to be let out of his cell for any part of the day and refused to see all visitors. "Many letters and telegrams and some packages came, but I opened none," he said. "I just wanted to be alone."[25]

As Chapin's trial approached, Levy arrived at the Tombs. He

had just met with the district attorney, and he came to tell Chapin that a deal was possible. Chapin's testimony before the lunacy commission had been circulated to all five Supreme Court judges, and they had the unanimous opinion the district attorney could not win a conviction for first-degree murder. As a result, Swann was willing to permit Chapin to plead guilty to a lesser offense and avoid the electric chair.

"I promptly told the district attorney," said Levy, "that I would agree to nothing in the way of compromise, and I further told him I am confident of acquitting you in the final trial of your case." But, he admitted, were he to pursue this strategy, it might be years before the case is finally resolved, and Chapin would be confined to the Tombs during that time. "Your friends insist that you have not the physical strength to stand such an ordeal. I will not attempt to advise you what course we shall pursue. You must now decide that for yourself." Chapin had now been confined in the Tombs nearly four months. He considered his options. "I witnessed and heard things that made my blood run cold. The horror of it no pen can describe. . . . I realized that if I had to endure it much longer, a commission wouldn't need to waste much time in finding me stark mad."[26]

Chapin consented to the deal. At 10:55 A.M. on January 14, Sheriff David Knott escorted Chapin into the Judge Bartow Weeks's courtroom. Chapin knew Weeks well. In fact, it had not been very long since the Joffre dinner when Weeks had wished they would get together more often. Wearing a dark blue serge suit, tan shoes, and holding a dark soft hat in his hands, Chapin now stood before the judge in vastly different circumstances than either of them could have imagined. In Weeks's possession was the two-page plea recommendation worked out between Levy and Swann. The document reviewed the facts of the case and said that no motive for the crime had been uncovered except for those Chapin himself had claimed. Although Chapin's reasons do not mitigate the enormity of the crime, read the carefully written plea, the district attorney has concluded that it is doubtful a jury would convict Chapin of a higher verdict than second-degree murder.

Chapin rose. Levy stood next to him, still convinced that no jury hearing Chapin's story would have rendered a verdict of any degree of murder. Clerk William Penney asked Chapin if he wished to change his plea of not guilty. Chapin smiled and nodded.

"Do you wish to plead guilty to a lesser degree?" continued Penney.

Again, Chapin smiled and nodded.

"Do you wish to be sentenced at once?" asked Penney.

"Defendant is ready for immediate sentence," said Levy.

Weeks then looked down at Chapin and said, "Charles E. Chapin, you are sentenced to imprisonment at hard labor for a minimum term of twenty years and a maximum term of your natural life."

Chapin's face twitched and he turned pale, but remained standing erect. Then he bowed slightly to the court, and Sheriff Knott escorted him out. In three minutes, the whole affair was over. The press was unprepared for the early dénouement, which, in the words of the *New York American*, "was swept off the calendar, without one turn of the machinery that usually accompanies an important criminal trial."[27]

Swann sat and recorded his last notes on the outside of the bill of indictment. "Defendant pleads guilty to murder in the second degree. State prison, minimum 20 years; maximum the natural life of said defendant." With his initials, Swann and the district attorney's office now considered Chapin's case closed. But a piece of the puzzle remained unplaced. During the almost five months of animated press coverage, police investigations, court proceedings, and lunacy commission hearings, not a single creditor had come forward. And the outstanding $2,000 bill at the Plaza? It had been settled.

Inside the Walls

For a prisoner lingering in one of the reception cells at Sing Sing Prison in 1919, the first clue of what awaited him was a poem etched on the wall. Its author was unknown, but its point was lost on no one who passed through.

> Stone walls do not a prison make,
> a poet once did sing.
> He must have been a blooming fake;
> He didn't know a thing.
> Perhaps 'twas true as he did say,
> When under inspiration;
> But the stone and bars they use today
> Make a damn good imitation[1]

Undoubtedly one of the most notorious prisons in America, Sing Sing had been home to New York's worst citizens since 1828, when convict labor completed the construction of a huge cellblock built entirely of stone quarried on site. The narrow, tall, rectangular structure held living quarters more confining and stifling than the tenements from which many of the prisoners had sought escape with a life of crime. Eight hundred cells were stacked six-high against the wall. A metal walkway, like an exterior fire escape, ran across the front of each level and was connected at each end with a set of open stairs. Each cell was seven feet deep, three feet three inches wide, and six feet seven inches tall. There was barely room for an inmate to stand adjacent to his bed; when changing his shirt, his wrists would invariably scrape the dank ceiling. Until the end of the nineteenth century, when large windows were cut into the eastern wall of the hall, darkness and dampness were as much a part of cell life as the stone itself. By 1919, Sing Sing had expanded greatly beyond this one structure, but the old cellblock remained in use. Crime, or at least the apprehension of criminals, continued to be a growth industry in New York. The state, desperate for space to house its inmates, poured money into Sing Sing. By 1919, the prison complex had filled in several acres of low riverfront land, and new cellblocks were being erected on the hills behind. As a result, Sing Sing came to straddle the rail line running north–south along the Hudson. This odd arrangement gave rise to the almost-hourly sight of train passengers, faces pressed against the glass, hoping to catch a glimpse of a famous gangster doing hard time.[2]

Two days after his sentencing, on January 17, 1919, Chapin entered this world. Sheriff Knott, who had sat by Chapin's side through all the lunacy commission hearings, brought him by car rather than consigning him to the normal gaggle of prisoners brought by train. At the Hunter Street gate, Knott removed Chapin's handcuffs, and Sing Sing guards relieved Knott of his charge. Chapin was then led to the record clerk for processing. He filled out the receiving blotter, putting down Don Seitz and his sister Marion under the section, "Names of relative or friend." His new identity was listed at the top left—"Number 69690." Then to complete the transformation, Chapin was led to a small building in the prison yard where he was stripped, ordered to shower, and had his mouth, toes, fingers and other regions checked for contraband. At this point, most inmates were issued a set of coarse underwear, a "hickory" shirt, a pair of brogan shoes, socks, gray pants, and a coat. Little effort was made by the guards to determine whether the clothes fit. In fact, as one warden observed, it was immaterial whether they fit. The point was to strip the prisoner of his personal identify and individuality. "Wish you could see my new pants," wrote one inmate to a friend. "They come to an end two inches below the knee. . . . On the level, Joe, I look like a soda water bottle in these togs."[3]

Chapin, however, was able to avoid some of this sartorial injury because regulations permitted prisoners with means to supply their own shirts, shoes, and underclothes. In fact, an inmate was permitted to wear a collar and tie. The trousers—"they call them pants here," observed Chapin—were the only part of the uniform that was compulsory. Chapin was given a cap, two sizes too small, that looked like those worn by railroad brakemen, a jacket he couldn't button, and pants that were too short and too tight. "But," he noted, "they were clean and had never been worn, which was something to be considered, in the view of the clothes I saw handed out to some of the men who came after me." Dressed in his new togs, Chapin caught a glimpse of himself in a small mirror. "I couldn't recognize the grotesque figure I saw reflected as the fastidiously attired chap I had always conceived myself to be," he said. The officers and the prisoners smiled when they spotted Chapin considering his new look; he laughed a bit himself. "It is good," he wrote later, "to begin a term of life imprisonment with a laugh."[4]

After the "dressing in," Chapin and the other new arrivals were taken to the prison hospital for a cursory examination. A dentist looked over his teeth, an oculist peered into his eyes, and a doctor drew some blood and poked around. At the prison school, the group was given an educational test. The tests completed, the inmates were photographed, and their Bertillon measures were taken. Developed by Frenchman Alphonse Bertillon, the idea was to measure a criminal's cranium, his height, the length of one foot, one arm and an index finger. The information would then be dutifully recorded on an index card and filed according to a complicated cranial-size system. At first, the French police considered this idea foolish, but soon the system led to arrests and convictions. A false beard might change one's appearance, but there is little a miscreant can do about his head size. The last stop for the pricked, tested, and measured inmates was a visit with the prison chaplain, Father William E. Cashin, for some counsel. It had been only a few years since Chapin and Cashin had dined together at Sing Sing when Chapin, the famed New York newspaperman, had come to the prison in the company of Judge Herbert. Now he had returned as a convicted murderer.

At last, after a brief pause to pick up a slop bucket, Chapin was brought to the old cellblock and was locked into cell 106. "I was shown to one of the cells that had filled me with loathing the time I inspected them with my friend, the judge," he said. "I could scarcely breathe in the foul atmosphere that permeated the stone hole." The cell contained an iron cot, a mattress stuffed with straw, a blanket and pillow, a tin drinking cup, and a place for his iron slop bucket. Wildlife, in the form of ticks in the mattress and bugs of all sorts in the crevices of the walls, shared the cell. The door, twenty-two inches wide, was solid steel with a checkerboard latticework at the top to let air and light in. It was said by officers at Sing Sing that if ever a man cried in prison, it was at this moment when the bolt was first drawn across the door and he was left alone to consider his fate. But before Chapin had a chance to be despondent, he heard a cheery voice through the grate. It was Father Cashin, who had come bearing magazines and words of cheer. Cashin told Chapin to come to his office in the morning, and he would have a surprise for him.[5]

When Chapin caught up with the priest the next day, he discovered his prison job would be to work in the prison library over which Cashin had dominion. The Father set aside a desk for him in the Chaplain's office—"as bright and cheerful and comfortable as any office I ever occupied outside of prison," said Chapin—and promised he would have ample time to step through the door and lose himself in the 12,000-volume library. "It was amid these surroundings that I began my sentence of 'twenty years to life at hard labor.'" Chapin had won the prison-job lottery. Very few inmates were exempted from the newcomer's job of shoveling coal in Yard Company No. 2, feeding the huge boilers that produced the prison's electric power and heat. Chapin's exemption did not go unnoticed. At a baseball game one Sunday afternoon, inmate Edward J. McGrath spotted Chapin seated below, dressed in a silk shirt, his eyes protected from the sun with a green eyeshade.[6]

"So that's Chapin!" said McGrath. "Say, what's he doing?"

"You've been here all these years and you ask me what he is doing," his companion replied with a laugh. "You don't think he's on the coal pile, do you? A big editor from New York has to have a good job."

In time, Chapin fell into the rhythm of prison life. Each morning at 6:00, the guards would ring a bell and conduct their morning count. Chapin would have to be out of his bunk and dressed within thirty minutes. At 6:30, the cells would be unlocked, and he would join the march to the open sewer where inmates dumped the contents of their buckets and placed them on a rack for the day. Breakfast, usually hash or cereal, would be eaten in the mess hall at 7:00. At 7:50, the prison whistle blew, and the men headed to work. By 8:00, Chapin had to be in the library. At noon, the whistle blew again, and the inmates, assembled in companies, marched to lunch. Usually it consisted of a piece of meat, a vegetable, bread, and coffee. No fresh vegetables or fruit were ever served because the daily allotment for an inmate's meals was only twenty-one cents. After lunch and a short break for a smoke, inmates returned to work until 4:00. After a dinner, often supplemented with care packages from home or items bought in the prison store, inmates were free to roam the prison yard. Some played baseball, others just whiled away the time talking. It was not long, however, before the whistle blew again, summoning the men to pick up their night buckets and march to their cells. As harsh as these conditions were, many inmates were old enough to remember the years of the dreaded lockstep, striped uniform, and regimen of silence.

Chapin's job in the library was, as Cashin promised, not taxing, and he had plenty of time to read. "Books were almost my only companion," he said. "But sometimes I would read for an hour without retaining a word and frequently would have to turn back and read the pages again, for I had read only with my eyes; my mind was focused elsewhere." Nothing he did could shake off the oppression of Sing Sing: the monotony, the loneliness, the hours of bitter regret, the heartache, the desolation, and, worst of all, the long nights of solitude. "In the new life in which I found myself there were duties to be performed during the day, or I must have gone mad with the morbid thoughts that were always surging through my brain," he said. "But there were the long evenings and longer nights, sleepless nights in a cell that is no bigger than a dead man's grave." On these nights, Chapin would lie awake on his cot and stare at the walls bathed in light from the bulb encased in green glass hanging from the ceiling of his cell. "While the light burns, a reflection of the green shade is cast though the latticed upper half of the cell door onto the big window that is immediately in front of it. The reflection is as brilliant as an emerald of enormous size—as big as a cabbage—and crisscrossing it are the dark shadows of the bars that form the checkered lattice. It is the last thing my eyes rest upon every night when the lights are turned off."[7]

However glum he might have felt, Chapin's living conditions were improving rapidly. A modest pension from the *Evening World* permitted him to purchase additional food and personal items from the prison store and through friends on the outside. He obtained a red carpet, new bed linens, and a blue satin, down-filled pillow. As a Grade "A" inmate, he was permitted four weekday visits and one Sunday visit a month. Soon, an old friend came to call and listened patiently as Chapin detailed his sad life at Sing Sing.

"Why don't you turn to writing during some of your leisure hours?" the friend suggested. "Why don't you write a book?"

"About what?" replied Chapin.

"Write an autobiography."

"I haven't that much egotism left."

"Tell the story of your forty years as a newspaper man."[8]

That night back in his cell, Chapin remained awake as usual, but for a different reason. "Forty years a newspaper man! Memories began to crowd in upon me. It seemed as if even the smallest events of my life were flashing through a kinetoscope." Subsequently, back at work in the library, Chapin came across a book called *Character* by the nineteenth-century self-help philosopher Samuel Smiles. In it, Chapin found an entire chapter devoted to prison writers. Smiles suggested that they had been roused into action by adversity. "It seems as if, in certain cases, genius, like iron struck by the flint, needed the sharp and sudden blow of adversity to bring out the divine spark," Chapin read. "There are natures which blossom and ripen amidst trials, which would only wither and decay in an atmosphere of ease and comfort." Chapin considered his fate and thought of the writers he read about in Smiles's book. Hadn't Miguel de Cervantes conceived *Don Quixote* while in prison? Novelist Daniel Defoe was certainly no stranger to English prisons. Dominican philosopher Tommaso Campanella spent thirty years in Italian jails. It was thought that poet Richard Lovelace's "To Althea, From Prison" was written during his confinement in the gatehouse at Westminster. "Solitude drives some men mad; it sharpens the wit of others," Chapin wrote. "Courageous men have often turned confinement into a

great personal achievement, while more faint-hearted ones, crushed and defeated by self-pity, have drifted quickly into a condition of impotent inertia." The idea of writing his life story lifted him from his despondent lethargy.[9]

"I began to write. In memory I lived my life over again." He wrote each day in the library with no fixed plan or purpose. He said he had no thought of publishing what he wrote. Instead, he was contented by the distraction it offered. He began his tale with his memories of Atchison at age fourteen. He recounted his years of barnstorming, Chicago journalism, his move to New York, Park Row news battles, his recollections of the Pulitzers, and his eventual collapse. Though he sometimes claimed a shade more credit than he was due, the manuscript was considerably honest. Writing without the use of calendars, diaries, or aides-mémoire, Chapin pieced together an accurate, though at times puzzling, rendition of his life. Conspicuously absent from the manuscript were two aspects of his life. The first was his parents, especially his father. A reader would have no idea that his father renounced the family and created a new life with another woman. The only clue—and one that could be noticed only by a reader who knew of the family breakup—was a kind of idolizing reverence Chapin accorded his mother. More important was the absence of Nellie. Aside from a short, but touching, remembrance of their courtship, Nellie disappeared entirely, except for the occasional mention as his companion, such as in "my wife and I were having Thanksgiving dinner at the Hotel Savoy." At the end of the manuscript, Nellie resurfaced, but only as Chapin explained the events leading to her death. But even in this section, he chose not to use her name, referring to her only as "wife."

While Chapin worked on his manuscript, his health declined. By fall, he was confined to the prison's infirmary. Sixty years old, feeble and gaunt, Chapin weighed only 133 pounds. Amos Squire, the prison doctor, concluded that he would not live much longer. Chapin concurred and wrote instructions that he be buried with his wife, setting aside what little funds he had for that purpose. And then he waited.[10]

Winds of political and social change were blowing in New

York, and they soon reached Sing Sing. During Chapin's confinement in the Tombs, New Yorkers had elected reform-minded Catholic Al Smith as governor. Soon after Chapin's confinement at Sing Sing, the wardenship of the prison became vacant. The opening itself was not unusual: during the past twenty years, the average tenure of a warden at the prison had been only eleven months. A popular quip at the time was that the quickest way to get out of Sing Sing was to come in as a warden. It had been regarded mostly as a patronage post belonging to Westchester County politicians. But business under Governor Smith was different. Already he had done the unheard-of by appointing a woman, Frances Perkins, to the Industrial Commission. Sing Sing was next to receive the Smith touch. On December 5, 1919, a telegram was sent to Lewis Lawes at the New Hampton Reformatory on Long Island. "Can you arrange to meet the Governor and me at the Biltmore Hotel on Tuesday, December 9th, at seven o'clock. (Signed) C. F. Rattigan, Superintendent of Prisons."[11]

Already, at the young age of thirty-six, Lawes was the poster child of prison reformists. Born in Elmira, New York, Lawes had been around inmates his whole life. As a child, he had spent hours watching the prison drill team at the New York State Reformatory near his home. Like Chapin, he had left home as a teenager and had sought to make his own way in the world. After a tour in the army, he became a guard at state prisons in Dannemora and Auburn and then returned home to assume a post in the Elmira reformatory. Lawes decided on an unusual course before turning thirty. He obtained a leave of absence and enrolled in the New York School of Social Work. There a prison guard who had come, on his own, to learn from leaders of social reform did not go unnoticed. His strategy worked. Shortly after resuming work in Elmira, Kathryn B. Davis, one of his instructors and the New York City Commissioner of Corrections, invited Lawes to return to the city and become warden of the troubled New York City Reformatory on Hart Island. Conditions at the reformatory were ripe for change. Situated between a penitentiary and Potter's Field, where New York's unclaimed dead were buried, the reformatory had just been the site of a riot led by an inmate known as "Mike the Rat Catcher."

Lawes accepted the challenge. Within a week, he found himself sitting in the cooler talking with Mike, the inmate responsible for the uprising. "I found the notorious 'bad boy' to be a slim, narrow chested, wan looking youngster, of medium height," said Lawes. "His eyes impressed me. They were bright and looked straight at you." Mike had earned his unusual moniker from his uncanny ability to catch rats without a trap. He even kept several as pets. "Mike's love for rats made him the hero of the reformatory," said Lawes. "With suitable advertisement he might, in later years, have landed in Congress or some other public office. There is often no accounting for the 'people's' acclaim." After talking with Mike, Lawes released him and his henchmen back into the prison population after extracting from them a promise of good behavior. Simultaneously, Lawes moved quickly to improve conditions, lifting many of the reformatory's odious restrictions, bringing games into the dormitory at night, and improving the food. "I had no further trouble with Mike and his cohorts during the year we stayed on the Island."[12]

The conditions of the reformatory were such that New York City consented to funding the construction of a new reformatory in Orange County. Under the supervision of a handful of guards, Lawes led 547 boys and young men by boat, then train and another boat to the open fields purchased by the city on which a few makeshift bunk houses had been erected. None of the wards escaped during the journey, though many might have regretted not doing so when they arrived at the muddy fields that would be their home. Within a few years, Lawes had built, using inmate labor, what was widely hailed as a model institution. This feat caught the attention of the then-sheriff of New York Al Smith.

"How about going up to Sing Sing and take charge?" said Smith as he greeted Lawes in his Biltmore suite for the promised meeting. Lawes said he was reluctant. Though complimented to be considered, he told the governor he thought it unwise to give up his civil-service post at New Hampton for a political one with a history of short tenure.

"Young fellow, it's all right with me," said Smith. "It's a tough spot. I don't blame you for being scared. It'll take a big man to go up there and stay."

Lawes consented to visit the prison while considering the offer.

Several days later, Lawes came into the prison infirmary on his inspection tour. As he walked through, he saw a forlorn, gray-haired man lying listlessly on a cot. "I noticed that his eyes were wide open and brilliant," said Lawes. "They followed me on my tour of the ward."

He approached the inmate, not knowing anything about who he was, and asked about his health. The two talked for a while, and introductions were finally made. Like many who lived in New York City, Lawes recognized Chapin's name. And Chapin, displaying the memory that had made him famous as an editor, placed that of Lawes.

"Oh, yes." said Chapin. "You are going to be the new warden?"

Lawes replied he had not yet decided.

"I'm praying you'll take it," said Chapin. "You know you are the first man who gave me a kindly nod since I came here."[13]

Two weeks later, Lawes assumed the wardenship of Sing Sing. At a meeting in his office, Lawes asked Dr. Squire for a report on Chapin's condition. Squire said he didn't think Chapin had long to live. He was failing rapidly, and it seemed as if he had lost his will to live. Lawes was moved. "Twenty years to life had been his sentence. Possibly he might not live to complete that sentence," he thought. "But surely the few remaining years of his life could be put to some good service." Lawes went to see him. "He was almost too weak to answer my greeting," said Lawes. "But his eyes still burned with life."

"Oh, it's you," said Chapin. "I thought you'd given me up. You've been here a week."

"I've been thinking about you just the same," Lawes said. "Charlie, how would you like to get out of bed?"

Chapin shook his head.

"I think I'll put you to work, Charlie," continued Lawes, ignoring Chapin's protests. "Something that I think you will like."

He then explained that the prison had an inmate newspaper and that it had fallen on hard times. Lawes said he thought an old newspaper editor might be able to liven it up. Chapin seemed interested, and his eyes carefully examined Lawes.

"But," said Lawes as he rose to leave, "you will have to get well in quick order, otherwise the offer is withdrawn. We can't wait too long."

Chapin was out of bed by the week's end.[14]

At the Editor's Desk, Again

By the time Lawes made his offer to Chapin, a prison newspaper had been published at Sing Sing off and on for more than thirty years. Starting in the 1870s, most major prisons in the United States had some kind of inmate-operated press. Some were lively, polished, independent publications, often the darling of prison reformers. Others were heavily censored, boosterish kinds of papers that made for dull reading. In December 1887, a small, illustrated magazine called *Solitaire* appeared at Sing Sing with the announcement on its masthead that it was "edited, designed, illustrated, and printed without type, without a printing press, or scissors." It was the loving work of Gay W. Foster, an inmate serving time at Sing Sing for reasons unknown except—what the *New York World* called—"his connection with bucket-shops and commercial enterprises of a questionable character." The first issue was fourteen pages long, half of which were filled with illustrations printed from hand-cut maple wood engraving. "To produce it," noted the *New York World*, "long hours of painstaking care and skill were required on the part of a man who is—as he expressed it—'dead by the law of man, yet speaketh.'"[1]

By 1899, when the *Star of Hope* was established, there was no trace of Foster's efforts. The new publication was launched, like most other prison newspapers, when printing presses were introduced to prison industries. An inmate, known only as No. 1500, was enamored with the new printing plant at Sing Sing. It "attract[ed] my own longing gaze every time I marched by it, which was some half-dozen times a day. If I only had that plant up state somewhere, I used to say to myself, what a happy activity for myself I could create!" Finally, the idea took shape in his mind that he might be able to publish a newspaper right there at the prison. "I had never heard of prison journalism," he admitted, "although I knew that in Stillwater, Minnesota, a little sheet called the *Prison Mirror* was published weekly. . . . So I set to work to frame up a prospectus of what I thought a prison journal might be." He suggested to the warden that an eight-page paper of material written by the inmates about Sing Sing, with some news of the outside, be printed bi-weekly in the new plant. "As for its staff, I offered myself as editor and publisher and the whole community of prisoners as its corps of contributors," he said.

With the permission of the warden and the general superintendent of the prisons, the *Star of Hope* was first published on April 22, 1899. Francis Quigley, one of the nation's more notorious counterfeiters, etched its nameplate. It depicted the countryside beyond the walls, and a star hovering above one of the guard towers of the prison. The paper alternatively thrived and withered for about fifteen years until it was merged with the *Bulletin*, published by the Mutual Welfare League, an inmate government much like a student government started at Sing Sing in 1913. By 1920, prison journalism had become an established part of life behind the walls of Sing Sing and at least two-thirds of America's prisons. Many wardens were convinced that a prison paper could serve them well in their efforts to reform their wards. At the same time, however, there was a limit to what prison officials would tolerate.[2]

It was in this ambivalent atmosphere in January 1920 that Chapin began his new career as an editor of a prison newspaper. He moved into the *Star-Bulletin*'s office, located on the ground floor of a large yellow building in the middle of the prison yard. It took ten inmates to carry his books and cache of luxuries supplied by friends outside. "I watched in amazement as he unpacked the boxes and packages," said fellow-inmate McGrath, who worked in the print shop. "With the opening of each one, the place looked more and more like a grocery-store. . . . There were cans of fruit, cans of vegetables, jars of jams, jellies and preserves, boxes of crackers, sugar, tea, coffee—everything that a man could possibly need." There was so much that when the moving crew prepared to leave, there were still two dozen cans that Chapin had no place to store.

"Don't we get something for helping you?" one of the men asked.

"Why should you?" replied Chapin, who turned his back to them.

The next day, as McGrath stood in the print shop, he spotted four men from the carpentry shop carrying a cabinet he had ordered to store binding material he used in his work.

"Fine, boys," said McGrath. "Put it right here in the corner."

"Sorry, Eddie," said the guard who was accompanying the crew. "This cabinet ain't for you. It's for the big shot next door."

"For Chapin? You're crazy. I ordered this cabinet a month ago!"

"That's right, but it ain't for you. It *was* for you, but Chapin is getting it. Look, don't you see them groceries over there in the corner? Well, he has to have some place to put them, and his cupboards are full now. Orders came to give this to Chapin and to make another one for you. Guess you'll have to wait another couple of weeks."³

Even if it weren't for the larder, Chapin's office would have been an incongruous oasis in a city of cold stone. Measuring twelve by fifteen feet, the space was actually an alcove with an arched ceiling, furnished with cabinets and a large, flat-top desk topped with a case of pigeon holes for papers and letters, and a separate typewriter desk. The walls were painted French gray, and the ceiling white, striped and decorated with green, red, and gold. Throughout the day, the room was awash in sunlight pouring in through windows that faced east and west. At night, it was lighted with an electric sunburst cluster suspended from the ceiling by gilded chains. Shortly after moving in, Chapin hung sash curtains, green and black draperies, and put down thick carpeting. In no time, Chapin regained his health. "I was delighted beyond expression to again be breathing into my nostrils the smell of printer's ink and hear the whiz and slam of the rotary press." His step quickened, his shoulders straightened, and he regaled himself in barking out orders. "He found renewed interest in life," said Lawes, who also was adjusting to life at Sing Sing. "He was a man made over." Lawes gave him free run of the prison and permitted him to make his own schedule. Chapin chose to remain in his new office from seven in the morning until he returned to his cell at ten in the evening, taking all his meals in his office, eating off a china dish set. He turned his full attention to his new paper.[4]

With Lawes's approval, Chapin remade the prison paper. It was re-christened the *Sing Sing Bulletin*, it was enlarged to twice its former size, and a new typeface was obtained to distinguish it from its predecessors. The first issue was off the press in February. It was eighteen pages long, cleanly designed, and well illustrated. On the front page it featured a flattering and lengthy profile of the prison's new warden written by "C.E.C. 69,690." Chapin's appointment as editor and his plans for the publication were described in an editorial on the inside. "Warden Lawes," wrote Chapin, "believes the *Bulletin* should be the leading prison publication and has promised to back it to the full extent of his resources." Inmates were urged to contribute to the "new" prison paper. Writing under the pseudonym "Man in the Library," Chapin told his readers, "what other men have accomplished under worse conditions should be an incentive to every inmate of Sing Sing to at least make an effort to write something worth while for our prison paper. Writing will help us forget our misery." Following his own advice, Chapin published the first installment of his memoirs, consuming two entire pages of the *Bulletin*.[5]

Like an editor at the *World* and *Evening World*, which had always championed the downtrodden, Chapin devoted more space for news of interest to inmates, such as court cases, and turned what little editorial power the *Bulletin* possessed toward advocating for inmate causes. The *Bulletin* joined other prison newspapers in campaigning for increased—or in some cases, any—wages for convict labor. "The state hasn't discharged its duty to society," wrote Chapin, "when it does nothing to correct evil-doers but confine them behind prison walls and embitter them by compulsory work without compensation." Chapin pushed for increased pay for guards to ensure more competent (and thus, one hoped, less dangerous) keepers. He composed elegant pleas against the death penalty, using his own case to illustrate that death may be a lesser punishment than life in prison. "We know the heartache it brings, the dreary loneliness, the deadly monotony, the never ending sorrow and regret. And we know there will never be anything different in all our lives. It will be the same tomorrows that follow after as long as we live, and until the period of our long sentence expires."[6]

The most evident change in Sing Sing's newspaper was that it began to reflect the aggressive, abrasive, and sometimes arrogant personality of its new editor. It wasn't long before Chapin abandoned his idea of having inmates write most of the articles. Their work, apparently, was not up to his standards. Although in print he praised his fellow inmates, privately his opinion of their intellect was certainly not high. "A prison editor must not soar above the dwarfed and shriveled minds of his readers," he wrote to a friend. By the fall, he was writing almost the entire paper by himself, "covering my identity," he explained, "by such delightful pen names as 'The Lifer,' 'Bill the Burglar,' 'The Man in the Library,' 'Jerry the Monk,' and whatever absurd name may pop into my mind at the moment." This attitude was evident to the inmates. "When it started, the *Star-Bulletin* was a medium of expression for any prisoner who was able to put his thoughts on paper in something approaching a decent literary form," said McGrath. "This didn't last when the old editor of the [*Evening*] *World* got his fist on the blue pencil. Instead, it was a paper written almost exclusively by 'the master' and covering only those things in which he personally was interested—mainly himself."[7]

In many ways, McGrath's view, though shaped by a disdain for Chapin, was correct. For Chapin, the *Bulletin* offered a personal escape from his confinement. His readers—at least the ones he cared most about—lay outside the walls. If he couldn't be among his old set in person, he could do so in type, the way he had always made his presence felt. He took great care to mail former colleagues, friends, and luminaries hundreds of copies of each edition, featuring not only his autobiography, but also essays on various subjects ranging from the prison's pauper graveyard to his new brier pipe. "Each night in the drab solitude of my rock-walled cell, I ease the heartache and sorrows of prison life, as I draw sweet solace through its cooling stem," he wrote. His essay on the pauper's graves revealed that Chapin still possessed the journalist's touch for scene setting that he had honed in Chicago forty years earlier. "On the brow of the windswept hill that rises above the frowning walls of Sing Sing is a cluster of grassy mounds, more lonely and neglected than any sullen felon in solitary confinement. It is Twenty-five gallery, the prison graveyard. . . . It gets this name from the old Cell Block, where the twelve hundred cells rise tier upon tier and are blocked off into twenty-four galleries. Twenty-five gallery, the final resting place of friendless convicts, is on the hill."[8]

These reflective pieces on prison life were interspersed throughout each issue of the *Bulletin*, the center of which was consumed by Chapin's lengthy installments of his autobiography. Publishing his memoirs certainly boosted outside interest in the paper among his old press colleagues. Letters came in from old friends such as Seymour, former reporters such as Terhune, and even past rivals. "The newspaper you are editing now has twice the human interest in it that the *Evening World* ever had," wrote Ashby Deering, the city editor of the *Morning Telegram*. The *Newark News* wryly commented, "one handicap he will have is that he can't fire reporters." To which Chapin joshingly replied, "Reporters of our prison paper don't come down at irregular hours and sing the editor a song about a blockade in the subway. They are never called away by sickness in the family or to attend the funeral of a mythical grandmother. There are no besetting temptations to lure them from duty, no racetracks, no poker games, no cabarets, no wild women."[9]

Shortly after Chapin assumed the editorship of the *Bulletin*, Basil King, an Episcopal minister turned best-selling author, came to Sing Sing to visit a young inmate with whom he had been corresponding. During the visit, the inmate asked King if would like to meet Chapin, now Sing Sing's most famous resident. King readily agreed. "Here my own books had prepared the way for me, and, as far as the conditions permitted, our coming together was not different from what it would have been had we met at a club," said King, who was imbued with an idealism common among those who took an interest in prisons in that era. They saw prisons as criminal, the criminals as suffering for society's sins, and society as guilty for permitting the whole affair to continue. For King, there was "no difference between the man whom we somewhat hideously call a convict and anybody else."

At first, Chapin and King politely conversed about the events of the day, literature, and prison life. But they quickly found they had much in common, especially in Chapin's dazzling knowledge of books. Soon, King was a regular visitor and the first new friend Chapin had made since being sent to prison. Chapin was appreciative. "One quickly learns not to count on earlier friendships after he gets in prison, one also realizes that he forfeited all rights to call any man his friend by placing himself here," he said.[10]

On a subsequent visit, Chapin showed King his manuscript. King was impressed with what he read and urged Chapin to submit it to a publisher. Chapin had no means to make copies, so instead he mailed the first installment printed in February's *Bulletin* to Putnam and Harpers publishing companies. Both houses asked to see the manuscript, but George Palmer Putnam made the first move. Putnam had once served on a parole board and frequently read prison newspapers. He came to Sing Sing by train with a contract, a $1,000 advance, and promised royalties of fifty cents a book. Chapin accepted the offer immediately. After reviewing the manuscript, Putnam stipulated that Chapin was to write two additional chapters to add bulk to the book. Chapin agreed to write one on newspaper ethics and another on the murder of Nellie. In his rapid, two-fingered typing style, he dashed off the two chapters, 5,000 and 7,500 words respectively, in two evenings and mailed them to Putnam on the third day without so much as reading over what he had written. Unlike King, who told Chapin he revised a work six or seven times before submitting it to a publisher, Chapin had no sense of what it took to prepare a book for publication. "My practice was to write what I had to tell and feed it to the typesetters a page at a time almost without reviewing, a very bad practice, as I very well know, but my writing had to be swiftly done to make an edition of a daily newspaper and I had no alternative but to rattle it off at the fastest speed I was capable of."[11]

Chapin's haste was most evident in the chapter on newspaper ethics. It began with a strong defense of American journalism, challenging Upton Sinclair's dismal appraisal of the press as being under the thumb of corporate America in his new book *The Brass Check*, which a magazine editor had recently mailed to Chapin. "It is my firm belief that at no time in the history of American journalism have newspapers been more enterprising, more reliable, or more influential," wrote Chapin. But as he began to offer support for his argument—such as Pulitzer's refusal to withhold or suppress a news item—the chapter dissipated into a hodgepodge of Park Row remembrances, ranging from the sinking of *La Bourgoyne* to the Equitable Insurance scandal.

The second new chapter was completely different. Called "A Lifer in Sing Sing," it was very personal and offered the first public explanation of his actions. "The amazing part of my story," he wrote, "is that I am alive to relate it." Why he did not finish what he set out to do that September morning and kill himself after ending his wife's life is a puzzle not only to his friends but to him, admitted Chapin. "It has been said by others that after taking the life of my wife I lacked the fortitude to kill myself. The assumption is justifiable, but it is untrue." It required greater courage to surrender, he said, because he believed he would face the electric chair. Instead, Charles said it was Nellie's lingering death that foiled his plans for suicide. He hadn't dared point the pistol at himself in case she survived. When she finally died, the fear, the desperation, the anxiety that had driven him to the act disappeared. "Then my brain went dead," he said. "What happened immediately afterward I but dimly remember. I have tried to piece together what I did throughout the day and all of the night, but it is like trying to gather the elusive threads of a fast-fading dream." At best, he remembered only wandering the city in a daze until he read about the murder in the morning papers. In the remainder of the chapter, Chapin detailed his trial, the lunacy commission, his time in the Tombs, and his arrival at Sing Sing. "For many months after I put on the gray garb of a felon, I was so ill and dazed that much of the time I could scarcely realize my surroundings. I wanted to crawl out of sight of everyone and cry." He feared that he would go insane and be sent to the state's insane asylum. But over time, he wrote, he had learned to appreciate his fellow inmates and the kindness of prison officials, and come to terms with his fate. "The past is behind me. What I have done I cannot undo." But for those who looked for contrition, the final words of this chapter and the book would leave them disappointed. "Almost two years have passed," wrote Chapin. "In the solitude of my cell I have subjected myself to a more searching examination than the most analytical prosecutor could put me through, and the verdict that is firmly fixed in my mind is that I did the only thing that was left to me to do. There was no other way of saving my wife."[12]

Chapin felt his final chapter was one of best things he had composed. Perhaps, as he suggested, it was because it was written "straight from the heart without pretense of composition." It had a very honest tone in comparison with the rest of the manuscript, which is not to say that the remainder of his reminiscence was inaccurate. In fact, Chapin was remarkably faithful to the events of his life, precisely recalling incidents from more than forty years earlier. In the end, however, his explanation for the murder would leave even his friends exasperated. His old star writer and friend Cobb, for instance, saw the book as "mostly alibis and extenuating circumstances."[13]

With the manuscript in Putnam's hands, Chapin turned his attention to a new challenge. His editorship of the *Bulletin* was threatening its very existence. Warden Lawes had given Chapin as much latitude as he felt he possibly could. "Frequently he chafed under institutional restrictions," said Lawes. "Having his editorial censored was something new to a man of Chapin's temperament. As Warden that was my duty, and I fulfilled it literally." But Lawes was considerably liberal and rarely suggested any changes. He had been pleased with Chapin's work and thought he had "built up a prison paper second to none in the country." The *Bulletin* had certainly become popular. Visitors to Sing Sing always asked for copies, and prison reform activists in New York City got themselves on the mailing list. The paper's visibility caused Chapin to boast that it had become so popular with the mail clerks alone that "many [issues] we send out never reach the ones to whom they are addressed." Officials in Albany, on the other hand, were not amused. They had been watching the increasing visibility of Chapin's paper with growing wariness. Now they complained that the *Bulletin* was becoming the voice of Chapin and not the convicts. The fact that he was publishing his memoir in the paper contributed to this impression, even though it was read by inmates who regarded him as a kind of local eccentric.[14]

Chapin knew that he was facing a serious crisis with the paper.

In April 1920, he had received the first volley from his critics. Charles Rattigan, state superintendent of the prisons, had ordered that the circulation of the *Bulletin* be cut. The April edition of the *Bulletin* announced unpersuasively that in order to "economize," the paper would be restricted to 1,500 copies per run, its normal number having been around 5,000 copies. "After this issue the mailing list will be practically eliminated," continued the announcement. Equally crippling was the decision that support from outside the prison would no longer be permitted because "the law forbids us to accept subscriptions."[15]

Obviously, Rattigan had not consulted any of Chapin's colleagues about what happened when the irascible editor felt pushed. Instead of lying low, Chapin decided that, if his reminiscences were popular, then he would enlist another memoir writer. This time, he chose Charlie Wilson, a bigamist. "On the outside were seven women vowing adoration, and swearing fealty. Wilson had married them all," explained a newspaper reporter. "Now for his sins and his loving heart, he was doing time." In the May issue, Wilson told his story with what one can only presume to have been Chapin's editing touches. "They say a good wife is a rare jewel." he began. "I have been a collector of jewels." But, Wilson admitted, he had some regrets. "I am doing five and a half for collecting my string of jewels. They were not worth the price." If Sing Sing readers chuckled, those in Albany did not get the joke. The June and July issues appeared as scheduled, but the calm was the kind that precedes a storm.[16]

During the dog days of summer, Rattigan came down from Albany. He told Lawes the Wilson article and Chapin's memoirs had prompted the trip. You have three choices, Rattigan told the warden: You can remove Chapin as editor, or submit all the content of the paper to Albany before publication, or suspend the paper. After Rattigan departed, Lawes went to the print shop to find Chapin. He told him to come with him. They walked, in silence, to the top of the hill where they could look out over the Hudson. "The superintendent of prisons," said Lawes, "has decided that he will censor our publication. From now on, he has ordered me to send all our material to him before it is printed. Nothing is to appear in our paper without his approval or sanction. In other words, he wants to be editor."

"Well, I know what I would do about it," replied Chapin, trying to control his temper. "But I'm not going to tell you what to do. I'm not going to get out a paper to please him."

The pair walked back to Chapin's office. "Of course, my advice doesn't amount to a damn, now, inside these walls," said Chapin. "But people used to come in to see me for advice—big people, too. There are broader implications in this thing than the control of a sheet that nobody ever heard of until we put life into it. Keep that in mind."[17]

In August, the *Bulletin* failed to appear. Lawes told visitors to Sing Sing who asked for copies that he had received orders to discontinue the newspaper. Chapin's allies rushed to his defense. B. Ogden Chisolm, a prison reformer from New York, fired off a letter to Governor Smith saying he regarded the stopping of the publication an "outrage" and demanded that the governor allow it to resume. Smith replied that he would investigate. Within two days, Rattigan denied that he had ever ordered that the paper be closed and promised to investigate the whole episode. The state prison commissioners weighed in. They announced that, although they understood the superintendent had not actually specifically ordered the suppression of the paper, they wanted it to resume publication. In the meantime, Chapin was told to go ahead and publish the *Bulletin*. He went to work on plans to publish the material in the missing August issue as a combined August/September issue. The battle did not escape the attention of the press. The *New York Times* reported that Rattigan's action resulted "in no appearance of the *Bulletin* this month, and in the fight that now is being waged, not only to restore the *Bulletin* to its former activities as a prison newspaper, but also to settle whether or not it is to be edited in Albany or Sing Sing." It would now be up to the governor to decide.[18]

Governor Smith ordered Rattigan and Lawes to work out their problems, but made it clear the *Bulletin* was to resume publication. Rattigan, accompanied by Deputy Superintendent of Prisons James Long, immediately boarded a train in Albany and once again headed down to Sing Sing. To observers of the prison scene, the fact that Long was on the trip was a signal that a peace treaty was in the works. Long was known as the "diplomatist" on Rattigan's staff. When they reached the prison, the two men walked silently past the gathered reporters and went directly into the warden's office. A while later, the three emerged. Rattigan told the reporters he had nothing to say, that Lawes would fill them in. He then turned and went into an adjoining room.

"The *Sing Sing Bulletin* will be continued," announced Lawes. "The suspension has been lifted, and the differences over it have been ironed out."

"It will be edited as it has been," added Long. "It will be carefully edited and censored."

"Edited and censored here or at Albany?" asked a reporter.

"Here," said Long.

"There is no conflict of authority between the Warden's and the Superintendent's office," said Lawes. "There is no hard feelings over the matter." That night, the print shop worked overtime preparing the combined August/September issue, in hopes of having it ready for the first of the month.[19]

The dispute, however, was not over. Lawes and Chapin had won the first skirmish, but Lawes felt the attack put in jeopardy the promise from the governor that he would have a free hand in running Sing Sing. Two days later, he and Smith met. Like the first time, their meeting was at the Biltmore. Any thoughts of what Lawes might say to the governor were jumbled when he stepped off the hotel elevator and found himself surrounded by dozens of well-dressed New York women. Certain he had mistakenly gotten off on the wrong floor, he began to retreat when an aide approached him.

"Warden Lawes?"

Lawes nodded.

"Come with me. The governor will see you first. These dames can wait. It's some welfare crowd, and they want to be photographed with the governor. They'll wait till the cows come home and then some."

"Here's the warden, Governor," said the aide as he ushered Lawes into the suite. The scene inside the suite was a remarkable contrast to that of the hall. Outside the door stood a gaggle of women with social registry pedigrees, all anxiously waiting to have their photographs taken with Smith. "At the table before me," said Lawes, "sat the object of their quest, in shirtsleeves, his striped suspenders loudly proclaiming the informality of the man.

As I entered, he was biting into an ear of corn with all the vigor of his indomitable personality."

"What's up, Warden?" he asked between bites. "I thought you could run that place. Are the boys too much for you? Pulling your leg, so to speak."

Lawes reminded the governor of his promise to let him run the prison unfettered. "If that is not to be continued, you can have my resignation at once."

The governor took another ear of corn and slowly buttered it, shook salt and pepper on it, then looked up. "Now, Warden, you go back and tell that crowd that you're to run that prison as I said you should. Without any interference. We've got to get this thing on a sensible basis. I won't let politics interfere with our prisons any longer. Now, you go back and tell 'em that, will you, like a good fellow?"

"My resignation stands, Governor, unless that word comes from you directly to them."

"All right," Smith said after a moment's pause. "I'll tell them. You go back home, and it will all come out fine."[20]

It was the end of the day by the time Lawes returned to Sing Sing. The prison grapevine announced his return, and soon the clerk from the switchboard called Lawes with the news that Chapin was on the phone and wanted to know if the warden wanted to see the page proofs.

"Tell him no," said Lawes.

"He wants to know if there are any other instructions."

"Yes, tell him—tell him he can peddle his papers."[21]

The remainder of the summer passed without incident. The combined issue appeared in September—as the *New York Times* put it, "on prison news stands"—though Albany officials continued to grumble that the serialization of Chapin's life story was "self-aggrandizement of an inmate." They must have reacted with a greater horror that month when Chapin's autobiography arrived in stores. Bound in blue cloth with gold lettering, the dust jacket proclaimed in twenty-two-point type, "In this unflinching revelation of the tragedy which terminated his career with life imprisonment, the author, for twenty years City editor of the *New York Evening World*, bares his soul." The volume was dedicated, though not by name, to Nellie. Rather, the dedication page was inscribed "To Her Who Ever Beckons To Me From Afar" and featured a stanza of poetry adapted from a poem by William Leggett, a nineteenth-century journalist.[22]

> Oh, how dark and lone and drear
> Will seem that brighter world of bliss
> If, while wandering through each radiant zone
> We fail to find the loved of this.[23]

The *New York Times* was the first to review it. The book, it said, offered readers considerable proof of the lure of newspaper work. "Through the author's eyes they will look behind the scenes of life in New York, Chicago, St. Louis and other cities; they will sit with the one-time city editor at his desk and feel the strands of history run through their fingers as cable, telephone and telegraph unwind them." The reviewer, however, was noncommittal about recommending it, though the paper listed it among the "Two Hundred Leading Books of the Season," right next to *The Autobiography of Andrew Carnegie*. Some other reviewers were quite taken with Chapin's work. "The recital of the morbid psychological conditions that led to the author's crime does not make wholesome reading," said the reviewer for *Outlook* magazine. "Nevertheless, the book is one of the most remarkable that ever came from within prison walls." The *Springfield Republican* said, "In comparison with some literary products, the work may seem 'choppy' at times, but the human story is there and written in a style easily understood and followed." Neither the *World* nor the *Evening World* reviewed it.[24]

In addition to the reviews, a number of newspapers serialized the book. The *Washington Post* ran four lengthy installments in September and October, publicizing the series with a display advertisement that toted the work as "a most graphic human document of a brilliant career that ended in a tragic crime." The first installment the paper published was the one in which Chapin detailed the murder and the events leading to it, which the *Post* sympathetically described as revealing in "startling pity" what "caused him to take his wife's life rather than leave her to the miseries of poverty." No telling how Marion and Frank Chapin, who still lived in Washington, reacted when they opened their copy of the *Post*, or if they even took the paper.[25]

That fall as his second year in Sing Sing came to a close, Chapin's circumstances were considerably different from when Sheriff Knott had delivered him to the prison. Chapin was healthy; his weight was back up to nearly 150 pounds. "I am stronger physically and mentally than I have been in years," he said. He had secured luxuries and accommodations that, in comparison to the lot of his fellow inmates, made his version of Sing Sing seem like the Plaza. He had been accorded privileges from the warden that freed him from most prison regulations. His social life included many regular visitors—far above the number normally permitted—and frequent dinners with the Lawes family. In fact, a photographer captured his exceptional situation that fall on the verandah of the warden's house. In the photograph, Chapin is reposing in a rocking chair, reading a copy of a magazine, dressed in a beautifully knit sweater, bow tie, gray flannels, and polished shoes with spats.[26]

On the other hand, it could hardly be said that Chapin had faded away into the anonymity of penal life. Far from it. His battle with the state over the *Bulletin* and the publication of his autobiography gave him a newfound fame. The volume of mail addressed to inmate No. 69690 grew exponentially. Virtually all the correspondents had one aim in mind—saving Chapin's soul. "The pigeon holes of my desk are stuffed with their letters," said Chapin. "I never knew until now there was so much cant. It is the worst part of my punishment." But in late November 1920, Chapin received a very different letter. It came from Viola Irene Cooper, a twenty-four-year-old Californian living in Minnesota who had read about Chapin in the newspaper. It was different from the other unknown correspondents in that she expressed no interest in his soul, rather only a desire to learn his "habits of the mind." On Thanksgiving, Chapin sat at his desk in his office and began tapping out a response on his typewriter. "Dear Viola Irene," he began. "You ask: 'Are we going to be friends?' and my heart responds with a bound, for I have waited a very long time to hear from you."[27]

"It was good of you to write," he continued. "I am indeed grateful, for I was so lonely—not for someone, for they are many—but for *the* one, for Viola Irene. . . . I am repeating the name aloud and my voice never sounded so musical—'Viola

Irene.'" Please, he urged her, don't think him "mushy" for his reaction to her letter. But the conditions of his life impelled him to
be so direct. "I am more lonely than any person you may know,
so lonely that I am even now reaching out my arm to clasp your
hand, hoping that you will let me hold it in mine for just a little
while, you lady with intellect, and heart, and understanding—
Viola (a violet) Irene (peaceful)." Chapin offered to send Cooper
a copy of his autobiography, though he feared she might not like
"the man who bared his soul in its pages, and I shall not again
hear from you." He promised to send copies of the *Bulletin*,
though he warned it was "not written for intellects such as yours."
Fifteen-hundred words later, Chapin closed his missive with one
final plea. "I am waiting for your answer—waiting like a timid
lover, unmindful of who and where I am—doubting—fearing—
hopeful, yet—?"

The next morning, Chapin posted the letter. Then he counted
the days until an answer could plausibly arrive. He calculated it
would be Thursday, December 2, and he marked a red cross on
his calendar. Twice, he dreamed of Cooper, but he began to fear
that he might not get a response. "I wondered if I might not have
been too precipitate in writing," he said. Maybe he had taken for
granted more than Cooper intended. Maybe his forwardness
would cause the letter "to be dropped like an old coat at the door
so that all the rest of my life I should go on hungering for one
who called me back to life for just a brief moment and then fluttered away."

On Thursday, Cooper's answer arrived. "The letter came at the
very hour I hoped it would," said Chapin. "My faith has been
rewarded."[28]

Viola

Viola Irene Cooper's letters marked the beginning of Chapin's literary escape from Sing Sing. If he couldn't physically leave the prison, he could certainly write his way out. On Thursday, December 2, 1920, the day he received Cooper's reply to his Thanksgiving supplication, he retreated to his office to savor its every word. He waited until the last whistle had blown and quiet had descended on Sing Sing before placing a sheet into his typewriter. "I am alone, dear one, with you," he wrote. "I'll not write to another or permit any save you to come into my thoughts tonight. This is your night—consecrated wholly and exclusively to you—just you. So cuddle up close, so close that I may look deep into your eyes, and tell me again, and over again, what I have just read in the sweetest letter that has ever come into my Gethsemene."[1]

In her letter, Cooper called Chapin "pal o' mine." The expression "so fraught with meaning" made Chapin delirious as he read it aloud. "How I wish you were seated in that comfortable chair before me now, as I almost feel that you invisibly are, and I could hear you say it, 'pal o' mine.'"

"Would [there] be room for me in your friendship?" asked Cooper.

"There is room for you, my Viola Irene, so come in if you will and we will lock the door and throw away the key. Will you come? I want no other. It seems as if you have belonged to me from almost the protoplasmic stage of your existence, psychogenically mine, in the sense of the operation of a higher agency than natural selection."

But a new fear now crept into Chapin's mind. The book. If Cooper read it and was repulsed by "the man who bared his soul in its pages," he would never hear from her again. "I am growing to detest the sight of it," he wrote. "Why should you need to read it, or know, or even care? Why cannot we both slam the door on all of the yesterdays in both of our lives and get all we can out of each day as we live it—you and I?"

In the morning, he walked over to the warden's office and entrusted his letter to the secretary who, thanks to Warden Lawes, personally mailed all of Chapin's correspondence, thereby sparing him a reading by the censor. Not that the censor would have necessarily excised what he had written. But knowing that another's eyes would read it might have cooled his ardor. In the privacy of letter writing that Lawes gave him, Chapin could blurt out, as he did in the closing lines of his letter, "God! how utterly unconscious one can become of his age when his heart remains young and is hungering for the one he long has sought and now, perhaps, found too late."[2]

In unseasonably warm weather for December, Chapin traversed the prison yard to his office, where he spent the day finishing a short story for the Christmas issue of the *Bulletin*. This was a new pursuit for Chapin. Not having written fiction while a free man, the incarcerated Chapin recently found solace in it. In fact, he often became so lost, pecking out his stories on his Underwood in his two-fingered style, that only the sounds of the prison dynamos reminded him that he was still in Sing Sing and not in his imagined locale. He had published the first of his efforts in the combined August/September issue of the *Bulletin*. It consisted of two stories set in Colorado, a place he knew well from his days of vacationing in the West. They were romantic tales, one concerning an outlaw, the other a painter who rescues a rarified woman from her dismal rural existence and brings her back to New York City.[3]

The story Chapin worked on this day was "Jim's Christmas Visitor," the tale of Jim Gauline, whose tranquil reveries in the prison library are disturbed one day with the news of a surprise visitor. It is Agnes, his old girlfriend, who has come from New York City in a limousine to see him. For five years, Agnes has shunned Jim because she believed he was guilty, but she was recently persuaded otherwise and would now use her influence to prove his innocence. Soon, he is pardoned by the governor and leaves prison for a passionate reunion with Agnes at the Biltmore. Over time, however, he finds he can't live with idea of being supported by Agnes. He writes her a letter explaining his departure and leaves to take up life in a cabin in the wilderness with another ex-convict, where he hopes to support himself writing prison stories. Unwilling to give up Jim again, Agnes shows up to take up life with him in his new surroundings.

In the evening, King came by for a visit. The two laughed over an encounter King had while in California earlier that year during the filming of a movie based on his novel *Earthbound.* When introduced to a young woman, King had mentioned somehow that he had arrived in California a day late because of a visit to Sing Sing to see a former newspaper editor.

"Do you mean Mr. Chapin?" asked the woman.

"Yes, do you know him?" replied the astonished King.

"Know him, why I love him. He gave me my start."

The woman, it turned out, was the daughter of Chapin's childhood sweetheart. She had come to know Chapin when she looked him up in New York years ago, and he had found her work in a movie company.[4]

That night, Chapin slept fitfully. At one point he propped himself up, lit his pipe, and thought of a cabin he knew in Cespe Canyon, California, resembling the one in his short story, where he had once been fishing and hunting. When he awoke the next morning, Chapin went to his office and took off his shelf the special edition of his book, bound in red Moroccan leather, which Putnam made for its authors. He inscribed the fly leaf with the words "Dearest, keep this until ———," and mailed it to Cooper. "It goes to you with many misgivings that after you have read it you may not wish again to write to me, and I can imagine nothing that could hurt so much as losing you," he wrote to Cooper later in the day. For the first time, Chapin suggested he was a changed man. "The man whose story it tells was an entirely different man from the one who is now so eager to have you as a friend."[5]

After consigning the book to the mail, Chapin was eaten up with a new anxiety. Two days later, he wrote again to Cooper: "Before this letter reaches you my poor life story will be in your hands, and you may have already found time to read it. I tremblingly await the verdict." A response by mail will be too agonizingly slow, wrote Chapin. "May I have the verdict by night telegram?" Chapin passed more sleepless nights, made worse Thursday night by the sound of the electric dynamos in the power house building up current for the electrocution of five condemned men. Friday morning's mail brought Cooper's verdict—"a full and unconditional pardon—more sweet to me than any pardon a Governor might grant," said Chapin. "It gave me more than life; it gave me love." With the fear dissipated, Chapin poured out his affection to a woman, forty years his junior, whom he had never set eyes on. "Indeed," he wrote, "I never in all my life wanted so much to live as I do now, as always I mean to, for the life you breathed into my dead heart has made it pulse with joy, and I am young again. . . . I am going to live for you—only for you—and I am not going to care a snap of my finger for prison bars or for anything or anyone save only you. Nothing else matters."[6]

Remarkably, Cooper did not seem frightened by what she had unleashed. Quite to the contrary, she encased her letters in pink envelopes and sent Chapin four photographs. Now he had a vision of his maiden of the mail. Cooper had dark hair, cut in a pageboy style, a rather dominant nose, and thin lips. She was solid in build, but not heavy. Nor would one describe her as thin. Chapin took two of the photographs and placed them in frames on his desk in such a way that no one else's eyes might see them. She joined an exclusive gallery. On the wall, Chapin had replaced the collection of movie actresses he found when he was given the office. In their stead he hung photographs of Governor Smith, Warden Lawes, New York Archbishop Patrick J. Hayes, Sir Thomas Lipton, who had visited Chapin at Sing Sing, and his old publisher, Joseph Pulitzer. "It would sadden him could he know," said Chapin of his Pulitzer photograph. He was beside himself with happiness. "I fear I bore you with my new found joy, but, girl o' mine, you and all that you mean to me so fill my thoughts that my typewriter balks at writing of anything else."[7]

The following Monday, Chapin received three letters from

Cooper. "Oh, the ecstasy of living, when there is someone to live for!" Chapin not only felt happier and better, but his health was now much improved. His December was so busy that he hardly had a moment to consider any woes. The Christmas issue of the *Bulletin* demanded most of his time. Chapin was writing almost all of the copy for the larger-than-normal issue, again using his pen names "Bill the Burglar" or "Moonlight Harry," among others. He still wrote at a speed that left little time for reflection. "Each of the four long stories," he wrote to Cooper, "was written in a single evening, without five minutes' previous thought as to what the 'plot' would be, and as fast as a page of copy was written, it was fed to the linotypes almost without revision or even reading." Chapin also took a short story that Cooper sent him and, after padding it a bit, included it in the issue. Amazingly, considering his hasty approach to writing, Chapin had the temerity to suggest that Cooper approach writing stories by outlining the plot one night, drafting sentences the second night, polishing them on a third, then turning to the typewriter—"But not too rapidly to miss opportunities for improving as you progress."[8]

"I am sure I will always be your harshest critic, probably because I would fear that prejudice would make me too indulgent," he wrote. "Belasco dragged Leslie Carter about by the hair of her head before he could get her to discover herself; then it was a case of act or get hurt."

Literary or theatrical references, like this one to playwright and producer David Belasco, were common in Chapin's growing correspondence with Cooper; she was an aspiring writer and he an extraordinarily well-read person with a vast memory trove from his life on the stage. Over time, the letters were filled with lengthy discourses on various authors, books, stories, plays, and ideas about writing, interspersed, of course, with lengthy romantic passages of undying affection. Cooper may have offered young, naive love to the aging Chapin. But in return, Chapin provided the immense pleasure of correspondence with a dazzling mind in an age when letter writing was taken as an art. "This was the fortune particularly of those of us who were ambitious to adopt a career similar to that which had brought him to the pinnacle of newspaperdom," Cooper later said. Normally, she said, there was no chance that one as inexperienced as she would become intimately acquainted with an "Olympian" like Chapin. "To bring this about a miracle of a tragedy must generally transpire." In his case, it was the murder of his wife. "Lying in the bottom of the pit, stunned, miserable and unhappy, he who might have been arrogant before was now grateful for the mercy of a passerby. The price of acquaintanceship was only a little human kindness."[9]

On December 18, 1920, Zona Gale, now a literary figure of some standing, came to visit her old boss. Since leaving the *Evening World* in 1903, Gale had gone on to a successful career as a writer, first with a collection of stories, *Romance Island*, in 1906 and most recently with *Miss Lulu Bett*, a novel about a spinster's rebellion against her village's family and marriage customs. Chapin always had—in his words—a "paternal pride in her achievement." Earlier in the year, when *Miss Lulu Bett* was published, Chapin had sent Gale a note of congratulations. She flattered him in her reply, claiming her success was due to the training she got under him. In the visiting room, the two reminisced about old times in the *World* building. Her hair was touched with frost now, but otherwise, Chapin didn't notice any change in his old reporter. She reminded Chapin it had been twenty years ago this month that he had hired her. She asked if he remembered the time she ate breakfast at her desk and made faces at him.

Gale now lived in Portage, Wisconsin. She had come East because she had turned her last novel into a play, and Brock Pemberton, a New York producer and *Evening World* alum, was going to stage it. More remarkably, the premiere would be at Sing Sing. Since 1914, a custom had developed at the prison for a New York theater company to put on a performance at Christmas. The conditions were rudimentary, but in 1920, Belasco furnished the prison with a proper stage, sets, and lights in anticipation of putting on a play titled *Call the Doctor*. A last-minute scheduling conflict caused Belasco to cancel, though he still donated the equipment, and Gale, a socially conscious writer who was friends with the famed social reformer Jane Addams, jumped at the chance of bringing her play to the prisoners instead.[10]

Cooper's letters, Gale's visit, and the special edition of the *Bulletin* all contributed to a vastly improved Christmas for Chapin. During the past two years, Christmas had been one of the hardest parts of his confinement. While in the Tombs, he had refused on Christmas to see anyone or to open any packages or letters. At Sing Sing, the day had been no better. This year, Chapin excitedly prepared for Christmas. He took a stack of books from his stock that Putnam had been sending him and packaged them up for Cooper. Among them was Jerome K. Jerome's *All Roads Lead to Calvary* and Zofia Na'lkowska's *Kobiety* ("decidedly a woman's novel"). Along with the books, he also sent a magenta silk sweater that Kathleen Lawes, the warden's wife, purchased for Chapin in New York City. They had to guess at the size; the color was Lawes's call. The only touch of sadness that entered Chapin's Christmas preparations was a notice in the newspaper that Horatio Seymour, whom he had first met in Chicago and eventually brought onto Pulitzer's staff, and Abe Levy, his friend and attorney, had died. "So many I knew have died since I came to prison that soon there will be no one left of my friends of other days."[11]

On Christmas Eve, Chapin retired to his office. Around him were stacks of Christmas letters, telegrams, cards, and endless packages. Among them was a burnished brass clock that tolled the hour by striking a ship's bell, given to him by one of the officers of the Atlantic Yacht Club. Although the messages and packages gave him a sense of importance, Chapin's joy was tempered by the belief that many of them were sent to him out of pity. The prison was unusually quiet. All the men had gone to their cells for the evening count, and soon would be led to the chapel, festooned with a beautiful tree. There inmates would see a movie, enjoy music by a prison band, and receive armfuls of gifts. "Outside my office windows all is darkness, save for the electric arc lamps that are scattered through the yard," Chapin typed. "There is not a soul in sight; not a sound disturbs the silence. It is Christmas eve, and you and I are alone." In her last letter, Cooper had proposed a game of visiting one another by "moonbeam flights." Chapin was enamored of the idea. Every Saturday night, at 2:30 her time, 3:30 his, they should clear their minds of all thoughts other than of each other. This was only the first of many fantasy games the couple would play.[12]

Christmas greeted Chapin with a telegraphic message of love from Cooper. "If Santa Claus had told me I might pick my Christmas present from the treasures of the earth, I could not have chosen one that would give me so much happiness, now and always, as the gift that came in your charmingly worded Telegram," Chapin wrote. Because it made him so happy, Chapin chose to spend the day alone in his office. "I felt I could not bear to have anyone talk to me."[13]

On December 26, 1,000 inmates gathered before the new stage in the chapel to see the premiere of *Miss Lulu Bett*. Gale, Pemberton, and other New Yorkers sat in a special box. Ten minutes before the curtain was to go up, Chapin had not shown up despite promising Gale he would attend. "I don't feel that I can sit in the audience under existing conditions," Chapin wrote to Cooper from his office. "So here I am, and here I mean to remain until it is time to go to bed." His typing, however, was interrupted by an urgent and insistent message to come to the chapel. Chapin complied and took his seat with Gale in the box. "There were others I knew, and my embarrassment soon wore off, for they did all they could to make me feel like a regular human being, just as I was in the days they knew me." The play itself was an enormous success. "A distinct hit," said Chapin. Still, being in the theater was a strain for Chapin. Just before the curtain rose on the final act, Gale went to the stage and spoke to the inmates. "While she was speaking, I slipped out unobserved and went quietly to bed." The play opened in New York the following night at the Belmont Theatre and was awarded the Pulitzer Prize for drama a few months later.[14]

After Christmas, talk of the possibility of life outside of prison began to creep into Chapin's letters, especially when he wove his fantasies of life in a cabin in the woods with Cooper. "My thoughts can always kiss you, though my lips may not touch yours, and I will come to you on a moonbeam as often as I may," he wrote. "Someday I'll come on the Limited, and you will be waiting for me at the station, the real flesh and blood girl of my dreams." Sometimes, Cooper sent Chapin travel brochures, and the two weighed the many options that would be open to them when he was free. "Tell you what let's do, go to Baltimore and take one of the big steamers that run direct from there to Honolulu by way of the Panama Canal," suggested Chapin in one letter. In another, it was a windjammer to faraway seas. The notion of a sea escape came up repeatedly. "I am fully in sympathy with you about the sea voyage coming before the cabin. I would like it to begin on a big, square rigged sailing ship. . . . I have always longed for a trip on a windjammer." Its destination was usually the South Seas. "Wait 'till we are on the windjammer, honey, and we'll astonish even ourselves."[15]

The pair was awakened from their daydreaming by the realities of life in Sing Sing. First, new regulations threatened to curtail their literary exchanges. Only books sent directly from publishers would now be permitted after guards discovered drugs in a carved-out section of one book. Further, packages of food from the outside would no longer be permitted. Second, the new regulations would limit visitors to immediate family. Third, correspondence was going to be more seriously censored. Chapin had already encountered similar restrictions. For instance, Father Cashin, who reviewed all books sent to inmates, had withheld a book of Cobb's short stories. Thus far, Chapin had circumvented most of the rules by sending and receiving his mail and packages uncensored through Lawes's secretary. This, however, sometimes created a problem of its own. Once, she put all his letters into the wrong envelopes, so all his correspondents received letters intended for others. The question now for Chapin was whether his influence in the warden's office would be sufficient to overcome the new regulations. While he pondered this new problem, Chapin also fell ill. Cold weather had finally settled in after a mild early winter. In early January, the prison was covered in snow. Though he avoided the prison hospital, Chapin was laid low for a week with the flu. On top of it all, the *Bulletin* was running late. Chapin's 1921 did not look promising.[16]

"About letters, dear," wrote Chapin when feeling better. "I do not imagine that regulations will ever restrict the number of letters you may write to me, perhaps not even the number I may be privileged to write to you, but there may come a day, perhaps sooner that we may now expect, when I could not write to you with as much freedom as I do now."[17]

If Chapin now felt restricted in what he could express in his letters, he certainly faced no such restrictions in writing for the *Bulletin*. In February, he published a sequel to his Jim and Agnes story putting as a byline the initials V. I. C., the same as Viola Irene Cooper's. The story, "Beyond the Hurt of Hating Men," was transparent in intent, though no one would have been wise to its hidden meaning at the time. The story picks up with Jim and Agnes, living in a wilderness cabin complete with a yachtsman's brass clock. Unfortunately, their plan of writing stories together never gets off the ground because no one wants to give an ex-con a chance. Society continues to be vengeful, and Jim becomes desolate. At the end of the tale, Agnes turns to the other former inmate who lives with them. "I will take Jim to the beautiful island of Ceylon," she says. "We'll have a bungalow high up on the side of the mountain beyond the hurt of hating men. There is no lovelier climate in the world. We can write our books together and be happy in each other's love. What do you say, Jim?"

299
Viola

"Jim smiled and nodded his head."[18]

As amateurish as these stories were, publisher Putnam believed he could make a book of them. In the contract for Chapin's life story, Putnam had agreed to publish a second Chapin book. In February, Putnam was planning to return to Sing Sing to check on Chapin's progress. "He has an encouraging way of awakening ambition in me, and I suppose when he goes home he will have my promise to get a manuscript ready for him almost immediately." The book, however, never came to fruition. Chapin had other more pressing problems.[19]

What prison superintendent Rattigan had sought the previous summer, he now accomplished through fiscal means. John Parsons Joyce, the superintendent of the prison industries at Sing Sing, came to Lawes in early March with a bill for $1,800 for printing the *Bulletin*. The bill covered only the cost of the paper and ink, overhead, and a small margin of profit. When Lawes balked, Joyce reminded him that his department paid out of the industry's budget the one and one-half cents daily salary that Chapin and others connected with the *Bulletin* received. The only way to keep the *Bulletin* going would be to have the state fund it, and Lawes knew that Rattigan would prevent any such move. Outside supporters could not help either. The state was legally prohibited from receiving donated funds. Perhaps, said Lawes as he told reporters of the new threat to the *Bulletin*, there was a hope that some wealthy friends of Chapin could donate the paper, ink, and other necessary materials. More than a dozen offers came in to supply the needed materials for the paper to continue publishing, but Chapin refused them all. "I would prefer to shovel coal," he told a friend, "rather than edit a prison paper that existed solely by the generosity of men who take a kindly interest in it. If the state cannot supply the funds to buy the necessary materials, I would have no heart in trying to carry on."[20]

The end of the paper was a blow for Chapin. At the height of his fifteen-month tenure as editor, he had written Cooper, "I am making of our little paper something of far greater importance to me than anything I have ever done. In doing it I am keeping myself occupied and thus able to make the days and months, and even the years, move swiftly along." It wasn't simply that the paper had distracted Chapin. Lawes knew there was more to the *Bulletin* than that. "Here was a man groping for an interest in life," he said. "It seemed to me his heart longed to justify himself in the eyes of his fellows."[21]

Though the paper was gone, Chapin still had Cooper. In fact, she became a more important part of his life. She had moved from Minneapolis to New York City. Now she would be able to see Chapin in the flesh, as he had once hoped, though still behind bars. The two began to plan for their first meeting. "I know I am going to be shy and conscious of my white hair and increasing years," Chapin wrote Cooper as the day approached. "So won't you please not be shy, but hold out your arms and your lips to me, as you did when you were a very little girl? Greet me as though we had parted only yesterday and not a thousand years ago."[22]

Visits were one of the most significant moments in the life of a Sing Sing inmate. In one of his *Bulletin* essays, Chapin described how a refined and cultured woman had once looked over the well-dressed and groomed inmates in the visiting room and asked if there was a regulation to which they were abiding. There wasn't. Rather, inmates gained permission for extra baths, visits to the barber, cleaned and ironed clothes, and shined shoes—and borrowed what they lacked from other inmates—in anticipation of a visit. Chapin described the preparation in an issue of the *Sing Sing Bulletin*, "There is a final brush of rebellious locks of hair, vanity glimpse into a bit of looking-glass, and the prisoner steps expectantly into the Visiting Room like a dandy on parade. No bridegroom was ever more fussy in preparing for his wedding." Although Chapin had more visitors than probably any inmate in

Sing Sing at the time, Cooper's visit was different. "I am so eager for your coming that I find it difficult to curb my impatience," he wrote. "Moonbeam visits are very nice substitutes when a thousand miles lie between us, but they are so much like dreams that come in the night, and so hard to remember."

By the time the date arrived and Cooper entered the visiting room, the two had worked out all the details of the fantasy they would weave that day. They acted as if they were meeting in the lobby of the St. Francis Hotel in San Francisco or the Biltmore in New York. Chapin played the role of one who had been abroad for a long time and was now convalescing in a hospital. Cooper's task was to pretend she had come a long distance to visit, and the doctors had urged her to remain nearby until he was fully recovered. The news that Cooper would come as often as she could—both in fantasy and reality—thrilled Chapin. "I am so happy that you have come that I will get well quicker than the doctors thought, and then we—you and I—when the doctors decide I may go, will find a big sailing ship that is destined for some far away port in a remote part of the world, and we will be the passengers."[23]

The visits, though glorious, were in the end short and intermittent. At best, they filled a few hours. He still had years of unoccupied time ahead of him. The termination of the *Bulletin*, which had given Chapin such purpose, left him with empty days. Creditors garnished what few royalties were due from Putnam. "Again he began to droop," recalled Lawes. "He walked through the yard with a lagging step. A man just turned sixty, a failing body, a brain still active and willing, faced with years and years of endless nothingness. I was convinced that we would have to find a task well suited for his driving powers or he would again take to his bed."[24]

The Roses

As Chapin discovered, death was a regular part of life at Sing Sing, especially on Thursday nights. At least once a month, and sometimes more frequently, the weeknight was the chosen time for electrocution of those on death row whose turn had come. The proceedings, held in a small squat building less than a hundred feet from Chapin's cell, began as soon as all the inmates were confined to their cells for the night. There was, however, no escaping the nocturnal business.

On Thursday, December 9, 1920, an unusually high number of inmates were scheduled to die. All day long, there was still hope among the prisoners that a reprieve for the five facing the chair might still come in time from the governor. Eight months earlier, four of the inmates had been within three hours of being electrocuted when Governor Smith had issued a stay. By nightfall, it became apparent there would be no reprieves this time. "As I dragged myself wearily over to the old cell block," Chapin wrote Cooper, "I could get a sense of impending death in the very atmosphere, for already the great dynamos in the power house were grinding their grist of death dealing current for the execution." He went to bed and lay there in the dark, listening to the whirring of the dynamos. "No other sound broke the silence. Eleven hundred men were in the Cell Block, so close I could have touched them by reaching out my arms but for the stone wall between us. Many were doubtless as sleepless as I, yet not a sound came from one. You couldn't even hear the sound of their breathing, so tense was the stillness." Shortly after 11:00 P.M., the procession began. "I heard the slam of an iron door and then the tread of multiple feet," said Chapin. "From such experiences, I knew the spectators were going into the execution chamber. The dynamos kept on grinding." By 11:57 all five were dead.[1]

Among the spectators that night, and every such night, were Lawes and Father Cashin. The priest had accompanied more than one hundred inmates to the chair since his posting at the prison a decade earlier. Immensely popular among inmates of all faiths, Cashin was nicknamed the "Bishop of Sing Sing" and was almost as well known outside Sing Sing as the publicity-seeking warden. Reporters loved the quiet, soft-spoken priest and milked Cashin for good copy. Walter Davenport, who wrote for *Collier's*, *Liberty*, and other popular magazines, told his readers about his introduction to the priest as a cub reporter when his city editor asked him if he had ever seen a man die.

"No," replied Davenport.

"Well, a reporter isn't equipped to begin unless he has seen a man die," said the editor.

Davenport was then given a pass to see an execution at Sing Sing, and he went to Cashin's house. The execution wasn't for hours, so Cashin took the young Davenport to a room upstairs.

"Lie down here. Sleep a while. I'll wake you up," Cashin said. But when Davenport awoke, the sun was shining. He had missed the execution. Full of reproaches, Davenport started in on Cashin, who had just returned from the prison.

"Did you want to see him die?" asked Cashin.

"No, but . . ."

"I know, son. I'll tell you what happened. That will be enough, I guess. You are very young. Probably your life will not be less full for having missed this one tragedy."[2]

Born in Hyde Park in 1872 to immigrant parents from County Kilkenny, Ireland, Cashin had been originally destined for a workingman's life. After completing eighth grade, he secured an apprenticeship in a paint plant, working twelve hours a day for forty-two and a half cents a day. He then worked in a succession of menial jobs until, at the age of twenty-three, a wealthy benefactor sent him to a preparatory school connected with St. Charles College in Baltimore to study for the priesthood. Cashin, who was considerably older than his classmates, finished quickly and moved on to seminary and university. In 1903, when he turned thirty-one, Cashin was ordained a priest. He taught for a while at Catholic University in Washington, D.C., then was sent to take charge of a boys' school in Staten Island. In 1912, he was assigned to Sing Sing. In the decade since, Cashin had ministered to all types of murderers, gangsters, rapists, and thieves. By his own admission, he had taken a particular interest in Chapin since his arrival at Sing Sing.[3]

Now that the *Bulletin* was closed, the two found themselves together again in 1922. Chapin's despondency had not ameliorated in the year since he lost his newspaper. "I believed," said Chapin, "I would die or go crazy before very long and preferred to beat the craziness by dying as soon as possible." He didn't want to see anyone, hated leaving his cell in the morning, and spent the day waiting to return. At a loss about what to do with Chapin, Lawes had assigned him some light clerical work and sent him back to the library with the intent of getting him back under Father Cashin's supervision. Chapin had not forgotten the kindness the priest had shown him on his first night in Sing Sing. As for Cashin, he saw the transfer as another opportunity to work on Chapin's soul. Daily, he extolled the power of prayer, regeneration through the Holy Ghost, rebirth of the soul, and all the bits and pieces of catechism he could summon. "His theology interested me," conceded Chapin, "but I had no desire to discuss religion." Instead, he would change the topic whenever he could to prison reform or capital punishment. Chapin was not one for organized religion. As a child, he had attended a Methodist church and as an adult, an Episcopal church. In his forties, he gave up attending church, except for Easter morning or Christmas Eve. It was not that Chapin didn't believe in God. "One might as well say there is no God, because He is not visible to the human eye, but that doesn't prove there is no God," he once told Cooper. He was bored by what he saw as dogmatic interpretations of Christianity. When Chapin first came to Sing Sing, he made an exception to his practice and attended a few Catholic services, but only out of respect for Cashin. "The little prayer I offer every night in the solitude of my cell," he said, "gives greater satisfaction than stupid sermons and prayers chanted in a language I cannot understand."[4]

One morning in early June 1922, Father Cashin scolded Chapin
for remaining cooped up in the library and his office. He told him
he should get some fresh air and exercise. His aging mother, said
Cashin, had recently taken up gardening with a set of tools he
had bought for her. "Maybe if you could dig a little garden, Charlie, you would feel better."

"The hell I would," replied Chapin.[5]

Undeterred, Cashin returned that afternoon with a set of tools
like those he had purchased for his mother. "So yesterday morning," Chapin wrote to Cooper, "I worked for three hours among
the flowers and I intend to keep it up for a part of each morning
through the summer. . . . In the evening, after the sun is almost
down and the men have gone in, I am to play the hose on the
flowers and the grass. This will probably be good for me, and perhaps I will be of some use to the grass and flowers."[6]

What little cultivation existed at Sing Sing was confined to a
small patch of grass, a lone flowerbed in front of the warden's
office, and a few more strips of lawn in front of the cellblock. As
Chapin worked the little green patches and flowerbeds, he found
he enjoyed the puttering about. Among the odd bits of gardening
equipment, he discovered a few old seed catalogs and they gave
him an idea. He went looking for Lawes.[7]

"Listen, chief," Chapin said. "I've got an idea. I'm not going to
tell you all about it yet. It's a special job. I would like to be assigned to take care of the lawns."

"You're the Chief of the Lawns," said Lawes.[8]

Actually, when the paperwork was completed, Chapin was
given the title of prison horticulturist. His dominion, Lawes decided, would be primarily an area between the south gate, where
prisoners enter Sing Sing, and the former death house, where
many once departed. The latter, a low, yellow brick building, was
now Chapin's home. A new and larger death house had been built
closer to the Hudson River, and thus further from the inmates'
cells. Lawes had moved Chapin and a half-dozen trusted inmates
into the old one. Conditions in the converted death house were
luxurious in comparison to Chapin's old seven-by-three-foot

damp cell with its slop bucket. His new room was the size of a drawing room on a Pullman car, with running water and a toilet.[9]

Chapin immediately began his new job. If he possessed any horticultural ambition, it certainly had to be of the visionary kind. The land had no suitable soil for gardening. Open spaces in Sing Sing consisted of landfill comprising crushed rock, trodden cinders, and old metal scraps that occasionally surfaced. Further, beyond the tools Cashin had given him and an old hose, there were no implements—especially none that might double as a weapon. Lastly, there was no money. Lawes was able to help remedy the first problem. He assigned inmates to dig up and load the rubble into prison trucks that returned with topsoil and fertilizer from outside the walls. The work was hard and the summer heat stifling, as few river breezes reached that part of the prison yard. But soon, Chapin had some passable flowerbeds and soil for lawns. Putting something in the soil, however, posed yet another problem. Sing Sing's paltry landscaping budget had been consumed with the purchase of a lawn mover and a garden hose. It would be another three months before any more state funds could be used. Chapin resorted to his own money. "The only alternative was to dig deep into my tobacco money and buy the seed myself," he said. "When the grass began to grow I dug deeply again and filled a few beds with flowers." But he didn't begrudge the expense. With his money, and that of another inmate, Chapin bought a few dozen gladiolus corms and got them in before the end of July. In September, their small towers of flowers rose in the prison yard. "The greatest joy I had known during the years I had been in prison was when I saw the lovely blooms," he said.[10]

Hooked and possessing a nascent green thumb, Chapin wrestled the second quarter's budget from Lawes and mailed a small order to Frank R. Pierson's nursery a few miles away in Tarrytown. Pierson had operated a commercial nursery since at least the 1880s. He was a man of considerable means who lived in an elegant Hudson River Valley manor and was active in civic affairs. He also was well read and recognized Chapin's name as an author. Puzzled about what an inmate would be doing with flowers, Pierson went to Sing Sing, where he learned firsthand of Chapin's ambitious plans.

"Of course," said Pierson, "you won't be able to do much with what you've ordered."

"It's all I can afford, but it's a start," said Chapin.

Two days later, Pierson sent a truckload of plants with his compliments. That night, encouraged by Pierson's gesture, Chapin composed a letter to Adolph Lewisohn, a philanthropist who lived nearby and was well known to the inmates. "I hope to have some very beautiful flowers next spring if only I can procure what I need in the way of bulbs, shrubs or plants," wrote Chapin. "I bought some geraniums and some gladiola bulbs from Mr. Pierson and when a friend wrote him what I was doing, he sent me a load of plants and also came over himself to give me some practical suggestions." The letter hit home. After receiving Chapin's letter, Lewisohn ordered his chauffeur to get the car and drive to Sing Sing.[11]

For Lewisohn, Chapin represented the confluence of two of his main interests in life—prison reform and flowers. Raised on German translations of Victor Hugo and Charles Dickens, Lewisohn had been sympathetic to the fate of prisoners since his childhood. Now in his seventies, retired, and possessing a fortune made in the copper industry, he had the means and the time to do whatever he wanted. In 1919, he volunteered to serve on a prison survey commission, paying the commission's entire $30,000 budget out of his pocket. Imbued with the reform spirit of the era, Lewisohn advocated some novel ideas, such as the creation of a penological college, like a medical school, to be attached to Sing Sing so that students could go on "rounds" with Lawes and learn the science of penology. But it was his second passion, for flowers, that brought him and Chapin together. As with prisons, Lewisohn's interest in flowers developed in his childhood when he collected them and had a herbarium. For Lewisohn, there was a touch of the divine in growing one's own flowers, like trying to improve the lives of convicts. "You can watch them as they blossom into perfection; you can improve them from year to year; and finally, when they are brought out of your own earth to be shown, you feel a peculiar pride in finding the fruits of your own selection and your own people's devotion have proven worthy to be called the fairest among so many beauties."[12]

It wasn't long before both Lewisohn and Pierson were sending truckloads of donations to Sing Sing and telling their horticultural friends of Chapin's work. Bertrand R. Farr, a famed Pennsylvania iris grower, heard from them about the gardens and wrote to Chapin. He then sent a copy of Chapin's response to Richardson Wright, editor of *House & Garden*. As word spread, so did support. At first, it was one package with a dozen iris plants. The next day, two boxes with 500 plants by express mail. These only marked the beginning of a floral deluge. Every day brought another donation. A peony specialist in Minnesota sent a single root by parcel post, while other growers in Massachusetts and Nebraska sent three dozen each. Soon, Chapin had more than 150 peonies to plant. It was arduous work. For each peony tuber, a three-foot deep hole nearly two-feet wide had to be dug in the rock and gravel surface, and then filled with soil and fertilizer. While the work crew Lawes had assigned to Chapin was engaged in this excavation, other flowers and money arrived each day. Now armed with $50, Chapin sat in his office, studying his florists' catalogues. Although such a sum was a princely amount at Sing Sing, it wouldn't pay for many of the plants he examined. "I felt like a child with a penny to spend shopping for bonbons at Maillard's." After placing a modest order for shrubs, Chapin ran into Father Cashin. Pray for bulbs, Chapin told him. The very next day a bulb importer on Long Island, who had gotten wind of Chapin's gardens, wrote, "Although our house was robbed last week I am sending you 500 tulip bulbs to help beautify your prison and hope they will gladden the hearts of your associates."[13]

Within a short time, Chapin had more than 1,000 iris plants, 6,000 spring-flowering bulbs, and hundreds of other perennials, many coming from as far away as California. To accommodate all the bulbs, Chapin and his crew prepared a 469-foot border running the entire length of the old cellblock, plus a new bed in a remote part of the prison for the overflow. In the long border, Chapin also planted a blue spruce that he had purchased. "I was so proud of it that I would come into the garden at five o'clock in the morning to admire is beautiful foliage." A friend visited and paid for five additional spruces. When those were planted, another visitor asked why Chapin didn't continue the trees until the end of the cellblock. "There is but one reason," Chapin replied.

The visitor succumbed, joined the ranks of the horticultural benefactors, and ordered the remaining trees. "The trees had begun a
life sentence in Sing Sing before the final whistle blew the following day," said Chapin.[14]

In September, Chapin decided he might plant some rose
bushes. He had tended a few roses almost thirty years earlier at
the house he rented in St. Louis, and it had remained a favorite
flower. Coincidently, Lawes, who was pleased with Chapin's
work, agreed to turn over most of the prison yard between the
new 469-foot bed and the prison factories near the Hudson. An
issue of *House & Garden*—which Chapin gave the Panglosian
title of "best of all possible magazines"—carried a photograph of
a garden with 400 rose bushes in full bloom. "Instantly, I decided
that our garden should have 400 bushes," he wrote editor Wright.
"I hadn't a remote idea of where the bushes would come from,
but I had faith; and I believed that if only part of the potential 400
arrived in time for planting this fall the remainder would come in
the spring, and if not in the spring then in the early fall and the
following spring."[15]

It was no longer a matter of finding a bit of dirt for a dozen or
so bulbs. To accommodate his new ambition, Chapin would have
to change his scale. He retreated to his office. Where he had once
laid out gray type, he now carefully drew up plans for a 69-by-
172-foot flower garden. For inspiration, he drew from the catalogs
and the modest collection of books he had acquired. When he
completed the drawing, an ambitious project lay on the desk. At
the center would be a 24-foot-diameter concrete fountain, surrounded by a gravel walk. On each side of the rectangular garden
would be a series of five seven-by-sixteen-foot beds with hybrid
tea roses. At the north, a large screen covered with ramblers
would create a backdrop for a massive curved bed containing June
roses, with Spirea shrubs at the center of the bend. A six-foot
gravel border dotted with flowering shrubs would frame the entire
length of the garden. The selection of the roses was important, as
Chapin discovered. He first wanted to plant American Beauties,
but was dissuaded by Pierson, who explained that from the
50,000 American Beauty bushes he maintained, he was lucky to
cut fifty roses a day. "I have since read of other varieties that in the
summer time yield a hundred roses at a time, and I am thinking it

is such that will make our rose garden look like the one in my dreams," Chapin wrote Wright. "A rose bush with a hundred blooms on it would look like a million dollars to my famished, rose-hungry eyes."[16]

He mailed his drawings to the American Rose Society, whose president J. Horace McFarland also had begun corresponding with Chapin. The plans were published in the American Rose Annual for 1923, and members of the society lined up to donate the roses in time for spring planting. Frederick L. Atkins, of Bobbink & Atkins nursery in New Jersey, wrote to ask how many bushes it would take to complete the garden. The generosity of the rose enthusiasts now posed a new problem. Planting roses requires bone meal. "Never having so much as heard of bone meal until I took up gardening a few months ago," Chapin wrote to Wright, "I am unacquainted with any of the magnates who either manufacturer or deal in the commodity." The few bags that Chapin procured that summer cost as much as sugar, and he joked that he would have to switch from burning tobacco in his pipe to Alfala or dried Mullen leaf. Wright raised $18 in a crap game and bought 600 pounds. Then he convinced Henry A. Dreer, owner of a large horticultural business in Philadelphia, and others to contribute one-and-a-half tons of bone meal. The soil was soon ready for the roses.[17]

Before winter descended on Sing Sing, Lawes had a new greenhouse built along the wall of the old death house where Chapin resided. He also increased the work crew to thirty-six men, occasionally supplemented by the new inmates who previously were confined to their cells for their first few weeks. "You can imagine what cheerful helpers they make when they are brought into the open and permitted to exercise for several hours with shovels, spades, and hoes," said Chapin. The greenhouse was opened just in time to house 100 roses donated by Pierson. The donations and flurry of activity caught the attention of some of Chapin's former colleagues. In December, a reporter from the *New York Herald Tribune* sat in the visiting room waiting to meet with Chapin. A mother with three children sat in a far corner, and in another, a young girl worked at cheering up a young boy with his head in his hands.[18]

"So you've heard about my flower garden," said Chapin as he

came in and sat down on one of the small black stools. "I was out in the greenhouse in my rubber boots; that's the reason it took me so long to get here. I had to change my clothes."

The two walked out of the room and into the prison proper while Chapin explained he had gotten permission to take the reporter back to see the plants in the greenhouse. "There, that was my first cell—No. 106," Chapin said, pointing to the old cellblock to the right as they exited the narrow corridor that led into the prison yard. "I didn't have much hope during those first two years. I didn't care much what happened. It is only since I've started my garden that hope seems to be coming back."

"Look at those Blue Spruce—aren't they beauties," said Chapin as they continued their tour in the December cold. The yard was still barren, but its promise was clear. Already, an inmate skilled in stone and concrete work had completed a fountain and a pool in the center of a large patch of the yard that had been tilled for a garden. Chapin described the work that went into preparing the soil for the gardens. The rose beds were dug to a depth of three feet. Bone meal was added to the soil, but the soil itself was in desperate need of fertilizer. "It is at night I do my best thinking and planning," Chapin said as they walked. "I had been thinking for weeks about that rose garden, pondering how it might be accomplished. One night the name of an owner of blooded cattle came to me. I wrote that man at sun-up." The man was politician and newspaper owner V. Everit Macy, whom Chapin had known in his *Evening World* days. Within a few days, Macy sent nine tons of manure from his stables, and it was poured into the new beds with the bone meal. "Wait until spring," said Chapin. "It will be a bower of beauty then."

The pair reached the new greenhouse, where Chapin paused, looked around, and turned to the reporter. "This is where the electric chair used to stand. I expected to sit in that chair," he said as he led them into the hothouse. At last inside, Chapin showed off his first roses. When Pierson's plants had first arrived, Chapin had kept them disbudded to strengthen their stock, but now he was permitting them to bloom. Chapin picked one of the first Priscilla roses and presented it to the reporter, before he departed, impressed with what he had seen. The story made great copy—as Chapin would have said—for the Christmas Eve edition of the

Herald Tribune. "There will be Christmas roses at Sing Sing this year," wrote the reporter. "Priscilla and the Pilgrim have already bloomed, have shaken out their delicately tinted skirts before the frowning walls of that gray stone pile of buildings up the Hudson."[19]

For someone who, a few months earlier, couldn't have told a zinnia from a hollyhock, Chapin admitted to Wright that his plans sounded "like the mad raving of an opium-using enthusiast." Nonetheless, he threw himself at the enterprise, marshaling his celebrated work ethic and notorious supervisory habits from his days at the helm of the *Evening World.* He rose every day at 5:00 A.M. and worked straight through until the last whistle at 10:00 P.M. None of his diggers, weeders, or planters could match the energy of this sixty-four-year-old convict. In the spring of 1923, Chapin wrote to Lawes, "I would suggest that all men assigned to work in the garden be given to understand that they are not to shirk. Most of them disappear if I am not around an hour before the whistle blows. I expect them to work from 8:00 A.M. until 11:30, and from 1:00 P.M. to 3:30, except in stormy weather, and they should be given to understand that shirking will not be tolerated."[20]

Chapin knew that effort alone would not grow the garden he sought. Where he had once depended on years of on-the-job reporting experience to do his work, he now turned to books. The antiquated seed catalogs he used at first gave way to a set of Luther Burbank's famed books sent by Loren Palmer, editor of *Collier's Weekly*; Taylor's *The Complete Garden,* donated by Glen Frank, editor of *Century Magazine*; Fritz Mahr's *Commercial Floriculture,* a gift from Pierson; and Wright's *Book of Gardens.* Chapin never planted anything without consulting his library. He often read late into the night, remembering only to extinguish his light when his clock warned him of the approaching five o'clock awakening. "Sleeping seems a waste of precious hours when one has work to do, seems that way even to a life in prison," he wrote Wright.[21]

Work progressed through the summer of 1923. It wasn't long before Chapin walked into Lawes's office one day with a cluster of cut roses in his arms. "First choice, Warden," he said. "A thanksgiving offering to you for your cooperation." While the roses grew bountifully, Chapin's relationship with Viola Cooper was wilting. Though she had continued to come to Sing Sing in 1922, this year her visits were increasingly less frequent, as she began a series of journeys that would eventually lead to an ocean voyage a few years later. On September 17, 1926, Cooper and another woman, Jean Schoen, left Vancouver, B. C., as crew members of the *Bougainville*, one of the last windjammers still sailing. The first women to ship out on the clipper, Cooper and Schoen were also among the last of her crew. The *Bougainville*'s South Sea destination was a port where she would rust away as a warehouse barge. "We have no idea when we'll get back," Cooper told an Associated Press reporter as she packed her sea bag. "But we're young. There's a lot of time, and somehow we'll come slipping back into New York one of these days." The pair remained in the South Seas for at least another year, perhaps longer, island hopping, meeting cannibals, dancing with natives, while Cooper wrote what would eventually be published as a book of their travels.[22]

Cooper never returned to Sing Sing. "Looking back," she said years later, "I know now that my present love of the sea was born out of dreams that began in our letters and were nurtured through hours of visiting when we joined in a common purpose—to obliterate actual environment and create in its stead one of freedom's own design. Only youth could so casually have gone away, as I was eventually to do on the very kind of voyage we had so often imagined, leaving her pal alone."[23]

Constance

In January 1924, Constance Nelson was at her desk as usual in the Federal Reserve Bank, a modern rendition of an Italian Renaissance *palazzo* in downtown Cleveland, Ohio. A single professional woman in a man's business, Nelson was the editor of the bank's *Federal Reserve Notes*. Wallace K. Pinniger, a sixty-nine-year-old man who worked in the stockroom and who had a habit of finding unusual things, came to her desk bearing a blue cloth-bound book with gold lettering. "This will tell you some things about editing," Pinniger said, as he handed her Chapin's autobiography. "Chapin was the best city editor of his day. It is the story of his forty years as a newspaperman. It was written in Sing Sing, where he is now. It's great."[1]

Nelson opened the book eagerly, hoping to learn some tricks of the trade. Within a few pages, however, she forgot her reason for reading and instead became enthralled with Chapin's story. "I was profoundly touched, and wished that I knew the man and might help him." Only days earlier, Nelson had finished Oscar Wilde's *De Profundis*. Now she now recalled a passage in which Wilde is brought to prison from bankruptcy court. Bound in handcuffs with his head bowed in shame, he passed by a man who raised his hat. "When people are able to understand," wrote Wilde, "not only how beautiful this lovely act was, but why it means so much to me, and always will mean so much, then, perhaps, they will realize how and in what spirit they should approach me." In the same spirit, Nelson impulsively decided to approach Chapin, who, unknown to her, was also a fancier of Wilde. She took out a piece of stationary and wrote him an admiring letter, never mentioning his imprisonment or crime, and asked for help with her magazine. She addressed the packet to George Putnam, Chapin's publisher, and sent it off. She enclosed a note to Putnam, asking if he would forward her letter and the copy of *Federal Reserve Notes* she had enclosed to Sing Sing. "Somehow," she said, "I never thought of a prison as a place with a mail address. Prisons were grim gray things—somewhere. I didn't even know where." Then she waited.[2]

In February, Nelson spotted a curious piece of correspondence in the pile of morning mail on her desk. It was an odd-looking letter, a kind of cross between a bill and a membership reminder like one might receive from a professional organization. Behind its cellophane windowpane, she could see her name and address, typed in blue ink on the correspondence itself. The carmine George Washington two-cent postage stamp bore an Ossining, New York, cancellation. Eagerly she tore the envelope open.[3]

"Dear Miss Nelson," it began, "I am honored that you ask me to aid you with your editorial work, but my knowledge of banking is so limited that I very much fear you would find me of little use." Nonetheless, after complimenting Nelson on her writing, Chapin said that if she insisted, he would be glad to be of counsel. "Come to me with your problems as often as you will, but be prepared for disappointment, for a man who has been buried alive for more than five years is a poor counselor to aspiring youth." Nelson wrote back immediately. It took only two letters before Chapin was requesting Nelson's photograph, three letters before "Miss Nelson" became "My dear Constance," and four before Chapin was once again entirely smitten and angst ridden.[4]

Like Cooper before her, Nelson was not deterred by the flood of letters she triggered nor by the professions of affection from a lonely, old convict. "Soon letters were winging thick and fast between Cleveland and Ossining," she said. Constance's letters arrived at a point when correspondence was Chapin's only form of writing. The *Bulletin*, of course, was long gone. Sometimes Chapin helped Lawes with a speech or an article. But the second manuscript he had promised to Putnam lay untouched. "I haven't the time or inclination now, as my entire time is occupied with the cultivation of flowers, a relaxation that has grown into a mania," wrote Chapin.[5]

Each day he rose by 5:00 A.M. and before doing anything else, completed an inspection tour of his dominion of greenhouses and gardens. "Yes," he wrote Nelson, "even in winter, for I must know that the rose bushes and spring flowering bulbs have not been uncovered by the night winds." By this point, Chapin had more than 1,000 rose bushes in the ground and more than 20,000 flowering plants stuffed into his greenhouses, awaiting the warm weather when they could be planted outside. So far, his vigilance had paid off. He lost only six of the thousand bushes to winterkill, a figure that would be the envy of any Northeastern rose grower. On the other hand, Chapin had nothing but unfettered time on his hands to tend and protect his plants. At 7:00 A.M., Chapin would breakfast in the Roserie, as he called the greenhouse adjacent to his cell, where he took all his meals. He no longer ate prison fare. Larry, an inmate who was assigned to attend Chapin, instead prepared his meals from a vast supply of food items sent to him by friends or purchased by a former *Evening World* employee who shopped for him. Chapin's day was consumed with work in the greenhouses and supervising his growing crew. In the evening, if not to a greenhouse, Chapin retired to the old *Bulletin* office in the print shop, which Lawes permitted him to keep.

Though Nelson responded endearingly to his letters, Chapin seemed confused at first about his role this time. Nelson's photograph, which arrived in the mail on February 22, revealed a plump thirty-one-year-old woman, with bright eyes, soft smile, strong nose, and roundish face framed with long dark hair gathered in a mass above the nape. It had quite an effect on Chapin. "My dear Constance," he wrote back immediately. "You are not a bit like the girl I had pictured. Now I am confounded by my impudence." His tone turned paternal. "I never had the good fortune to have a child, but it was a dream of my younger years that some day a daughter might come to me and call me dad," he wrote. As he gazed at Nelson's photograph, Chapin said he was tempted to play "make-believe." He noted that though she talked of her mother and grandmother, she made no mention of a father. "I suppose that most girls have a sure enough dad and have little use for a make-believe one, even as a dark secret, but can you guess the hungry longing that this lovely picture has stirred in the depths of the starved man you so generously have held out your hand to?"[6]

His next three attempts to write a letter ended up in the waste-paper basket after he read them "in the saner light of early morning." Alone, at night, he had poured out his heart to his new "Girl of My Dreams," but in the morning he destroyed what he had written "when I see myself reflected in the small mirror just above the wash basin in my cell, and with it comes realization that I am a thousand years older than the girl to whom I spoke my heart in the letter I wrote the night before." This was not what Nelson intended. She had a father and didn't need another. She chastised Chapin for having torn up his more passionate missives.[7]

Chapin got the message, and within a week his letters were full or ardor, his gardens tilled with a new purpose, and his imagination unshackled. On Saturday night, March 15, Chapin retired to the Roserie where he set his table for two. His pocket watch, containing a photograph of Nelson cut out from her magazine, sat on the empty place setting. By it, as if he had pinned it in her hair, Chapin placed a golden yellow rose, a Mrs. Calvin Coolidge, developed that year and soon to be exhibited by Pierson, one of Chapin's floral benefactors, at the New York Flower Show. On the plates, Chapin put fresh strawberries and two slices of layer cake, typical fare from the larder he maintained. After supper, he "took" Nelson for a walk through the greenhouse, then to his office. "You are sitting very comfortably in my big swivel office chair, your feet elevated on a drawer of my desk I drew out for you." Gone was his hesitancy and confusion. Instead with each letter, Chapin unleashed his passion, confessing that he cried himself to sleep after listening to a radio broadcast from Cleveland, proclaiming he was the happiest he had been in six years—then changing his mind, to "say truthfully, than ever I have been"—and finally declaring his unequivocal love. In turn, Nelson announced that she would come to Sing Sing. "Your coming will be the biggest bribe held out to me to 'carry on,' for there is no one in all the world I so long to see," Chapin wrote Nelson upon hearing the news.[8]

Meanwhile, the amorous pair agreed to add a literary dimension to their courtship by exchanging novels they had read marked with their own commentary. The recipient would add his or her comments, then return it to the sender. Chapin had read of such an idea in a novel that winter, and he told Nelson "it made me wish there was a girl like the one in the story who could care that much for me. And now my wish is to come true." Nelson began first. She mailed Chapin a copy of one of her favorite books, George Gissing's *The Private Papers of Henry Ryecroft*. Chapin took the package back to his room in the annex. He made no attempt to read the book as one normally does. Instead he read Nelson's commentary and the passages she marked. "It took a lot of time and a lot of thought to prepare this dear book for my eyes," he wrote Nelson. "I thank you, I thank you!" He also broke their rules by refusing to mark his passages and return it, claiming he could not bear to part with it even for a few days. Other books did make the round trip. Among the first were Somerset Maugham's *Of Human Bondage* and *Moon and Sixpence* and Anatole France's *Red Lily*. But not *The Private Papers of Henry Ryecroft*. No wonder, it was as if Gissing wrote the book for Chapin. In the fictional memoir, the author recounts the dramatic changes in his protagonist after his exodus from London. "In a single day I had matured astonishingly; which means, no doubt, that I suddenly entered into conscious enjoyment of powers and sensibilities which had been developing unknown to me. To instance only one point: till then I had cared very little about plants and flowers, but now I found myself eagerly interested in every blossom, in every growth of the wayside. . . . To me the flowers became symbolical of a great release, of a wonderful awakening. My eyes had all at once been opened; till then I had walked in darkness, yet knew it not."[9]

In addition to the books, Chapin also concocted another way to bridge the gap between Ossining and Cleveland. Pierson, who now was a regular caller on Chapin, was soon to leave for the National Flower Show in Cleveland. Chapin hurriedly wrote to Nelson, asking her to attend the show and seek out Pierson. When Pierson returned, Chapin reasoned he would be able to shake his hand, knowing it had shaken hers. Unfortunately, when Pierson came home from the show, he was delayed in coming for a visit. Chapin waited impatiently until finally on April 14 Pierson came to Sing Sing and Chapin received his handshake and Pierson's appraisal of Nelson. "Why you are not at all what you tried to make me believe," Chapin wrote Nelson, "but, according to my friend's appraisal, a very charming young woman, tall and stately."[10]

Books exchanged and hands shaken, though indirectly, Chapin and Nelson's planning now turned to *the visit*. Friday, June 20, 1924, was selected. "The Gods are with us!" Chapin wrote her, after receiving a letter from Bobbink & Atkins, a nursery that had contributed 800 rose bushes. They predicted his roses would be at their best on June the twentieth. This would be the second full summer for his gardens, and Chapin held high expectations for what it would bring, after working day and night all fall and winter. The major part of the garden had been prepared and planted in 1923, but work continued through the spring on beds he held especially dear. Pierson and Chapin, for instance, designed a new bed for his favorite new rose, the Constance, a yellow flower developed in France in 1915 that turned golden as it aged. Digging the 50-by-8-foot bed began in April. It would be planted with 100 Constance roses sent by Frederick Atkins, the nationally known nurseryman and one-half of the firm Bobbink & Atkins that had been among the first to supply Chapin's gardens. Around the edge of the bed, Chapin planted Polyantha roses. Almost all of a ton of freshly donated bone meal was poured into the new bed. It was hard work. "Getting out extras on election night is child's play compared with what a gardener is obliged to do when the spring planting season is on," said Chapin.[11]

By May, a thousand purple iris flowers bloomed, and peony buds began to open. All the while, new plants continued to arrive. William Tricker, who originated commercial water lily culture in the United States, sent a collection of water plants for the basin of the new fountain at the center of the garden. Pierson sent 350 new rose plants to replace those moved from the greenhouses into the gardens. Each day's seemingly endless gardening task brought Chapin closer to June 20. "Hurry, hurry June 20, the Day of Days!" he wrote to Nelson on May 13. "Three weeks from tonight SHE will be here; three weeks from tomorrow morning I shall be with HER," he wrote on May 30. June arrived and he could hardly contain himself. "Thoughts of the great day that soon will be here are causing my pulse to beat fast." Three days before her arrival, Chapin's Constance roses began opening.[12]

On Friday, June 20, 1924, Nelson disembarked from the train in Ossining and took a cab to the Briarcliff Lodge, a luxurious hotel where Chapin had reserved a room through the warden's secretary. It cost Nelson the extravagant sum of $13 a night. The next day, which was summer solstice, Constance Nelson presented herself at the north gate of Sing Sing promptly at nine. After answering questions from the guard on duty, she was directed to one of the benches along the wall of the anteroom. The seats were filled, mostly with women. Children played. Mothers tried to quiet them, almost in fear that the guards would send them away if they were too noisy. Across from Constance sat a young woman, tears running down her cheeks, which she furtively brushed away with the back of her hand. A guard handed her an admission card, and she bravely tried to smile. At last, it was Nelson's turn. A guard escorted her down the stairs, opened the iron gate, and led her into the visitor's room. On the right were shelves where the visitors left any gifts they brought so that they could be inspected before reaching the inmates. At the end of the room sat another guard, armed with a pistol and blackjack. Nelson gave the man her card, took a seat on a stool in one of the small cordoned off areas and again waited. The door opened and Chapin entered, carrying a yellow rose. He came to her, took her in his arms, and kissed her. "If I waited any longer, they'd have to put me in a straight-jacket," he said.

They sat down on the stools. Nelson pinned the Constance rose Chapin had brought on her dress. The two morning hours allotted for visiting passed rapidly. Chapin insisted that they not extend their time, even though the guards would have permitted it, plus Nelson was expected at the warden's house for lunch. There she found that Chapin had decorated the porch, where he often sat reading, with some of his best plants and flowers. Nelson met Lewis and Kathleen Lawes and their daughter Cheri, and sat for a lunch served by an inmate. After the meal, she was taken into the prison grounds for a promised tour of the gardens, where she rejoined Chapin. They retreated to his office. There she saw the rolltop desk, stacked with letters and gardening books, his view of the Hudson River, the geraniums that grew on the sills, and the canary, Don, often mentioned in his letters. When they had entered the office, the guard who was assigned to accompany Nelson turned and stood at a distance to give the pair privacy. Instead of making use of the moment, Chapin continued his firm adherence to prison rules and went to his desk and busied himself with some papers. "You're a stubborn cuss, Mr. Chapin. You won't even take an inch," said the guard in frustration. Chapin ignored the remark and reached for a book on the shelf. It was *Candide*. "There is no one else to whom I would give my mother's favorite book, but to you, Constance." They parted company and the guard took Nelson to see Chapin's room in the annex before leaving Sing Sing for the night. As she inspected his spacious room, Nelson plucked the petals from the rose he had given her and arranged them in such a way on his pillow that they spelled out the words "I love you."

Sunday, Monday, and Tuesday the pair met at the appointed time for their two hours together. Only one of their visits was interrupted when Larry, Chapin's inmate-attendant, rushed in to tell Chapin that a rotten bench in one of the greenhouses had given way, dumping more than one hundred fragile plants onto the ground. Otherwise they passed the time in quiet devotion to each other. In intimate interludes, they gave each other new nick-names. Nelson would be known as "Captain" and Chapin as "Mate," to symbolize his devotion to her. "I would never have believed that anyone on earth could make me glory in submission as I do now," he said. On the last day of her visit, Nelson turned to Chapin. "After dinner," she said, "I will walk down in the twi-light and sit for a few moments on the hill outside the walls, so that you can know I am there and thinking of our visit."

"That will be nice, but you must not expect me to go out and talk to you," he replied.

Though he could have obtained permission, Chapin explained that he never accepted a personal favor from the warden unless it was for his gardens and made Nelson pledge that she would not seek any for him.[13]

The next morning Nelson boarded the *Washington Irving*, a large, ten-year-old steamer, to travel north on the Hudson River to Albany, where she would catch a train back to Cleveland. Chapin stood on the banks of the Hudson and watched the steamboat make its way upstream and disappear into the morning mist. Nelson had said she would walk the top deck of the boat as it passed the prison. Chapin removed his jacket so that the white of his shirt would make him more visible against the gray backdrop of the prison. "It gave me throbbing joy to know that your eyes were looking," he wrote Nelson. "I bit my lips until they hurt, but not a tear." Chapin then retreated to his office where he remained all afternoon with the door locked.[14]

Chapin was not permitted, however, the luxury of wallowing in self-pity for very long. What had been a trickle of visitors that spring grew into an almost ceaseless flood after Nelson's departure. First to arrive was Richardson Wright of *House & Garden*, coming for his long-promised visit. He was impressed by what he saw, calling Chapin's roses the finest he had seen that year. He decided to publish an article on the gardens in his magazine, just like those he regularly ran on the gardens of the wealthy and famous. Upon his return to the city he assigned Mattie Hewitt, one the most successful landscape photographers, to take the photographs. Wright was soon followed by the editor of the *Florists Exchange*, a trade publication. Chapin's visitors were not solely floral professionals but also enthusiasts. On July 5, 1924, thirty-four women from a garden club arrived in a procession of automobiles, expecting Chapin to conduct "a Cook's tour" of his gardens. "At the finish the entire club formed a line and each in turn shook my hand and said something nice in parting," he wrote Nelson. "I doubt if anything quite like it ever happened in prison before, and I hope it will not happen very often to me, for I was never so embarrassed."[15]

The visitors were not let down by what they discovered. The gardens exceeded their reputation, and the roses, which now numbered in the thousands, displayed a colorful pageantry unlike any public gardens in the United States. The names alone testified to the immense variety Chapin had planted. Among what were then called hybrid perpetual stood Général Jacqueminots, tall and leggy rose bushes that were considered by growers to be the "greatest stud of the rose world," and Frau Karl Druschkis, developed twenty-five years before and hailed as the finest white rose yet cultivated with its huge statuesque blossoms. If the ladies from the garden club did not yet know these varieties, they certainly recognized the many American Beauty roses. With a deep pink, almost red, blossom, they were what one purchased when one asked for "roses" in a New York florist's shop. More impressive were the vast number of hybrid tea roses. Grown for the beauty of their individual flowers, these bushes rarely produced more than three or four blossoms at any one time. There were Duchess of Wellington, Maman Turbat, and Triomphe Orleans. The favorite of hybrid tea growers, Madame Butterfly, whose creamy pink blossoms filled silver bowls in the best houses, grew alongside massive Bloomfield Abundance bushes that, in contrast, held huge airy sprays with as many as one hundred blush-pink flowers.

At the base of a dozen steel arbors, erected in straight rows like rays emanating from the fountain, were climbers such Paul's Scarlet, Dorothy Perkins, and Silver Moon. Paul's Scarlet was one of the easiest climbers to grow, but contrary to its name, its blossoms were blood red without any hint of purple. Dorothy Perkins, when it matured and bloomed in late summer, would provide cascades of small candy-pink pompons. Daringly, Chapin also had planted Silver Moon roses that would eventually give off hundreds of ivory-colored flowers arrayed on dark green foliage. Introduced only fourteen years earlier, this variety was hard to grow in a climate with cold and frosty winters.

Leading toward the river were the newest gardens, filled with snapdragons, tagetes (marigolds), perennial and annual phloxes, and asters. At the end stood the building containing the execution chambers, whose peculiar "V" shape recessed its entrance. On both sides of the door were large beds of coppery yellow cannas around which perennials such as hollyhocks, Sweet Williams, physostegias, and delphiniums bloomed earlier in the year. The three greenhouses, usually the last stop on a tour, were overflowing with carnations and chrysanthemums. The middle one, however, was planted with roses, including such new varieties as Mrs. Calvin Coolidge from Pierson's nursery.

First his autobiography, and now his gardens had given Chapin a new fame. Rather than notorious, he was becoming the nation's most celebrated inmate. Visiting or writing him became the vogue. In 1924 alone, Chapin's visitors numbered in the hundreds. Among them were author Booth Tarkington, actor

Thomas Meighan, and magician Harry Houdini. The latter had written to Chapin after reading his book and later came to Sing Sing to perform for the inmates. Each visitor had his or her own interpretation of Chapin's new life. For some, he represented the tragic figure; for others, the redeemed, the sower of beauty, or the wrongly imprisoned. After his visit, Tarkington inscribed a copy of *The Midlanders* to Chapin: "In grateful appreciation not only of what a book of his has meant to me, but of the beauty he has put into the lives of his fellow men, and offered also to the sight and reflection of a visitor, who will not, could not, forget it." Dr. Harold Pattison, a pastor of Washington Heights Baptist Church in New York City, delivered an entire sermon after visiting Chapin. He called it "Growing Roses Where Only Cinders Were Before." Proudest of Chapin was Warden Lawes. "I do not claim that flowers reform men, not that the gardens or the roses reformed Chapin," he wrote. "But they gave him a new perspective."[16]

Nelson continued to contribute to Chapin's "new perspective," too. On July 23 she managed a quick visit on her way home from the American Institute of Banking's national convention in Baltimore. There she had given a speech to the delegates who were involved in publishing company newsletters and magazines. She had begun her talk by quoting Chapin, "Originality of idea makes for editorial brilliance. Expression is of less importance." Chapin got a good laugh when he read the speech, knowing the delegates would have had no idea of their relationship. "If only they could have seen the heroine of the convention in our visiting room a few days later," he wrote.[17]

"It was dear of you to arrange to return home this way," wrote Chapin after Nelson departed. "And when the Fountain Pen is filled—well, I know that I'll be completely spoiled." The "fountain pen" was Chapin's code word for a gubernatorial pardon and "springtime" his euphemism for life outside of Sing Sing. Increasingly, this hope crept into their plans for the future. "That might be in a year; surely in ten," he wrote. The publicity about the gardens certainly gave him reason to consider such was a possibility. Even Albany liked Chapin now, with officials calling his rose garden "an inspiration to dark and troubled souls." On the other hand, Chapin warned Nelson (and himself) not to stake "all our future happiness on anything so potentially uncertain as the signature of one who, at the crucial moment, may suddenly be crippled by 'writer's cramp.' If it comes, good; if it doesn't, you and I are brave enough to make the best of conditions. How about it, Captain?"[18]

As the summer came to a close, Chapin worked overtime to prepare the gardens for *House & Garden* photographer Hewitt's camera. There also was work on a new greenhouse, to help cope with a never-ceasing stream of donated plants. One shipment came from England in a crate marked "roses," but turned out to be English ivy. On the sixth anniversary of Nellie Chapin's death, Nelson sent a sympathetic note. "Others may have remembered," Chapin wrote back, "but yours is the one handclasp. Love is wonderful, for it fosters understanding and nestles and warms."[19]

September also brought the departure of the one man at Sing Sing who, aside from Lawes, had most assiduously worked at rebuilding Chapin's life. Cardinal Patrick J. Hayes decided that the services of the "Bishop of Sing Sing" were needed at St. Andrew's in New York City. He informed Cashin that he would have to make the move no later than the first week of October. On September 30, 1924, Cashin addressed a letter to the superintendent of prisons. "I present this formal resignation with reluctance and in obedience to the will of my ecclesiastical superiors," he wrote. After more than a dozen years, Cashin said, parting with the inmates would be hard. "I have entertained the secret hope that I might be permitted to devote my life to this work. But now my plans are shattered and in the phraseology of the prison, 'I'll have to go out and go to work.'"[20]

That Sunday, Father Cashin delivered his farewell sermon to an overflow crowd in the chapel. As he stood before an altar covered in roses from Chapin's garden, some of the inmates could be heard crying. Cashin said he was sorry he was being denied his hope to remain among them but asked that they give the same loyalty to his successor. "There is more loyalty, sympathy and understanding inside these walls than in any other place of equal area in the world," he said. "Bring out the good in you. It is there, and I have worked here long enough to see what others cannot. Be square with yourselves, and you'll be square with God."[21]

In early October, Nelson was back again for another three-day visit. This time she also found time to tour Pierson's nursery in Tarrytown, visit Washington Irving's grave, and make several motor trips into New York with Kathleen Lawes. Her departure was again painful. Chapin took three days to write. "My control at parting, honey, is largely bluff," he wrote from his office, which she had decorated with leaves collected during a walk along the Hudson. "A few minutes later you'd have called me a silly old man could you have peeped into my office and seen the pitiful figure that, crushed and broken, sat sobbing at my desk with head buried in his arms. Could I write a letter under such conditions?"[22]

Chapin's mood was restored when, a few days later, he and Irvin Cobb had their reunion when Chapin's former *Evening World* colleague came to do his story for *Cosmopolitan*. His visit was quickly followed by that of George McManus, an old staffer and now famous cartoonist, and of three different friends, one bearing roast chicken, mince pie, iced cake, and a basket of fruit. "I guess so many visits are a bit wearing, especially when I have someone come and all the while keep secretly wishing the someone was you," he wrote Nelson. In November, it was her turn. Nelson stopped at Sing Sing on her way back from Washington, D.C., where she spoke to a group of women bankers. Between the lunch and the dinner at which she was to speak, Nelson had gone to Rhode Island Avenue and knocked at Marion and Frank Chapin's house. It was Marion's birthday, and she was out at a matinee with a friend. Chapin's brother Frank was dressed in his old clothes because he was heading out to plant bulbs at Glenwood Cemetery. Nelson followed him to the cemetery, where she put roses on Nellie Chapin's grave, causing her to be late for the dinner. At Sing Sing, Nelson told Chapin the tale of placing roses on his wife's grave and being late to the dinner. He said the women would have been scandalized had they known the cause of her tardiness.[23]

The remainder of Chapin's fall was consumed with preparing the rose bushes, which numbered more than two thousand, for winter. A foot of soil had to be built up around each rose bush. More than a dozen trucks of soil were required to bring in sufficient dirt. Then on top of the dirt, Chapin's crew placed a thick layer of manure and covered each hill with corn stalks. The work was necessary not to keep the roses from freezing, which they could survive, but to prevent them from thawing and freezing again. "No matter how severe the winter may be I feel pretty confident that our losses will be nominal," Chapin wrote Nelson when the job was complete. "I wish I might protect you as well as I have the roses."[24]

With the approach of Christmas, hope for a pardon arose again. That summer and autumn friends had repeatedly encouraged Chapin to believe that once the elections were over, Governor Smith would place Chapin on his list of Christmas pardons. One friend went so far as to say the governor had personally assured her. "But one's friends sometimes promise more than they can fulfill," he wrote Nelson, as he heard nothing more on the subject from his supporters. "It is so easy to talk about such things when they are doing their utmost to shed sunshine where there is so much gloom." Finally on December 14, Chapin read the list of thirty Christmas pardons published in the newspapers. "I failed to find the name you'd most like to have been there," Chapin wrote Nelson. "Well, perhaps next Christmas, or some Christmas."[25]

Letters and Christmas cards for Chapin poured into Sing Sing. The inmates who shared the annex erected a tall tree, covered in small electric lights, reaching nearly to the skylight, in front of Chapin's cell. In the greenhouses, however, Chapin's roses were being uncooperative. The overcast days had been insufficient incentive for them to bloom. Instead, Chapin had to resort to other flowers when he decorated the altar for Christmas morning services to be led by Father McCaffrey, Cashin's replacement. On Christmas Eve, Houdini came to the prison to put on a show for the inmates. Chapin, in keeping with his vow not to attend shows, remained in his cell, piled high with Christmas packages. After opening a number of them, he got under his blanket, lit his pipe and opened Eleanor Hallowell Abbot's *Old-Dad*, one of the books he got as a present, and was soon lulled to sleep by the Christmas music playing on the radio. At ten that night he was awakened by Houdini. The magician stayed for a half-hour and asked Chapin to put him on his visiting list.

Nineteen-twenty-five brought Wright's article, illustrated with Hewitt's beautiful photographs, in *House & Garden*, published among the usual feature articles on lavish homes from Hollywood to Port Washington, Long Island. Now as never before, the public got a clear idea of the immense scope and beauty of Chapin's gardens. The more than a half-dozen photographs showed off the neatly planted beds, the arbors with their young rose bushes at their feet, the fountain and basin, the row of blue spruces, and the gardens leading down to the Hudson. "We do not expect any great revolution in penology to come from the publication of this story—and yet you can never tell," wrote Wright in the front of the magazine, where he urged his subscribers to read the article. The effect of the creation of a world of fragrance and color in a cruel and dark environment can't be predicted, said Wright at the end of his lengthy description of the gardens. "This we do know, however, that what was once crushed rock and trodden cinders now blossoms with the rose; that whereas men once gazed out upon dank gray walls and the miasma of a prison yard, they now can watch the awakening of shrubs, the swelling of buds, the coloring of blossoms. They smell the fragrance of flowers and hear birds call in the trees. They see the long shadows on close-cropped lawns. To them the arrival of spring means something new, a new thing the burgeoning of summer and the flaming tints of autumn."[26]

Wright's paean to Chapin was soon followed by Cobb's take on Chapin's gardening in *Cosmopolitan*. Chapin and Nelson had grown concerned about his old reporter's plans when the magazine began advertising the article with the line: "Irvin Cobb tells of a life prisoner who made a garden on his road to Hell." Though Chapin received an advance copy, he asked Nelson to read the story first. If her verdict was negative, Chapin promised he would destroy the issue without reading it. In early February, Nelson mailed her judgment to Chapin. "It is frank and rather merciless, but read it and tell me your honest reaction," she said. "My own chief objection is to the word *ophidian*." Cobb had used the word in describing Chapin's eyes. ("The light which lit them seemed not to come from within his skull but from without," wrote Cobb.) "I wasn't sure of the meaning and looked it up in the dictionary," Nelson told Chapin. "It means snake. I hate Cobb for that." After receiving Nelson's letter, Chapin retrieved the copy of *Cosmopolitan* hidden in his desk drawer and took it back to his cell to read. "It doesn't sting," he wrote to Nelson. "I'm going to write Cobb and tell him that I like his story, that it is remarkably fair and as truthful as he knew how to make it, wonderfully well written and without gush." As to the business of his eyes, Chapin assuaged Nelson that Cobb only knew him as the fearsome editor and has never known the man she knew.[27]

Chapin came down with the flu, but by the end of February he was back at work planting seeds (his desk was groaning under the weight of seed packets) and transplanting seedlings. Not only were the demands of his garden dragging him from his bed, but also Nelson was on her way to Sing Sing for her fifth visit in less than a year. When she arrived on March 5, Nelson found a love note from Chapin waiting for her at the hotel. "I know how glad you will be, too, to again feel the pressure of my hand in yours," he wrote. "Did it ever occur to you what a very unusual romance ours is? I wonder if there ever was another girl since the beginning of time who wore her last winter's coat and misered her earnings that she might travel many miles to visit a white-haired old man. What would Cobb say to that, do you think?"[28]

At 9:00 A.M. on Monday, March 2, 1925, Nelson and Chapin held hands again in the visiting room. Each day, they repeated the pattern of the previous visits. Nelson would come for the morning visiting hours and then amuse herself in the afternoon. Chapin continued to refuse to ask for special dispensation, which Lawes would have given gladly. As the week came to an end, Chapin brought from his office the remaining copy of the pair of special author's editions of his autobiography that Putnam had given him, the other having been given to Cooper. In Nelson's presence, he inscribed it.

> My Constance,
> With deepest affection always
> Charles Chapin.

As Chapin finished engrossing the book, Lawes arrived from his office with a copy of Cobb's newest book *Alias Ben Alibi*, a fictional account of the greatest genius Park Row ever knew. Chapin took the book from Lawes and flipped through some of the pages and read some passages in silence.

"Alias Ben Alibi seems to have been a tough customer, and Cobb means me, you know, Constance."

"Then he is lying!" she replied.

"Now, now, honey. I wasn't always the estimable gentleman I am now. Don't get cross with Cobb. I've no doubt he's done a good job."[29]

Chapin's reaction was calmer, in part, because he had known for a while that Cobb had been writing a thinly disguised novel about him. Cobb, ever mindful of his old boss, had sought permission from Chapin before writing a word. That night, after Nelson had left for Cleveland, Chapin read *Alias Ben Alibi*, marked up passages as he and Nelson continued to do, and the following morning sent the book on to her. "I doubt if you will find it very interesting," he wrote to Nelson. "While I can recognize myself in Ben Alibi, so much is fiction, and so comparatively little real that I don't care nearly so much for it as I did his *Cosmopolitan* article." Contrary to Chapin's expectations, Nelson found the book sufficiently fascinating to publish a full-page review in the *Cleveland Banker*, which she edited in addition to the *Federal Reserve Notes*. Nelson knew the region's bankers would be puzzled by the incongruous review, not knowing Nelson's connection to Chapin. "Well, what, I can hear, has this to do with banking and with me," wrote Nelson toward the end of her review. "Just this." Cobb had created a portrait, said Nelson, of a man whose vim, fire, and success should be respected, admired, and emulated by young people no matter what profession.[30]

Although Nelson accepted Cobb's work as a tribute to her love, another piece of writing appeared that was far more disruptive to her relationship with Chapin. Kenneth Coolbaugh, an old *Evening World* reporter, wrote in *Liberty* magazine about a city editor who fired reporters simply because he "enjoyed the process." The editor was unnamed, but it became clear two paragraphs later who he had in mind. "The gray-haired, the weak, and unfortunate were always his especial victims," wrote Coolbaugh. "They are no longer, however, for the bleak walls of the penitentiary and life sentence for murdering his wife have shorn him of power either to fire or hire." Nelson dispatched a sympathetic note to Chapin, thinking Coolbaugh's malicious pen might have upset him. Chapin misconstrued Nelson's intent and told her if she couldn't handle a nasty remark in print, what would she do when people gossiped, pointed at her, and generally ostracized her for her association with him? Hurt by his tart reply, Nelson became resentful, and Chapin had to work hard to regain her confidence. He wrote immediately, saying that he never intended to suggest that she believed Coolbaugh's portrayal of him or that he doubted for a minute her faith in him. "Such a thought never entered my mind, nor has there been a one day, or one minute, in almost a year's time that I doubted the genuineness of your avowed affection for me." The damage was repaired.[31]

Spring brought a glorious renewal of Chapin's garden, more press attention, another deluge of floral donations, a few lover's squabbles with Nelson, and hope. Max Neuberger, a wealthy New York friend who had known Chapin and his wife since 1910, came to the prison on April 15 after wintering in Florida. Neuberger had led the 1924 pardon effort but had fallen ill in the fall. "He hasn't been idle in the meantime, but has been, and still is, energetically at work to accomplish that which will mean so much to both of us," Chapin announced joyfully to Nelson. Neuberger discussed with Chapin his plans for a renewal of the pardon campaign, and by the time his visit was over, Chapin was once again convinced that a pardon could be had. "If everything works out as he expects, I shall probably have my next birthday dinner with you," he told Nelson.[32]

In May, Cobb returned, this time with his wife Laura. They brought Chapin a Brazilian cardinalis in a Japanese cage that they had owned for two years. Chapin hung the cage in the greenhouse by the annex, where three other rare birds also lived. "When I left a little while ago all four were singing their heads off," Chapin said. A few weeks later the warden increased Chapin's singing bird population by giving him a Carolina parakeet and a South American parrot. Chapin put the two in one of the greenhouses by the river. The growing population of birds sparked Chapin's ambition. He went to Lawes with the idea that a bird house would complete the gardens. The warden told him he was free to try, but there would be absolutely no state or prison money for such a project. There was, however, little time for Chapin to think about it. The warmer weather meant that thousands of seedlings that had been started in the greenhouses during the winter had to be planted. Concurrently, thousands of spent tulips and narcissus bulbs had to be dug up and stored until fall. By the end of May, all the new plants were planted except for a last-minute donation of another 100 rose plants from Bobbink & Atkins.[33]

The end of June brought Nelson back to Sing Sing. As usual Chapin mailed a note to the hotel so a letter would await her arrival. "When you are handed this little note of welcome, you will know there is a white-haired old man expectantly waiting for you to come to him." Promptly at 9:00 A.M., Monday, June 29, Nelson made the now-familiar walk past the guards to Sing Sing's visiting room. Heartened by Neuberger's efforts, Chapin shared his hope that next winter's roses would be tended by another inmate. They talked a great deal about the future. Also present that week was actor Meighan who had returned to make "The Man Who Found Himself," a silent film based on a story by novelist Tarkington. The movie, about a man who takes the fall for his brother's crime, was to be filmed in part in Sing Sing. Nelson lunched with Meighan and the Lawes family. After lunch, the cameras were set up in the gardens where Meighan, as the imprisoned protagonist, is put to work. A *New York Times* reporter who witnessed the filming described the scene as captured by the camera. "The lovely rose bushes on which he was working were in the foreground, behind them was the fountain with its silver spray thrown by the wind out over the kaleidoscope of flowers and greenery, and for a background the cold, gray walls of the old cell block, broken at intervals by deep and very narrow windows, heavily barred."

Between scenes Chapin joked with Meighan. "Too bad to see a likely looking young fellow like you in here," he said. "How did it happen?"

"The movies put me here, brother," Meighan said as he shook his head in mock regret. "But in this case, the law got the wrong man. I'm innocent."

"So's every one else in here, to hear them tell it. Look at 'em," said Chapin waiving his arm toward the buildings of the compound. From all the windows the convicts could be seen looking down at the nearly 100 actors, electricians, cameramen, and lighting crew members.[34]

On Thursday, Nelson's visit ended, and she returned by night train to Cleveland. The two made plans to meet again in Septem-

ber and in October. Shortly after her departure, John Kennedy, a wealthy banker and president of the State Prison Commission, came to Sing Sing after being recruited to the cause by Neuberger.
Kennedy knew Chapin, and his daughter had written a flattering article for the *Brooklyn Eagle* the previous winter. Kennedy told Chapin he would do whatever he could to help and said he planned to make a personal appeal to Governor Smith. "So perhaps we will hang up our silk stockings together at Christmas, though we will not count on it until we are certain that the fountain pen has gone into action," Chapin wrote Nelson after Kennedy departed.[35]

Immediately after Kennedy left, the Chapin clemency movement prepared to make its formal plea. The law firm of Broadwin & Manneheimer drew up an application for a pardon to Governor Smith. In their petition, the lawyers argued that Chapin's crime had "none of the depraved impulses which customarily prompt crimes of violence. His act was parallel to that of a son who kills his mother to free her from the agony she is suffering in the death throes of an incurable ailment." The lengthy petition reviewed Chapin's life, quoted extensively from the proceedings of the sanity commission, and highlighted the point that the recent and widely publicized transformation of Sing Sing's grounds occurred without any cost to the state. If pardoned, said the petition, Chapin would dedicate himself to writing. "If it be the function of the law to attempt the rehabilitation of the wrongdoer—and this we take to be its loftiest aim—then, indeed, should Chapin be freed: for even from within the prison walls his condemned soul created beauty—gave evidence of his complete restoration. No mortal can safely gauge his potentialities. Certain it is, however, that this indomitable spirit—if free—would at least transform its subsisting power to useful achievement and distinction." Momentum seemed to be building in Chapin's favor. Another state report, issued later that year, cited Chapin as most responsible for the transformation of Sing Sing from one of the most oppressive prisons to one of the most beautiful. "Flower beds, shrubs, and grass plots are everywhere," said the official report. "The rose garden in the center of the quadrangle would grace any institution."[36]

The effort left Chapin torn between his increasing confidence that he would be freed soon and his place in the special world he had created at Sing Sing. Work had begun on a bird house, to be built with contributions from outside and construction scraps from inside, the new seedlings for 1926 had to be tended, and more trees were being delivered. Until a pardon was signed, Chapin told Nelson, he would adopt an attitude that he would remain at Sing Sing for years to come. "But down deep in our hearts we will both be secretly wishing that the time is getting close at hand when we can politely ask the porter to get the state-room ready."[37]

23

The End

The pardon application was finally before the governor, and positive reports from the field heightened the intoxicating scent of freedom in the summer air of 1925. "Just heard from Mr. N. that friends of yours are coming out strong and others who are not even acquaintances some of them high up in political circles," a devoted friend wrote excitedly to Chapin in late July. "He is much encouraged." But in the end, it wouldn't be Chapin's freedom that would alter his life that summer. Rather, it was that which was given to Larry, the trusted inmate who for years had cooked Chapin's meals, catalogued his books, tended his orchids, and, on occasion, read poetry with him. Unlike Chapin's, Larry's prison sentence was ending. In August he was set free. With a new suit and $10, he was shown to the gate and wished good luck.[1]

A few weeks later, Nelson was at her desk when the telephone rang. It was Larry calling.

"I'm a friend of Mr. Chapin, and I would like to see you," said the voice at the other end of the line. Nelson thought the voice sounded familiar, but wasn't entirely sure.

"I think when we meet you will remember me," Larry said.

Nelson agreed to meet, and Larry soon presented himself at the bank. He had a job working as a clerk in a summer hotel on Lake Erie. He was dressed in worn, but neatly pressed, clothes, but, like many who have been imprisoned, he had a demeanor that betrayed his convict past.

"I'm a square peg in a round hole," he said. "The hotel is small and unimportant, and I feel like an upper-class servant. I've an inferiority complex, and it's got me beaten."

Nelson felt sorry for him, especially considering how loyal he had been to Chapin. She gave him some money, lent him some more, found him a room, and obtained a tutoring position for him. She thought nothing more of the matter, especially after finding a pitiful letter from Chapin in her mail. He had fallen ill. Describing himself as having "less pep than a wet dishrag," Chapin concluded with "Oh honey, I'm so tired and lonesome—so sick and sad. Good night, and all the love of my lonely heart." Nelson immediately booked a train East, ironically having to borrow money from a friend after having loaned hers to Larry. She reached Ossining at eight in the morning and spent the day at Sing Sing. After determining Chapin would recover, Nelson returned that afternoon to Cleveland.[2]

A few days after getting back, she opened another letter from Chapin. This one startled her more than the previous one. Chapin was no longer physically sick, but it must have seemed to Nelson as if he had lost his mind. The letter was vicious and dripping with venom. Chapin had learned that Larry was in Cleveland and had met with Nelson. He accused Nelson of betraying him, assuming all the worst of the encounter. In his anger, he reached deep into the recesses of his theatrical past and aimed a verbal dagger at her heart. "I had rather be a toad and live upon the vapor of a dungeon," he said quoting *Othello*, "than keep a corner of the thing I love for others' uses."[3]

Nelson was beside herself. Once again, she was a passenger on an eastbound train. This time, when she reached Sing Sing, Chapin refused to see her. She took a room at the Briarcliff, the same place where she had stayed on her first visit and where Chapin once had left an affectionate note to greet her. She returned again and again to the prison until he finally consented to talk with her. "Talk," however, was an inaccurate description. They met in his office. He remained hard, cold, and angry, referring to Larry as a "pup" and masticating a mangled cigar. "The young pup. I'll have his ears cut off," he kept repeating over and over until Nelson decided to retreat. As in Dodge City, almost fifty years ago, Chapin was blinded by unfounded jealous rage.

Chapin's volcanic eruption exposed his lack of equilibrium and his continued frail hold on reality. Whenever he felt slighted, he would let the wound fester until it poisoned him. Cobb, his only true friend in the city room, remembered watching this on more than one occasion. "He would carry a grievance for days, though, hugging it to him like a possession dear and fragile, before he loosed the vials of his wrath." More to the point, his singular vision of the world as a stage upon which humans play out dramas in black and white, with no shades of gray, blinded him in his personal life. It seemed unfair. This trait had served him well—in fact, made him a star—in the newspaper world. "When a story was running," said Cobb, "human beings were not human beings. . . . Now they were just copy." All human drama could be reduced to the simplicity of a headline. But when it came to personal matters, his inability to see the full complexity of life had led to the death of Nellie and now to the extinguishing of Constance's love. As an editor, he imposed order on the world. Here, he was powerless except to lash out. By no fault of her own, Nelson would be the victim.

Back at the inn, she wrote Chapin plaintively and told him she would leave for home the next day and never return unless he promised to give her a chance to explain. She sent the note by messenger and waited through the afternoon and evening. No answer came. In the morning she called Kathleen Lawes.

"Have you seen him today? Is he still obdurate? Is there anything I can do?" asked Nelson.

"He's hard as nails, the way he was when he came here," replied Lawes. "Won't eat his food, or look at his flowers. I think he cried all night."

"And there's nothing I can do?"

"Nothing, my dear. The man's beside himself, and there's no use talking to him."[4]

Nelson left that day by Hudson River steamer, the same that had taken her past Sing Sing the year before when Chapin walked to the riverbank and took off his coat so that she could spot him. Back in Cleveland, Nelson wrote Chapin each day, but no answer came. Then in late September, a reply. "Your letters rather surprise me," wrote Chapin. "You say that true love never doubts. Had it ever occurred to you, my dear, that Jealousy is the very cornerstone of affection? When Jealousy flies out the window, it usually takes love along with it for company."[5]

The fire had been extinguished. The letters that now began again to pass between them turned to polite and meaningless chatter. When Nelson mentioned the possibility of visiting, Chapin dissuaded her with talk of saving money. Occasionally a flash of the past ardor surfaced, as when Chapin confessed he hoped the letters she used to send would resume. "I miss them, girl o' mine." But the damage was done. Chapin certainly was no longer the same man. The change may have been prompted by his growing sense of isolation, stemming from the death of his compatriots outside of prison. Or it may have simply been the realization that his end was drawing near and that Sing Sing would be his final home. Adding to his sense of gloom, Neuberger was now uncommunicative about the pardon effort. "Guess he found the task he set for himself more difficult of accomplishment than he anticipated," remarked Chapin in October.[6]

Cobb, too, sensed the change in Chapin when he came to see him. Lewisohn had contacted Cobb because he had heard that he was on good terms with Governor Smith. He asked if Cobb would use his influence to get Chapin's pardon application moved up on the clemency board's agenda. He further told Cobb that, if the plan succeeded, Chapin would have a job tending his extensive Westchester gardens. Cobb agreed to give it a try and telephoned the executive mansion in Albany that he would arrive the next day to make a personal request of the governor. In the morning, Cobb stopped at Sing Sing to see Chapin. He found him supervising the construction of the new bird house, which had become more imperative now that dozens of exotic birds had been donated. Cobb filled him in on Lewisohn's plan.

"Listen, give that gentleman my thanks, but beg him please, not to bother me again until I give the word," said Chapin. "This job's not half finished. Anyhow, I don't fancy the idea of being a pensioner on some millionaire's bounty, coddled one day and the next being pointed out as Chapin the life termer."

"As I went away," said Cobb, "bound for New York now, and not for Albany, he was snapping out orders like a drill master."[7]

In late November, novelist Theodore Dreiser came to Sing Sing. He had persuaded the *World* to give him press credentials so that he could tour the death house as part of the research for his next novel, *An American Tragedy*. Over the years, Dreiser's and Chapin's lives had intersected at many journalistic junctures. In Chicago, Dreiser had been in the lobby of the *Herald*, hoping to get a job interview with Chapin. In St. Louis, in the 1890s, they had worked as reporters for competing papers. In New York, they had both passed through the *World* city room. Chapin was apparently unaware of their close encounters. He certainly wasn't a fan of the writer. He dismissed Dreiser's literary work, referring to his fiction as "silly slush fit only to be flung into the garbage can." The two only saw each other briefly during Dreiser's visit. When Chapin read what the *World* published, based on Dreiser's interview with a death-row inmate, he extended his appraisal of Dreiser's literary skills to that of his journalism.[8]

On Christmas, Lawes tried to lift Chapin's spirits with some seasonal cheer. At midnight, the warden dressed as Santa Claus and entered Chapin's cell with a flashlight, woke him, and gave him a package wrapped in red paper with a gilt cord. After Lawes left, Chapin opened the package and discovered a suede windbreaker, lined with satin, to be worn under a sweater to defeat the cold winter winds coming off the Hudson.[9]

In early 1926, a tremor of passion was stirred in Chapin. He and Nelson resumed some affectionate name-calling, exchanged marked-up novels, and even planned a visit. But the romantic renaissance was soon interrupted. Nelson had lost her job at the Federal Reserve and was frantic. There was the possibility of work in Philadelphia or Boston, and her attention was diverted as she decided what to do. During this jobless interlude, Chapin reevaluated his situation. He was now sixty-seven, and the extended silence from Neuberger made his fate seem clear. "So far as I can now tell, I will probably stay here as long as I am alive," he wrote to Nelson. "I don't like your thinking that my affections have changed. They are the same and always will be. But it made a marked difference in the general aspect when I found out there was nothing in the promises of release at Christmas. With nothing to look forward to, I'm not brute enough to encourage affection that seems so hopeless of fruition." Chapin told her he had to look at the facts and not dream of happiness that can never be had. "The best I can now look forward to is an early end of this life and a long rest at Glenwood," he said, referring to the Washington, D.C., cemetery where Nellie and his mother were buried.[10]

In her job hunt, Nelson opted for Boston. In March, she stopped at Sing Sing on her way. The visit, unlike the earlier ones, was dour. Chapin was glum; in his words, "I am now up to my chin in mental depression and see but little prospect of ever getting back onto solid ground." The only thing to come from the visit was a new pair of shoelaces that Nelson sent him upon reaching Boston. She had noticed that Chapin, once Park Row's dandy, had replaced the broken laces in his black shoes with tan ones.

Within a month of being in Boston, Nelson fell ill and returned home to Wisconsin. She sent Chapin a note that she would be unable to make the planned April visit. Angry, he ceased to write. Then it was Chapin's turn to become sick. In late July, acute gastritis confined him to bed. Often associated with stress or trauma, acute gastritis in the 1920s was one of the eight leading causes of death. Lawes became anxious. "He refuses to go to the hospital, but he has not been out of his cell for five days," he told a reporter for the *New York Times*. Lawes called in two doctors to tend Chapin, a move unheard of for an inmate. They reported that his rheumatism, as well as the gastritis, had greatly weakened him. Newspapers around the nation carried reports of Chapin's illness. Nelson, who saw an article, immediately wired Lawes. On Monday, July 26, 1926, after the flurry of press reports, Lawes went to see Chapin. He read him the various newspaper accounts and the frantic telegram he had received from Nelson.[11]

Lawes used Chapin's weakened state to stir the coals of the pardon movement. "He has been losing weight for some time." Lawes told the press. "He is fast slipping and cannot last long if kept in confinement." But when pressed by a reporter, Lawes acknowledged he no longer knew of an existing movement to get Chapin a pardon except for Cobb's checked effort the previous year. The sixty-eight-year-old Chapin would not be eligible for parole for another seven and half years. Chapin's decline continued, and on Sunday Lawes ordered that he be moved to the prison hospital. Dr. C. C. Sweet, the acting prison surgeon, reported that the gastritis and auto-toxication were taking their toll.

Chapin's blood pressure was low, his heart was weak, and his general condition was very feeble. But the move to the hospital worked. A week later Chapin left his bed for the first time in more than two weeks and stepped outside briefly.

Though both Nelson and Chapin were mending physically, their relationship continued its disintegration. In late November, when Chapin finally responded to one of Nelson's letters, he offered a dog-ate-my-homework reason for his silence. He claimed that, while in his feeble state, he had dictated a reply to Nelson's telegram. "The young man I gave dictation to confessed to me he lost his notes, and he lacked the nerve to tell me at the time or return to have the letters dictated a second time." The formal tone of their letters left little doubt in either's mind as to the final state of their relationship.[12]

As 1927 opened, it seemed to Lawes that his prison was becoming one of the most popular sightseeing spots in New York state. On certain days, 3,000 visitors—many of them actors, priests, doctors, philanthropists, and even college students—came calling in hope of touring Sing Sing. Finally, it became too much for the prison guards to watch both the kept and the peepers. Lawes banned sightseers. The ebbing tide of visitors would have little effect on Chapin, however. His own coterie of visitors had dwindled to a handful, many of whom were becoming too infirm to make the trek much longer. Even if they could, it wouldn't matter. With each coming year, Chapin was closing far more significant gates than the metal ones that held the outside world at bay. It was the beginning of the end, and Chapin knew it. He would turn seventy the next year and soon would be the age at which his father died. Almost a decade had passed since he killed Nellie, and he was still in prison. And he had pushed Nelson away. All that was left to him were his flowers. After five years of care, they now appeared each spring with predicable beauty. The beds had a permanent air about them, the paths that ran along them were well trod, and the benches were aged by weather.[13]

On January 7, 1927, Chapin escaped the winter cold to tend the smallish pile of correspondence that lay on the desk in his office. Few letters came anymore. Without his glasses, which were sent out for repairs six weeks earlier, reading a lot of letters would have been out of the question anyway. Among the few that were on his desk was one with a Boston postmark that was growing cold from inattention. "My dear Constance," he typed. "I am conscience stricken for having so long delayed replying to your nice letter, but I am sure of forgiveness when I tell you that I am still bereft of reading glasses." The truth about his conscience, however, was soon conveyed as Chapin told her about the one book he had managed to read that winter, a collection of letters between Victorian thinkers John Ruskin and Jessie Leete. Leete disappointed Ruskin at one point on a visit. "I think that no man is so great that he doesn't like sometimes to quit posing and be treated like a human being, especially by a girl he has taken a liking to," Chapin wrote. "She attempts to blame his changing attitude toward her on his failing health, but Ruskin lingered along for twenty years after her visit to him." The bitterness of this book report to Nelson revealed how Chapin continued to lick his self-inflicted wound. "Now that the holidays are over, I will probably not have many letters to answer, except from my garden friends. They at least are faithful—my garden friends." Nelson did not rise to the bait, and 1927 was entirely devoid of letters or visits from her. Chapin was left alone with his garden.[14]

Indeed, the impression of "a gentle old man puttering about his flowers and birds" was the one that first greeted Lamar Middleton of the *New York Evening Post* when he saw Chapin that March. Middleton was touring the prison in the company of the warden. The place was busy. Architect George Starin Cowles, serving time for having forged his uncle's will, was supervising the construction of Chapin's long-awaited bird house. The circular stucco and wood house, forty-feet in diameter, promised to accommodate one thousand birds when completed. The space was needed for the burgeoning population of birds that had been donated as a result of the publicity given to a parrot whose curses even shocked the sensibilities of convicts. Lawes just finished explaining all this to Middleton when Chapin himself joined them.[15]

"Crystal has grown some spring feathers, Warden," said Chapin referring to a red and blue macaw that lived in a large cage in the greenhouse attached to Chapin's quarters. "If you come to the greenhouse, I'll show you to her."

The party then followed Chapin. He became reluctant to talk,

however, when Lawes introduced Middleton as a reporter. Chapin had not granted an interview since the first flurry of interest in his gardens years before. His responses were brief. "He gave
the impression of speaking in the unadorned idiom of newspaper prose," said Middleton. They talked only about the care of the birds and gardens. Middleton was particularly struck by Chapin's comments regarding the birds. "His references to the birds' 'good cages' was psychologically peculiar in light of his own imprisonment," he said. But as Middleton's short visit concluded, he saw in Chapin's eyes and demeanor that not all of his famous irascible personality had been extinguished. "The prison years have only tempered him, absorbed some of the harshness. In many characteristics, he is still the old war horse of his newspaper days."

In the fall, Chapin received bad news. Max Neuberger had been found dead in a suite at the Hotel Clendening, on West 103rd Street, with a bullet hole in his right temple and an automatic lying beside his hand. He had disappeared two days earlier, and his worried wife had hired a private detective to find him. He had no financial worries, but had suffered a nervous breakdown.[16]

In June 1928, writer Andrew S. Wing came to check up on Chapin and the gardens for *Farm & Fireside*, a national farming magazine. Wing waited for Chapin in Lawes's office. "A faded, grayish old man came in, dressed in rough gray prison trousers and sweater coat," said Wing. "It was Chapin." He greeted the warden cheerily. Over all these years, even though he was Chapin's keeper, Lawes had remained his truest friend and protector. Chapin then grasped Wing's hand and led him to the prison gates. "Take a good look at this man so you can let him out again," Chapin said to the guards as he and Wing passed through the walls. "I've found it easier to get into this place than to get out," he said rather dryly to Wing.

When they entered the yard proper, Chapin took Wing first into the old cellblock where he had been kept when he arrived in Sing Sing, "We entered this, the original prison," said Wing. "The stone floor between the cell rows and the outer wall was worn deep from the passing of countless thousands of feet. I stepped inside one of the cells and could just stand upright." Wing felt enormous relief to be in the fresh air of the yard again, as was perhaps Chapin's intent. Now before him stretched the gardens, the pool, the shrubs, and the trees. "But for the high prison walls in the background one could imagine himself in a millionaire's estate," said Wing. As they walked, Wing lost the feeling of talking with a prisoner. "We chatted on many subjects, man to man, as human beings of equal status." Wing also noticed, as they made their way around, how the prison guards treated Chapin with enormous respect.

From the gardens they passed through the greenhouses, filled with plants whose flowers were cut daily for the prison hospital, chapel, and dining room. They stopped in Chapin's office, where he filled his pipe from a stash of tobacco in the desk drawer. They visited the bird house, where now 120 birds, ranging from canaries to a talking parrot, made their home among the tropical plants. Like most visitors, Wing was impressed. The tour complete, the pair stood in the yard while men filed by in platoons on their way to the mess hall. "How young the prisoners seemed!" said Wing. "Occasionally a bright, intelligent face would stand out. I asked Chapin about one of these—a red-haired lad."

"I don't know him," Chapin replied. "There was a time when I knew all the men here. But not anymore. I don't think about them or about myself. I spend my time and thoughts with my birds and flowers."

"I asked him what he would do if his sentence were commuted and he were free to go," said Wing.

"That is something I have never permitted myself to think about," Chapin said disingenuously. But he continued in a more honest vein. "I do not believe that I would care to leave here if I could. There are too many pointing fingers in the world outside our walls. Here there are none. I doubt if I would be as much interested elsewhere as I am now in our prison flower garden; anyway, I am too fond of the garden I have created to ever wish to turn my back on it. I hope to continue as now for as long as I may live." The visit was over. "We shook hands and said good-bye; he to return to the life of the prison, I to the freer air beyond the walls," Wing wrote.[17]

In the fall, Chapin faced his seventieth birthday. His only visitor that day was Bess Houdini. Chapin and Harry Houdini had been friends since the magician wrote him following the publication of *Charles Chapin's Story*. Houdini also had sent Chapin books, performed for the inmates at Chapin's request, and even met Nelson after a performance in Cleveland. Following his death in 1926, Bess and Charles became friends, particularly after she

came to Sing Sing to make arrangements for the transfer of the criminology collection that Houdini had willed to Lawes. The two took a sincere liking to each other, and Bess came to believe that Charles's crime was a "mercy killing." Every few months, Bess came to visit by taxi from her home in Inwood, New York. In turn, Charles regularly sent her flowers from his garden and even arranged for some of his inmate-gardeners to do some landscaping at her cottage in Rye, twenty miles away. At one point their relationship became the center of gossip when the *New York Graphic* tried to get copies of Charles's letters to Bess on the rumor they explained his murder of Nellie.[18]

A few days after Bess's visit, alone at his desk, Chapin dug out a yellowed letter that had come from Cleveland many years earlier. He then placed a sheet of writing paper in his now rarely used typewriter. "My dear Constance," he typed. Two years had now passed since the two had corresponded, and Chapin offered as excuse that he was now writing at the urging of Kathleen Lawes. He told Nelson of finding the old letter. "The contents that once thrilled me now seemed but a mockery," he wrote. "It protested much and gave no hint that I would so soon be forsaken. Life is full of just such mutable twists, isn't it?" Once again, a few furtive letters were exchanged. Rather than rekindling affection, the effort only aggravated the old wounds. Chapin said he had been "awakened" to Nelson's true feelings when he discovered that she had come near Sing Sing by car on her way to Boston and not stopped. He was unaware that she had tried to visit, but had come after visiting hours, and that Lawes, who would have permitted the visit, was away. "And again in your recent letter," he wrote in December 1928, "telling me that you were in New York last summer and didn't run up, although it takes less than an hour. It was so unlike the Cleveland girl I had known and cared for." He bitterly attacked her consideration of a job in California instead of accepting one in New York. "Had you accepted the New York job, it would have shown me that you did care after all." There was little point in replying. Instead, she kindly sent several long newsy letters about her life in Boston though she persisted to talk of the possibility of moving to California. The latter continued to irk Chapin. "Yes, I am sorry, Constance," he wrote, "sorry to completely lose you, for I realize if you go to California I shall never see you again."[19]

The inauguration of a new governor prompted a last effort to win a pardon for Chapin. But before friends could even contact Governor Franklin D. Roosevelt, Chapin put a stop to it. "I would not accept a pardon even if one is offered to me," he told the *New York Times*.[20]

Spring, which had become in recent years his busiest and most anticipated season, brought little cheer to Chapin in 1929. On St. Patrick's Day, he warned Nelson that if she tarried long in the West, she would never see him again. "Not much left for me to live for, anyway," he wrote. "I enjoy the flowers, the trees I have planted, my large collection of beautiful birds, and most of all my wonderful radio, but there are so many hours of deadly loneliness I often feel that I will be very glad when I can go to sleep and forget about everything. Don't think me morbid, I'm not—just tired of it all and ready to quit." Finally, he admitted that he had been selfish. "I had hoped that you would come to New York and be nearer to me, for no one needs you as much as I do. But I know that an old man mustn't expect to be coddled, so I'll just sit tight and be as placid and content as possible until the trumpet calls me to Glenwood, ever grateful for all I have had." It was the last letter he would ever write to her.[21]

At the end of the summer in 1930, work began on many long overdue improvements to Sing Sing, including a new drainage system. The contractor brought a massive steam shovel into the main yard to dig the necessary trenches. With no care as to what might be of value in the yard, the operator gave his engine a full head of steam and drove it straight through the gardens cutting wide swaths of devastation as he surged forward. "Everything went down before that iron fury," said Lawes who toured the carnage. "Rose hedges were uprooted and destroyed—annihilated." Chapin stood by and watched sorrowfully, but he knew the words of a tottering old convict would not stop a callous contractor. Already Chapin was in a weakened state. In May, he had been hospitalized again for a stomach disorder and severe cold. He collapsed again. "He was suddenly the helpless invalid, unable to carry on," said Lawes, "his burden of life too heavy."[22]

In late October, the world outside of Sing Sing began to get word of Chapin's decline. The *New York Times* reported that Chapin was "critically ill after a general breakdown and may never again regain his health." He refused to be taken to the prison hospital and instead lay in his bed in a small room on the upper floor of the old death house. Everett Herriot, an inmate assigned to the infirmary, nursed him each day. Chapin began to make his final plans. He asked William Halpin, a guard with whom he had become friends, if he would do the duty of accompanying his body to Washington, D.C., and handle the burial arrangements. Halpin agreed. In a moment of strength, Chapin wrote one last letter to be given to Lawes upon his death. "As you know, I have been fighting death for nearly a year and now feel I have about reached the limit of my resistance," he wrote. "I grow feeble every day." Old newspaper friends, even old rivals such as Arthur Brisbane of the *Evening Journal*, were quietly ushered in to see him. Father Cashin also came from New York. But by the end of November, Chapin began falling in and out of a coma and could no longer eat.[23]

On the evening of December 13, 1930, Lawes was at Chapin's bedside, as he had been when they first met eleven years earlier.

"Do you need anything, Charlie?" asked Lawes.

"Yes," Chapin replied weakly. "I want to die. I want to get it over with." His request was promptly answered. Finally, after six weeks of illness, Chapin succumbed at 11:45 P.M. The official cause was listed as bronchial pneumonia.

Grief struck, Lawes left the death house and went to meet the reporters who had been keeping a death watch. He told them he had always held Chapin in high regard, though he knew little of his life as a newspaperman. "But in all his life he could not have done as much to alleviate human suffering and help humanity as he has done here in the last twelve years," Lawes said. "While he was physically in prison, he was mentally never in prison."[24]

In his office, Lawes opened Chapin's letter to him. It contained his final instructions. He wished to be buried with his wife at Glenwood. He asked that his sister Marion be notified so as to have the grave dug and the casket met at the train station. "I especially desire that there be no service here or in Washington," wrote Chapin. "I wish the casket to be the least expensive obtainable enclosed in a box never to be opened." His savings were to be applied to the cost of his funeral. Having earned twenty-five cents a day for his work tending the garden, Chapin had $91.57 credited to him on the prison ledgers at the time. The contents of his office, including his prized radio, he left to Halpin. The contents of his cell, he left to Herriot. The garden books, which he so treasured, were to be given to whomever Lawes selected to continue the work. "In conclusion," wrote Chapin, "I thank you and the members of your fine family for much kindness and consideration during my long years in your charge."[25]

From Washington came a telegram from Marion. "Please ship remains to Washington. Will make arrangements for burial here."

His most devoted supporters viewed Chapin's final request to rejoin his wife as proof of his defense twelve years earlier that he had killed Nellie with the intention of taking his own life as well. But even his own *Evening World* remained unconvinced. "His own picture of himself as a superdevoted husband mercifully killing his wife to save her from poverty hardly squared with his known characteristics and habits," said the paper in an editorial two days after Chapin's death. "The kindest explanation of the crime is that money losses caused in him that temporary insanity which covers such a multitude of sins."[26]

Among reporters, stories of Chapin were dusted off again. Even columnist Heywood Broun devoted his Monday installment in the *New York Telegram* to tales of Chapin. "It is a curious trail of fame which will continue," he wrote. "Charles E. Chapin has died in Sing Sing. As long as newspapers exist, reporters will regale one another with Chapin anecdotes. And it may be that a good story is as enduring a monument as any granite."[27]

On December 15, the casket and a funeral arrangement of roses from his own greenhouses left by train for Washington. Chapin would be guarded, for the last time, by Halpin. Gravediggers cut into the hard winter soil on a hill in Glenwood Cemetery, as December winds tossed the remaining fallen leaves of autumn. Only Marion, Frank, and Halpin were at the graveside when Chapin's casket was lowered. Though they had written to each other continuously, it was the first time that Marion and Frank had been with their brother in more than a decade, as he had strictly forbidden them to ever visit him at Sing Sing. They were not even able see him this one last time in keeping with his request that the casket remain closed. There was to be no ceremony. "Just a simple burial," said Marion. "Charley would have wanted that." The gravestone, so carefully chosen by Chapin years earlier, would now be cut with its final inscription. Below his name and above the words, "His wife, Nellie L. Chapin. Died Sept. 16, 1918," would be written the final words of Chapin's story: "Died Dec. 13, 1930."

Epilogue

Less than a week after Chapin's death, New York literary agent George T. Bye received a letter from Eleanor Early, a writer in Boston. The contents intrigued him. "I know a girl who carried on a correspondence with Mr. Chapin in Sing Sing," Early wrote. Would Bye be interested in selling them to a publisher? Maybe they could be called "Letters from a Prison Garden"? Early had selected the right agent. Bye counted many newspapermen among his clients, having been one himself until he opened his agency in 1923, and his specialty was books by people in the news. He immediately replied to Early by telegram. "By all means send on Chapin letters undoubtedly important project."[1]

Chapin had kept all his correspondence under lock and key in his prison office desk, but it all disappeared with his death. Nelson, however, had preserved his letters to her in a safe-deposit box in Wisconsin and now felt compelled to publish them to counter what she saw as an unfair portrayal of Chapin in the press. "In the letters Charles Chapin had written to me," she said, "he had revealed his soul and shown a side which the world never knew." Nelson also believed Chapin would approve. "Dear child," he once said to Nelson when she mentioned the idea of publishing his letters, "if you can find anyone to publish them, or what would be harder—to read them, and it would please you, I hope you do so." After all the hurt Chapin had caused her, Nelson still clung to her charitable vision of him. In the book, and to the press on the day it was be released, she said, "If these letters can make you know, as I did, the other side of a forceful figure, and make you see him as I did, a great and gallant man who even in tragedy never dipped his colors, then I know I have rendered him the last and greatest service in my power."[2]

Within a month, Bye sold the project to Simon and Schuster. Max Schuster still remembered Chapin from his youth when he worked as a copy boy for the *Evening World*. Bye also tried to entice the editor of *Ladies Home Journal*, who had worked as a reporter under Chapin, to do a feature on the letters. The editor declined because he thought the business of Chapin killing his wife might not go over well with his readers. Bye found, too, that Hollywood had only a "lukewarm" interest in the film rights to the letters. Simon and Schuster, however, remained enthusiastic. They advanced $750 to Early and Nelson to compile and edit the letters, and for Early to write a lengthy introduction. The plan to which they agreed was that Nelson's identity would be shielded. The book would appear under the name *The Constance Letters of Charles Chapin*, edited by Eleanor Early and Constance.

The two women worked together rapidly. Early interviewed Nelson at length, and the pair pored over the letters. They completed their work by June 1931. As the publication date neared, the relationship between the two became testy, and Nelson began reconsidering her anonymity. Early was panicked that this might kill the project, so she urgently wrote Bye to enlist him in keeping Nelson to the original plan.

"If she remains a lovely lady of mystery, people will be interested, and do a lot of conjecturing," she wrote. "But if she comes right flat out—225 pounds of her—where is the lovely romance? I believe if Constance is visioned as the frail young girl—beautiful in soul, body, and mind—that the letters conjure, people are going to enjoy them. But do you think they are going to be very thrilled about an affair between a 70-year-old man and a fat, middle-age woman?" Nelson was talked out of it, and the public never learned who she was.[3]

Meanwhile, Cooper also was approaching publishers with her collection of Chapin letters. As Nelson had done, Cooper sought to remain anonymous by titling her collection *The Uncensored Letters of Charles Chapin* and using only "Viola Irene" as her name. Rudolph Field agreed to bring out the slim volume comprising Chapin's letters to Cooper from 1920 and 1921, before prison regulations on mail were tightened. Cooper said she selected that period because Chapin's letters lost their "naturalness" and "spontaneity" after new censorship rules were imposed. In truth, Chapin had quickly circumvented the new rules, and the change in tone had been due more to the turmoil during his editorship of the *Bulletin* and, equally important, Cooper's departure on a windjammer.

In the fall of 1931, the two collections of Chapin's letters appeared in stores. They soon disappeared from the shelves, not from reader demand, but lack of it. It seemed no one was interested in Chapin anymore. "Only the assiduous students of Chapinian will find anything in this volume to repay study," said the *Saturday Review of Literature* in its appraisal of *The Constance Letters of Charles Chapin*. That was charitable. *American Mecury's* review said the letters revealed Chapin as "a shabby vain character."

It was left to the venerable *New York Times*, which had always been charitable toward Chapin, to find some virtue in the letters in its review of both volumes. "The letters, revealing no great literary gift or wealth of imagination, do yet touch the heart," wrote Robert L. Dufus, a Vermonter by birth, recruited to newspaper work by Ida Tarbell. He detoured from his assessment of Chapin's letters to offer one of the man himself. "Charles Chapin is thoroughly human and understandable if one takes his career phase by phase and emotion by emotion. He became desperate because he had thrown away his own money and some that was not his own in wild speculation. Because he was desperate, he decided to kill himself. Because he did not believe his wife could face existence alone, he decided to kill her. Having killed her, he lacked the courage to kill himself. For the murder, he was sent to prison. Because he there had time to think and to grow lonely, he softened. When the friendship of women was offered to him in his womanless prison, he responded eagerly. Let those who are disposed to throw stones ask themselves how well they would have succeeded in keeping their own emotional balance under the circumstances."[4]

Nelson's collection of Chapin's letters became her last known literary accomplishment. After leaving the Federal Reserve Bank in Cleveland, she took a job working for the Boston Society for Psychic Research, an unusual organization that investigated psychic phenomena. Beyond that job, there is no trace of what happened to her. Social Security death records list the death of a Constance Nelson, with the same birth date, in December 1972 in Providence, Rhode Island. As it listed her death under her maiden name, one might presume she never married.

Viola Cooper never married either. After returning from her windjammer journey, she settled in New York and wrote a charming book about her trip, which was a critical success and went through several printings. She also penned a play that was never produced, and co-authored a book about wartime medicine during World War II. Eventually, Cooper became a literary agent. She died in 1951.[5]

Warden Lawes went on to pursue some of his literary interests. In 1932, he published a successful book called *Twenty Thousand Years in Sing Sing*. Warner Brothers made a movie that was based on the book and released at the end of 1932. It starred Spencer Tracy, Bette Davis, and Lyle Talbot. Much of it was filmed at Sing Sing, and Chapin's gardens are visible in the opening scenes. Eight years later, a remake called *Castle on the Hudson* was released. During the 1930s, Lawes became extremely well known. He had a weekly radio program on NBC that ran from 1932 until 1938. In 1937, a play he wrote was staged on Broadway by Brock Pemberton, who produced the Zona Gale play that premiered at Sing Sing. Lawes died in 1947 and is buried at Sleepy Hollow Cemetery in Tarrytown, New York.

Another person who played an important role in Chapin's life also joined the Hollywood set. Winfield Sheehan, Police Commissioner Waldo's assistant, who provided Chapin with the pistol, left his job to become William Fox's personal secretary as the latter was building Fox Pictures into a major Hollywood studio. Eventually, Sheehan became the studio's general manager and a well-known film mogul.

The remarkable team on the *Evening World* rewrite desk, known as the "Big Four," eventually broke up and went their separate ways, especially after both the *World* and the *Evening World* closed in 1931. Lindsay Denison went on to work for the King Features Syndicate, and teamed up with Max Fischel to publish a collection of stories about New York neighborhoods that was widely used in New York public schools. Denison died in 1934.

Martin Green moved on to the *New York Sun,* where he was working when he died in 1939. Chapin's friend Irvin Cobb, who had left the paper in 1912, added the titles "movie actor" and "screenwriter" to his list of accomplishments, and served as master of ceremonies of the 1935 Academy Awards. In 1936, he got his own radio show. He died in 1944 and was buried in Paducah, Kentucky, next to a rough-hewn granite boulder with the inscription "Back Home." Only Barton Currie lived on for many years. He left *Ladies Home Journal* in 1928 and became an author and biographer until his death in 1962.[6]

Over time, public memory of Chapin has faded. Cobb's witty remark about Chapin was eventually dropped from *Bartlett's Familiar Quotations.* Chapin's name still surfaces occasionally, usually attached to an inaccurate legend, or simply in reference to the vanished world of Park Row, where editors were king. The *Evening World* itself has been almost completely forgotten; in fact, few people these days have even seen an afternoon newspaper. Only the morning *World* remains alive in histories. I discovered, though, on a trip across the country, that Junior's memory lingers in an unusual fashion. On the wall of some of the Subway franchise sandwich shops, a full page of the *Evening World* appears in its wallpaper comprising scenes from old New York.[7]

At Sing Sing, some guards remember hearing stories of Chapin, and photographs of the gardens hang in a guard recreational hall. In recent years, inmates have excavated the fountain that was once at the center of the gardens. By its side stand two of the metal arbors on which Chapin's roses grew. During a visit to Sing Sing, I spotted a small rose plant at the base of one of these arbors. I like to think it was one of Chapin's.

Appendix

The following is a list of roses known to have been grown in Chapin's gardens at Sing Sing. In addition, Chapin cultivated dahlias, peonies, tulips, carnations, chrysanthemums, hollyhocks, delphiniums, and hyacinths, among dozens of other plant varieties.

Roses

American Beauty
Anna de Diesbach
Baron de Bonstettin
Baroness Rothschild
Captain Christy
Clio
Frau Karl Druschki

Général Jacqueminot
Hybrid Perpetuals
Magna Charta
Mrs. R. G. Sherman-Crawford
Paul Neyron
Ulrich Brunner

Hybrid Teas

America
Augustus Hartman Betty
Bloomfield Abundance
Chateau de Clos Vougeot
Columbia
Commonwealth
Constance
Crusader

Duchess of Wellington
Francis Scott Key
General MacArthur
George C. Waud
Gruss an Teplitz
Hermosa
K of K Golden Ophelia
Killarney

La Tosca
Lady Alice Stanley
Lady Ursula
Laurent Carle
Los Angeles
Madame Butterfly
Madame Edouard Herriot
Madame Meha Sabatier
Mrs. Aaron Ward
Mrs. Calvin Coolidge

Mrs. W. G. Harding
Ophelia
Pilgrim
Premier
Priscilla
Radiance
Red Radiance
Rose Marie
Souvenir de Claudia Pernet
Sylvia

POLYANTHA

Aennchen Muller
Andrew Lenoble
Baby Tausendschon
Cecile Brunner
Edith Cavell
Glory of Hurst
Jessie
Katherina Zeimet

Maman Turbat
Marechal Foch
Mrs. W. H. Cutbush
Orleans
Red Cap
Tip Top
Triomphe Orleans

CLIMBERS

American Beauty
American Pillar
Bess Lovett
Christine Wright
Dorothy Perkins
Dr. W. Van Fleet
Electra
Evangeline

Excelsa
Gardenia
Hiawatha
Paul's Scarlet Climber
Silver Moon
Snowdrift
Waltham Rambler

RUGOSA

Hugonis

Guide to Notes and Abbreviations

Endnote numbers appear at the end of paragraphs and often include multiple sources, so the reader wishing to identify the source of a particular quotation or fact should note its placement within the paragraph. Also when a series of quotations were taken from a single source, I refrained from creating multiple citations by indicating its extensive use.

Commonplace items such as weather and small anecdotes that provide color but are not significant to the story are not footnoted when they are drawn from the newspapers and other records of the time and can easily be confirmed.

I have not made up any of the conversations that are reproduced here. All dialogue is drawn from remembrances, letters, newspaper accounts, and other sources and is footnoted. Lastly, rest assured that when the figures in this biography gaze, think, ponder, or otherwise take action, I have made such declarations based on their own accounts.

Works and manuscript collections have been identified by the following abbreviations:

Chapin, *Story* Chapin, Charles. *Charles Chapin's Story: Written in Sing Sing Prison.* New York: G.P. Putnam's Sons. 1920.

CC to CN Chapin, Charles. *The Constance Letters of Charles Chapin.* Ed. Eleanor Early. New York: Simon and Schuster, 1931.

CC to VC Chapin, Charles. *The Uncensored Letters of*

Charles Chapin. New York: Rudolph Field, Inc., 1931.

AoNY-A.	Archdiocese of New York Archives, St. Joseph Seminary, Yonkers, N.Y.
P-CU	Joseph Pulitzer papers, Columbia University, New York, N.Y.
P-LC	Joseph Pulitzer papers, Library of Congress, Washington, D.C.
W-CU	*New York World* archival records, Columbia University, New York, N.Y.
LAWES	Papers of Lewis E. Lawes, Lloyd Sealy Library, John Jay College of Criminal Justice, New York, N.Y.
NA-CW	Pension files and Civil War records relating to Earl Chapin, found in the National Archives. Cecelia Ann Chapin, pension claim no. 889,965. War records of Earl Chapin, Co. C 103d U.S.C.V.I., Record Group 15.
Brown	James Oliver Brown literary agency files, Columbia University, New York, N.Y.
FHS-MO	Francis Hurd Stadler Collection, Missouri Historical Society, St. Louis, Mo.

People who are frequently cited have been identified by the following abbreviations:

CC	Charles Chapin
JP	Joseph Pulitzer
CN	Constance Nelson
VC	Viola Cooper

Notes

CHAPTER 1: THE GARDENS

Researching Cobb's fame in the 1920s and 1930s was a reminder of how fleeting fame is. Today he is almost completely forgotten, and only one of his more than sixty books is still in print.

1. See New York newspapers, October 24–30, 1924; "Treasury Fails to Act on Tax Chaos," *New York Times*, 26 October 1924, 1.

2. *Current Opinion*, February 1923, 231–32. The profile of Cobb was headlined "Irvin Cobb, Our Leading Literary Heavyweight." The rumor of being the best-paid writer was also fed by Cobb himself, for obvious beneficial reasons. A few months later, a popular magazine ran a photograph of Cobb in front of his country house with the caption "Irvin Cobb is one of the highest-paid writers of his or any other time." *Good Housekeeping*, February 1925, 42.

3. Irvin S. Cobb, *Exit Laughing* (New York: The Bobbs-Merrill Company, 1941), 226; Alexander Woolcott, foreword to *City Editor* by Stanley Walker (New York: F.A. States Co., 1935), vii.

4. See M. H. Dunlop, *Gilded City: Scandal and Sensation in Turn-of-the-Century New York* (New York: William Morrow, 2000) for an excellent discussion of the significance of city newspapers; Figures taken from Richard Harwood "The Golden Age of Press Diversity," *Washington Post*, 22 July 1994, 23.

5. The Bedford Forrest comparison belongs to Cobb, "The Convict Who Made a Garden on the Road to Hell," *Cosmopolitan*, March 1925, 180; Credit for the marvelous, but certainly apocryphal, headline said to be written by Chapin also goes to Cobb. Cobb, *Exit Laughing*, 140.

6. Cobb, *Exit Laughing*, 119; For the story of Chapin and Pulitzer's son Joe, see Chapter 12; Walker, *City Editor*, 6. This is only one of about

six such tales that show up in various memoirs. Though the quotation was dropped from *Bartlett's Familiar Quotations* in the 1930s, the comment that Cobb made is still found on at least 166 Web-based collections of quotations. See Chapter 12 for the story of the remark he made about Chapin.

7. Cobb, *Exit Laughing*, 119; Walker, *City Editor*, 1, 6.

8. Walker, *City Editor*, 4; Frank O'Malley quoted in Walker, *City Editor*, 6; Donald Henderson Clarke, *Man of the World* (New York: Vanguard Press, 1950), 248.

9. A letter from Cobb to his friend Robert Davis, dated September 17, 1924, written from the Laurentian Club, Lac La Peche, Quebec, Canada. Crabbe Library, Eastern Kentucky University.

10. Cobb, "The Convict Who Made a Garden," 180. Descriptions and dialogue reported in this chapter, as well as comments by Cobb, are drawn from this article unless otherwise indicated.

11. "Makes Prison Yard a Thing of Beauty," *New York Times*, 19 October 1924, 27.

12. *CC to CN*, 22 October 1924, 161.

13. "To be sent up the river" is an American colloquialism that stems from Sing Sing's riverbank location. *Brewer's Dictionary of Phrases and Fables* (New York: Harper & Row Publishers, 1981), 953.

14. *CC to CN*, 28 October 1924, 163; The dialogue reported here and comments made by Cobb are all drawn from Cobb, "The Convict Who Made a Garden," 183.

15. Cobb's story about Sing Sing was "Local Color," published in 1916 in a collection of stories by the same name.

16. *CC to CN*, 28 October 1924, 163.

17. Ibid.

18. *CC to CN*, 12 June 1924, 93, and 15 June 1924, 94.

CHAPTER 2: YOUTH

Census records, local histories, newspapers, and other sources confirm and clarify Chapin's remembrances of his youth and fill in the many parts of the early past he never told. At times, the record of events did not match Chapin's own account. In all such cases, I was, however, able to find an explanation for the discrepancy. For instance, Chapin believed he visited Wilbur Story in 1875. It was more likely the visit occurred in late 1874. That Chapin made this kind of mistake is not surprising considering he was in his sixties when he wrote the account of his life and had no written record to consult.

Two key pieces of documentary evidence were crucial in being able to reconstruct Chapin's youth. The first was a massive pension file in the National Archives. Contained in it was considerable information about the many moves that the family made while Chapin was young. It also permitted me to eventually identify the "western town" in which Chapin first caught the newspaper bug. The second remarkable find was preserved copies of a newspaper that he published as a teenager. The fact that these papers still exist is a testament to the pack-rat nature of the United States and the wonders of the World Wide Web. It was through the latter that I discovered the American Private Press Association Library and the existence of four copies of *Our Compliments*.

1. Though I searched through birth records, examined his death certificate, and reviewed court and prison records, Chapin's middle name remains a mystery. At first I thought it might be Earl, the name of his father. However, in his father's will I found that Chapin's brother's middle name was Earl. Excitedly, I believed that at long last the will would disclose Chapin's middle name. Sadly, he was listed again as "Charles E. Chapin."

2. Information on Chapin's family history is drawn from a variety of sources found in the Oneida Public Library, the Madison County Historical Society, Earl Chapin's Civil War Pension files in the National Archives, and from a lineage chart by Deanne Driscoll; *Biographical Review: The Leading Citizens of Madison County (New York)* (Boston: Biographical Review Publishing Co.), 1894, 96; Russell Sage, of course, would later become a famous American financier. Paul Sarnoff, *Russell Sage: The Money King* (New York: Ivan Obolensky, Inc., 1965), 15.

3. Mrs. Whitney Luna M. Hammond, *History of Madison County, State of New York* (Syracuse, N.Y.: Truair, Smith & Co., Book and Job Printers, 1872), 524.

4. Hammond, *History*, 525; "Death of Samuel Chapin," *Oneida Dispatch*, 7 April 1903, 1; Advertisement for S. Chapin & Son, *Oneida Sachem*, 21 October 1858, 3.

5. Affidavit of Aaron E. Yale, 7 March 1908, *NA-CW*.

6. *Oneida Dispatch*, 25 September 1858, and 8 October 1858; Samuel Eliot Morrison, *The Oxford History of the American People* (New York: Oxford University Press, 1965), 595.

7. Morrison, *Oxford History*, 611; George Ticknor and Sidney George Fisher quoted in James M. McPherson, *For Causes & Comrade: Why Men Fought in the Civil War* (New York: Oxford University Press, 1997), 16; *History of Oneida* (Oneida, N.Y.: Oneida Free Press, 1880), 42. Typed manuscript in the Oneida Public Library local history collection.

8. The burning of the Chapins' house is cited in several affidavits contained in the Cecelia Ann Chapin pension files, *NA-CW*; Isabel Bracy, *The 157th New York Volunteer (Infantry) Regiment 1862–1865, Madison and Cortland Counties, New York* (Interlaken, N.Y.: Heart of the Lakes Publishing, 1991), 45–46.

9. Enlistment and discharge records for Earl Chapin, Civil War, *NA-CW*.

10. Frank Ziegler Glick, *They Came to Smoky Hill: History of Three Generations* (Manhattan, Kan.: Sunflower University Press, 1986), 1. Census records for Geary County, Kansas, 1870; The growth of Junction City is documented in John B. Jeffries, "An Early History of Junction City, Kansas: The First Generation" (master's thesis, Kansas State University, 1963). "By the early 1870s, Junction City was passing from its role of frontier village to that of a settled city, with most of the cultural advantages found in other cities of like size," p. 137; and in Susan Lloyd Franzen, *Behind the Facade of Fort Riley's Hometown: The Inside Story of Junction City, Kansas* (Ames, Iowa: Pivot Press, 1998). Chapin seems to have liked school. Late in his life, he still had fond remembrances of school pranks and of a pair of trousers with velvet piping in the outside seam, worn by a school chum. *CC to VC*, January 1921, 50–51.

11. Information regarding the prosperity of Atchison and how it might have drawn someone like Earl Chapin taken from interview with Chris Taylor, executive director of the Atchison Historical Society, 8 July 2002. The advertisement for Chapin's store ran on page 4 of issues of the *Daily Champion* beginning 9 November 1872.

12. Chapin, *Sing Sing Bulletin*, 21, no. 8, February 1920, 10.

13. Sheffield Ingalls, *History of Atchison County* (Lawrence, Kan.: Standard Publishing Co., 1916), 219; Chapin, *Story*, 2.

14. Chapin recalled the telegraph office as being in the same building at the *Daily Champion,* but records of the time show that the two existing telegraph companies were both a block away. There was, however, certainly considerable need on their part for a messenger boy. Together the Western Union and Great Western telegraph companies received 18,000 telegrams in Atchison in 1872, according to the 1872–73 city directory; Thomas W. Herringshaw, *Prominent Men and Women of the Day* (A. S. B. Gehman & Co., 1888); Description of the house is drawn from Burton J. Williams, *Senator John James Ingalls: Kansas Iridescent Republican* (Lawrence, Kan.: University Press of Kansas, 1972), 59–60; footnote 24, 172; 67.

15. Chapin, *Story*, 5–6.

16. Chapin, *Story*, 8.

17. His reading list can be found in Chapin, *Story*, 9. His love of *Can-*

dide is often mentioned in his correspondence late in life. Although his reading list is remarkable, there is little doubt that he did indeed read many of the works he cites. An examination of the literary devices he uses in his journalism confirms his claim.

18. See Fred Fedler, *Lessons From the Past: Journalists' Lives and Work, 1850–1905* (Prospect Heights, Ill.: Waveland Press, Inc., 2000), 1. This drive for self-improvement permeated antebellum nineteenth-century life, according to Jo Radner, an American Antiquarian Society Mellon Postdoctoral Fellow who is researching a book on the creation and performance of handwritten literary "newspapers" in nineteenth-century New England. Radner, letter to author, 11 November 2002.

19. Chapin, *Story*, 11.

20. Chapin, *Story*, 12.

21. Chapin, *Story*, 17–18; Newspapers frequently reprinted little bright items from other papers as fillers, crediting the paper from which it was taken. I undertook a search for the article but failed to locate a copy. Nonetheless, there is no reason to doubt Chapin's recollection, as the event was a considerable thrill for him. "Nothing I ever did afterward in the field of journalism brought me so much happiness," he said. The pattern of illness in Chapin's adult life, and his own comments about his "tubercular throat," may be an indication that he contracted tuberculosis. It seems unlikely, however, especially as it did not resurface as a health problem when he was old and imprisoned. More likely was that the condition of his health was related to the state of his nerves and that he, as did many others, referred to his throat problems as "tubercular." See Sheila M. Rothman, *Living in the Shadow of Death* (New York: Basic Books, 1994.)

22. Chapin, *Story*, 19.

23. *CC to CN*, 30 March 1924, 52.

24. Chapin, *Story*, 20–22; Chapin, *Sing Sing Bulletin* 21, no. 9, March 1920, 10.

25. In 1992, the Smithsonian Institute National Museum of American History mounted an exhibit called "The Boy and His Press" that told the story of this nineteenth-century fad that was paralleled in the twentieth century by the Ham Radio. Information about printing presses was drawn from the exhibit's catalog. The quotation from the Kelsey catalog is drawn from Elizabeth Harris, *The Boy and His Press*, (Washington: Smithsonian Institute, 1992), 4; Chapin, *Story*, 23–24.

26. Advertisement in *Our Compliments*, May 1875, 7; Chapin's role in this movement merited a mention in Truman Joseph Spencer, *The History of Amateur Journalism* (New York: The Fossils, Inc., 1957), 172. This citation led me to obtain actual copies of *Our Compliments* that are

among the collection of The American Private Press Association Library, Stayton, Oregon.

27. Advertisement in *Our Compliments*, May 1875, 5; *Our Compliments*, August 1875, 7; While I can't prove that the serial was written by Chapin, it seems unlikely that he could obtain the services of a published author. Further, the style has some similarities to his later writings, which become much easier to identify. Fascinatingly, there are some strong parallels between his career as a teenage editor and his career as a prison editor. Chapin, *Story*, 24.

28. Chapin "Attention Amateurs!" *Our Compliments*, November 1875, 3; Spencer, *History of Amateur Journalism*, 172; See also A. C. Alft, *Elgin: An American History* (Elgin, Ill.: Crossroads Communications, 1984).

CHAPTER 3: TRAVELING THESPIAN

When I first learned of Chapin's acting career from his memoirs, I feared that he exaggerated and that I would find little to corroborate his account. Two finds, however, substantiated his memory. First, I discovered that the library in Deadwood, South Dakota, indexed many of the newspapers from the time when Chapin claimed to have acted in the mining town. Sure enough, his comings and goings, as well as his performances, were duly noted in the *Black Hills Daily Times*. Second, I ran across the work of a Kansas historian who had written about the Lord acting troupe. Using his work, I was able to locate numerous articles in Kansas newspapers that contained information about Chapin the actor.

Material about Chapin's father's desertion of his family is drawn from the set of pension records in the National Archives cited in Chapter 2 Notes. Following Earl's death in 1906, his legal widow Cecelia applied for a survivor's pension. The pension bureau appointed several special examiners, who took depositions from the family and friends. These documents tell a fascinating tale about nineteenth-century morality, government procedures, and more relevant to the task at hand, Chapin's family.

1. Chapin, *Story*, 25; Chapin identifies his friend only as "Rodney." I was able to obtain his last name by comparing the playbill for *Lemons*, which listed two actors with the first initial of "R" and the list of the company when it was in Dodge City; Chapin, *Story*, 26; William C. Young, ed., *Famous Actors and Actresses on the American Stage: Documents of American Theater History*, vol. 1 (New York: R. R. Bowker Company, 1975), 53; Donald Mullin, ed., *Victorian Actors and Actresses in Review: A*

Dictionary of Contemporary Views of Representative British and American Actors and Actresses, 1837–1901 (Westport, Conn.: Greenwood, 1983), 41–43.

2. Information on Louis H. Yarwood drawn from Hazel Belle Perry, "Old Elgin Tales," *Courier News*, 13 August 1969, and David Siegenthaler, Elgin Area Historical Society, letter to author, 8 August 2002; Chapin, *Story*, 26.

3. Quoted in Ray Ginger's *Age of Excess: The United States from 1877 to 1914* (New York: Macmillan, 1965), 132; Samuel Eliot Morrison, *The Oxford History of the American People* (New York: Oxford University Press, 1965), 780–81; Donald Mullin, introduction to *Victorian Actors and Actresses in Review*, xxi; George C. D. Odell, *Annals of the New York Stage*, vol. 9 (1937; reprint, New York: AMS Press, 1970), 431; The drama critic of the Leavenworth *Daily Commercial* commented on Louie's hair and voice. Her hair, he said, "rivaled Godiva's rippled ringlet to her knee." Quoted in James C. Malin, "James A. and Louie Lord: Theatrical Team—Their Personal Story, 1869–1889," *Kansas Historical Quarterly* 22, no. 3, Autumn 1956, 251; Chapin, *Story*, 27.

4. *Ford County Globe*, 28 May 1878, reported the troupe ended its nine-month-two-week road trip in late May; Donald Mullin, introduction to *Victorian Actors and Actresses in Review*, xxii–xxv.

5. Chapin, *Story*, 27–28; Quoted in Malin, "James A. and Louie Lord," 246.

6. Chapin, *Story*, 29; Topeka information taken from Malin, "James A. and Louie Lord," 250; "Lord's Troupe," *Hays Sentinel*, 1 February 1878, 3; Glen Hughes, *A History of the American Theatre 1700–1950* (London: Samuel French, 1951), 300–302; Chapin, *Story*, 29.

7. "Lord's Dramatic Company," *Junction City Union*, 23 March 1878, 5; "The Theater," *Junction City Union*, 29 November 1878, 5.

8. *Dodge City Times*, 19 January 1878, 25 May 1878, and 1 June 1878; *Ford County Globe*, 28 May 1878; Eddie Foy, *Clowning Through Life* (New York: E. P. Dutton & Co., 1928), 107–8; Armond Field, *Eddie Foy: A Biography of the Early Popular Stage Comedian* (Jefferson, N.C.: McFarland & Company, 1999), 30–31. Chapin never mentioned the incident in his autobiography. He did, however, tell Cobb about it. "He told me also about the time in Tombstone—or perhaps it was in Dodge City?—when he took potshots at another itinerant trouper, one Edward Fitzgerald, subsequently called Eddie Foy. They were playing in rival repertoire companies and pique between them arose over a frail sister of the community." Cobb, *Exit Laughing*, 140. Foy and Chapin met one more time, in the early 1900s when they crossed paths at Jack's restaurant in New York. "His hair had turned white, but I recognized him

immediately, and so he did me," said Foy. "We hesitated a moment and then stopped and shook hands." Foy, *Clowning Through Life*, 108.

9. Malin, "James A. and Louise Lord," 247, 261–62; "The Fire, and All About It," *Hays Sentinel*, 11 January 1879, 3.

10. Chapin, *Story*, 35–36.

11. Chapin, *Story*, 36; Information concerning the Thornton Combination is drawn from the *Brookfield Gazette*, 30 October 1879, and 6 November 1879.

12. Chapin, *Story*, 34–37; Information drawn from marriage certificate, which listed Nellie by her stage name of "Nellie Thorn," which was misspelled. Copy of certificate on file at Brookfield Public Library, Brookfield, Mo.

13. *Elgin Daily News*, 8 November 1879, carried a small item about the wedding because his family lived there. Either Chapin sent the paper a letter, or his family shared one with the editors because the item included "Charlie writes that he is now a leading man in the dramatic company with which he travels"; *The Brookfield Gazette* also ran an item. "On the evening before their last performance Mr. Chas. Chapin and Miss Nellie Thorne went around to Rev. Mr. Filey's and were united in wedlock. Rumor has it that—but confound 'Rumor,' anyway." *The Brookfield Gazette*, 13 November 1879; Chapin, *Story*, 38.

14. Deposition of Fannie Chapin Skinner, 16 December 1908, 5, *NA-CW*. In her deposition, Cecelia Chapin said that she "heard indirectly of him only through the Chapin family." (Deposition of Cecelia Ann Chapin, 29 August 1908, 6). There is no evidence that either Fannie or Charles told Cecelia what they learned about their father until 1906; Fannie Chapin Skinner deposition, 16 December 1908, 5; Cecelia Ann Chapin deposition, 29 August 1908, 6. "It, Sir, has been a mystery to our family," said Frank E. Chapin in his deposition when asked why his father left home (Deposition of Frank E. Chapin, 31 August 1908, 2). Census records taken in June of 1880 show Cecelia living in Elgin with Charles, Fannie, Fred, and four boarders who worked at the watch factory, and Earl living in a hotel in Springfield.

15. Census records 1900; 1880 Census records for Illinois also list a Mary McCoy as a servant living close to Springfield; Fannie Chapin Skinner deposition; *The Hoyes City Directory 1888–1889* for Springfield, Missouri, lists Earl Chapin employed as an engraver with J. G. Willeke, a jeweler on Public Square in Springfield.

16. Nellie Thorne was a stage name also used later by a Broadway actress. Lawrence Stine, "A History of Theatre and Theatrical Activities in Deadwood, South Dakota, 1876–90" (Ph.D. diss., State University of Iowa, 1962), 2. A reporter for the *Sidney Telegram* (Sidney, Nebraska),

22 May 1877, quoted in Stine, "A History of Theatre," 18; *Black Hills Daily Times*, 14 January 1879.

17. Stine, "A History of Theatre," 153; "The New Theatre," *Black Hills Daily Times*, 16 November 1880, 4.

18. "Personal News," *Black Hills Daily Times*, 16 November 1880, 4.

19. The play is remembered today only for the line "Life's too short for chess."

20. "Nye's Opera House," *Black Hills Daily Times*, 21 November 1880, 4.

21. Chapin, *Story*, 31. For a long time I doubted the veracity of this tale, especially as Calamity Jane's own biography puts her elsewhere at the time. In fact, I developed a theory that he had based it on an item about Calamity Jane that appeared in the *Black Hills Daily Times* while he was in Deadwood and had adopted the story as his own. But I then discovered that Calamity Jane was actually back in Deadwood on the exact dates that Chapin recalled. So in the end I have included Chapin's tale of the evening.

22. "Sick in her rooms in Avenue House," *Black Hills Daily Times*, 14 December 1880, 4.

23. *Black Hills Daily Times*, 22 April 1881, 4.

24. Chapin, *Story*, 33; "Nye's Opera House," *Black Hills Daily Times*, 15 July 1881, 4.

25. "Personal News," *Black Hills Daily Times*, 28 July 1881, 4; Chapin, *Story*, 34.

26. Chapin, *Story*, 38–39.

CHAPTER 4: AT LAST A REPORTER!

In this chapter, Chapin completes his transition to the fourth estate. I was struck in researching this transformation by the remark of another biographer. "Actors, like newspapermen, lived on the borderline of polite society," wrote Arthur Lubow in his biography of Richard Harding Davis.

The account of this chapter's main event, the Willson murders, was based mostly on Chapin's reporting rather than his memoir. Writing forty years after the events, he gives himself a far more important role than the events warranted.

Note: As the modern headline had not come into widespread use yet, many of Chapin's stories carried the same heading. The date thus becomes the more important part of the identifying notes below.

1. Chapin, *Sing Sing Bulletin*, 21, no. 9, March 1920, 11; I could not establish the exact date when Chapin began his reporting career in Chicago. From all evidence, it is most likely he arrived in the late summer or early fall of 1881. Chicago newspapers, which were growing at an extraordinary rate, would continue to be a source of employment for would-be journalists until the end of the decade. In 1886, a column in the *Journalist* called "Scraps from Chicago" reported "a great dearth of good newspaper men here. Lots of openings." Vol. 3, no. 10, 29 May 1865, 5. At the same time, not everyone who wanted a newspaper job got one easily. Theodore Dreiser, for instance, had quite a struggle. Why Chapin, with little reporting experience, succeeded in landing a job on the best paper in town is not known. Chapin, *Story*, 40.

2. Walker, *City Editor*, 15; William Salisbury, *The Career of a Journalist* (New York: B. W. Dodge & Co., 1908), 141.

3. Theodore Dreiser, *Newspaper Days: An Autobiography*, T. D. Nostwich, ed. (Santa Rosa, Calif.: Black Sparrow Press, 2000), 21. Fascinatingly, Chapin and Dreiser's lives continued to intersect for years. Dreiser moved next to St. Louis and left just as Chapin arrived. Then Dreiser worked for the *New York World* while Chapin was away. They had many reporter and writer friends in common, certainly knew of each other, and perhaps even met on occasion. The only meeting on record, however, was in 1925 when Chapin was in prison.

4. "Chicago Studies: No.1 The Tribune," *Journalist* 8, no. 5, 20 October 1888, 4.

5. Dreiser, *Newspaper Days*, 44.

6. *CC to CN*, 22 October 1924, 160; Chapin's fondness for Hall was evident even at the end of his life. While writing his memoirs in prison, Chapin said the following about Hall: "When I last heard of him he had been retired on a pension, after almost a half-century in the *Tribune* office. His wife had been horribly killed in a motor boat explosion, his only daughter married and moved away and he was alone with his books and his memory. I know but one man more lonely than he is. Both of us have lived too long." Chapin, *Story*, 53–54; The description of Hall is based on a description found in "Chicago Studies: No.1 The Tribune," *Journalist* 8, no. 5, 20 October 1888, 4, as well as Chapin's own account in *Story*, 52;

7. Chapin, *Story*, 55; Chapin, *Story*, 40.

8. Chapin, *Story*, 41.

9. Chapin, *Story*, 40; 111–12.

10. *Chicago Tribune*, 14 February 1884, 3. The account of the murder that follows, unless otherwise cited, is taken from the *Chicago Tribune*, Chapin's memoirs, and other Chicago newspapers.

11. See Russell A. Mann, "Investigative Journalism in the Gilded Age: A Study of the Detective Journalism of Melville E. Stone and the Chicago Morning News, 1881–1888" (Ph.D. diss., Southern Illinois University, 1977), 56–72; James Weber Linn, *James Keeley: Newspaperman* (Indianapolis: Bobbs-Merrill Co., 1937), 40.

12. "One of the buttons was picked up by a *Tribune* reporter and handed to the Coroner three hours before the detectives arrived at the scene of the murder." Chapin, "Thou Art the Man, *Chicago Tribune*, 29 February 1884, 7. In his memoirs, Chapin wrote that he cautioned the coroner to take good care of the button because it might be an important clue. (*Story*, 84). It seems unlikely, however, that an inexperienced reporter would be telling an official how to do his job—though I wouldn't put it past Chapin to do so.

13. See Norman Howard Sims, "The Chicago Style of Journalism" (Ph.D. diss., University of Illinois at Urbana-Champaign, 1979). The story actually ran on page 3. The actual front page of the *Tribune* in that era was covered with advertisements, so it is not entirely inaccurate to call it a "front-page story." *Chicago Tribune*, 14 February 1884, 3; Chapin, "Winnetka's Horror," *Chicago Tribune*, 14 February 1884, 3.

14. Chapin identifies her as a schoolteacher in his memoir (86–87). Her profession is not identified in his newspaper articles; Chapin, "Winnetka's Horror," *Chicago Tribune*, 14 February 1884, 3.

15. Chapin, *Story*, 84.

16. Chapin, "The Winnetka Murders," *Chicago Tribune*, 15 February 1884, 2; Chapin, "Winnetka's Murders," *Chicago Tribune*, 17 February 1884, 3.

17. Chapin, "Winnetka's Butcher," *Chicago Tribune*, 23 February 1884, 2; Chapin, *Story*, 90.

18. Chapin, "Winnetka's Murders," *Chicago Tribune*, 17 February 1884, 3.

19. Chapin, "The Butcher," *Chicago Tribune*, 24 February 1884, 5.

20. Chapin, "The Man in Jail," *Chicago Tribune*, 25 February 1884, 8; Chapin, "Prisoner McKeague," *Chicago Tribune*, 26 February 1884, 2.

21. Chapin, "Thou Art the Man!" *Chicago Tribune*, 29 February 1884, 7. Over time, Chapin mistakenly remembered this article as the one in which he revealed key facts he uncovered on his own. He did not, however, have the luxury of reading it again when he penned his memoirs.

22. Chapin, "The Willson Murders," *Chicago Tribune*, 6 May 1884, 6; Chapin, "Thou Art the Man!" *Chicago Tribune*, 29 February 1884, 7.

23. Brazilian pebbles are spectacles made from a transparent, colorless rock crystal. Chapin, "Neal M'Keague," *Chicago Tribune*, 13 May 1884, 9; Chapin, "Neal M'Keague," *Chicago Tribune*, 14 May 1884, 10.

24. Chapin, "Neal M'Keague," *Chicago Tribune*, 16 May 1884, 12.

25. Chapin, "Neal M'Keague," *Chicago Tribune*, 22 May 1884, 10; Chapin, "Neal M'Keague," *Chicago Tribune*, 23 May 1884, 9. In almost every story, Chapin commented on the number of women in attendance.

26. Chapin, "Neal M'Keague," *Chicago Tribune*, 29 May 1884, 7. Chapin reported in his autobiography with pleasure that McKeague was eventually killed in a barroom brawl.

27. Lloyd Wendt, *Chicago Tribune: The Rise of a Great American Newspaper* (Chicago: Rand McNally, 1979), 278; Comparison to Bennett and the famous editorial are contained in John Tebbel, *The Compact History of the American Newspaper* (New York: Hawthorn Books, Inc., 1969), 130.

28. Chapin, *Story*, 48–49.

29. See Paul Avrich, *The Haymarket Tragedy* (Princeton, N.J.: Princeton University Press, 1984); Henry David, *The History of the Haymarket Affair: A Study in the American Social-Revolutionary and Labor Movements*, 2d ed. (New York: Russell & Russell, 1958).

30. See Edward Chiasson Jr., *The Press on Trial: Crimes and Trials as Media Events* (Westport, Conn.: Greenwood Press, 1997); Chapin described his role as that of being "active in the rounding up of the leaders." Chapin, *Story*, 104; Chapin et al., "Down with Anarchy," *Chicago Tribune*, 7 May 1886, 2.

31. Another reporter from the *Stats-Zeitung* may have accompanied them. In his trial testimony, Hume described the interview he and Chapin conducted, but he was not sure if a third reporter came with them. *Illinois vs. August Spies et al.* trial transcript no. 1. Testimony of Hugh Hume, 28 July 1886, vol. K, 375–404.

32. Chapin, "Their Records," *Chicago Tribune*, 6 May 1886, 1.

CHAPTER 5: MARINE REPORTER

Sifting fact from fiction in this chapter was arduous. The McGarigle story has become part of Chicago lore, and participants have exaggerated their role in it over the ensuing years. Unquestionably, Chapin gained the upper hand in the race to cover the escape. However, his memory of events often did not coincide with the contemporary accounts he published in the *Tribune*. Nor, for that matter, did many other memoirs. What I have done is forgive him for his excesses and share them with the reader in the footnotes. The chronicle I present is as close to the facts as one can get more than a century later. In some cases, where I felt Chapin was honest but I could not find a second source to confirm this fact, I presented it as his version of the events.

1. Being a marine reporter remained an important part of Chapin's life. Thirty years later, in New York, he continued to attend dinners of marine reporters. The city directory lists the Chapins at a new address each year. While visiting one of the addresses, I learned from the current owners that they discovered during renovations that it had once served as a boarding house. I then compared the addresses for Chapin with listings for boarding houses and concluded that the Chapins' lifelong habit of living in temporary quarters, such as hotels, was developed early in their married life.

2. The history of Chicago as a port city is detailed in David M. Young, *Chicago Maritime: An Illustrated History* (DeKalb, Ill.: Northern Illinois University Press, 2001).

3. "Getting at the Truth," *Chicago Tribune*, 28 July 1887, 1; Chapin, *Story*, 63–64.

4. Chapin, "A Canadian Exile," *Chicago Tribune*, 31 January 1889, 1.

5. Chapin, "Getting at the Truth," *Chicago Tribune*, 28 July 1887, 1.

6. Chapin, *Story*, 65. *Boodle*, and thus *boodler*, were nineteenth-century terms that have since fallen out of favor. *Boodle* was the popular word for bribe or other illicit payments, and the behavior of Chicago public officials helped put the word in the dictionary. See Richard Lindberg, *Chicago by Gaslight: A History of Chicago's Netherworld, 1880–1920* (Chicago: Academy Chicago Publishers, 1996), 47–69; Chapin, *Story*, 66.

7. Russell A. Mann, "Investigative Journalism in the Gilded Age: A Study of the Detective Journalism of Melville E. Stone and the *Chicago Morning News*, 1881–1888" (Ph.D. diss., Southern Illinois University, 1977), 156; Chapin, "The Detectives Were Badly Fooled," *Chicago Tribune*, 29 July 1887, 1.

8. Chapin, *Story*, 69–70.

9. "A Doubt as to Her Real Whereabouts," *Chicago Tribune*, 31 July 1887, 1.

10. Chapin, "Just Over the Line," *Chicago Tribune*, 1 August 1887, 1. Unless otherwise indicated, subsequent quotations about this episode also are taken from this article. During the last twenty-five years of the nineteenth century, shippers began to use schooners as barges, and towed them from port to port rather than sailing them. In some cases, even old schooners were de-masted. So, the sight of three or four schooners in tow was not unusual. Young, *Chicago Maritime*, 76–77.

11. Chapin, *Story*, 75.

12. Melville E. Stone, *Fifty Years a Journalist* (Garden City, N.Y.: Doubleday, Page and Company, 1921), 164–65.

13. Chapin, *Story*, 75.

14. Chapin wrote about the launch in the *Chicago Tribune* on August 17, 1886. Many of the details about the *Vernon* and the circumstances of her demise are drawn from an excellent two-part article published by the Wisconsin Underwater Archeology Association. Richard Boyd, "The Dark Voyage of the Propeller *Vernon*," *Wisconsin's Underwater Heritage* 10, no. 2, 1, 7–11, and no. 3, 1, 7–11, June and September 2000.

15. Boyd, "Dark Voyage," 9.

16. Chapin, *Story*, 79.

17. Chapin, "The Vernon's Survivor," *Chicago Tribune*, 3 November 1887, 1. Unless otherwise indicated, all subsequent quotations concerning Stone's story are taken from this article.

18. Chapin, *Story*, 80; Chapin had several facts mixed up in his re-membrance of the events, but those have been corrected by the contemporary record.

CHAPTER 6: DEATH WATCH

By an accident of fate, the young Chapin portrayed in this chapter may have penned his most often-quoted words. Because the use of bylines was still a number of years away, historians by the droves have quoted Chapin's account of the Haymarket executions without citing him by name. Virtually all accounts of the hanging refer to the descriptions, chronology, and details that Chapin published in the *Tribune* on November 12, 1887.

1. Chapin, *Story*, 104; Joseph Pulitzer telegram to Cook County Sheriff Canute Matson, 7 November 1887. Chicago Historical Society; In fact, several newspapers, such as the *New York Times*, reserved the entire front page of Saturday's edition for their correspondent's account of the coming event. The ensuing publicity about the execution helped spawn the international holiday commemorating the Haymarket martyrs, known as May Day.

2. *The Accused, the accusers: the famous speeches of the eight Chicago anarchists in court when asked if they had anything to say why sentence should not be passed upon them. On October 7th, 8th and 9th, 1886* (Chicago: Socialistic Publishing Society, 1886[?]), 42; Letter reprinted widely in Chicago newspapers. *Chicago Tribune*, 11 November 1887, 1.

3. Unless otherwise indicated, this and all subsequent quotations re-

garding Lingg's death in this chapter attributed to Chapin are taken from his article "Lingg's Fearful Death," *The Chicago Tribune*, 11 November 1887, 1–2.

4. Very few reporters were inside the jail at this time, and Chapin remembers being "one of the first to reach the cell of Louis Ling [sic], when he cheated the hangman by blowing off his head with a dynamite cartridge, exploding the cartridge between his teeth." Chapin, *Story*, 104. According to historian Henry David, Oscar Neebe, one of the convicted Haymarket martyrs sentenced to prison, later claimed that on the morning of Lingg's death, a stranger was seen near his cell. Upon Neebe's release from prison, he searched vainly for the man. Henry David, *The History of the Haymarket Affair: A Study in the American Social-Revolutionary and Labor Movements*, 2d ed. (New York: Russell & Russell, 1958), xi. The mystery man may have been Lingg's friend Dyer Lum, according to Paul Avrich, who wrote the most definitive history of the event. Paul Avrich, *The Haymarket Tragedy* (Princeton, N.J.: Princeton University Press, 1984), 376–77. None of this, of course, was known at the time Chapin was reporting the suicide.

5. Chapin, "Dropped to Eternity," *Chicago Tribune*, 12 November 1887, 1. Chapin claimed in his autobiography that he covered the execution. A careful reading of the account shows it to be unquestionably authored by him. All subsequent quotations regarding the execution are drawn from this account unless otherwise credited. For information on systems of identifying texts, see Don Foster, *Author Unknown: On the Trail of Anonymous* (New York: Henry Holt, 2000).

6. The unattributed quotation is drawn from "The Men on the Scaffold: How Their Appearance Impressed Different Reporters" *Chicago Tribune*, 12 November 1887, 1.

7. Chapin, *Story*, 105.

8. Chapin, "Dropped to Eternity," 1; Chapin, *Story*, 106.

9. Chapin, *Story*, 107–8.

10. Chapin, *Story*, 98.

11. The Chicago & St. Louis Railroad Company was built with cash from a syndicate put together by these men. Cummings, of Chicago, was frequently interviewed by reporters; Chapin, *Story*, 44–45; Howard is listed as a member of the Union League Club, as of 1884 onward, in the club annuals on file at the New-York Historical Society. An account of Brown, Howard & Co.'s seven-million-dollar contract to build a 13.5-mile section of the aqueduct may be found in the *New York Times*, 27 September 1888, 8. Chapin, in his memoir, said of Thomas's remark: "From what I learned afterwards I am inclined to think he meant it." Chapin, *Story*, 45.

12. David M. Young, *Chicago Maritime: An Illustrated History* (De-Kalb, Ill.: Northern Illinois University Press, 2001), 77–78; "An American Christmas: Decade by Decade" an exhibit maintained by the Herbert Hoover Museum, West Branch, Iowa.

13. Chapin, "Mrs. Macaulley's Crime," *Chicago Tribune*, 25 December 1887, 1.

14. Chapin, *Story*, 115.

15. Chapin, *Story*, 114.

16. The account of the crime in this and subsequent paragraphs is drawn from Chapin, "Mrs. Macaulley's Crime," unless otherwise cited.

17. Chapin, "Mrs. Macaulley's Crime"; Chapin, *Story*, 116.

Chapter 7: At the Editor's Desk

From the start, Chapin's Utah trip was a puzzle. Chapin mentioned it as an aside in his autobiography, but it seemed out of character that he would have done such a thing. However, as so many of his stories turned out, the records corroborated the events he listed. Though I failed to find anything that specifically connected him to being in Utah at that time, he could have only known of the events he claimed to have witnessed by having actually been there. I was left to conclude this was one more odd, but true, episode in his life.

1. Henry M. Hunt, "Chicago," *Journalist* 6, no. 7, 5 November 1887, 4. Hunt and Chapin were quite alike in some ways. They were both in their thirties and both consummate newspapermen. Like Chapin, Hunt was mostly self-educated, in his instance by candlelight as an errand boy in a small newspaper in his native England. And, also like Chapin, Hunt had taken a detour—in his case into radical European politics—before becoming a Chicago reporter. Stanley Waterloo, "Henry M. Hunt" *Journalist* 8, no. 22, 16 February 1888, 2; Chapin, *Story*, 127–28; Chapin, "Fighting a Fierce Fire," *Chicago Tribune*, 8 January 1888, 1.

2. Fascinatingly, Chapin titled the chapter of his memoir about this episode, "City Editor at Twenty-Five." There is no question, however, that he was twenty-nine at the time. I have never figured out why he did that. Chapin, *Story*, 128.

3. "The corps of reporters is also a large one," observed the *Journalist*, "and many of them are doubtless anxious regarding what the immediate future may bring forth," said Hunt, "Chicago," *Journalist* 6, no. 7, 5 November 1887, 4; Chapin, *Story*, 129. Chapin certainly held this view

late in life at the *Evening World* when he contemplated his future with no pension, no savings, and worse, no newsroom.

4. A hotel reporter was a newspaperman whose beat was hotels, keeping track of who came and went and looking for interviews with the noted guests. Chapin never disputed his propensity to fire reporters, but the figure of 100 may be an exaggeration. It was, nonetheless, a high number of many dozen. Chapin, *Story*, 132–33; The dismissal of Scott, along with some details, such as his beat, appeared in the *Journalist* 6, no. 18, 21 January 1888, 4.

5. Chapin, *Story*, 132. Neither of the two biographies of Dunne mentions Chapin. Instead, they attribute the hire to West. Chapin's account is, however, substantially confirmed in the *Journalist*. Equally important, when Chapin later quits the *Times*, Dunne leaves with him and follows him to the *Tribune*, which suggests Dunne was loyal to Chapin rather than to West. *Journalist* 8, no. 16, 5 January 1889, 6.

6. John Tebbel, *The Compact History of the American Newspaper* (New York: Hawthorn Books, Inc., 1969), 156–57.

7. Chapin, *Story*, 133; The articles, said Cusak, were written "at the request of the editor of the *Chicago Times*." Nell Nelson, *The White Slave Girls of Chicago* (Chicago: Barkley Publishing, 1888), i. Brooke Kroeger, *Nellie Bly: Daredevil, Reporter, Feminist* (New York: Times Books, 1994), 120.

8. Nell Nelson, "City Slave Girls," *Chicago Times*, 30 July 1888, 1; Chapin's editing is so evident in the first paragraphs that it almost seems like his prose. The iron mask metaphor and the cadence of the second paragraph are typical of his work as a newspaper writer.

9. *Chicago Times*, 31 July 1888, 6; *Chicago Times*, 1 August 1888, 6. Nell Nelson, "White Slave Girls," *New York World*, 23 September 1888; What happened to Cusak after working for the *World* is not known. Chapin claims she married the editor of a New York newspaper, who became a wealthy publisher, and she lived the remainder of her life in a mansion. Chapin, *Story*, 133–34.

10. Chapin, *Story*, 134–35; It remains a mystery why Chapin so vehemently objected to this exposé. The only difference between the slave-girls articles he commissioned and championed and this one was the issue of sex. His attitude about sex was very Victorian, as revealed in letters he wrote to women at the end of his life. He also seemed to worship his wife Nellie, but at a distance. They had no children for reasons never disclosed. The significance of the series is explained in Leslie J. Reagan, *When Abortion was a Crime: Women, Medicine, and Law in the United States, 1867–1973.* (Berkeley: University of California Press, 1997).

11. Henry M. Hunt, "Chicago," *Journalist* 8, no. 16, 5 January 1889, 6; Chapin, *Story*, 129.

12. *CC to CN*, 28 January 1925, 222–23.

13. Dr. Robert George Brett opened the sanitarium at age thirty-five after helping found a medical college in Manitoba. He remained in Banff, became successful in a number of businesses and eventually politics, rising to become the lieutenant-governor of Alberta. Letter and documents sent to author from Lena Goon, White Museum of Canadian Rockies, 24 January 2002. Chapin, "A Canadian Exile," *Chicago Tribune*, 31 January 1889. All subsequent quotations and descriptions of the reunion are drawn from this article unless otherwise indicated.

14. *CC to VC*, 7 December 1920, 36.

15. Reverend Charles Williams and F. G. Christmas were the names of the ministers. The mounted police officer was only identified as Mr. Brown. The caves in which they bathed still exist and may be seen, but bathers are no longer permitted. See "Journeys: 36 Hours In Banff," *New York Times*, 29 November 2002.

16. The "night of pleasure" remark is drawn from *CC to VC*, 7 December 1920, 36.

17. Chapin, *Story*, 137.

18. O'Brien-Bain, "Washington, D.C.," *Journalist* 8, no. 13, 15 February 1889, 13.

19. James Bryce, *The American Commonwealth*, vol. 3 (London: MacMillan & Co., 1888), 623; S. Reynolds Hole, *A Little Tour in America* (New York: E. Arnold, 1895), 309–10; also quoted in Constance McLaughlin Green, *Washington: Capital City, 1879–1950* (Princeton, N.J.: Princeton University Press, 1963), 77. This volume is an excellent source of information on Washington history; Green, *Washington: Capital City, 1879–1950*, 78.

20. Edmund Morris, *The Rise of Theodore Roosevelt* (New York: Ballantine Books, 1979), 397. Aside from being in Washington for a short time, reporters of the era had to work hard to develop sources, as much of the government's business was conducted behind closed doors. Personal relationships were about the only means a reporter had to obtain information. "A correspondent, no matter how able and brilliant, is at a great disadvantage if he does not personally know the leaders on both sides in Congress," noted E. J. Gibson, "The Washington Correspondent," *Lippincott's Magazine*, November 1894, 716. See Donald A. Ritchie, *Press Gallery: Congress and the Washington Correspondents* (Cambridge, Mass.: Harvard University Press, 1991), 41; Chapin, *Story*, 137; Farwell lived at 1233 17th St., NW, just beneath Massachusetts Avenue. The house is now gone, but similar houses still stand.

21. Chapin, "Marched in the Rain," *Chicago Times*, 5 March 1889, 1. Although there were no bylines in the issue, I established Chapin's authorship through an analysis of the style of each article.

22. Morris, *Rise of Roosevelt*, 401; Chapin, "Mr. Enander Resigns," *Chicago Times*, 9 May 1889, 1; Estimates of Wanamaker's support for Harrison begin at $50,000. See Harry Sievers, *Benjamin Harrison: Hoosier President, The White House and After*, vol. 3 (Indianapolis: Bobbs-Merrill Co., 1968), 16; Morris, *Rise of Roosevelt*, 400; Chapin, "Tiring Office-Seekers Out," *Chicago Times*, 11 April 1889, 1.

23. Chapin, *Story*, 137–38; Farwell was imperial in his spoils demands. First, he told the president that he wanted a spoils system based on the number of Republican votes cast in a state. Second, he tolerated no questions once he made his recommendation for a post. See Sievers, *Benjamin Harrison*, 42–43, especially on 29, 43; Chapin, "Col. Sexton The Man," *Chicago Times*, 11 April 1889, 1.

24. Morris uses the number "thousands." Morris, *Rise of Roosevelt*, 400; Chapin, "Capt. Meredith Feels Hopeful," *Chicago Times*, 1 April 1889, 2.

25. Chapin, *Story*, 141–42; Chapin was not alone in his description of Harrison. Many descriptions of Harrison are equally as unflattering.

26. Most interesting is that shortly afterward, Chapin's brother obtained a job with the Government Printing Office and moved to Washington.

27. Chapin, "Palmer is the Man," *Chicago Times*, 4 May 1889, 1.

28. Chapin, "Palmer is Appointed," *Chicago Times*, 8 May 1889, 1; Frank Chapin, deposition 31 August 1908, *NA-CW*.

29. See David G. McCullough, *The Johnstown Flood* (New York: Simon & Schuster, 1987); O'Brien-Bain, "Washington," *Journalist* 9, no. 12, 8 June 1889, 4.

30. The account of the junket is based on O'Brien-Bain's description in the *Journalist* 9, no. 15, 29 June 1889, 5.

31. O'Brien-Bain, "Washington," *Journalist* 9, no. 12, 8 June 1889, 4.

32. Henry M. Hunt, "Chicago," *Journalist* 9, no. 20, 3 August 1889, 6; Chapin, *Story*, 144–45.

33. *Chicago News*, 20 July 1889; *Journalist* 9, no. 20, 3 August 1889, 6; *Journalist* 9, no. 25, 7 September 1889, 6. Did he resign, or was he replaced? It's hard to know. The *Journalist* portrayed Brooks as "liked by everyone." Chapin's departure from Washington was reported in August "as the result of changes which have taken place in the home office." O'Brien-Bain, "Washington," *Journalist* 9, no. 22, 17 August 1889, 6.

34. Chapin, *Story*, 145–46. The items that Chapin described in his autobiography match those found in the Utah press of the time. It is very unlikely Chapin could have known about them or even remembered this election years later in prison had he not been a participant. The election, in fact, was hardly mentioned in the Eastern press. All of this seems to confirm this odd chapter in his life.

35. I have concluded that the events I am describing took place on this trip for the following reasons: first, records in Springfield's City Directory list Earl Chapin as residing there at the time with Mary; second, later records show they gave birth to a son in Springfield; third, Chapin does take a trip to Utah that could logically take him through Springfield; fourth, it is unlikely that any of his previous jobs until this point would have permitted such a long trip. Even if my dates are, however, wrong, other evidence indicates the reunion would have occurred at approximately this time. In January 1890, for instance, Chapin said he was in Fort Riley, where he witnessed the same-day execution of six murderers (16 January 1890); Fannie Chapin Skinner deposition, 16 December 1908, 6, *NA-CW*; In her deposition, Cecelia said, "none of the children heard from him directly at anytime." Cecelia Ann Chapin deposition, 29 August 1908, 6, *NA-CW*. Fannie's account, made under oath and certain to be read by Cecelia, related Charles Chapin's encounter with his father, leaving one to presume that Cecelia is truthful because she had never been told.

36. Dreiser, *Newspaper Days*, 6; Chapin, *Story*, 147; "A Chicago Criticism," *Journalist* 3, no. 11, 5 June 1886, 3.

37. A report in the *Journalist* (25 January 1890) cites Chapin as Lyman B. Glover's replacement. Glover had been the paper's music and drama critic for a number of years. An account of Fannie Chapin's wedding in May 1890 lists Chapin as a drama critic on the *Herald*. *Elgin Every Saturday*, 17 May 1890, 1. Late in life, Chapin also mentions having reviewed a performance of the famed opera singer Adela Patti, which would also coincide with these dates.

38. Many of the details of the Whitechapel cited here are drawn from Larry Lorenz, "The Whitechapel Club: Defining Chicago's Newspaperman in the 1890s," *American Journalism* 15, no. 1, Winter 1998, 83–102, and Brand Whitlock, *Forty Years of It* (New York: D. Appleton and Co., 1914), 42–49.

39. Dreiser, *Newspaper Days*, 5.

40. "Dying in Bitter Cold," *Chicago Herald*, 4 February 1891, 1.

41. "Crying out for Help," *Chicago Herald*, 5 February 1891, 1; Chapin, *Story*, 153–54. Chapin is somewhat inaccurate in his recollection of the charity drive in that he recalls it being prompted by a $1,000 anonymous gift. The gift came at the end of the drive.

42. "Aid for the Hungry," *Chicago Herald*, 6 February 1891, 9.

CHAPTER 8: PARK ROW

1. Chapin, *Story*, 155; Edwin G. Burrows and Mike Wallace, *Gotham: A History of New York City to 1898* (New York: Oxford University Press, 1999), 1051; Hy B. Turner, *When Giants Ruled: The Story of*

Park Row (New York: Fordham University Press, 1999), 114. Number of visitors found in brochure in Pulitzer Papers at Columbia University.

2. Many of the construction details may be found in a special supplement to the *New York World*, 10 December 1891. Corsehill stone is a fine-grained, red-brown sedimentary rock.

3. Allen Churchill, *Park Row: A Vivid Re-creation of Turn of the Century Newspaper Days* (New York: Rinehart & Company, 1958), 44, 31.

4. Supplement to the *New York World*, December 10, 1891, 3.

5. W. A. Swanberg, *Pulitzer* (New York: Charles Scribner's Sons, 1967), 193, 190; Don Seitz, *Joseph Pulitzer: His Life and Letters* (New York: Simon and Schuster, 1929), 188.

6. Chapin, *Story*, 156.

7. A. J. Liebling noted the connection between the dizzying height of the *World* building and the power Pulitzer's staff felt it had at its disposal; Churchill, *Park Row*, 52. The description of the newsroom is based on one contained in the supplement to the *World*, December 10, 1891 and, in part, on one written by Theodore Dreiser when he came to work at the *World* three years later. Dreiser, *Newspaper Days*, 623–25.

8. "New York Reporters," *The Journalist* 9, no. 26, 14 September 1889, 10.

9. Lorimer was quoted in Justin Kaplan, *Lincoln Steffens: A Biography* (New York: Simon and Schuster, 1974), 60.

10. "A Smash on the Central," *New York World*, 20 August 1891, 1. All the subsequent quotations and descriptions of the wreck are taken from this article. Chapin's autobiography and an analysis of the article's style confirm that he wrote it.

11. Chapin, *Story*, 156; Denis Brian, *Pulitzer: A Life* (New York: John Wiley & Sons, 2001), 160.

12. Chapin, "Dismay in Kingston," *New York World*, 4 October 1891, 1.

13. Information on how Chapin secured the interview and quotations taken from Chapin, "20 Years of Theft," *New York World*, 7 October 1891, 1–2; *Journalist* 14, no. 6, 24 October 1891, 4.

14. *New York World*, 22 July 1891, 10.

15. "Mr. Sage in Wall Street," *New York Times*, 5 December 1891, 2; Sarnoff, *Russell Sage*, 4–5; Chapin, *Story*, 267.

16. This and subsequent quotations are taken from "A Chat with Russell Sage: How the Veteran Financier Looks and Acts After His Terrible Experiences," *New York World*, 8 December 1891, 6. Though there was no byline, it is certain that it was Chapin's work because the article was so identified when introduced as evidence in a later lawsuit; Chapin, *Story*, 272.

17. Sage revealed in the Laidlaw civil trial (see Chapter 10) that he

had given Chapin a job on his railroad in Colorado. *New York Herald*, 29 March 1894, 5; "Choate Again Worries Sage," *New York Times*, 30 March 1894, 8.

CHAPTER 9: ST. LOUIS

Chapin was very vague in his autobiography about his years in St. Louis. Most of his recollections centered on several events in 1896, but he said nothing, for instance, about his coverage of Kelley's Navy. For more on Dreiser in St. Louis see my article "A Writer Comes of Age in St. Louis," *Missouri Life*, November 1981, 29–31.

1. Jack London, *The Road* (Santa Barbara, Calif.: Peregrine Smith, Inc., 1978), 193.
2. Francis Behymer believes Chapin came to St. Louis as a kind of freelance correspondent traveling with Kelley's Navy. While this seems possible, evidence suggests that he had joined the *Post-Dispatch* before the Navy reached St. Louis. Francis A. Behymer, "Simon Legree of the City Desk," *Page One Ball of 1948*, St. Louis Newspaper Guild, 1948. For histories of Coxey's Army and Kelley's Navy see Carlos A. Schwantes, *Coxey's Army* (Lincoln, Neb.: University of Nebraska Press, 1985) and Donald L. McMurry, *Coxey's Army: A Study of the Industrial Army Movement of 1894* (1929; reprint with an introduction by John D. Hicks, Seattle: University of Washington Press, 1968); Thomas Scharf, *History of St. Louis City and County* (Philadelphia: Louis H. Everts & Co., 1883), 938.
3. Chapin, *Story*, 157.
4. Chapin, "Kelley's Navy," *St. Louis Post-Dispatch*, 27 May 1894, 25.
5. Chapin, "In Camp Here," *St. Louis Post-Dispatch*, 29 May 1894, 1. The enthusiasm dissipated quickly, as Kelley's Navy soon thereafter suffered a split among the ranks. See Schwantes, *Coxey's Army*, 226–27.
6. Chapin, "Joan of Arc," *St. Louis Post-Dispatch*, 3 June 1894, 24.
7. The Harrigan stories, which still make for great reading, appeared in late July and early August 1894; Chapin, "Henry Samuel Priest, Our New Federal Judge," *St. Louis Post-Dispatch*, 9 September 1894, 21.
8. Chapin's elevation to city editor is reported in "From St. Louis," *Journalist* 19, no. 52, 16 March 1895.
9. Edgar C. Scott Jr., "Writer with Kindly Heart Owes Training to Chapin," *Editor & Publisher*, 5 March 1949, 24.
10. The closest rival to the *Post-Dispatch* was the venerable *Globe-*

Democrat. Its average daily circulation was 69,835 as compared to the *Post-Dispatch*'s 78,289, from *The American Newspaper Annual* (New York: N.W. Ayer & Son, 1897); Dreiser, *Newspaper Days*, 175–76.

11. Behymer, "Simon Legree," 11.

12. Chapin, *Story*, 162; Brian, *Pulitzer*, 189; Behymer, "Simon Legree," 11; Brian, *Pulitzer*, 189; Swanberg, *Pulitzer*, 251.

13. The account that follows is drawn from "Judge Murphy Raps City Editor Chapin," *Republic*, 18 January 1896, 1; "Judge Murphy Very Mad," *St. Louis Globe-Democrat*, 18 January 1896, 8; "He Acted Like a Blatherskite," *St. Louis Post-Dispatch*, 18 January 1896, 1–2; Chapin, *Story*, 162–67.

14. All the newspapers printed _____ where the objectionable words have now been inserted. I assumed modern tastes would permit their use.

15. *St. Louis Post-Dispatch*, 27 May 1896, 1.

16. Chapin, *Story*, 158–59.

17. Chapin, *Story*, 159.

18. Martin Green, "Death and desolation," *Republic*, 28 May 1896, 1–2.

19. Editor's introduction to Lucy Hosmer, "Factory Girls in a Big City," *St. Louis Post-Dispatch*, 26 November 1896, 1.

20. Chapin remained friends with Ringling and his widow until the end of his life. Ringling, said Chapin, "was one of my most intimate men friends for twenty-five years." *CC to VC*, 18 December 1920, 70; Margaret G. Henderson, Ethel Dewey Speerschneider and Helen L. Ferslev, "The Greatest Show on Earth," *It Happened Here: Stories of Wisconsin*. (Madison: State Historical Society of Wisconsin, 1949), 218–21; Chapin, *Story*, 171.

CHAPTER 10: NEW YORK TO STAY

Like many historians, I remained completely unaware of how literally colorful the Yellow Journalism described in this chapter was until I came across *Double Fold: Libraries and the Assault on Paper* by Nicholson Baker. I had stared at scratchy, black and white microfilm copies of late nineteenth-century New York papers for years, unaware that the publishers made deft use of both color and colored paper. I'm thankful that, in addition to leading the movement to cease the destruction of the original copies of these priceless newspapers, Baker has taken on the role of preserving the newspapers that libraries were destroying once they were microfilmed. For more information on the American Newspaper Repository and Baker's efforts, consult www.oldpapers.org.

1. Description of Chamberlain's features from Churchill, *Park Row*, 113; Albert Payson Terhune, *To the Best of My Memory* (New York: Harper & Brothers Publishers, 1930), 94; *New York World*, 17 February 1898; Swanberg, *Pulitzer*, 285.

2. Terhune, *To the Best of My Memory*, 146.

3. Terhune, *To the Best of My Memory*, 94–95; James Wyman Barrett, *Joseph Pulitzer and His World* (New York: Vanguard Press, 1941), 176; Swanberg, *Pulitzer*, 286; The story of Chamberlain's decline—or "brain fever"—also may be found in *Harper's Weekly*, 26 March 1898, 295; Terhune tells of a pathetic encounter he had with Chamberlain at home before he died, when the sick editor dictated copy for a full page advertisement for a book to be published by a firm whose directors would include Pulitzer, the president of France, J. Pierpont Morgan, and Terhune, among others. "No, it was not funny. There was a lump in my throat as I wrote down the idiocy that was voiced so sanely." Terhune, *To the Best of my Memory*, 95.

4. The role of Hearst's mother is described in Judith Robinson's *The Hearts: An American Dynasty* (New York: Avon Books, 1991); Arthur Lubow, *The Reporter Who Would be King: A Biography of Richard Harding Davis* (New York: Charles Scribner's Sons, 1992), 130; Terhune, *To the Best of My Memory*, 111–12 and 115–16; *Journalist* 26, no. 1, 21 October 1899, 446; The competition and staff raiding that went on between the two papers is also well described in David Nasaw, *The Chief: The Life of William Randolph Hearst* (Boston: Houghton Mifflin, 2000); Newspaper editor Selah Clarke detailed, in a sketch of life on Park Row that was privately published after his death, the wide array of cheap eats that could be had in lower Manhattan. As these establishments often combined drinking with food, they were frequent evening hangouts for reporters. At Martinelli's Cellar, for instance, the proprietor was known for his vermouth cocktail served in a glass frosted with sugar. Selah Merrill Clarke, *Frivolous Recollections of the Humble Side of Old Days in New York Newspaperdom* (New York. Privately printed, 1932), 18. Piccalilli, by the way, is a green tomato relish.

5. Hearst rewarded some of his best reporters with bicycles as gifts. Churchill, *Park Row*, 87; Chapin, *Story*, 179; Terhune, *To the Best of My Memory*, 133–34; *New York World*, 2 July 1898, 1; Turner, *When Giants Ruled*, 136; Brian, *Pulitzer*, 234; Ben Proctor, *William Randolph Hearst: The Early Years, 1863–1910*. (New York: Oxford University Press, 1998), 124.

6. Before reading lights were widely available, circulation of the *World* grew and shrank with the length of the days in summer and winter; Turner, *When Giants Ruled*, 122–24; Churchill, *Park Row*, 66–84; Edwin and Michael Emery, *The Press and America: An Interpretive history of the Mass Media, 5th ed.* (New York: Prentice-Hall, Inc., 1984), 285–88; Allan Forman, "The Evening Papers," *Journalist* 35, no. 13, 16 July 1904; Chapin, *Story*, 179; *Journalist* 35, no. 20, 3 September 1904; Terhune, *To the Best of My Memory*, 132; Chapin, *Story*, 179; Barrett, *Joseph Pulitzer and His World*, 177; Brian, *Pulitzer*, 234.

7. Terhune, *To the Best of My Memory*, 112; *CC to VC*, 21 December 1920, 82; Chapin, *Story*, 177.

8. Terhune, *To the Best of My Memory*, 96. Terhune recounts also that Duneka had "an all encompassing horror of death and of anything pertaining to it" and was buried in a snow-white suit with a flaming scarlet tie; Chapin, *Story*, 177.

9. Swanberg, *Pulitzer*, 309; A description of this system may be found in Swanberg, *Pulitzer*, 279–82, 309. Certain editions of Swanberg's biography feature some of the code names inside the cover. The full list is in the Columbia University collection of Pulitzer's papers.

10. Brian, *Pulitzer*, 231; Chapin, *Story*, 179. For the modern reader, the headlines look amateurish and at times hokey, but they were such a radical departure from the past that they were incredibly eye catching.

11. *New York Evening World*, 7 May 1898; Chapin, *Story*, 184.

12. Don Carlos Seitz, *Joseph Pulitzer: His Life and Letters* (New York: Simon & Schuster, 1924), 242.

13. Chapin, *Story*, 178; Address drawn from city directory. It was probably a boarding house, as there were no hotels listed with that address.

14. Chapin, *Story*, 257; John Dillon to Ana Price Dillon, 5 July 1898, reprinted in *Ana Price Dillon: Memoir and Memorials* (New York: The De Vinne Press, 1900), 453–54. This was a privately printed tribute to Dillon's wife who died on *La Bourgoyne*. Chapin never identifies the passengers whom he was seeing off.

15. J. Watson Fraser, "How the Great Beat was Obtained for the Evening World," *New York Evening World*, 7 July 1898, 5; Chapin, *Story*, 257–58.

16. Chapin, *Story*, 258–59; Churchill, *Park Row*, 256–57; Chapin, "The Evening World was First with News of the Disaster," *New York Evening World*, 6 July 1898, 3. The competitive atmosphere of Park Row had many newspapers publishing stories touting how they beat the competition. The *Evening World* ran at least three such stories in the month of July alone, illustrating one with a cartoon about Hearst's *Evening*

Journal called the "Yallowest Yet of the Illuminated Rags." *New York Evening World*, 11 July 1898, 3. Churchill's *Park Row* wrongly claims that Chapin's use of the passenger list gave the *Evening World* the best coverage for several days. It was only hours before others reprinted the *Evening World*'s list.

17. Introduction to Charles H. Garrett, "Lived Three Months on Five Cents a Day," *New York Evening World*, 18 July 1898, 1; Catherine King, "Girl Toilers of the City," *New York Evening World*, 26 July 1898, 7.

18. Don Carlos Seitz to JP, 20 October 1898, *P-LC*; JP to Coates, Duneka, and Chapin, 30 October 1899, *P-LC*.

19. Chapin, *Story*, 260–61; "Mrs. Suzanne Dillon Warriner," *New York Times*, 22 February 1904, 5. Chapin did not provide Warriner's name, referring to her only as Dillon's married daughter. Aside from the daughter he lost at sea, Dillon only had one other daughter. She was married and died a few years later, as Chapin said.

20. Van Bethuysen to JP, 2 February 1900, *W-CU*.

21. Foster Coates to JP. 15 February 1900; William Van Benthuysen to JP, 20 February 1900, *W-CU*.

22. Chapin, *Story*, 219–21; Brian, *Pulitzer*, 256–57.

23. Bradford Merrill to JP, undated, early March, 1900, *W-CU*.

24. Chapin, "Crazy Man Shoots Himself for Love of Miss Russell," *Evening World*, 30 March 1900, 2.

25. Foster Coates to JP, 30 March 1900, *W-CU*.

26. "Laidlaw Begins his Suit," *New York Times*, 24 March 1892, 10; An *Evening World* interview with Sage, secured no doubt by Chapin, gained wide notice and was reprinted in the *Wall Street Journal*. "Mr. Sage on the Situation," *Wall Street Journal*, 22 October 1898, 1; The first trial was held in 1892 and the last in 1895. The appeals lasted almost to the end of the century. Laidlaw was awarded $25,000 in one trial, but the judgment was set aside. The final trial jury awarded $40,000. Neither sum was ever collected. Choate was the lead attorney in *Pollock v. Farmers Loan & Trust Co.* (1898), in which the U.S. Supreme Court threw out the nation's federal income tax. The Sixteenth Amendment later made income taxes constitutional.

27. "Choate Again Worries Sage," *New York Times*, 30 March 1894, 8.

28. Questions and answers drawn from "Some Posers for Mr. Sage," *New York World*, 29 March 1894, 10.

29. *New York Herald*, 29 March 1894, 5; "Mr. Sage Tells his Story," *New York Times*, 29 March 1894, 3.

30. Questions and answers drawn from "Choate Again Worries Sage," *New York Times*, 30 March 1894, 8.

31. Chapin, *Story*, 268.

32. Chapin, *Story*, 270.

CHAPTER 11: A NEW CENTURY

1. Pulitzer biographers W. A. Swanberg and Denis Brian wrongly assumed that it was the morning *World* that was carried to the President on new year's day. Park Row historian Hy B. Turner, however, describes it correctly in his book *When Giants Ruled*. *New York Evening World*, 1 January 1901, 3; Turner, *When Giants Ruled*, 138; Van Benthuysen to JP, 2 January 1901, *W-CU*.

2. Terhune, *To the Best of My Memory*, 132; White to JP, 7 January 1901, *W-CU.*; Swanberg, *Pulitzer*, 320; JP to staff, undated (January–July 1901), *P-LC;* Chapin was actually anxious to fight back. At one point, Pulitzer's and Hearst's top men brokered a short-lived ceasefire. Now Coates, Chapin's former boss who had crossed over, called Seitz to ask if the agreement was over. "Why?" asked Seitz. "Because," replied Coates, "Chapin has just stolen our artist," Don Carlos Seitz to JP, 18 January 1901, *W-CU.*

3. Donald Henderson Clarke, *Man of the World* (New York: Vanguard Press, 1950), 114; The facts about the amount of trees and lead used by the *World* is drawn from a 1903 brochure celebrating the newspaper's twentieth anniversary under Pulitzer's ownership, contained in the Library of Congress Pulitzer Papers.

4. "M'Kinley Outlines Official Policy," *New York Evening World*, 5 September 1901, 8; "M'Kinley's condition now is SERIOUS," *New York Evening World*, extra no. 6, 6 September 1901, 1; Chapin, *Story*, 162; The Giants lost both games that day.

5. The introduction of telephones came very rapidly in New York. Examining telephone directories from 1898, for example, the number of telephone subscribers grew from 50,000 to 60,000 in nine months. The advertising pitch in the directories certainly has a vintage sound to the modern reader. "Look him up in the list before you write or telegraph or go to see him," urged the directory. "He may have a telephone and you may save half an hour or half a day." *Telephone Directory of the New York Telephone Company*, December 1898.

6. See Fedler, *Lessons From the Past*, 143–45, for a discussion of the introduction of the telephone into newsrooms; *Story*, 186; For more on the introduction of the "legman and rewrite" approach to news coverage see Marcus Errico, "The Evolution of the Summary News Lead," *Media*

History Monographs 1, no. 1, 1997–98, or online journal (http://www
.elon.edu/dcopeland/mhm/).

7. Martin Green, "Park Row in Those Days, Park Row! Alas for Us Who Never Worked There," *Shoeleather and Printers' Ink: 1924–1974*, ed. George Britt, (New York: Quadrangle/New York Times Book Co., 1974), 208; Bradford Merrill to JP, 3 October 1902, *W-CU;* The *Evening World*, whose expenses were half those of the *World*, was often twice as profitable, according to year-end statements on file in the *World* archives; Memo by Florence White, 14 March 1902, *W-CU*. White, however, also nagged Pulitzer about letting Chapin spend so much money on staff. For instance, even when the *Evening World* expenses fell, he faulted Chapin for his "high priced men" that prevented the expenses from being even lower. White to JP, 1 June 1900, *W-CU*.

8. "Minister Shot Down on the Street May Die," *New York Times*, 4 February 1901, 1; August Derleth, *Still Small Voice: The Biography of Zona Gale* (New York: Appleton-Century Co., 1940), 59; Gale to her mother, reprinted in Derleth's biography, 63–64.

9. *CC to CN*, 3 November 1924, 167. Gale seems to have left the *Evening World* around 1903, but continued to freelance for the *World*. In 1903, she wrote an article about Mrs. Katherine Mackay who was expecting. The publication of an article that identified a woman as being pregnant—even though the word was not used—so incensed Pulitzer that he demanded the reporter be fired immediately as an example to others. Seitz reported to Pulitzer that he would fire her, but there is no record of whether he did so. Ellin Mackay, the child who was born to the Mackays, later eloped with Irvin Berlin and was disowned by her father, Clarence Mackay, for doing so. The correspondence is contained in the files of February 1903, *W-CU*.

10. Chapin, *Story*, 195–96; "Tunnel Wreck," *New York Evening World*, 8 January 1902, 1.

11. Seitz to JP, 9 January 1902, *W-CU;* White memo, 14 March 1902, *W-CU*.

12. "What is Doing in Society," *New York Times*, 4 March 1902, 7; "Thousand Island Resorts Are Unusually Crowded," *New York Times*, 13 July 1902, 8; Merrill to JP, 25 September 1902, *W-CU;* Swanberg, *Pulitzer*, 324; The promise of a $10,000 bonus was in an undated October 1904 JP memo, *W-CU*.

13. White to JP, 8 April 1903, *W-CU*.

14. CC to JP, 10 April 1903, *W-CU*.

15. CC to JP, 14 April 1903, *W-CU*. The gruesome piece on the barrel murder appeared on April 14, 1898. White and Chapin often had differing views on their respective contributions to the enterprise; Seitz to JP, 14 April 1903. *W-CU*.

16. "Mrs. Sage Hates Girls to Smoke," *New York Evening World*, 15 April 1903, 5.

17. "Former Chicagoans Dine," *New York Times*, 17 April 1904, 9.

18. Newman Levy, *The Nan Patterson* Case (New York: Simon & Schuster, 1959), 68. *Floradora* featured a scene with six women, each five-foot-four and 130 pounds, who sang "Tell Me Pretty Maiden" with the male chorus. The show was the rage of New York and London, where it originated. As a result, glamorous young women were often called "Floradora" girls.

19. Churchill, *Park Row*, 233–35; *New York Evening World*, 15 June 1904, and other newspapers. Eugene Moran's tugboat company, which Chapin's reporter called, is still in existence today, providing tug service to almost a dozen U.S. ports.

20. Merrill to JP, 16 June 1904, *W-CU*.

21. Terhune, *To the Best of My Memory*, 136–38.

22. Copies of the contract and correspondence with Judge Dittenhoefer are to be found in the November 1904 folder, *W-CU*. Some of the documents date back to May 1903.

23. "Men, Women, and Things," *Journalist* 36, no. 19, 25 February 1905, 307; *Journalist* 36, no. 24, 1 April 1905, 386.

24. Emmeline Pendennis, "Where Can a Girl Alone in New York Find Assistance?" *New York Evening World*, 4 February 1905, and subsequent issues.

25. Coney Island European Tour ride information comes from "Coney Island—Dreamland," an unpublished history by Jeffrey Stanton; Edith Wharton, *A Motor-Flight Through France* (DeKalb: Northern Illinois University Press, 1991), 1. Her use of the word "posting" seemingly means "fleeting."

26. White to JP, 26 July 1905; Seitz, supplemental diary, 23 May 1905. Contract renewal contained in Seitz's diary, 11 April 1905, *W-CU*.

27. *CC to VC*, 18 December 1930, 65, 66; *CC to CN*, 18 August 1925, 306; *CC to CN*, 11 January 1925, 212; The description of the meeting between Pulitzer and Chapin is drawn entirely from Chapin's memoirs (*Story*, 223–24). Pulitzer biographer Denis Brian dated this encounter to April 1900. It seems unlikely, however, that Chapin could have afforded a trip that early in his career with the *Evening World*. It also made little sense that Chapin would have been at the end of a European motor trip that early in the spring. Instead, other evidence led me to date this encounter to 1905. First, Chapin recounts that Pulitzer had arrived in London from the continent. This is the trip Pulitzer took in 1905 and not in 1900. Second, and more important, the Ellis Island immigration records show Charles and Nellie returning to New York in 1905, but have no records of previous journeys.

28. A description of Tite Street may be found in Stanley Weintraub, *The London Yankees: Portraits of American Writers and Artists in England, 1894–1914* (New York: Harcourt Brace Jovanovich, 1979); Description of Pulitzer's visit drawn from Swanberg, *Pulitzer*, 363; Brian, *Pulitzer*, 302–3; Quotation from Sargent appears in Charles Merrill Mount, *John Singer Sargent: A Biography* (New York: W. W. Norton , 1955), 264.

29. Anita Lawson, *Irvin S. Cobb*, (Bowling Green, Ohio: Bowling Green State University Popular Press, 1984), 62.

30. Quoted in Lawson, *Cobb*, 53–54.

31. Chapin, *Story*, 189.

CHAPTER 12: A GRAND LIFE

1. Swanberg, *Pulitzer*, 376; Brian, *Pulitzer*, 311; Daniel W. Pfaff, *Joseph Pulitzer II and the Post-Dispatch* (University Park, Penn.: The Pennsylvania State University Press, 1991), 60. The word "yanked" is drawn from the transcript of an interview of Joseph Pulitzer II by Louis M. Starr, 7 October 1954. Oral History Collection, Columbia University, 19; Use of the telephone, Brian, *Pulitzer*, 312; *CC to CN*, January 12, 1925, 241; Chapin, *Story*, 225.

2. "The *Evening World* is the black sheep of the family, about whose whereabouts and mode of life one does not inquire too carefully," according to editor Oswald Garrison Villard. Oswald Garrison Villard, *Some Newspapers and Newspaper-men* (New York: Knopf, 1926), 48; Chapin, *Story*, 225–26.

3. Chapin, *Story*, 217; "I have always believed he was fond of me," *CC to VC*, 20 January 1921, 189. Letters in the Pulitzer archives support Chapin's belief.

4. Some of this description of Chapin, especially of his eyes, is owed to Cobb, *Exit Laughing*, 139 and "The Convict Who Made a Garden," *Cosmopolitan*, March 1925, 181.

5. Joe Pulitzer described his arrival in a letter to his father, Joseph Pulitzer II to JP, 28 May 1906, *P-CU*; Chapin, *Story*, 226; Terhune, *To the Best of my Memory*, 136; Clarke, *Man of the World*, 252, 248–49.

6. Cobb, *Exit Laughing*, footnote, 141; John Henry Goldfrap (1879–1917) wrote the Bungalow Boys series under the pen name Dexter J. Forrester, the Boy Scout series under the pen name Howard Payson, and the Motor Rangers series under the pen name Marvin West, among many other dime novels.

7. Story about reinstatement contained in an unsigned, undated memo, 1903, *P-CU*; Cobb, *Exit Laughing*, 139; *CC to VC*, 20 January

1921, 191; Terhune, *To the Best of my Memory*, 147. Chapin's temperance was also alluded to at a dinner where New York Governor Charles S. Whitman said to Chapin, "I assume that you, who never indulge in intoxicants, think that I drink more than I should." Chapin, *Story*, 249.

8. Terhune, *To the Best of my Memory*, 146; Clarke, *Man of the World*, 85; Barry Faris, "Perry's Drugstore? Bar? Where Friendship Ripened," in *Shoeleather and Printers' Ink*, ed. George Britt, 213. Chapin was credited with having accomplished the same reduction in drinking at the *Post-Dispatch*, see Daniel W. Pfaff, *Joseph Pulitzer II and the Post-Dispatch* (University Park, Penn.: Pennsylvania State University Press, 1991), note, 410.

9. Chapin, *Story*, 226; Alfred Butes to JP, 30 May 1906, *W-CU;* Joseph Pulitzer II to JP, 4 June 1906, *P-CU.* The ditty's racist refrain was, "Damn, damn, damn the Filipinos, cross-eyed kakiack ladrones; / Underneath our starry flag, civilize 'em with a Krag, / And return us to our own beloved homes."

10. Chapin, *Story*, 228–29. Joe Pulitzer went on to be a success in St. Louis and ran the *Post-Dispatch* until his death in 1955.

11. Profit calculations made using year-end statement for 1904, *W-CU*; Don Carlos Seitz to JP, 17 February 1906, *W-CU*; Bradford Merrill to JP, 19 February 1906, *W-CU.* An obvious twist on the phrase made famous by Chapin's friend Finley Peter Dunne that the job of the press is to comfort the afflicted and afflict the comfortable.

12. Terhune's and Green's eyewitness accounts also appeared in the *Evening World*, 26 June 1906, 1.

13. Seitz to JP, 10 July 1906, *W-CU.*

14. Quoted in Allen Churchill, *Park Row: A Vivid Re-creation of Turn of the Century Newspaper Days* (New York: Rinehart & Company, 1958), 252.

15. White complained of Chapin hogging the tickets in a letter to JP, 8 April 1903; "A. G. Vanderbilt Wins Again," *New York Times*, 19 April 1906, 4; "Vanderbilt's Horses Lead," *New York Times*, 20 April 1906, 13.

16. "Russell Sage Dies, Leaving $80,000," *New York Times*, 23 July 1906, 2.

17. Cobb, *Exit Laughing*, 144. It is unlikely that Cobb could have remembered this conversation word for word as he describes here. But as the sentiment fits Chapin's continued attitude that he was "robbed" of his inheritance, I have included it.

18. "Sage Will to Prove Surprise, His Friends Say," *New York Evening World*, 23 July 1906, 2.

19. "Sage Will to Prove Surprise, His Friends Say," *New York Evening World*, 23 July 1906, 1; Cobb, *Exit Laughing*, 143. Cobb is, of course,

in error calling Chapin a nephew of Sage. He was Sage's grand-nephew, but many thought he was a nephew, a presumption Chapin may have encouraged, especially with creditors.

20. Annual Report to the Lot Proprietors, Kensico Cemetery, 1897; Details of the funeral arrangements from *New York Times*, 26 July 1906, "Ghoul Proof Vault Holds Body of Sage," *New York Evening World*, 25 July 1906, 3,

21. "How Stewart Body was Stolen Away after his Burial," and "Ghoul Proof Vault Holds Body of Sage," *New York Evening World*, 25 July 1906, 3.

22. "A Score of Men Needed to Lower Sage Coffin," *New York Times*, 26 July 1906, 1; "Sage's Will to be Filed for Probate To-Morrow," *New York Evening World*, 26 July 1906, 2.

23. "Sage's Will to be Filed for Probate To-Morrow," *New York Evening World*, July 26, 1906, 2.

24. "Mrs. Sage in Ignorance of Husband's Will," *New York Evening World*, 24 July 1906, 1; "Sage Gave to Wife $10,000,000 Before Death," *New York Evening World*, 30 July 1906, 1; "Erasure Made in Sage Will May Break it," *New York Evening World*, 2 August 1906, 2.

25. Medical records in pension files NA-CW; "Sage Heir is Dead," *Milwaukee Sentinel*, 27 September 1906, 7.

26. Fannie Chapin Skinner deposition, 16 December 1908, 6, *NA-CW*.

27. Louisa Harrison deposition, 13 November 1908; Sarah Ramaker deposition, 14 November 1908. *NA-CW*.

28. Earl Chapin to Cornelius Wheeler, 24 February 1903, *NA-CW*.

29. Earl boasted of Charles's achievements to the jeweler for whom he worked and to a neighbor. The 1910 census lists Marjorie Chapin as a "ward" of Fannie and William Skinner.

30. Chapin, *Story*, 279–80; Cobb, *Exit Laughing*, 145–46. A similar theory was offered, but never substantiated, by a Hearst newspaper years later. The *New York American* claimed that Chapin earned 3.5% of the additional $425,000–$850,000 paid to each of the seventeen beneficiaries, which would be between $15,000 and $30,000 on top of the $50,000 the paper erroneously concluded he had inherited. "Chapin Tells How and Why he Shot Wife," *New York American*, 18 September 1918, 5.

31. "Yachts Change Hands in Midwinter Season," *New York Times*, 6 January 1907, 14; The price Chapin paid is unknown. But he would have paid no more than $2,000, according to Wendy Schnur, reference manager at the G. W. Blunt Library of the Mystic Seaport Museum in Connecticut, who reviewed the prices of other yachts sold that year.

Letter to author, 13 November 2002; Information about the Atlantic Yacht Club is drawn from *The History of American Yacht and Yachtsmen* (New York: Spirit of the Times Publishing Co., 1901), 34–35; A depiction of Chapin's signal is found in *Lloyd's Register of American Yachts*, 1910; The Atlantic Yacht Club Yearbook for 1909 lists Chapin as chair of the library committee and a member of the nominating committee; "Light Breeze in Atlantic Y.C. Race," *New York Herald*, 6 September 1910; "Yachtsmen, Ahoy!" *New York Evening World*, 27 March 1906. During the years Chapin owned *Eidolon*, the *Evening World* did indeed carry considerable yachting news. The Walt Whitman poem is "Sail out for good, Eidolon yacht," contained in *Leaves of Grass*.

32. "A Phase of the Thaw Case," *New York Evening World*, 22 January 1907, 14. The moniker "Trial of the Century" was used for thirty-three different cases by 1999, according to Gerald Uelman, professor of law at Santa Clara University Law School. Linda Deutsch, "Famous Trials Force Society to Face its Ills," Associated Press, 28 December 1999.

33. Headline in *New York Evening World*, 23 January 1907, 3; See Phillis L. Abramson's *Sob Sister Journalism* (New York: Greenwood Press, 1990).

34. Irvin Cobb, "Pen Pictures of Thaw, His Wife and Chief Counsel," *Evening World*, 24 January 1907, 2; Cobb, *Exit Laughing*, 227; Chapin, *Story*, 190; Lawson, *Cobb*, 66–67; One of Cobb's articles from the trial was also included in Louis L. Snyder and Richard B. Morris, *A Treasury of Great Reporting* (New York: Simon and Schuster, 1949).

35. "Pulitzer's 60th Birthday," *New York Times*, 11 April 1907, 5; Swanberg, *Pulitzer*, 387.

36. Swanberg, *Pulitzer*, 387; Swanberg also tells an amusing story about Pulitzer's modesty. It seems that Rodin asked Pulitzer to bare his shoulders. At first Pulitzer refused, but he finally consented when Rodin threatened to return to Paris.

37. Chapin, *Story*, 212–13.

38. Joseph Pulitzer II to JP, 8 May 1907, *P-CU*.

39. From every account, St. Louis turned out to be the perfect place for Joe Pulitzer. Chapin himself said of the father's sending the son to St. Louis, "This is just what Joe wanted, for that is where his heart was." Chapin, *Story*, 229. Joe's relationship with his father, however, was still poor. Correspondence between the two was marked by long periods of silence on the father's side, followed by sudden outbursts of anger, then an apology. See Brian, *Pulitzer*, 322–25; Joseph Pulitzer II to JP, 9 May 1907, *P-CU*.

40. Ralph Pulitzer to CC, telegram, 31 May 1907; S. M. Williams to JP, 19 June 1907. Other references to Seymour and Pulitzer's interest in

him may be found in several earlier *World* files, *W-CU*; One assumes the "croaker" reference is to the fish.

41. Chapin, *Story*, 214; Details of Seymour's contract contained in a letter from Seymour to CC, 8 June 1907, *W-CU*; CC to JP, 14 June 1907; CC to Seymour, 10 June 1907, *W-CU*.

42. Cobb, "The Convict Who Made a Garden," 181; "Another Fine Hotel now on the City's List," *New York Times*, 29 September 1907. While Chapin is not mentioned as one of the guests in the press coverage of the opening of the Plaza, I was able to establish his early move there by consulting an October 1907 edition of the New York telephone directory, which showed him already installed in the hotel; The incomplete dining room is cited in *CC to VC*, 10 January 1921, 160–61. Each family had a table reserved for their use in the secluded dining room so they wouldn't be bothered by transient guests or New Yorkers dining out. For those who chose to eat in their suites, savory dishes of piping hot food were shot skyward in one of four dumb waiters equipped with special locks so that food couldn't be purloined while in transit.

43. Cobb, *Exit Laughing*, 141–42; *CC to CN*, 21 October 1924, 159.

44. Lincoln Steffens, *The Autobiography of Lincoln Steffens* (New York: Harcourt, Brace and Company, 1931), 205; Cobb, *Exit Laughing*, 256–57; "Max Fischel Dies; Police Reporter," *New York Times*, 25 March 1939, 15.

45. Cobb, *Exit Laughing*, 121, footnote, 136; Cobb, "The Convict Who Made a Garden," 182.

46. Chapin, *Story*, 187–90. Chapin tells this story first in his autobiography (p. 190) and then retells it in one of his letters from prison. But in the latter case, he claims it was Denison who made the remark. The version with Cobb as the speaker became so well known it appeared in numerous editions of *Bartlett's Famous Quotations* and continues to be found in Web-based collections of famous quotations.

47. Terhune, *To the Best of My Memory*, 206.

Chapter 13: On Senior's Desk

1. See Swanberg, *Pulitzer*, 412–30 and Brian, *Pulitzer*, 343–49.

2. Cobb, *Exit Laughing*, 156–61. Cobb also tells another expense account story. Later that year, he went north to cover a sanity hearing for Thaw, who had been sent to the state asylum. During the hearing, Cobb discovered that the cost of Thaw's stay in the county jail for the hearing included white lilies and vanilla éclairs. His scoop, on the front page of a "Lobster Trick" edition, earned him a rebuke from Tennant for having

overspent his expense account and congratulations from Chapin. "The contrasting actions were characteristic of the two men," said Cobb. Cobb, *Exit Laughing*, 245.

3. Barrett, *Joseph Pulitzer and His World*, 275.

4. Barrett, *The World, the Flesh, and Messrs. Pulitzer* (New York: Vanguard Press, 1931), 7.

5. Pulitzer put Seymour in his own office in the dome. Barrett, *Joseph Pulitzer and His World*, 276; CC to JP, 9 March 1909; CC to JP, 11 March 1909, *W-CU*.

6. JP to CC, 10 March 1909, *W-CU*.

7. CC to JP, 11 March 1909. *W-CU*. The term "Black Hand" referred to a group, prevalent in Chapin's time, that extorted money from immigrants.

8. JP to Caleb Van Ham, 7 March 1909; Van Hamm to JP, 14 March 1909, *W-CU*.

9. Chapin, *Story*, 222.

10. Content of conversation covered in memo from CC to JP, 17 March 1909, *W-CU*.

11. Samuel Williams to JP, 19 March 1909; CC to JP, 19 March 1909, *W-CU*.

12. Seymour to JP, 6 July 1909, *W-CU*.

13. JP to Ralph Pulitzer, 25 June 1909, *P-LC*; Notes dictated by JP at Carlsbad, Germany, 12 June 1909, *W-CU*.

14. Barrett, *Pulitzer*, 276; Seymour to JP, 9 November 1909, *W-CU*.

15. *American Heritage* 45, no. 6, October 1994; *Harper's Weekly*, 13 August 1910, 3; Cobb, *Exit Laughing*, 143.

16. Louis Heaton Pink, *Gaynor: The Tammany Mayor Who Swallowed the Tiger* (New York: The International Press, 1931).

17. Alleyene Ireland, *An Adventure with a Genius* (New York: W. O. Dutton, 1920), 235–36; Swanberg, *Pulitzer*, 471.

18. "Joseph Pulitzer Laid in Woodlawn," *New York Times*, 2 November 1911, 11; Chapin, *Story*, 217.

Chapter 14: A Titanic Scoop

The number of books that have been published about the sinking of the *Titanic* is immense, made even larger as a result of the 1997 movie on the disaster. Equally large is the number of myths that surround this event. In dissecting the press coverage of the disaster, one of the most useful books was Paul Heyer's *Titanic Legacy: Disaster as Media Event and Myth* (Westport, Conn.: Praeger, 1995).

1. "Way of the World," *Journalist* 3, no. 25, 11 September 1886, 11; Turner, *When Giants Ruled*, 127.

2. "Carlos F. Hurd, 73, St. Louis Reporter," *New York Times*, 2 June 1950, 23.

3. Chapin, *Story*, 209; Allen Churchill wrote that the walls of all Park Row buildings "echoed and trembled" when the presses ran. Churchill, *Park Row*, 12; Chapin, *Story*, 209; Sue Ann Wood, "A Symphony of Sorrow," *Everyday Magazine, St. Louis Post-Dispatch*, 14 April 1997, 01E; Vera and John Gillespie, *The "Titanic Man," Carlos F. Hurd: Covering the Most Famous of All Shipwrecks, S.S. Titanic* (Grover, Mo.: V. & J. Gillespie, 1996), 6.

4. "Titanic Tears the New York from Dock," *New York World*, 11 April 1912, 7. Frances Hurd Stadler, "My Father's Scoop of a Lifetime," *Mature American*, Spring 1988, 18. Carlos F. Hurd, "When the Titanic Sank," *The Quill*, June 1932, 1.

5. The description of the city room at the *New York Times* is drawn from Meyer Berger, *The Story of the New York Times: 1851–1951* (New York: Simon & Schuster, 1951), 193–94.

6. Although it was commonly believed that "CQD" meant "Come Quick Danger," it really represented an agreed-upon code by wireless operators for distress. The "CQ" was a convention adopted by the Marconi company for a general call, and the "D" stood for distress. A recipient of such a message would understand the three letters in this arrangement to mean "All stations, Distress"; "How Titanic Story was Reported," *Editor and Publisher and Journalist*, 20 April 1912, 1.

7. Hurd, "When the Titanic Sank," 1; Kathleen Hurd, "Stories of Women Who Survived Titanic Disaster Gathered by Mrs. Hurd," *St. Louis Post-Dispatch*, 19 April 1912, 6.

8. *New York Evening World*, Final Edition, 15 April 1912.

9. Chapin, *Story*, 208.

10. According to Hurd, an illustrator for the *New York Tribune* was on board but didn't want any part of reporting the story; Hurd, "When the Titanic Sank," 4.

11. Hurd, "When the Titanic Sank," 4; Arthur H. Rostron, "The Rescue of the *Titanic* Survivors," *Scribners Monthly*, March 1913, 364; Rostron, in a letter to survivors on board the *Carpathia*, explained that they could not send Marconigrams. The letter was found in a scrapbook belonging to Dr. Frank H. Blackmarr. In the hearings following the disaster, Rostron was asked about his having censored news reports:

> SENATOR SMITH: And no one attempted in any way to put a censorship over the wireless service on your ship?

MR. ROSTRON: Absolutely no censorship whatever. I controlled the whole thing, through my orders. I said I placed official messages first. After they had gone, and the first press message, then the names of the passengers. After the names of the passengers and crew had been sent my orders were to send all private messages from the *Titanic*'s passengers first in the order in which they were given in to the purser; no preference to any message.

12. Carlos F. Hurd, "St. Louisan tells of Tragic Scenes at Titanic's Grave," *St. Louis Post-Dispatch*, 21 April 1912. Carlos F. Hurd, "When the Titanic Sank," *The Quill*, June 1932, 1; Carlos F. Hurd, "Hurd's Narrative Tied to a Buoy, Is Thrown to a Tug," *St. Louis Post-Dispatch*, 19 April 1912, 12.

13. Carlos F. Hurd, *St. Louis Post-Dispatch*, 19 April 1912, 9.

14. Hurd, "When the Titanic Sank," 15.

15. An analytical account of the New York papers' pursuit of the story is contained in Paul Heyer, *Titanic Legacy: Disaster as Media Event and Myth* (Westport, Conn.: Praeger, 1995); *New York Evening World*, Extra and Final, 16 April 1912, 1.

16. *New York Evening World*, Extra and Final, 17 April 1912, 1, 8.

17. Richard Kluger, *The Paper: The Life and Death of the New York Herald Tribune* (New York: Knopf, 1986), 181; Berger, *The Story of the New York Times*, 197–99.

18. Ralph Pulitzer to Carlos Hurd, 18 April 1912, *FHS-MO*.

19. The telegrams may be found in the Marconi Collection house at Chelmsford, United Kingdom, or may be viewed on the Web at http://www.marconicalling.com/museum/html/archivehome.html.

20. *Editor and Publisher and Journalist*, 20 April 1912, 2. Gaynor's orders were later changed to permit each major newspaper to have a representative on the pier. *New York World*, 18 April 1912, 1.

21. *St. Louis Post-Dispatch*, 21 April 1912; Hurd, "When the Titanic Sank," 15; Stadler, "My Father's Scoop," 18.

22. James French Dorrance, "The Sea-going Reporter. Tugging the Titanic Story," *The Publishers' Guide*, October 1912, 37–38.

23. Rostron, "The Rescue of the *Titanic* Survivors," 364.

24. Hurd, "When the Titanic Sank," 17.

25. *New York Times*, 19 April 1912, 1.

26. *St. Louis Post-Dispatch*, 19 April 1912, 12; Hurd, "When the Titanic Sank," 17; Stadler, "My Father's Scoop," 18.

27. The only extant copy of this extra is in the possession of the Missouri Historical Society. A microfilm version is available from the New

York Public Library. The mistake of "knots an hour" is certainly a reflection of the speed at which the issue was assembled; knots are a measure of nautical miles per hour. Among the reporters on the pier that night was Cobb, who had since left the *Evening World* and was helping out some reporters gratis.

28. *The Fourth Estate*, 20 April 1912, 30.

29. The scrap is in the possession of the Missouri Historical Society.

30. Chapin, *Story*, 211.

CHAPTER 15: THE CRISIS

This chapter depends heavily on Chapin's own accounting of events. In all key points, his descriptions of events have been verified by other sources. I have, however, chosen to use Chapin as the primary source to provide the reader with a better sense of his mind set. In the end, it is what is going on inside Chapin's mind, rather the events themselves, that will matter the most.

1. Accounting for inflation, a $1,000 bonus in 1912 would be the equivalent of a check for more than $17,000 at the end of the century, according to the Consumer Price Index maintained by the U.S. Government.

2. Van Benthuysen to JP, 3 March 1905, *W-CU*; See Charles R. Geisst, *Wall Street: A History* (New York: Oxford University Press, 1997); Walter Lord, *The Good Years: From 1900 to the First World War* (New York: Harper & Row, 1960), 69; Charles R. Geisst, *100 Years of Wall Street* (New York: McGraw-Hill, 2000), 2–3.

3. Purchase of the plots is recorded in the books of Glenwood Cemetery, Washington, D.C., as December 12, 1912.

4. "Big Dinner to Martin Green," *Editor & Publisher*, 3 May 1913, 4.

5. See Thomas Dormandy, *The White Death: A History of Tuberculosis* (New York: New York University Press, 2000) for descriptions of contemporary treatments; Chapin, *Story*, 282–84.

6. Chapin, *Story*, 285. While in San Francisco, Chapin claims to have dined with Jack London in a club and stayed up late into the night listening to his stories. *CC to VC*, 10 December 1920, 46–47.

7. Chapin, *Story*, 285–86; The sugar market had remained relatively steady for several years until Chapin made his investment. The fall in prices can be seen in the average retail price for sugar in 1912 and 1913. It went from 31.5 cents a pound to 27.5 cents a pound. *Historical Statistics of the United States: Colonial Times to 1970*, vol. 1 (Washington, D.C.:

U.S. Department of Commerce, 1970), 213; Chapin, *Story,* 287; Court records of the 1918 trial for murder refer to the sale of the automobile and yacht.

8. Chapin, *Story,* 288. Geisst, *100 Years of Wall Street,* 4.

9. Chapin, *Story,* 290.

10. Chapin, *Story,* 290–91.

11. Cobb, *Exit Laughing,* 140.

12. *CC to CN,* 15 February 1925, 233; *CC to CN,* 10 February 1925, 230; Chapin described his relationship with Nellie: "We lived within ourselves, for one another," he said. Lunacy Commission Report, 484–86, quoted in Petition for Pardon on behalf of Charles E. Chapin, July 1925.

13. Cobb, *Exit Laughing,* 146–47.

14. Chapin, *Story,* 292; James Lardner and Thomas Repetto, *NYPD: A City and Its Police* (New York: Henry Holt and Company, 2000), 157.

15. Chapin, *Story,* 293.

16. Chapin, *Story,* 294; Lunacy Commission Report, 19–20, quoted in application for clemency, 5. Purchase of cemetery plots noted in records of Glenwood Cemetery, Washington, D.C.

17. Chapin, *Story,* 295.

18. Quoted in Arthur S. Link, *Wilson: The New Freedom* (Princeton, N.J.: Princeton University Press, 1956), 80.

19. See John M. Blum, *Joe Tumulty and the Wilson Era* (Boston: Houghton Mifflin Company, 1951), 62–67; Chapin, *Story,* 296. Though it sounds incredible, it is plausible that Chapin could have entered the White House with a revolver at that time.

20. In checking on the veracity of Chapin's account of these events, I found that he remembered with considerable accuracy the shows he attended in Washington and Baltimore.

21. Chapin, *Story,* 298.

22. Chapin, *Story,* 299.

23. Chapin, *Story,* 302. The tour would be Cohan's last. In Detroit, he announced he was quitting the stage. He did, however, come out of retirement many times later.

24. Chapin, *Story,* 303–4.

25. Chapin, *Story,* 305.

26. "Tells Lotos Club About Goethals," *New York Times,* 25 January 1914, 11; "Reporters Hosts to City Officials," *New York Times,* 22 February 1914, 11; Chapin, *Story,* 250–51; "Plan Last Honors for Sailor Dead," *New York Times,* 8 May 1914.

27. *Tenadores* Ship Manifest, 23 June 1914. The American Family Immigration History Center, Ellis Island, New York (http://www.ellis island.org); *New York Journal,* 17 September 1918, 3; "Favors in form of Turkey," *New York Times,* 26 November 1914, 11.

28. Lawson, *Cobb*, 131–34. The film was called "From Paducah to Prosperity or the Life of Irvin S. Cobb." I could not locate a recipe for Savannah au rhum.

29. "Balfour and Vivani Welcome U.S. as Ally in the War for Civilization; Stir Diners to wildest Enthusiasm," *New York Times*, 12 May 1917, 1–2; "Great Banquet To-Night," *New York Evening World*, 11 May 1917, 2.

30. "Rev. W. Cashin Sing Sing Chaplain," *New York Times*, 6 April 1912, 1; Chapin, *Story*, 255–56.

31. Emmet Crozier, "Boss Chapin's Arrest for Murder: Guess Which Reporter Covered it?" in *Shoeleather and Printers' Ink*, ed. George Britt, 95–96.

32. Chapin, *Story*, 309–10.

CHAPTER 16: THE DEED

To reconstruct the crime, I relied primarily on accounts in the newspapers, the indictment, the plea agreement, the pardon request filed in 1925, and Chapin's memoir. While I quote from Chapin's autobiography to provide the reader with a sense of Chapin's mind at the time, his recounting of the facts is unreliable in comparison to the police account he provided the day of his arrest. The autobiography was written two years after the murder.

Specific quotations or facts are footnoted. General information concerning the crime, often appearing in several newspapers at the same time, was compiled from the following publications:

New York American	*New York Journal*
New York Evening Journal	*New York Sun*
New York Evening Telegram	*New York Times*
New York Evening World	*New York Tribune*
New York Herald	*New York World*

1. "City is Loyal Again on Gasless Sunday," *New York Times*, 16 September 1918, 18; Oliver E. Allen, *New York, New York*. (New York: Atheneum, 1990), 256; *New York Times*, 15 September 1918.

2. "City is Loyal Again on Gasless Sunday," *New York Times*, 16 September 1918, 18.

3. Cobb, "The Convict Who Made a Garden," 181. Cobb also observed, "He had never manifested real tenderness except in his attitude toward the fragile, faded little woman who was to die by his hands."

4. Chapin, *Story*, 311. Chapin also shared the encounter with the old woman in his testimony before the Lunacy Commission, but did not divulge it during his confession.

5. Chapin, *Story*, 311–12.

6. Chapin, *Story*, 315–16; Lunacy Commission Report, 25–26, quoted in Pardon Request, July 1925, 6. It is likely that had Chapin been alive today, he would have been diagnosed with bipolar disorder. If that were the case, then his remembrance of Nellie living on for thirty minutes could be fictional, according to Edwin N. Carter, a clinical psychologist in private practice in Northern Virginia. He suggests that such a tale would fit the pattern of someone with this disorder.

7. "Chapin Confesses He Planned Murder," *New York Times*, 18 September 1918, 24.

8. "Wife of Editor Shot Dead in Bed," *New York Times*, 17 September 1918, 7.

9. Quoted in application for clemency, July 1925, 6.

10. Caruthers' statement to police, quoted in "World Editor Missing After Wife is Slain," *New York Herald*, 17 September 1918, 12.

11. "Search for Chapin Fails," *New York Evening Journal*, 17 September 1918, 1.

12. Chapin, *Story*, 316.

13. *Motion Picture Herald*, 25 March 1944, 1; Lawson, *Cobb*, 162; Conversation between Frank Chapin and *World* reporters contained in special dispatch from Washington; "Wife of Editor Shot Dead in Bed," *New York Times*, 17 September 1918, 7; "Bullet Kills Wife, Editor Disappears," *New York World*, 17 September 1918, 24.

14. "Chapin Surrenders and Defends Crime," *New York Sun*, 18 September 1918, 12.

15. Chapin, *Story*, 317–18. The *New York Times* reported that it was its paper he purchased.

16. "Wife of Editor Shot Dead in Bed," *New York Times*, 17 September 1918, 7. Most of the papers were running the story of the murder on the front page or on the front of the metropolitan news section. Only the *New York Times* was restrained, especially in comparison to the Hearst papers.

17. Chapin, *Story*, 318.

18. "Chapin Led by Financial Ruin to Slay Wife," *New York Tribune*, 18 September 1918, 12.

19. "Search for Chapin Fails," *New York Evening Journal*, 17 September 1918, 1.

20. "A New York Crime," *London Times*, 18 September 1918, 8c; "Search for Chapin Fails," *New York Evening Journal*, 17 September 1918, 2.

21. Chapin, *Story*, 319.

22. Confession reprinted in "Chapin Surrenders and Defends Crime," *New York Sun*, 18 September 1918, 12.

CHAPTER 17: A DATE IN COURT

The voluminous report inquiring into Chapin's sanity did not survive. An extensive search of New York City municipal archives and New York State archives revealed no trace of the report. The only sections still existing are those that are quoted in Chapin's 1925 application for a clemency. The psychological explanation for Chapin's behavior offered in the chapter is based on the work of Louis B. Schlesinger, John Jay College of Criminal Justice, New York, N.Y.

1. "C.E. Chapin Gives Up After Tragic Death of His Wife," *New York Evening World*, 17 September 1918. 6; "Debt Drove Editor to Kill His wife," *New York World*, 18 September 1919, 5.

2. "Chapin Confesses he Planned Murder," *New York Times*, 18 September 1918, 24; Emmet Crozier, "Boss Chapin's Arrest for Murder: Guess Which Reporter Covered it?" in *Shoeleather and Printers' Ink*, ed. George Britt, 96–97. Crozier told this story years later to Gene Fowler, who said, "My God! I never had any of that kind of luck with my city editors"; Chapin, *Story*, 320.

3. "Chapin Defends Killing of his Wife," *New York Journal*, 18 September 1918; "Chapin Tells How and Why he Shot Wife," *New York American*, 18 September 1918, 5; "Chapin Confesses he Planned Murder," *New York Times*, 18 September 1918, 24; "Chapin led by Financial Ruin to Slay Wife," *New York Herald*, 18 September 1918, 12; "Debt Drove Editor to Kill his Wife," *New York World*, 18 September 1919, 5.

4. "Chapin Indicted for Killing Wife," *New York Tribune*, 19 September 1918, 9.

5. "Chapin Indicted for Killing Wife," *New York Tribune*, 19 September 1918, 9.

6. "Chapin to Make Insanity Plea," *New York Journal*, 19 September 1918, 3; Description of clothing and line-up from the *New York Evening Journal*, 19 September 1918, 1, and "C. E. Chapin, Arraigned, Enters Not Guilty Plea," *New York Evening World*, 19 September 1918, 7. Chapin knew Rand from his days of visiting Sage. Though newspaper accounts list him as chairman of the grand jury, his signature does not appear on any documents. He may have recused himself from the case.

7. "C. E. Chapin, Arraigned, Enters Not Guilty Plea," *New York*

Evening World, 19 September 1918, 7; "Chapin is Sane, Prosecutor's View; Editor 'Not Guilty,'" *New York Herald*, 20 September 1918, 5; "No Record that Chapin Lost in Speculation," *New York Times*, 20 September 1918, 14; *New York Evening Journal*, 19 September 1918, 1; "Inquiry Being Made Into Past," *New York Sun*, 20 September 1918, 10; *New York Herald*, 20 September 1918, 5.

8. "Chapin to Make Insanity Plea," *New York Journal*, 19 September 1918, 3; "Chapin Tells How and Why he Shot Wife," *New York American*, 18 September 1918, 5; "No Record that Chapin Lost in Speculation," *New York Times*, 20 September 1918, 20; "Inquiry Being Made Into Past," *New York Sun*, 20 September 1918, 10. Chapin's actual salary was calculated by using his earlier contracts and assuming an annual raise conservatively computed to match that of others on staff. The per-capita income of New Yorkers was estimated by examining the per-capita income of New Yorkers in 1929, the earliest year available in the *Historical Statistics of the United States: Colonial Times to 1970*.

9. *New York Times*, 18 December 1920, 15.

10. Chapin, *Story*, 321–22.

11. *New York Evening Journal*, 20 September 1918, 3; "No Record that Chapin Lost in Speculation," *New York Times*, 20 September 1918, 14.

12. Testimony before Lunacy Commission, 579–80, quoted in Application for Clemency, July 1925.

13. "Chapin Pleads Insanity," *New York Times*, 27 September 1918, 5.

14. "Appoint Lunacy Commission," *New York Times*, 18 October 1918, 24. Court documents, Supreme Court (Criminal Branch) Trial Term, Part I, *The People of the State of New York against Charles E. Chapin.*

15. "Dr. Smith Jelliffe, Psychiatrist, Dies," *New York Times*, 26 September 1945, 23.

16. Louis B. Schlesinger, "The Catathymic Crisis, 1912–Present: A Review and Clinical Study," *Aggression and Violent Behavior* 1, no. 4, 1996, 307; Sigmund Freud, "Twenty-third Lecture: The Paths of Symptom-Formation," *A General Introduction to Psychoanalysis* (New York: Garden City Publishing, 1938), 322.

17. Frederic Wertham, "The Catathymic Crisis," *Violence: Perspectives on Murder and Aggression*, eds. Irwin L Kutash, et al. (San Francisco: Jossey-Bass, Publishers, 1978), 165–66.

18. "Waldo Says Chapin was not Eccentric," *New York Sun*, 2 November 1818, 12; [title of article illegible], *New York American*, 2 November 1918, 7.

19. Chapin, *Story*, 323.

20. "Chapin Sane Legally When he Slew Wife," *New York American*,

15 December 1918, 9; *New York Times*, 18 October 1918, 24; Chapin, *Story*, 326.

21. "Chapin Sane Legally When he Slew Wife," *New York American*, 15 December 1918, 9.

22. Minutes of Lunacy Commission, 582–83, quoted in Application for Clemency, July 1925.

23. Minutes of Lunacy Commission, 584, quoted in Application for Clemency, July 1925.

24. Chapin, *Story*, 328–29.

25. *CC to VC*, 13 December 1920, 52.

26. Chapin, *Story*, 331–32.

27. "Chapin Sentenced to Prison for Life," *New York Times*, 15 January 1919; "Chapin Gets 20 Years for Slaying Wife," *New York American*, 16 January 1919.

CHAPTER 18: INSIDE THE WALLS

A shell of the cellblock in which Chapin was confined at Sing Sing still stands, the inside having been destroyed in a fire. Officials, however, hope to restore parts of it for a planned museum in the interior of the prison to be staffed by inmates.

Among the potential sources for Chapin's years in Sing Sing is an unpublished biography of Lewis Lawes by Emile Gauvreau, editor of the *New York Evening Graphic* and later the *New York Mirror*. It is, however, a very unreliable document, either because it was never finished, and thus is only an early draft, or because of a kind of blurring of the lines between fiction and fact for which his *New York Graphic* was famous. I have used it in only a few instances, where either other sources corroborated the account or, in one case, where my judgment led me to believe the dialogue was accurate.

1. Poem was transcribed by an inmate in a letter in the Supplement to the Papers of Lewis Lawes, *LAWES*. The letter was also reproduced in Lewis Lawes, *Life and Death in Sing Sing* (New York: Sundial Press, 1937), 59.

2. *Sing Sing Prison: Its history, Purpose, Makeup and Program* (Albany, N.Y.: Department of Corrections, 1953); Lewis Lawes, *Life and Death in Sing Sing*; Blake McKelvey, *American Prisons: A History of Good Intentions* (Montclair, N.J.: P. Smith, 1977). An excellent chapter on the prison's history may also be found in Ted Conover, *Newjack: Guarding Sing Sing* (New York: Random House, 2000).

3. The receiving blotter with Chapin's entry may be found in the New York State Archives, Albany, N.Y., but it is also reproduced in Lewis Lawes, *Twenty Thousand Years in Sing Sing* (New York: Ray Long & Richard Smith, Inc., 1932), 222; Knott became fond of Chapin and even visited Chapin at Sing Sing in 1921. *CC to VC*, 21 January 1921, 199; The description of the reception process for new inmates is taken from Lewis Lawes, *Life and Death in Sing Sing*, 51–64, as well as his notes contained in his papers.

4. Chapin, "Real Sing Sing Prison of Today As a 'Lifer' Found It," *Sing Sing Bulletin* 22, no. 3, June 1920, 1.

5. Chapin, "Real Sing Sing," 2; Comment about crying is drawn from Lawes, *Life and Death*, 57.

6. Chapin, "Real Sing Sing," 2; Edward J. McGrath, *I was Condemned to the Chair* (New York: Frederick A. Stokes, 1934), 219–20. McGrath's memory may be a bit suspect because he said Chapin's tie was blown over his shoulder. Chapin usually sported a bow tie. On the whole, however, McGrath's observations about Chapin tend to be corroborated by other evidence.

7. Chapin, *Story*, xviii, xvii; *CC to VC*, 21 January 1921, 195.

8. The pension is mentioned in his letters from prison. See *CC to VC*, 4 December 1920, 31; Many of the items Chapin obtained from outside prison came through one particular friend, Mimi, whose identify he never shared. A writer, married to an artist, she would keep Chapin supplied with luxuries, from preserves to knit socks. Though I have no proof, I believe the friend who suggested writing the book was Don Seitz, his former boss at the *Evening World*. I know that he visited Chapin at some point during his first year or so of confinement, and the advice fits his character. Seitz, himself, ends up writing several books, including a biography of Pulitzer.

9. Samuel Smiles, *Character* (London: John Murray, 1872), 350; Chapin writing under the pen name "The Man in the Library," "Great Books Have Been Written by Men in Prison," *Sing Sing Bulletin* 21, no. 8, February 1920, 16; Chapin, *Story*, xxii.

10. *CC to VC*, 4 December 1920, 27; Lawes, *Twenty Thousand Years*, 225; *CC to VC*, 3 January 1921, 130.

11. Quip found in Lawes, *Twenty Thousand Years*, 109. Rattigan telegram found on page 65.

12. Lawes, *Twenty Thousand Years*, 46–47.

13. Ibid., 224.

14. Ibid., 225–26; A similar description of the meeting is found in the Gauvreau manuscript, supplement "X101," *LAWES*.

1. For a complete history of the American prison press see my *Jailhouse Journalism: The Fourth Estate Behind Bars* (Rutgers: Transaction Publishers, 2002); The only known information about *Solitaire* is contained in "A Journal from Sing Sing," *New York World*, 18 December 1887. Foster had a partner, William H. Parsons, who was also in prison for fraud, but he died before the first issue appeared.

2. No. 1500, *Life in Sing Sing* (Indianapolis: Bobbs-Merrill, Co., 1904), 85–86, 88.

3. McGrath, *I was condemned to the Chair*, 221–22. McGrath writes that a few weeks later, some of the inmates took the back off one of Chapin's cabinets and cleaned him out of many delicacies.

4. *CC to VC*, 22 December 1920, 87; *Sing Sing Bulletin* 22, no. 3, June 1920, 2; Lewis Lawes, *Twenty Thousand Years in Sing Sing* (New York: Ray Long & Richard Smith, Inc., 1932), 226.

5. *Sing Sing Bulletin* 21, no. 8, February 1920, 8, 16.

6. *Sing Sing Bulletin* 21, no. 4, July 1920, 8; *Sing Sing Bulletin* 22, no. 1, April 1920, 10.

7. *CC to VC*, 25 November 1920, 18; McGrath, *I was condemned to the Chair*, 225.

8. Chapin, "My New Brier Pipe," *Sing Sing Bulletin* 22, no. 3, June 1920, 2; Chapin, "Twenty-five Gallery," *Sing Sing Bulletin* 22, no. 4, July 1920, 1. The piece he wrote about his new pipe remained his favorite for years.

9. *Sing Sing Bulletin* 21, no. 1, April 1920, 9; *Sing Sing Bulletin* 21, no. 9, March 1920, 8.

10. King (1859–1928) wrote thirty-two novels, many of which were best sellers of his era, and at least one was made into a movie. *The City of Comrades*, one of his more famous novels, was published the year he went to Sing Sing; *CC to CN*, 15 February 1925, 233.

11. "Books and Authors," *New York Times Book Review*, 5 September 1920, 15; *CC to VC*, 13 January 1921, 166; Typing style revealed in letter, *CC to VC*, 20 January 1921, 191; *CC to VC*, 15 December 1920, 59.

12. Chapin, *Story*, 316, 334.

13. *CC to VC*, 13 January 1921, 168; Cobb, *Exit Laughing*, footnote, 147.

14. Lawes, *Twenty Thousand Years*, 226; *CC to VC*, 28 January 1920, 205.

15. *Sing Sing Bulletin* 22, no. 1, April 1920, 1.

16. Eleanor Early, "Short History of Charles Chapin," introduction

to *The Constance Letters of Charles Chapin*, ed. Eleanor Early (New York: Simon and Schuster, 1931), 21.

17. This dialogue is drawn from the unpublished Gauvreau manuscript, v-8, 47–48. Although I have pointed out elsewhere that the manuscript is riddled with errors, the tone and words are so in keeping with the character of Lawes and Chapin that I decided, in the end, to include this conversation.

18. "Chapin's Sing Sing Paper Suspended," *New York Times*, 17 August 1920, 11

19. 'Sing Sing's Paper Will Be Resumed," *New York Times*, 25 August 1920, 28.

20. Lawes, *Twenty Thousand Years*, 128–30. A similar account appears in the Gauvreau manuscript.

21. Gauvreau manuscript, vi-11, 60.

22. "Prison Paper Reappears," *New York Times*, 16 September 1920, 6.

23. Chapin, *Story*, iii. Chapin does not identify the author, but thanks to the search engines now available on the Internet, I located an almost identical poem by William Leggett (1801–39) who worked for William Cullen Bryant at the New York *Evening Post*:

> But oh! How dark, how drear and lone,
> Would seem the brightest world of bliss,
> If wandering through each radiant one,
> If there no more the ties shall twine
> That death's cold hand along could sever
> Ah! then those scars in mockery shine—
> Ah! then those scars in mockery shine—
> More hateful as they shine for ever!

Printed in the *Montréal Vindicator*, January 1829 (http://www.arts.uwo.ca/ canpoetry/newspaper/Montreal_Vindicator_1829_january.htm).

24. "Autobiography from Sing Sing," *New York Times Book Review*, 12 September 1920, 12; *Outlook*, 20 October 1920, 334; *Springfield Republican*, October 17, 1920, 9. "Two Hundred Leading Books of the Season," *New York Times Book Review*, October 17, 1920, 18; A search through the *World* and *Evening World* for the fall of 1920 uncovered no reviews of the book.

25. "The Remarkable Story of a Misspent Life," display advertisement in *Washington Post*, 11 September 1920, 4.

26. *CC to VC*, 4 December 1920, 27. Photograph appears opposite title page of *The Constance Letters*, and of this book.

27. *CC to VC*, 25 November 1920, 15.

28. *CC to VC*, 2 December 1920, 21.

1. *CC to VC*, 2 December 1920, 21.

2. *CC to VC*, 25 November 1920, 17; *CC to VC*, 2 December 1920, 23.

3. *CC to VC*, 28 January 1921, 205; Chapin, "A Wild Mountain Rose That Grew in a Lonely Cabin" and "Rocky Mountain Outlaw with Glittering Gold Teeth," *Sing Sing Bulletin* 22, no. 5 & 6, August/September 1920, 8, 17.

4. *CC to VC*, 4 December 1920, 27.

5. Ibid., 26.

6. *CC to VC*, 7 December 1920, 37–38; *CC to VC*, 10 December 1920, 41.

7. *CC to VC*, 20 January 1921, 188. Chapin's selection of photographs is interesting. The puzzling one is the photograph of Hayes. Chapin was not Catholic, though he had a close relationship with Cashin. It may also be possible that the Archbishop and Chapin had communicated. In a letter to Hayes from Neuberger, who campaigned for Chapin's release, some mention is made of a "kindness" done to Chapin by Hayes. Neuburger to Hayes, 29 June 1925, *AoNY-A*; *CC to VC*, 11 December 1920, 51.

8. *CC to VC*, 15 December 1920, 59–60.

9. Ibid.; [Viola Irene Cooper,] "Foreword," *The Uncensored Letters of Charles Chapin*, (New York: Rudolph Field, Inc. 1931), 12.

10. Chapin, "Zona Gale," *Sing Sing Bulletin* 21, no. 10, January 1921, 14.

11. *CC to VC*, 13 December 1920, 53; *CC to VC*, 19 December 1920, 75, 78; *CC to VC*, 19 January 1921, 185.

12. *CC to VC*, 27 December 1920, 104; *CC to VC*, 24 December 1920, 94.

13. *CC to VC*, 26 December 1920, 99.

14. Ibid., 99, 101; Chapin, "Zona Gale," *Sing Sing Bulletin* 21, no. 10, January 1921, 14.

15. *CC to VC*, 27 December 1920, 104; *CC to VC*, 5 January 1921, 140; *CC to VC*, 18 December 1920, 64; *CC to VC*, 23 January 1921, 202; *CC to VC*, 15 December 1920, 60.

16. *CC to VC*, 3 January 1921, 125; *CC to VC*, 5 January 1920, 136.

17. *CC to VC*, 5 January 1920, 135.

18. Chapin, "Beyond the Hurt of Hating Men," *Sing Sing Bulletin* 22, no. 11, February 1921, 10–12.

19. *CC to VC*, 13 January 1921, 168. The idea for the second book is also described in *CC to VC*, 20 January 1921, 187.

20. "Sing Sing Newspapers Ceases Publication," *New York Times*, 20 March 1921, 8; *CC to VC*, April 1921 (no specific date), 8.

21. *CC to VC*, 15 December 1920, 57; Lawes, *Twenty Thousand Years*, 226.

22. [Viola Irene Cooper,] "Foreword," *Uncensored Letters*, 10.

23. Description of preparations for visits drawn from *Sing Sing Bulletin* 22, no. 4, July 1920, 8; Comments describing the fantasy first visit drawn from an undated letter to Cooper, Spring/Summer 1921, 10–11.

24. Lawyers from an unidentified bank to which Chapin owed $500 contacted him at the end of 1921; Lawes, *Twenty Thousand Years*, 226.

CHAPTER 21: THE ROSES

1. *CC to VC*, 10 December 1920, 40; "5 Die in 52 Minutes in Sing Sing Chair," *New York Times*, 10 December 1920, 1.

2. Walter Davenport, "The Bishop of Sing Sing," *Liberty*, 15 November 1924, 9–10.

3. According to Gauvreau, Cashin once told Lawes, "He's the only man I ever saw who looks as if he'd lost his soul, and God forgive me for saying it. I've never worked harder on a prisoner, and that's not because some Protestants can be tougher than others." ii-6, 15.

4. Cobb, "The Convict Who Made a Garden," 184; Early, "Short History of Chapin," 22; *CC to VC*, 28 December 1920, 108.

5. Early, "Short History of Chapin," 22.

6. *CC to VC*, 4 June 1922, 9.

7. Who actually first gave Chapin the idea to garden is not entirely clear. It may have been Lawes who made the first suggestion, as he claimed in his memoir. Chapin once, years later, also gave him credit but continued to say the tools came from Cashin. In the end, I decided the contemporaneous letter written to Cooper was the most reliable account.

8. Gauvreau, xi-6, 100–01, Lewis Lawes, "Sing Sing Rose Man," *American Rose Annual*, 1931, 157.

9. "Chapin Beautifies Prison," *New York Times*, 25 September 1922, 16; *CC to CN*, 8 March 1924, 46.

10. CC to Richardson Wright, February 1923, 136.

11. Lawes, *Twenty Thousand Years*, 230; *CC to CN*, 14 April 1924, 64.

12. Adolph Lewisohn, *Memories of a Happy Life*, unpublished manuscript, New York Public Library, Manuscript and Archives Division, 268–69, 276, 288, 231; *CC to CN*, 15 November 1925, 313.

13. Henry Maillard ran an old New York confectionery, known for its

elegant, hand-decorated chocolates, crystallized fruits, Venetian mints, jellies, and what one person described as "the best bridge mix in the country," consisting of nuts coated in milk and dark chocolate; *Brooklyn Eagle Sunday Magazine*, 5 April 1925, 5.

14. *House & Garden*, February 1923, 136.

15. *House & Garden*, February 1923, 136–38.

16. Chapin also said he recalled his mother having American Beauties. That is unlikely, as they were not introduced until 1875; CC to Richardson Wright, 23 April 1924; *House & Garden*, April 1923, 174.

17. *House & Garden*, April 1923, 172; *House & Garden*, January 1925, 92.

18. Chapin to Richardson Wright, April 1923, 176–78.

19. "Convict 'Burbank' Provides Prison Christmas Flowers," *New York Herald Tribune*, 24 December 1922, section 8, 2. "Burbank" in the headline was a reference to the famed horticulturalist Luther Burbank. The term "blooded cattle" means purebred. I corrected one of the names the reporter gave to the roses he saw. He misidentified the Pilgrim rose.

20. Lawes, *Twenty Thousand Years*, 231.

21. *House & Garden*, April 1923, 76.

22. Lawes, *Twenty Thousand Years*, 231; "Women go to South Seas," *New York Times*, 18 September 1926, 15. Viola Irene Cooper, *Windjamming to Fiji* (New York: Rae D. Henkle Co, 1929).

23. [Viola Irene Cooper,] "Foreword," *Uncensored Letters*, 11.

CHAPTER 22: CONSTANCE

While we know a considerable amount about Chapin's life in prison from his letters and the articles about him, piecing together information about Constance Nelson was far more difficult. First, as with Viola Cooper, Nelson kept her identity from the public. One day, in the 1980s, I was perusing a card catalog in the manuscript division of the library at Columbia University, and I came across an entry for a letter by Chapin that was contained in the collection of a literary agent. The files turned out to be those of Brown Literary Agency, which represented Nelson in her sale of the letters to Simon and Schuster. Armed with her last name and the fact that she had worked for the Federal Reserve in Cleveland, I contacted Lynn Sniderman, Associate Librarian and Archivist at the Federal Reserve Bank in Cleveland. With her assistance, I was able to piece together many of the missing parts of the Nelson story that are presented here.

1. Information on Pinniger drawn from cemetery record, Cleveland Necrology File, Reel #064, Cleveland Public Library, Cleveland, Ohio; [Constance Nelson,] "Why these Letters are Published," in *The Constance Letters of Charles Chapin*, ed. Eleanor Early, vii.

2. [Nelson,] "Why these Letters are Published," viii, ix; Nelson misquoted Oscar Wilde. The actual quotation is, "When you are able to understand, not merely how beautiful Robbie's action was, but why it meant so much to me, and always will mean so much, then, perhaps, you will realize how and in what spirit you should have approached me for permission to dedicate to me your verses." Oscar Wilde, *De Profundis, The Portable Oscar Wilde* (New York: Viking, 1981), 569.

3. [Nelson,] "Why these Letters are Published," vii.

4. *CC to CN*, undated but probably January 1924, 39; [Nelson,] "Why these Letters are Published," ix.

5. McGrath, *I was Condemned to the Chair*, 225; *CC to CN*, 15 February 1924, 41.

6. *CC to CN*, 22 February 1924, 42.

7. *CC to CN*, 8 March 1924, 44.

8. *CC to CN*, 15 March 1924, 47–48; *CC to CN*, 30 March 1924, 51; *CC to CN*, 21 March 1924, 50; *CC to CN*, 8 April 1924, 55.

9. *CC to CN*, 21 March 1924, 50; George Gissing, *The Private Papers of Henry Ryecroft* (New York: New American Library, 1961), 35–36.

10. *CC to CN* 14 April 1924, 64.

11. *CC to CN*, 30 April 1924, 73.

12. *CC to CN*, 13 May 1924, 77; *CC to CN*, 30 May 1924, 83; *CC to CN*, 1 June 1924, 85.

13. *CC to CN*, 30 April 1925, 268; Description of visit drawn from Early, ed., *The Constance Letters*, 98–101 and footnotes on 101–02, 88.

14. *CC to CN*, 26 June 1924, 104.

15. *CC to CN*, 6 July 1924, 114.

16. *CC to CN*, 30 April 1924, 73–74; *CC to CN*, 26 October 1924, 162; Lawes, *Twenty Thousand Years*, 232.

17. Constance Nelson, "Capturing Ideas," *Federal Reserve Notes*, August 1924, 18; *CC to CN*, 18 August 1924, 142.

18. *CC to CN*, 23 July 1924, 123; "Makes Prison Yard 'A Thing of Beauty,'" *New York Times*, 19 October 1924, 27; *CC to CN*, 18 August 1924, 137.

19. *CC to CN*, 16 September 1924, 148.

20. William E. Cashin to James L. Long, 30 September 1924, AANY, *AoNY-A*.

21. Quoted in unpublished Gauvreau manuscript, x-5, 91.

22. *CC to CN*, 19 October 1924, 156.

23. *CC to CN*, 23 November 1924, 178; Early note, *The Constance Letters*, 149–50. I surmised that Frank Chapin and Nelson went to the grave together, which is why Nelson was late for the dinner. He told his sister he had planted bulbs at the cemetery that afternoon. According to Nelson, she stopped at the house and went to the grave; thus, it seemed very likely they went together.

24. *CC to CN*, 3 December 1924, 181–82.

25. *CC to CN*, 7 December 1924, 183; *CC to CN*, 14 December 1924, 189.

26. Richardson Wright, "Bulletin Board" and "The Garden Between the Walls," *House & Garden*, January 1925, 45, 94.

27. CC to CN, undated, February 1925, 229; *CC to CN*, 10 February 1925, 229.

28. *CC to CN*, 26 February 1925, 238.

29. Quoted in *The Constance Letters*, 239.

30. *CC to CN*, 6 March 1925, 240; Constance Nelson, "A Book and a Job," *The Cleveland Banker*, July 1925, 27.

31. Kenneth Coolbaugh, "Gentle Art of Firing," *Liberty*, 14 March 1925, 20; Early, footnote, *The Constance Letters*, 248; *CC to CN*, 17 March 1925, 249.

32. Chapin never refers to Neuberger by name, but I was able to identify him through documents in the Archives of the New York Archdiocese and a reference to Mr. N. in another letter; *CC to CN*, 15 April 1925, 261.

33. *CC to CN*, 18 May 1925, 276–77; Lawes, *Twenty Thousand Years*, 233.

34. Mardaunt Hall, "The Screen," *New York Times*, 24 August 1925, 17; "Meighan's Picture in Sing Sing," *New York Times*, 12 July 1925, x2. The movie was not a success. The *Times'* Hall said the scenes in Sing Sing did not turn out any more interesting than the usual screen version of prison life. In the end, he concluded, "Only a great admiration for Mr. Meighan will keep this picture from wearying a spectator." According to the Library of Congress Moving Image Section, there are no surviving copies of the film.

35. *CC to CN*, 9 July 1925, 292.

36. Application for Clemency, July 1925; "Goldfish and Roses Lighten Sing Sing," *New York Times*, 16 December 1925, 21.

37. *CC to CN*, 9 July 1925, 292.

CHAPTER 23: THE END

1. *CC to CN*, 23 July 1925, 297. Chapin is quoting his friend Mimi, whom he never identifies. She is evidently a writer, married to a sculptor, who remains devoted to Chapin during his years at Sing Sing. She

is the one who supplied him with the delicacies for his imaginary meals with Constance. Governor Smith's office contacted various people in August concerning the application for clemency. The district attorney in New York City, for instance, received a letter from the governor's office on August 19, 1924. After providing the governor with a summary of the case, the district attorney said, "No further facts have been presented to me since the sentence of the petition, and I have no recommendation to make to your Excellency in regard to his application for clemency." Edward Swann (unsigned but probable) to Gov. Alfred E. Smith, 23 August 1924. *The People of the State of New York against Charles E. Chapin, 1918*, New York City Municipal Archives.

2. Information on the encounter between Larry and Nelson is drawn from Early, "Short History of Chapin," 32–33. Early interviewed Nelson. *CC to CN*, 24 August 1925, 307–8; Early, notes, 308.

3. Early, notes, 308. The line comes from Shakespeare, *Othello*, iii. 3, 276–78. Othello utters it in a moment when he vacillates between his love of Desdemona and a welling hatred of her for her imagined infidelity. As a man who could put people away in dungeons, Othello knows of what he speaks when he uses this metaphor. Of course for Chapin, confinement was an all too real aspect of his life. Chapin does, however, misquote Othello slightly. The actual line is "a corner *in* the thing I love." But one assumes he drew the line from memory. In the play, the horror of our watching this scene is that Othello is persuading himself of just what he wants to hear, enjoying his own pain, and that he suggests he deserves this treatment because he is so much older than his wife, according to Michael Olmert, a Shakespeare scholar at the University of Maryland. "So it's doubly ironic that your Rose Man alludes to this moment," Olmert said. Letter to author, 30 April 2002.

4. Early, "Short History of Chapin," 33–34

5. *CC to CN*, 27 September 1925, 309.

6. *CC to CN*, 3 January 1926, 316; *CC to CN*, 11 October 1925, 311.

7. Cobb, *Exit Laughing*, footnote, 148–49. The timing of Cobb's story coincides with other evidence concerning the collapse of the effort to win Chapin a pardon.

8. Chapin only mentions Dreiser once in all his writings. I think he must have had some contact with him when the two were in St. Louis, or at least have known about him then. But I have no evidence of such. The visit to Sing Sing is mentioned in *CC to CN*, 27 December 1925, 314. H. L. Mencken arranged for the *World* credentials. The paper expected an article from Dreiser, who had no intention of writing anything for his old newspaper. The resulting fracas, which embarrassed Mencken, was resolved by having a *World* reporter interview Dreiser about his visit to death row. The story is told in W. A. Swanberg, *Dreiser*, (New

York: Charles Scribner's Sons, 1965), 357–59, and in Richard R. Linge-man, *Dreiser*, vol. 2 (New York: Putnam, 1990), 255.

9. *CC to CN*, 27 December 1925, 314.

10. *CC to CN*, 28 January 1926, 321.

11. *CC to CN*, 28 March 1926, 325; Early, notes, 327; "Ex-Editor Charles Chapin is Ill in Sing Sing," *New York Times*, 26 July 1926, 2. In 1920, diseases in these eight groups—tuberculosis; influenza and pneumonia; nephritis and renal sclerosis; gastritis, duodenitis, enteritis, and colitis; syphilis; diphtheria; whooping cough; and measles—killed more than 540,000 Americans. Telegram from Nelson cited in Early, notes, 237, and *CC to CN*, 30 November 1926, 330.

12. *CC to CN*, 30 November 1926, 330.

13. "Sightseeing at Sing Sing Prison is Stopped; Warden Says it Adds to Hazard of Escapes," *New York Times*, 24 June 1927, 3.

14. *CC to CN*, 7 January 1927, 337–39.

15. "Sing Sing Builds Bird House for 100 Pets of Prisoners," *New York Times*, 11 November 1928, 33; Middleton's visit and dialogue taken from "Charles Chapin, Failing Now, Tends His 71 Birds in Prison," *New York Evening Post*, 18 March 1927. Page unknown, contained in Lawes papers.

16. "Fur Merchant Found Dead in Hotel Room," *New York Times*, 7 October 1927, 56.

17. Andrew S. Wing, "This Life Prisoner Turned Sing Sing's Cinder Heap into a Rose Garden," *Farm & Fireside*, July 1928, 6–7, 43–45, 49.

18. Interview with Marie H. Blood, 20 February 2000; also, Marie H. Blood in Kenneth Silverman, *Houdini!!! The Career of Ehrich Weiss* (New York: Harper Collins, 1996), 426.

19. *CC to CN*, 4 November 1928, 340; *CC to CN*, 5 December 1928, 342; *CC to CN*, 8 March 1929, 345.

20. "Chapin Opposes Pardon," *New York Times*, 2 January 1929, 15.

21. *CC to CN*, 17 March 1929, 345.

22. Lawes, *Twenty Thousand Years*, 234.

23. "Chapin Critically Ill in Prison," *New York Times*, 1 June 1930, 16; "Chapin Critically Ill in Prison," *New York Times*, 31 October 1930, 3; "Chapin 'Very Ill' at Sing Sing," *New York Times*, 2 November 1930, 14; "Chapin Sinking in Prison," *New York Times*, 20 November 1930, 22; The Brisbane visit is quite remarkable considering how long it had been since he left the *World* to join Hearst. Brisbane had been to Sing Sing as a young reporter in 1891 to witness one of the first electrocutions. A state law that had previously prohibited any newspaper from printing more than eight lines concerning an execution had been lifted. Brisbane was so sickened by witnessing the execution that he couldn't stay for

the autopsy. Oliver Carlson, *Brisbane: A Candid Biography* (New York: Stackpole Sons, 1937), 97.

24. "Charles E. Chapin Dies in Sing Sing," *New York Times*, 14 December 1930, 24. Lawes's own account varies only slightly. He says Chapin responded to his questions with "Nothing. I am tired and want to die." Lawes, *Twenty Thousand Years*, 234.

25. Chapin's final letter was published in several newspapers. The quotations here are taken from "Charles Chapin Will Be Buried Beside His Wife," *New York Herald Tribune*, 15 December 1930, 17. The amount of Chapin's savings was published in the *New York Evening World*, 15 December 1930, 17.

26. "Chapin Asked Burial Beside Wife he Killed," *New York Times*, 15 December 1930, 23; "Charles E. Chapin," *New York Evening World*, 15 December 1930, 16.

27. Heywood Broun, "It Seems to Me," *New York Telegram*, 15 December 1930.

EPILOGUE

1. Eleanor Early to George T. Bye, 16 December 1930, and telegram from Bye to Early, 17 December 1930, *Brown*; "George T. Bye, 70, Literary Agent," *New York Times*, 25 November 1957, 31. Bye's last newspaper job was at the *World* from 1921–23. Early was a freelance writer in Boston. After this book, she would write almost a dozen books, mostly about travel and one romance novel.

2. [Nelson,] "Why These Letters are Published," x; "Chapin Love Notes in Book," *New York Times*, October 14, 1931, 21.

3. Early to Bye, 14 July 1931, *Brown*.

4. R. L. Dufus, "Charles Chapin's Prison Letters," *New York Times*, 6 December 1931, 28.

5. Viola Irene Cooper, *Windjamming to Fiji*, (New York: Rae D. Henckle Co., 1929); "Viola Irene Cooper," *New York Times*, 23 March 1951, 21.

6. Lawson, *Cobb*, 242.

7. The wallpaper was designed by the in-house art department of the Subway Corporation. It was created by making a collage of pictures from the New York City Public Library. Karen DeRosa, Subway Corporation, letter to author, 29 November 2002.

Bibliography

Only works that have been directly used in the making of this book are listed here. Manuscripts and unpublished materials are listed only in the endnotes.

NEWSPAPERS

New York City

Fourth Estate
The Journalist
New York American
New York Evening Journal
New York Evening World
New York Herald

New York Journal
New York Sun
New York Times
New York Tribune
New York World
Town Topics

Chicago

Chicago Herald
Chicago Inter Ocean

Chicago Times
Chicago Tribune

St. Louis

Missouri Republican
St. Louis Globe-Democrat

St. Louis Post-Dispatch
St. Louis Republic

Other

Atchison Champion, Kansas
Black Hills Daily Times, South
    Dakota

Brookfield Gazette, Missouri
Dodge City Times, Kansas
Elgin Courier News, Illinois

Elgin Daily News, Illinois
Ford County Globe, Kansas
Hays Sentinel, Kansas
Junction City Union, Kansas

London Times, England
Milwaukee Journal, Wisconsin
Oneida Dispatch, New York
Sing Sing Bulletin, New York

MAGAZINE AND JOURNAL ARTICLES

Behymer, Francis A. "Simon Legree of the City Desk." *Page One Ball of 1948*. St. Louis: St. Louis Newspaper Guild, 1948.

Boyd, Richard. "The Dark Voyage of the Propeller *Vernon*." *Wisconsin's Underwater Heritage*, 10, no. 2 & 3, June & September 2000

Cobb, Irvin S. "The Convict Who Made a Garden on the Road to Hell." *Cosmopolitan*, March 1925.

Davenport, Walter. "The Bishop of Sing Sing." *Liberty*, November 15, 1924.

Dorrance, James French. "The Sea-Going Reporter. Tugging the Titanic Story." *The Publishers' Guide*. October 1912.

Gibson, E. J. "The Washington Correspondent." *Lippincott's Magazine*. November 1894.

"How Titanic Story was Reported." *The Editor and Publisher*. April 20, 1912.

Hurd, Carlos. "When the Titanic Sank." *The Quill*. June 1932.

Lawes, Lewis. "Life and Death in Sing Sing." *The World's Work*. May 1928.

———. "Sing Sing's Rose Man." *American Rose Annual*. 1931.

Lorenz, Larry. "The Whitechapel Club: Defining Chicago's Newspaperman in the 1890s." *American Journalism* 15, no. 1, Winter 1998.

Malin, James Claude. "James A. and Louie Lord, Theatrical Team: Their Personal Story, 1869–1889." *Kansas Historical Quarterly* 22, no. 3, Autumn 1956.

———. "Traveling Theatre in Kansas: The James A. Lord Chicago Dramatic Company, 1869–1871." *Kansas Historical Quarterly* 23, no. 3, Autumn 1957, and 23, no. 4, Winter 1956.

Matthews, Albert F. "The Metropolitan Newspaper Reporter." *Chautauquan*. November 1893.

Morris, James K. "A Writer Comes of Age in St. Louis." *Missouri Life*. November 1981.

Rostron, Arthur H. "The Rescue of the *Titanic* Survivors." *Scribners Monthly*. March 1913.

Schlesinger, Louis B. "The Catathymic Crisis, 1912–Present: A Review and Clinical Study." *Aggression and Violent Behavior* 1, no. 4, 1996.

"Sing Sing Past and Present." *Scientific American*. February 1929.

Smythe, Ted Curtis. "The Reporter, 1880–1900, Working Conditions and Their Influence on the News." *Journalism History* 7, no. 1, Spring 1980.

Snow, Richard. "Charles Chapin." *American Heritage*. December 1979.

Sprogle, J. L. "A Reporter's Recollections." *Lippincott's Magazine*. January 1899.

Stadler, Frances Hurd. "My Father's Scoop of a Lifetime." *Mature American*. Spring 1988.

Starr, Louis. "Joseph Pulitzer and His Most Indegoddampendent Editor," *American Heritage*. June 1968.

Stevens, Walter B. "The New Journalism in Missouri." *Missouri Historical Review*. April 1923–July 1925.

Wood, Sue Ann. "A Symphony of Sorrow." *Everyday Magazine, St. Louis Post-Dispatch*. April 14, 1997.

Wing, Andrew S. "This Life Prisoner Turned Sing Sing's Cinder Heap into a Rose Garden." *Farm & Fireside*. July 1928.

Wright, Richardson. "The Sing Sing Rose-Garden." *American Rose Annual*. 1923.

———. "The Garden Between the Walls," *House & Garden*. January 1925.

DISSERTATIONS

Jeffries, John B. "An Early History of Junction City, Kansas: The First Generation." Master's thesis, Kansas State University, 1963.

Mann, Russell A. "Investigative Journalism in the Gilded Age: A Study of the Detective Journalism of Melville E. Stone and the

Chicago Morning News, 1881–1888." Ph.D. dissertation, Southern Illinois University, 1977.

Sims, Norman Howard. "The Chicago Style of Journalism." Ph.D. dissertation, University of Illinois at Urbana-Champaign, 1983.

Stine, Lawrence. "A History of Theatre and Theatrical Activities in Deadwood, South Dakota, 1876–90." Ph.D. dissertation, State University of Iowa, 1962.

SELECTED BOOKS

The Accused, the accusers: the famous speeches of the eight Chicago anarchists in court when asked if they had anything to say why sentence should not be passed upon them. On October 7th, 8th and 9th, 1886. Chicago: Socialistic Publishing Society, 1886[?].

Abramson, Phyllis L. *Sob Sister Journalism.* New York: Greenwood Press, 1990.

Adams, Samuel Hopkins. *A. Woolcott: His Life and His World.* New York: Reynal & Hitchcock, 1945.

Alft, A.C. *Elgin: An American History.* Elgin, Ill.: Crossroads Communications, 1984.

Allen, Oliver E. *New York, New York.* New York: Atheneum, 1990.

Avrich, Paul. *The Haymarket Tragedy.* Princeton, N.J.: Princeton University Press, 1984.

Barrett, James Wyman, *Joseph Pulitzer and His World.* New York: Vanguard Press, 1941.

————. *The World, the flesh, and Messrs. Pulitzer.* New York: Vanguard Press, 1931.

Berger, Meyer. *The Story of the New York Times: 1851–1951.* New York: Simon and Schuster, 1951.

Biographical Review: The Leading Citizens of Madison County (New York). Boston: Biographical Review Publishing Co., 1894.

Blythe, Samuel G. *The Making of a Newspaper Man.* Philadelphia: Henry Altemus Co., 1912.

Blum, John M. *Joe Tumulty and the Wilson Era.* Boston: Houghton Mifflin Company, 1951.

Botanica's Roses: The Encyclopedia of Roses. North Rochester, U.K.: Grange Books, 1998.

Brands, H. W. *The Reckless Decade: America in the 1890s*. New York: St. Martin's Press, 1995.

Bracy, Isabel. *The 157th New York Volunteer (Infantry) Regiment 1862–1865, Madison and Cortland Counties, New York*. Interlaken, N.Y.: Heart of the Lakes Publishing, 1991.

Brian, Denis. *Pulitzer: A Life*. New York: John Wiley & Sons, 2001.

Britt, George, ed. *Shoeleather and Printers' Ink: 1924–1974*. New York: Quadrangle/New York Times Book Co., 1974.

Burrows, Edwin G., and Mike Wallace. *Gotham: A History of New York City to 1898*. New York: Oxford University Press, 1999.

Bryce, James. *The American Commonwealth, vol. 3*. London: MacMillan & Co., 1888.

Campbell, W. Joseph. *Yellow Journalism: Puncturing the Myths, Defining the Legacies*. Westport, Conn.: Praeger, 2001.

Carlson, Oliver. *Brisbane: A Candid Biography*. New York: Stackpole Sons, 1937.

Cashman, Sean Dennis. *America in the Gilded Age: From the Death of Lincoln to the Rise of Theodore Roosevelt*. New York: New York University Press, 1988.

Chapin, Charles. *Charles Chapin's Story*. New York: G. P. Putnam's Sons, 1920.

———. *The Constance Letters of Charles Chapin*. Ed. Eleanor Early. New York: Simon and Schuster, 1931.

———. *The Uncensored Letters of Charles Chapin*. New York: Rudolph Field, Inc., 1931.

Chiasson Jr., Lloyd, ed. *The Press on Trial: Crimes and Trials as Media Events*. Westport, Conn.: Greenwood Press, 1997.

Christopher, Thomas. *In Search of Lost Roses*. Chicago: University of Chicago Press, 2002.

Churchill, Allen. *Park Row: A Vivid Re-creation of Turn of the Century Newspaper Days*. New York: Rinehart & Company, 1958.

Clarke, Donald Henderson. *Man of the World*. New York: Vanguard Press, 1950.

Clarke, Selah Merrill. *Frivolous Recollections of the Humble Side of Old Days in New York Newspaperdom.* New York. Privately printed, 1932.

Cobb, Elizabeth. *My Wayward Parent.* Indianapolis: Bobbs-Merrill Co., 1945.

Cobb, Irvin S. *Alias Ben Alibi.* New York: George H. Doran Company, 1925.

———. *Exit Laughing.* New York: Bobbs-Merrill Co., 1941.

———. *Local Color.* New York: The Reviews of Reviews Corporation, 1916.

———. *Myself-To Date.* New York: The Reviews of Reviews Corporation, 1923.

Commission of Investigation on "General Slocum" Disaster. *Report of the United States Commission of Investigation upon the Disaster to the Steamer "General Slocum."* October 8, 1904.

Conover, Ted. *Newjack: Guarding Sing Sing.* New York: Random House, 2000.

Cooper, Viola Irene. *Windjamming to Fiji.* New York: Rae D. Henckle Co., 1929.

Creelman, James. *On the Great Highway: The Wanderings and Adventures of a Special Correspondent.* Boston: Lothrop, 1901.

David, Henry. *The History of the Haymarket Affair: A Study in the American Social-Revolutionary and Labor Movements,* 2d ed. New York: Russell & Russell, 1958.

Davie, Michael. *The Titanic: The Full Story of a Tragedy.* London: Bodley Head, 1986.

Davis, Robert H. *Over my Left Shoulder.* New York: D. Appleton & Company, 1926.

Derleth, August. *Still Small Voice: The Biography of Zona Gale.* New York: Appleton-Century Co., 1940.

Dillon, Ana Price. *Ana Price Dillon: Memoir and Memorials.* New York: The De Vinne Press, 1900.

Douglas, George H. *The Golden Age of the Newspaper.* Westport, Conn.: Greenwood Press, 1999.

Dormandy, Thomas. *The White Death: A History of Tuberculosis.* New York: New York University Press, 2000.

Dornfeld, A. A. *Behind the Front Page: The Story of the City News Bureau of Chicago.* Chicago: Academy of Chicago, 1983.

Dreiser, Theodore. *Dreiser-Mencken Letters: The Correspondence of*

Theodore Dreiser and H. L. Mencken, 1907–1945, vol. 2. Philadelphia: University of Pennsylvania Press, 1986.

————. *Newspaper Days: An Autobiography.* Ed. T. D. Nostwich.
Santa Rosa, Calif.: Black Sparrow Press, 2000.

Dunlop, M. H. *Gilded City: Scandal and Sensation in Turn-of-the-
Century New York.* New York: William Morrow, 2000.

Emery, Edwin, and Michael Emery. *The Press and America: An
Interpretive History of the Mass Media,* 5th ed. New York: Prentice-Hall, Inc., 1984.

Fedler, Fred. *Lessons From the Past: Journalists' Lives and Work,
1850–1905.* Prospect Heights, Ill.: Waveland Press, Inc., 2000.

Fields, Armond. *Eddie Foy: A Biography.* Jefferson, N.C.: McFarland & Company, 1999.

Foote, Stella. *A History of Calamity Jane: Our Country's First Lib-
erated Woman.* New York: Vantage Press, 1995.

Foster, Don. *Author Unknown: On the Trail of Anonymous.* New
York: Henry Holt, 2000.

Foy, Eddie. *Clowning Through Life.* New York: E. P. Dutton &
Co., 1928.

Franzen, Susan Lloyd. *Behind the Facade of Fort Riley's Hometown: The Inside Story of Junction City, Kansas.* Ames, Iowa:
Pivot Press, 1998.

Freud, Sigmund. *A General Introduction to Psychoanalysis.* New
York: Garden City Publishing, 1938.

Geisst, Charles R. *100 Years of Wall Street.* New York: McGraw-
Hill, 2000.

————. *Wall Street: A History.* New York: Oxford University
Press, 1997.

Gillespie, Vera and John. *The "Titanic Man," Carlos F. Hurd:
Covering the Most Famous of All Shipwrecks, S.S. Titanic.* Grover, Mo.: V. & J. Gillespie, 1996.

Ginger, Ray. *Age of Excess: The United States from 1877 to 1914.*
New York: Macmillan Co., 1965.

Glick, Frank Ziegler. *They Came to Smoky Hill: History of Three
Generations.* Manhattan, Kan.: Sunflower University Press,
1986.

Green, Constance McLaughlin. *Washington: Capital City, 1879–
1950.* Princeton, N.J.: Princeton University Press, 1963.

Hammond, Mrs. Whitney Luna. *History of Madison County, State of New York.* Syracuse, N.Y.: Truair, Smith & Co., Book and Job Printers, 1872.

Harris, Elizabeth. *The Boy and His Press*, Washington: Smithsonian Institute, 1992.

Harris, Neil, ed. *The Land of Contrasts: 1880–1901.* New York: George Braziller, 1970.

Henderson, Margaret G. *It Happened Here: Stories of Wisconsin.* Madison: State Historical Society of Wisconsin, 1949.

Herringshaw, Thomas W. *Prominent Men and Women of the Day.* A. S. B. Gehman & Co., 1888.

Heyer, Paul. *Titanic Legacy: Disaster as Media Event and Myth.* Westport, Conn.: Praeger, 1995.

Historical Statistics of the United States: Colonial Times to 1970, vol. 1. Washington, D.C.: U.S. Department of Commerce, 1970.

The History of American Yacht and Yachtsmen. New York: Spirit of the Times Publishing Co., 1901.

Hole, S. Reynolds. *A Little Tour in America.* New York: E. Arnold, 1895.

Howard, Joseph, ed. *The Union League Club Historical And Biographical, 1863–1900.* New York: J. J. Wholtman, 1900.

How to Grow Roses, Dedicated to the Flower-Loving People of America, 12th ed. West Grove, Penn.: The Conard & Jones Co., 1916.

Hughes, Glen. *A History of the American Theatre 1700–1950.* London: Samuel French, 1951.

Ingalls, Sheffield. *History of Atchison County.* Lawrence, Kan.: Standard Publishing Co., 1916.

Ireland, Alleyene. *An Adventure with a Genius.* New York: W. O. Dutton, 1920.

Irwin, Will. *The Making of A Reporter.* New York: G. P. Putnam's Sons, 1942.

Jekyll, Gertrude, and Edward Mawley, *Roses for English Gardens.* London: Country Life, 1902.

Juergens, George. *Joseph Pulitzer and the New York World.* Princeton, N.J.: Princeton University Press, 1966.

Kaplan, Justin. *Lincoln Steffens: A Biography.* New York: Simon and Schuster, 1974.

Kinsley, Philip. *The Chicago Tribune: Its First Hundred Years.* Chicago: Chicago Tribune, 1946.

Kluger, Richard. *The Paper: The Life and Death of the New York Herald Tribune.* New York: Alfred A. Knopf, 1986.

Knightley, Philip. *The First Casualty.* New York: Harcourt Brace Jovanovich, 1975.

Kroeger, Brooke. *Nellie Bly: Daredevil, Reporter, Feminist.* New York: Times Books, 1994.

Kutash, Irwin L., Samuel B. Kutash, and Louis B. Schlesinger, eds. *Violence: Perspectives on Murder and Aggression.* San Francisco: Jossey-Bass Publishers, 1978.

Lancaster, Paul. *Gentleman of the Press: The Life and Times of an Early Reporter, Julian Ralph of the Sun.* Syracuse, N.Y.: Syracuse University Press, 1992.

Lardner, James, and Thomas Repetto. *NYPD: A City and Its Police.* New York: Henry Holt and Company, 2000.

Lawes, Lewis. *Life and Death in Sing Sing.* New York: Sundial Press, 1937.

———. *Twenty Thousand Years in Sing Sing.* New York: Ray Long & Richard R. Smith, Inc., 1932.

Lawson, Anita. *Irvin S. Cobb.* Bowling Green, Ohio: Bowling Green State University Popular Press, 1984.

Leech, Margaret. *In the Days of McKinley.* New York: Harpers & Brothers, 1959.

Leonard, Thomas C. *News for All: America's Coming-of-Age with the Press.* New York: Oxford University Press, 1995.

Levy, Newman. *The Nan Patterson Case.* New York: Simon and Schuster, 1959.

Lewison, Edwin. *John Purroy Mitchel: The Boy Mayor of New York.* New York: Astra Books, 1965.

Lingeman, Richard R. *Theodore Dreiser.* Two volumes. New York: Putnam, 1986, 1990.

Link, Arthur S. *Wilson: The New Freedom.* Princeton, N.J.: Princeton University Press, 1956.

Linn, James Weber. *James Keeley: Newspaperman.* Indianapolis: Bobbs-Merrill Co., 1937.

London, Jack. *The Road.* Santa Barbara, Calif.: Peregrine Smith, Inc., 1978.

Lord, Walter. *The Good Years: From 1900 to the First World War.* New York: Harper & Row, 1960.

Lubow, Arthur. *The Reporter Who Would be King: A Biography of*

Richard Harding Davis. New York: Charles Scribner's Sons, 1992.

Markham, James W. *Bovard of the Post-Dispatch.* Baton Rouge: Louisiana State University Press, 1954.

Masson, Thomas L. *Our American Humorists.* Freeport, N.Y.: Books for Libraries Press, 1966. First printed 1931.

McCullough, David G. *The Johnstown Flood.* New York: Simon and Schuster, 1987.

McGrath, Edward J. *I was Condemned to the Chair.* New York: Frederick A. Stokes, 1934.

McKelvey, Blake. *American Prisons: A History of Good Intentions.* Montclair, N.J.: P. Smith, 1977.

McMurry, Donald L. *Coxey's Army: A Study of the Industrial Army Movement of 1894.* 1929; reprint with an introduction by John D. Hicks, Seattle: University of Washington Press, 1968.

McPhaul, John J. *Deadlines and Monkeyshine: The Fabled World of Chicago Journalism.* Englewood Cliffs, N.J.: Prentice–Hall, 1962.

McPherson, James M. *For Causes & Comrade: Why Men Fought in the Civil War.* New York: Oxford University Press, 1997.

Milton, Joyce. *The Yellow Kids: Foreign Correspondents in the Heyday of Yellow Journalism.* New York: Harper & Row, 1989.

Morris, Edmund. *The Rise of Theodore Roosevelt.* New York: Ballantine Books, 1979.

Morris, James McGrath. *Jailhouse Journalism: The Fourth Estate Behind Bars.* Transaction Books, 2002.

Morrison, Samuel Eliot. *The Oxford History of the American People.* New York: Oxford University Press, 1965.

Mount, Charles Merrill. *John Singer Sargent: A Life.* New York: W. W. Norton, 1955.

Mullin, Donald, ed., *Victorian Actors and Actresses in Review: A Dictionary of Contemporary Views of Representative British and American Actors and Actresses, 1837–1901.* Westport, Conn.: Greenwood, 1983.

Nasaw, David. *The Chief: The Life of William Randolph Hearst.* Boston: Houghton Mifflin Co., 2000.

Nelson, Nell. *The White Slave Girls of Chicago.* Chicago: Barkley Publishing, 1888.

Parker, Watson. *Deadwood: The Golden Years.* Lincoln, Neb.: University of Nebraska Press, 1981.

No. 1500, *Life in Sing Sing.* Indianapolis: Bobbs-Merrill Co., 1904.

Pfaff, Daniel W. *Joseph Pulitzer II and the Post-Dispatch.* University Park, Penn.: Pennsylvania State University Press, 1991.

Pink, Louis Heaton. *Gaynor: The Tammany Mayor Who Swallowed the Tiger.* New York: The International Press, 1931.

Primm, James Neal. *Lion of the Valley: St. Louis, Missouri, 1764–1980.* St. Louis: Missouri Historical Society, 1998.

Procter, Ben. *William Randolph Hearst: The Early Years, 1863–1910.* New York: Oxford University Press, 1998.

Rafter, Nicole Hahn. *Shots in the Mirror: Crime Films and Society.* New York: Oxford University Press, 2000.

Rammelkamp, Julian S. *Pulitzer's Post-Dispatch: 1878–1883.* Princeton, N.J.: Princeton University Press, 1967.

Reagan, Leslie J. *When Abortion was a Crime: Women, Medicine, and Law in the United States, 1867–1973.* Berkeley: University of California Press, 1997.

Ritchie, Donald A. *Press Gallery: Congress and the Washington Correspondents.* Cambridge, Mass.: Harvard University Press, 1991.

Robinson, Judith. *The Hearts: An American Dynasty.* New York: Avon Books, 1991.

Rothman, Sheila M. *Living in the Shadow of Death.* New York: Basic Books, 1994.

Rouse, John Jay. *Firm but Fair: The Life of Sing Sing Warden Lewis Lawes.* Xlibris, 2000.

Salisbury, William. *The Career of a Journalist.* New York: B. W. Dodge & Co., 1908.

Sarnoff, Paul. *Russell Sage: The Money King.* New York: Ivan Obolensky, Inc. 1965.

Scharf, Thomas. *History of St. Louis City and County.* Philadelphia: Louis H. Everts & Co., 1883.

Schlesinger, Louis B., ed. *Explorations in Criminal Psychopathology.* Springfield, Ill.: Charles C. Thomas, Publisher, 1996.

Schwantes, Carlos A. *Coxey's Army: An American Odyssey.* Lincoln, Neb.: University of Nebraska Press, 1985.

Seitz, Don Carlos. *Joseph Pulitzer: His Life and Letters*. New York: Simon and Schuster, 1924.

Sievers, Harry. *Benjamin Harrison: Hoosier President, The White House and After, vol. 3*. Indianapolis: Bobbs-Merrill Co., 1968.

Silverman, Kenneth. *Houdini!!! The Career of Ehrich Weiss*. New York: Harper Collins, 1996.

Sing Sing Prison: Its History, Purpose, Makeup and Program. Albany: Department of Corrections, 1953.

Smiles, Samuel. *Character*. London: John Murray, 1872.

Spencer, Truman Joseph. *The History of Amateur Journalism*. New York: The Fossils, 1957.

Steffens, Lincoln. *The Autobiography of Lincoln Steffens*. New York: Harcourt, Brace and Company, 1931.

Stevens, John D. *Sensationalism and the New York Press*. New York: Columbia University Press, 1991.

Stevens, Walter. *St. Louis, The History of the Fourth City, 1763–1909*. Chicago-St. Louis: S. J. Clarke Publishing, Co. 1909.

Stone, Melville E. *Fifty Years a Journalist*. Garden City, N.Y.: Doubleday, Page and Company, 1921.

Squire, Amos Osborne. *Sing Sing Doctor*. Garden City, N.Y.: Doubleday, 1935.

Swanberg, W. A. *Citizen Hearst*. New York: Charles Scribner's Sons, 1961.

———. *Dreiser*. New York: Charles Scribner's Sons, 1965.

———. *Pulitzer*. New York: Charles Scribner's Sons, 1967.

Tebbel, John. *The Compact History of the American Newspaper*. New York: Hawthorn Books, Inc., 1969.

Terhune, Albert Payson. *To the Best of My Memory*. New York: Harper & Brothers Publishers, 1930.

Turner, Hy B. *When Giants Ruled: The Story of Park Row*. New York: Fordham University Press, 1999.

Villard, Oswald Garrison. *Some Newspapers and newspaper-men*. New York: Knopf, 1926.

Wade, Wyn Craig. *The Titanic: End of a Dream*. New York: Penguin Books, 1986.

Walker, Stanley. *City Editor*. New York: Blue Ribbon Books, Inc., 1934.

Weaver, Paul H. *News and the Culture of Lying: How Journalism Really Works*. New York: Free Press, 1984.

Weintraub, Stanley. *The London Yankees: Portraits of American Writers and Artists in England, 1894–1914.* New York: Harcourt Brace Jovanovich, 1979.

Wendt, Lloyd. *Chicago Tribune: The Rise of a Great American Newspaper.* Chicago: Rand McNally, 1979.

Whitlock, Brand. *Forty Years of It.* New York: D. Appleton and Co., 1914.

Wilde, Oscar. *De Profundis, The Portable Oscar Wilde.* New York: Viking, 1981.

Wilensky, Harry. *The Story of the St. Louis Post-Dispatch.* St. Louis: St. Louis Post-Dispatch, 1981.

Williams, Burton J. *Senator John James Ingalls.* Lawrence, Kan.: University Press of Kansas, 1972.

Young, David M. *Chicago Maritime: An Illustrated History.* De-Kalb, Ill.: Northern Illinois University Press, 2001.

Young, William C., ed., *Famous Actors and Actresses on the American Stage: Documents of American Theater History.* New York: R. R. Bowker Company, 1975.

Index